Lasting Screen Stars

Lucy Bolton • Julie Lobalzo Wright
Editors

Lasting Screen Stars

Images that Fade and Personas that Endure

Editors
Lucy Bolton • Julie Lobalzo Wright
School of Languages, Linguistics and Film
Queen Mary University of London
London, UK

ISBN 978-1-349-68099-3   ISBN 978-1-137-40733-7   (eBook)
DOI 10.1057/978-1-137-40733-7

Library of Congress Control Number: 2016936089

© The Editor(s) (if applicable) and The Author(s) 2016
Softcover reprint of the hardcover 1st edition 2016 978-1-137-40732-0
The author(s) has/have asserted their right(s) to be identified as the author(s) of this work in accordance with the Copyright, Designs and Patents Act 1988.
This work is subject to copyright. All rights are solely and exclusively licensed by the Publisher, whether the whole or part of the material is concerned, specifically the rights of translation, reprinting, reuse of illustrations, recitation, broadcasting, reproduction on microfilms or in any other physical way, and transmission or information storage and retrieval, electronic adaptation, computer software, or by similar or dissimilar methodology now known or hereafter developed.
The use of general descriptive names, registered names, trademarks, service marks, etc. in this publication does not imply, even in the absence of a specific statement, that such names are exempt from the relevant protective laws and regulations and therefore free for general use.
The publisher, the authors and the editors are safe to assume that the advice and information in this book are believed to be true and accurate at the date of publication. Neither the publisher nor the authors or the editors give a warranty, express or implied, with respect to the material contained herein or for any errors or omissions that may have been made.

Printed on acid-free paper

This Palgrave Macmillan imprint is published by Springer Nature
The registered company is Macmillan Publishers Ltd. London

Foreword

Those of us who write about film stardom crave the kind of smart, probing analysis proposed here by Lucy Bolton and Julie Lobalzo Wright. Friends for many years, and experienced and energetic teachers and scholars, Lucy and Julie's passion for their subject is clear on every page of this excellent book. Their guiding question is a deceptively simple one: Why it is that some film stars endure in the hearts and minds of the public, while others fade away into obscurity or become permanently fixed in a historical moment? Is it down to talent? Luck? Good or bad management of a career? Why did Rudolph Valentino prevail as a screen icon after his death, while his cinematic peer Wallace Reid did not? Why does a film stock image of Marlon Brando appeal to twenty-first-century consumers of jeans? Why is the book's cover girl, Norma Shearer, only ever seen through the prism of the 1930s and, often, eclipsed by Bette Davis and Joan Crawford?

What Lucy and Julie reveal, through a series of detailed case studies, is that the surface alchemy of star glory is in fact a consequence of complex cultural, historical, political, and industrial forces; shifting forces that are all too frequently outside the control of the individual actor, and reside, instead, in the multiple ways in which we relate to the star image: as fans, viewers, imitators, consumers. Within this conceptual framework they, and their contributors, test some of the received wisdom and contradictions about career longevity, fleeting fame, and what it means to age in the public eye. The essays are exciting and illuminating: they extend and enrich our understanding of film stars from different eras, places, and genres, while reminding us of the sheer pleasure they give us as performers and characters. In our era of mass circulation of images, of celebrity appropriation of social media, of careers that seem to have no natural end point, this book asks topical and important questions that will provide a foundation for new work in the field of star studies. This is a book that will endure.

Sue Harris
Queen Mary University of London

Acknowledgements

We would like to thank our colleagues and students from the film studies departments of Queen Mary University of London (QMUL) and Kings College London for their support and inspiration over the last ten years that we have been teaching star studies at these institutions. In particular, we would like to thank Sue Harris, Pauline Small, Charles Drazin, Richard Dyer, and Ginette Vincendeau. We've certainly learnt our star studies from the best.

We would also like to thank all those who've helped us publish this volume, including Chris Penfold at Palgrave Macmillan, our helpful and constructive anonymous readers, and of course all our patient and diligent contributors for their fantastic chapters.

Thanks to all colleagues who have shared their thoughts and wisdom about stars at the various conferences where we have presented our work along the way, including Revisiting Star Studies at Newcastle in June 2013, Exploring British Film and Television Stardom at QMUL in November 2013 and the Celebrity Studies conference at Royal Holloway in June 2014.

Julie would like to thank friends, family, and colleagues for their support over the years, especially my co-editor whose passion for this project has been appreciated from the very beginning. Thanks also to Tristan Wright for his constant support, endless encouragement, and boundless enthusiasm for Ice Cube.

Lucy would like to thank colleagues in the Film History research cluster at QMUL, and past and present chairs of film studies during the writing of this book, Libby Saxton and Guy Westwell. I am also hugely grateful to David Edgar at the British Film Institute for involving me in so many events about stars, and reaching out to those who love them as much as I do. My love and thanks to Jean Bolton, Laura Adams, and Richard Menzies, and my never-ending gratitude to my stalwart co-editor.

And thanks to Jimmy Brady for his support and conversation during the final stages of the book. All that tea really helped.

Contents

1 Introduction   1
Lucy Bolton and Julie Lobalzo Wright

Section 1   Lasting Stardom   9

2 From Angry Young Man to Icon of Neo-liberal India: Extra-cinematic Strategies that Make Amitabh Bachchan India's Lasting Super-Star   11
Aparna Sharma

3 Sophia Loren and the Healing Power of Female Italian Ethnicity in *Grumpier Old Men*   27
Antonella Palmieri

4 Cutting a Dash in Interwar Hungary: Pál Jávor's Enduring Stardom   41
Gábor Gergely

5 From Boy N the Hood to Hollywood Mogul: Ice Cube's Lasting Stardom in Contemporary Hollywood   55
Julie Lobalzo Wright

Section 2 Faded Stardom   69

6 'What Price Widowhood?': The Faded Stardom of
   Norma Shearer   71
   Lies Lanckman

7 Robert Taylor: The 'Lost' Star with the Long Career   85
   Gillian Kelly

8 Melanie Griffith: Wild Girl and Working Woman   99
   Lucy Bolton

Section 3 Ageing   113

9 The Ageing Stars of European Art-House Cinema:
   Jean-Louis Trintignant and Emmanuelle Riva in *Amour*   115
   Fiona Handyside

10 The Great Stoneface Ruined: From *The Buster
   Keaton Story* to *Film*   127
   Paul Flaig

11 Ageing Masculinity in the Films of James Mason   141
   Adrian Garvey

Section 4 Posthumous Stardom   157

12 The Afterlives of Rudolph Valentino and Wallace Reid
   in the 1920s and 1930s   159
   Lisa Bode

13 Beyond the Bounds of Criticism: Preserving Spencer
   Tracy as a Liberal Hero   173
   Hannah Graves

14 Everybody's All-American: The Posthumous
   Rebranding of Marlon Brando   189
   Lisa Patti

Section 5   Characters, Series and Types   201

15 Mrs John Bull: The Later Life Stardom of
   Margaret Rutherford   203
   Claire Mortimer

16 This Never Happened to the Other Fellow: The
   Fluctuating Stardom of James Bond and George Lazenby   217
   Jaap Verheul

17 Don't You Forget about Me: Molly Ringwald, Nostalgia
   and Teen Girl Stardom   231
   Frances Smith

18 Redundancy and Ageing: Sylvester Stallone's Enduring
   Action Star Image   245
   Glen Donnar

Section 6   Reflections Beyond the Screen   259

19 Still Famous: Fixing the Star Image of Diana Dors
   in the Photography of Cornel Lucas   261
   Linda Marchant

20 From Action Babe to Mature Actress: The Place of Humanitarianism in Angelina Jolie's Lasting Screen Career   277
Joshua Gulam

21 Rearticulating Bruce Lee and His 'Hip Hop Fury' in Fan-Made Videos   291
Dorothy Wai-sim Lau

Index   305

Biography

Lisa Bode is Lecturer in Film and Television Studies at The University of Queensland, Australia. She has published research on posthumous stardom in *Cinema Journal* and *Celebrity Studies Journal*, and is currently writing a book on the history of screen performance and cinematic illusion.

Lucy Bolton is Senior Lecturer in Film Studies at Queen Mary University of London. She is the author of *Film and Female Consciousness: Irigaray, Cinema and Thinking Women* (Palgrave 2011) and of many articles and book chapters on film philosophy and on stardom. She is currently researching a monograph on the relationship between the philosophy of Iris Murdoch and cinema, and is writing about the film performances of Vivien Leigh, the lasting cultural presence of Marilyn Monroe, and women in the films of Clint Eastwood.

Glen Donnar is a Lecturer in the School of Media and Communication at RMIT University in Melbourne, Australia. He has published widely on popular cultural representations of masculinities, terror, monstrosity, and disaster in American film and television, including on 9/11, the JFK assassination, horror and post-apocalyptic film. He has also published on the mediation of terror in the Australian news media, the ethics of viewership, and contemporary learning and teaching practice in media education.

Paul Flaig is a Lecturer in Film & Visual Culture at the University of Aberdeen. He is co-editor of *New Silent Cinema* (2015) and has published essays in *Cinema Journal*, *Screen*, *The Brecht Yearbook*, and *A Journal of Culture and the Unconscious*, as well as several edited collections. He is currently completing a book manuscript entitled *Weimar Slapstick: American Eccentrics, German Grotesques and Hollywood Comedy Abroad*, based on his doctoral research.

Adrian Garvey is a PhD candidate in History at Queen Mary University of London, working on film performance and stardom in the transatlantic career of James Mason. He has published on various aspects of British cinema, including Ken Russell's The Boy Friend and the TV sitcom adaptation. He contributed an article, '"Steely Velvet": The Voice of James Mason,' to the stardom issue of the Journal of British Cinema and Television, and has a forthcoming entry on British silent stardom for the Routledge Companion to British Cinema.

Gábor Gergely has recently taken up a post of Lecturer in film at the University of Lincoln. Previously, he was a Leverhulme early career fellow at the University of Manchester, where this chapter was written as part of a research project on early Hungarian sound film.

Hannah Graves is a PhD candidate in the Department of History at the University of Warwick. Her research explores the production and reception of socially conscious film making during the mid twentieth century in Hollywood. Using the figure of the liberal hero as a locus for discussion, her thesis charts the rise and fall in popularity of this figure alongside the careers of the film makers who felt compelled to bring him to screens.

Joshua Gulam is a PhD student at the University of Manchester. His research, funded by the Arts & Humanities Research Council, examines the philanthropic activities of contemporary Hollywood film stars. Publications include a chapter on George Clooney's campaigning in *Star Power: The Impact of Branded Celebrity* (2014) and a short article in *Celebrity Studies* that explores the intersections between film stardom, gender, and philanthropy.

Fiona Handyside is Senior Lecturer in Film Studies at the University of Exeter. She has edited *Eric Rohmer: Interviews* (2013) and is the author of *Cinema at the Shore: The Beach in French Film* (2014). She is the co-editor with Kate Taylor-Jones of *International Cinema and the Girl: Local Issues, Transnational Contexts* (Palgrave, 2015) and is currently working on a monograph on Sofia Coppola.

Sue Harris is Reader in French Cinema Studies at Queen Mary University of London. She has written widely on French cinema and popular culture, and on French stars including Gérard Depardieu, Catherine Deneuve and Alain Delon. Other published work includes a monograph on *An American in Paris* (BFI Film Classics/Palgrave, 2015); *Bertrand Blier* (2001); *France in Focus: Film and National Identity* (edited with Elizabeth Ezra, 2000); *Film Architecture and the Transnational Imagination: Set Design in 1930s European Cinema* (with Tim Bergfelder and Sarah Street, 2007); *From Perversion to Purity: The Stardom of Catherine Deneuve* (edited with Lisa Downing, 2007).

Gillian Kelly was recently awarded her PhD in Theatre, Film and Television Studies from the University of Glasgow. Her thesis, entitled *A Taylor Made Star: Male Beauty, Changes in Masculinity and the 'Lost' Stardom of Robert Taylor,*

Hollywood 1934–1969, explores the initial construction and subsequent developments of Robert Taylor's star persona across the whole of his career, primarily using a visual approach to analyse Taylor's developing star image over four different decades. Kelly's main research interests include star studies, Hollywood cinema, screen performance, media celebrity and stardom, filmic and extra-filmic constructions of star personas, modern American history, and gender and masculinity. Her previous work includes studies of Gene Kelly as a 'performing auteur' and British actor Herbert Marshall's work in Hollywood cinema. Kelly also holds an MLitt in Film and Television Studies from the University of Glasgow and a BA (Hons) in Media: Theory and Production from the University of Paisley.

Lies Lanckman is a postgraduate researcher in film at the University of Kent, where she co-founded the Melodrama Research Group in 2013 and NoRMMA, the Network of Research: Movies, Magazines, Audiences, in 2014. The main focus of her research is Hollywood history of the 1920s–1940s; particular research interests include stardom and fandom, fan magazines, issues of censorship, and the career of Norma Shearer.

Dorothy Wai-sim Lau received her PhD at The University of Hong Kong and is now teaching at Academy of Film, Hong Kong Baptist University. Her research interests are film stardom, fandom, digital culture, transnational cinema and Chinese-language cinema. Her recent publications include 'The *Matrix* Hero on YouTube: Fan Vids as a Form of Transmedia Storytelling' in *Social Media: Global Perspectives, Applications and Benefits and Dangers* (2014); 'Actor or Ambassador? The Star Persona of Jackie Chan in Social Media' (2014); and 'Donnie Yen's Wing Chun Body as a Cyber-Intertext' (*Journal of Chinese Cinema*, 2013).

Julie Lobalzo Wright is a Teaching Fellow in Film Studies at the University of Surrey and has taught at Queen Mary, University of London and King's College London. Her main area of research concerns music stars in British and American cinema. She has published a chapter on David Bowie's film stardom in *David Bowie: Critical Perspectives* (2014) and has a forthcoming book based on her thesis, *Crossover Stardom: Popular Male Music Stars in American Cinema*. She has also published more widely on music and film ('The Good, the Bad and the Ugly 60s: The Opposing Gazes of *Woodstock* and *Gimme Shelter*' in *The Music Documentary: Acid Rock to Electropop* (2013)) and stardom ('The all-American golden boy: Robert Redford, blond hair and masculinity in Hollywood') in *Celebrity Studies* (2016).

Linda Marchant is Senior Lecturer in Photography at Nottingham Trent University. Her research centres around photography and celebrity, with a particular focus on film stills and the production culture of still photography within the film industry. She is currently working on a study of the work and career of British photographer Cornel Lucas. Previous research has encompassed ideas of 'visual gossip' in celebrity magazines, as well as Hollywood star photography of the 1930s and 1940s.

Claire Mortimer is researching a PhD in ageing women in British film comedy of the mid twentieth century at the University of East Anglia. Her publications include *Romantic Comedy* (2010), *Doing Film Studies* (2012) and a chapter on Alexander Mackendrick for *A Companion to Film Comedy* (2013). More recently, she has written on Peggy Mount.

Antonella Palmieri completed a PhD in Film Studies at the University of East Anglia in 2012. She is a Lecturer in Film, TV and Media at the University of Lincoln. Her research is concerned with the politics of gender, sexual, and ethnic representations in Hollywood cinema and in American and British television. She is also interested in Italian cinema and star studies. She has recently contributed to *The Routledge Encyclopedia of Films*, for which she has written on Italian and Brazilian cinemas; and to *Stars in World Cinema: Screen Icons and Star Systems across Cultures*, for which she has written on the dynamics of ethnic assimilation in Alida Valli's Hollywood persona. Her current project focuses on the construction of Virna Lisi's star image within anti-feminist narratives as a patriarchal provocation to the emergent women's liberation movement for gender equality in mid-1960s American society.

Lisa Patti is an Assistant Professor in the Media and Society Program at Hobart and William Smith Colleges. Her research focuses on global media, translation and stardom. She is co-author (with Glyn Davis, Kay Dickinson and Amy Villarejo) of *Film Studies: A Global Introduction* (2015) and co-editor (with Tijana Mamula) of *The Multilingual Screen: New Reflections on Cinema and Linguistic Difference* (forthcoming 2016).

Aparna Sharma is a documentary film maker and theorist. She works as Assistant Professor at the Department of World Arts and Cultures/Dance, University of California Los Angeles. Her films document narratives that are overlooked in the mainstream imagination of the Indian nation. She is presently working in India's northeastern region, documenting cultural practices of indigenous communities. As a film theorist, she is committed to writing about documentary and parallel cinema practices, alongside critically analysing mainstream cinemas from a feminist and post-colonial position. She has previously written on India-Pakistan ties through documentary and the representation of gender in Indian cinema. Her book-length study, *Documentary Films in India: Critical Aesthetics at Work* (2015) explores non-canonical documentary practices in India.

Frances Smith completed a PhD in Film and Television Studies at the University of Warwick in 2013, where her research discussed the construction of gender and class in the Hollywood teen movie. In addition to having written a number of journal articles and book chapters discussing gender and popular Hollywood cinema, she is the co-editor (with Prof Timothy Shary) of *Refocus: The Films of Amy Heckerling* (2016) and the author of *Rethinking the Hollywood Teen Movie* (2017), both forthcoming.

Jaap Verheul is a PhD candidate in Cinema Studies at New York University, where his dissertation focuses on popular European cinema as it chronicles the dynamics of regional and national film making in the European Union today. He has written articles on trauma and memory in Sidney Lumet's *The Pawnbroker* (*CineMagie*, Issue 260), on fascist aesthetics in the work of Busby Berkeley (*CineMagie*, Issue 266), on multiculturalism in popular American television (*CineMagie*, Issue 272), and on the representation of the European bourgeoisie in the work of Michael Haneke (*Brooklyn Rail*, December 2012). For edited collections, Jaap has also contributed chapters on paranoia and pre-emptive violence in the television series *24* (*Hollywood Politics*, 2010), on the Flemish-British co-production of a European heritage brand for television (*Screening European Heritage*, 2016), and on the dual monolingualism of contemporary Flemish cinema (*The Multilingual Screen*, 2016).

List of Illustrations

Fig. 2.1	Amitabh Bachchan in *Sholay* (1975) (courtesy of the Kobal Collection at Art Resource, NY)	14
Fig. 2.2	Amitabh Bachchan in *Kabhi Alvida Naa Kehna* (2006) (courtesy of the Kobal Collection at Art Resource, NY)	20
Fig. 7.1	Robert Taylor in *Small Town Girl* (1936)	90
Fig. 7.2	Robert Taylor in *Ivanhoe* (1952)	93
Fig. 8.1	Melanie Griffith in Cannes, by Rita Molnár (2000)	105
Fig. 11.1	James Mason in *Lolita* (1962)	147
Fig. 11.2	James Mason in *The Shooting Party* (1985)	151
Fig. 13.1	Sidney Poitier in *Guess Who's Coming to Dinner* (1967)	180
Fig. 13.2	Spencer Tracy in *Guess Who's Coming to Dinner* (1967)	181
Fig. 15.1	Margaret Rutherford in *Murder She Said* (1961)	213
Fig. 16.1	Poster for *On Her Majesty's Secret Service* (1969) (courtesy of the Kobal Collection at Art Resource, NY)	218
Fig. 18.1	Sylvester Stallone in *Rambo: First Blood Part II* (1985)	248
Fig. 18.2	Sylvester Stallone in *The Expendables* (2010)	254
Fig. 19.1	Diana Dors (c) Cornel Lucas. Reproduced by kind permission of Cornel Lucas Collection. Image supplied by BFI National Archive	263
Fig. 19.2	Diana Dors, Venice May 1955. (c) Cornel Lucas. Reproduced by kind permission of Cornel Lucas Collection	264
Fig. 19.3	Diana Dors. (c) Cornel Lucas. Reproduced by kind permission of Cornel Lucas Collection	271

Fig. 19.4	Diana Dors in *Yield to the Night* (1956) © 1956 STUDIOCANAL Films Ltd	273
Fig. 20.1	Angelina Jolie as a UNHCR Goodwill Ambassador (2005) (courtesy of UNHCR/J. Redden)	282
Fig. 20.2	Angelina Jolie in *Maleficent* (2014)	286

CHAPTER 1

Introduction

Lucy Bolton and Julie Lobalzo Wright

There are many varieties of star in the celestial firmament: shooting, hot, luminous, exotic, cool, giant, supergiant, and—of course—degenerate. These descriptions can be quite readily mapped onto human stars too, and the range and variable intensity of the array of stars in the movie firmament is part of the reason why the figure of the star has always fascinated and continues to do so today. One of the most inescapable realities of the realm of stardom is that some stars endure across the decades, enjoying lengthy and high-profile careers, while others fade away, either into obscurity or crystallised at a specific moment in time. It is the phenomenon of variable endurance and longevity that this book investigates and attempts to understand.

The impetus for exploring this idea came from the editors' appreciation of *High Society* (1956) and the enduring stardom of Frank Sinatra and Grace Kelly. As they slow-dance next to the swimming pool, gracefully intoxicated and dreamily romantic, Sinatra sings, 'Mind if I make love to you', and their images as the seductive blue-eyed crooner and the high-class 'Miss Frigidaire' with sexual fire in her belly, are captured in all their complexities and possibilities. The images of both stars varied hugely across

L. Bolton (✉) • J.L. Wright
School of Languages, Linguistics and Film, Queen Mary University of London, London, UK

their lifetimes, beyond their cinematic careers, and after their deaths (Kelly in 1982 and Sinatra in 1998). Sinatra emerged as an idol of the bobby-soxers, became a Hollywood movie actor, lived through desperate career lows, won an Oscar for his role in *From Here to Eternity* (1953), and went on to become Chairman of the Board and consolidate his position as one of the greatest entertainers of all time. Kelly's screen image was based on refinement, class, and poise, but always underscored with playfulness and a sense of mischief. Leaving Hollywood at the age of 26 and marrying a real-life prince ensured her image as Princess Grace was anointed with regal reality and European chic, and her status as icon of cool blonde beauty was accorded prominence despite her no longer having an on-screen career. Since her death, Kelly's image as an emblem of dignity and refinement has been subverted by tell-all biographies describing her promiscuity and sexual voraciousness as a young woman. Sinatra's posthumous reputation has become more overtly associated with the mafia and the Kennedys, but his musical career continues to flourish, with the show *Sinatra: The Man and his Music* playing at the London Palladium at the time of writing. Kelly was the subject of the widely derided *Grace of Monaco*, starring ice princess de jour Nicole Kidman, which opened the Cannes Film Festival in 2014. The star images of both Kelly and Sinatra not only endure then, but thrive, in the form of the continuing popularity of their own films and music, in contemporary incarnations, as well as in high-profile advertising campaigns: Kelly for L'Oreal hair colour and Sinatra for Jack Daniel's. The other stars of *High Society*, Celeste Holm and Bing Crosby, are far less well known today: Crosby is essentially confined to Christmas popular music, and Holm is all but anonymous. Considering these actors and the elements of their star personas that make Kelly and Sinatra endure while Holm and Crosby have faded away formed the foundation for this book's inquiry, which examines a wide range of star images from different eras and national cinemas, and asks why they have lasted, why they have disappeared, or how they have simply survived.

Other stars, such as Mickey Rourke, lead high-profile rollercoaster careers consisting of catastrophic falls from grace and great successes in different eras. As Keri Walsh sets out at the beginning of her British Film Institute (BFI) volume on Rourke, there are many ways of approaching the question of why we should want to watch him (2014, p. 1). Walsh concludes that Rourke is 'idiosyncratic and fascinatingly scarred' (p. 108). His career and life story are an amalgam of rumour, self-promotion, and drama, veering from the grotesquery of excessive plastic surgery to the eccentricity of being accompanied by a pet Chihuahua. Many things have been said about Rourke, but one thing is clear: he endures. Walsh's detailed analysis of his persona cannot account for this endurance other than that he fascinates. Perhaps no full explanation can be given about the lasting appeal of some stars without hypothesising about the psychological motivations and desires of fans and spectators. It is clear that 'star images have histories', as Richard Dyer observed, and his discipline-defining scholarship always stressed the temporality of the star's structured polysemy (1998, p. 63). But, as Martin Shingler identifies in his overarching *Star Studies: A Critical Guide*, there is 'considerable scope to extend the borders of knowledge and understanding' of the star studies terrain (2012, p. 15). That is the aim of this volume: to further and deepen the understanding of which factors affect the persistence or transience of star images in different contexts. This endeavour thereby extends the discipline of star studies into new conceptual territory, bringing questions of race, nationality, age, gender, and sexuality into dialogue with the question of longevity, while also drawing on concepts such as time, colour, female genealogy, and the grotesque to explore the stardom of the chosen individuals in each chapter.

The range of stars in this book is eclectic and is designed to introduce as broad a range of new concepts for thinking about stardom in the context of longevity as possible. The book is divided into six sections. Section 1, Lasting Stardom, considers stars who have endured either by their own business sense or industrial diversification, or by their association with a national stereotype. Aparna Sharma demonstrates how Bollywood superstar Amitabh Bachchan has created a 'brand Bachchan' that maintains his image in the public eye, enabling him to move from angry young man to a commanding prominent figure with a high presence on social media. Julie Lobalzo Wright shows how rapper Ice Cube has evolved from hip hop star to actor to auteur and major industrial player with his production company Cube Vision. Cube is now in a position to make his own biopic, with his son playing him, tracing his emergence in the early days of his band and his rap career. These chapters shed light on the extra-filmic work and diversification that can lead to a star becoming an industrial figure with cultural impact. Antonella Palmieri's chapter on Sophia Loren and Gabor Gergely's on Pál Jávor show how the two stars have come to embody certain aspects of Italian femininity and Hungarian masculinity respectively. For Loren, embodying the stereotype of the sexy Italian woman who can cook wonderful pasta ensures her popularity as an Italian-American ideal in *Grumpier Old Men* (1995). Jávor popularity is analysed in his own country, where he embodied a volatile and tempestuous type of masculinity seen as anti-establishment, apolitical but popular, and always as an honourable Hungarian.

Section 2, Faded Stardom, looks at actors who have been major Hollywood stars but who are not considered to be in the upper echelons of stardom today for very different reasons. Lies Lanckman explains how our cover star Norma Shearer, seen here as the epitome of 1930s glamour, became associated with very domesticated visions of love, and ultimately, widowhood, with a persona rooted in the tragic. Gillian Kelly analyses the perplexing anonymity of Robert Taylor, the handsome star, famed for his profile and irresistibility to women, whose career spanned the length of the studio system. Taylor may have had the longest contract at Metro-Goldwyn-Mayer (MGM), but is hardly known now, except to those who remember him from their cinema-going days in the 1940s and 1950s. Lucy Bolton looks at the complex and contradictory star image of Melanie Griffith and unravels the elements that have gone towards inhibiting her career. Griffith's stardom persists, and Bolton argues that this is the result of her uniquely high-profile female genealogy, as well as her off-screen life that continues to challenge and provoke as a combination of youthful rebellion and mature, maternal, femininity.

Directly engaging with questions of ageing on-screen, Section 3 looks at very different presentations of advancing years. Fiona Handyside examines the ways in which director Michael Haneke has explored how the technology of the medium of cinema can be used to draw attention to the star bodies of Emmanuelle Riva and Jean-Louis Trintingnant in *Amour* (2012). Siting this exploration as an authorial project, Handyside shows how the fimmaker focuses on the deterioration of star bodies, and reflects upon stars having their images on-screen for a lifetime, and on our relationship to viewing and remembering those images. There is no more agonising exploration of the aged star image than the trials of Buster Keaton in *Film* (1965), written by Samuel Beckett. Paul Flaig contrasts the power of this short with the conventional biopic *The Buster Keaton Story* (1957) in order to show how the former confronts the star's alienation from his own earlier self, as well as what he is now, whereas the latter peddles in traditional discourses about the march of time and the coming of sound. These powerful, original, and conceptual takes on the depiction of aged stars represent an intriguing new approach to thinking through the decayed star image and how the stars are themselves implicated in such depictions. From a more historical perspective, Adrian Garvey looks at the long career of James Mason, from Gainsborough melodrama, through his experimental sojourn in Hollywood, and final return to playing an elderly English gentleman. Garvey carefully traces the shifts in Mason's persona, particularly in terms of his masculinity, and observes how changing styles of film performance afforded Mason career longevity and adaptability despite the conflicts between the roles he could get and the ones he wanted. This section, then, takes the theme of ageing—which is becoming a popular topic in celebrity and cultural studies, with the work of scholars such as Deborah Jermyn (2013), Deborah Jermyn and Su Holmes (2015), and Imelda Whelehan and Joel Gwynne (2014)—and thinks through some of the issues that specifically pertain to cinema and film stars.

As mentioned in relation to Kelly and Sinatra, a good deal of morphing and mutilation of star images occurs posthumously, and this concept frames Section 4. Lisa Bode juxtaposes the iconic Rudolph Valentino and the now obscure Wallace Reid, and asks what happened to their careers and images to make their places in cultural memory so dichotomous. The answer, it seems, lies in posthumous manipulations of their images, one to become associated with eroticism and aesthetic progress, the other with scandal and a repression of his film work. The role of the stars' families in each case was significant in the manipulation, and in her chapter on Spencer Tracy, Hannah Graves highlights the role played by the producer Stanley Kramer in shaping Tracy's style of masculinity whilst alive and at the time of his death. Tracy's end-of-career image had become Kramer's political and auteurist project, and Graves explores the relationship between the various agendas at play in the formation and perpetuation of that image. With a more commercial aim in mind, the branding of stars' images after they are dead can be a lucrative business, capitalising as it can on the influential associations of the stars concerned. Lisa Patti considers the transnational, political, star image of Marlon Brando and its posthumous rebranding as all-American, particularly in a commercial for MasterCard. This section, therefore, asks us to consider the range of other people invested in a star's image, and the possibilities it offers for appropriation, manipulation, and commercialisation.

Section 5, looks at stars who share their image with a fictional character, a series or a type, and considers how this relationship affects the existence of the star outside this shared image. Considering the later-life stardom of Margaret Rutherford, Claire Mortimer shows how Rutherford's persona lent itself perfectly to the emblematic British eccentric, and how this enabled her to achieve international stardom in a series of performances based on her age, gender and social class. The once dismissed 'non-Bond', George Lazenby, is recuperated in Jaap Verheul's analysis of the casting, shooting, promotion, and remembering of *On Her Majesty's Secret Service* (1969). Now perceived as one of the Bonds closest to Daniel Craig's ruthless, no-frills incarnation, Lazenby might be considered to be the aficionado's Bond, with a respect and affection hitherto reserved for Sean Connery. In her exploration of the image of Molly Ringwald, Frances Smith demonstrates how a star can encapsulate the unfixed nature of stardom by both fading and enduring. Ringwald's greatest film stardom was in the 1980s, when she epitomised for many a certain type of teenage girlhood, and yet she still works as an actress, singer, and newspaper columnist, with an active profile on social media. Sylvester Stallone's type, however, is shown to endure into a new age of 'geri-action' movies. Glen Donnar shows how Stallone's embracing of the limits of his action-star image, and his deliberate replaying of both the genre and the type, enable him to extend his film performances beyond that which a more diverse range of roles would allow. Therefore, the association of a star with a type, or a character, outside their own personal traits and individuality can be seen to hinder, enable, or indeed engender a rebirth in a star's image.

The final section looks at ways in which factors from outside the film industry can have a monumental impact on the endurance of a star's image. Linda Marchant discusses the hugely prolific photographer Cornel Lucas and demonstrates the impact his portraits and stills had on the circulation of images of Diana Dors. As Marchant demonstrates, the role of production stills and portraits in maintaining the visibility of a star persona in popular culture is immeasurable. Joshua Gulam analyses the way in which Angelina Jolie's acting career has intersected with her high-profile humanitarian campaigning, revealing a striking and instrumental interrelationship between the two. In the final chapter, on the rearticulation of Bruce Lee's stardom by hip hop fans and vidders, Dorothy Wai-sim Lau makes it clear that stars' images, and indeed their work, are digitally available to be accessed, reworked and recirculated on the internet to global fan audiences in ways that the stars and their caretakers or commercial exploiters have very little control over. Democratising the star image so that fans can rearticulate what Lee means for them, fan vids offer Lee reincarnated in contemporary media for fans who weren't alive when he died.

As Richard Dyer writes in *Heavenly Bodies*, 'star images are always extensive, multimedia, intertextual' (2005, p. 3). A summary of the chapters in this book will, hopefully, be a preview of the coming attractions, but also inevitably asks more questions than it answers. Many other stars could be considered in light of the concepts we have included: Meg Ryan as a star imprisoned by her persona as America's sweetheart; Catherine Deneuve as embodying a nation's conception of femininity through the decades; and many of today's stars who are successfully marketing their own 'brand' across multimedia platforms and in various commercial contexts. Countless other concepts remain to be explored, such as the memorialisation of certain stars in exhibitions and museums (such as Ava Gardner or James Stewart); the paralysing linkage of a star with one particular role (such as Anthony Perkins as Norman Bates); or the ambivalent co-dependence of star and director (Tim Burton and Johnny Depp). Our hope for this book is that it begins to suggest probable reasons for the endurance of some stars, the fading of others, and the ups and downs of several more, and paves the way for many more star studies works to come.

REFERENCES

Amour. (2012). Film. Directed by Michael Haneke. [DVD]. UK. Artificial Eye.
Dyer, R. 1998. *Stars*, New edn. London: British Film Institute.
——— 2005. *Heavenly bodies: Film stars and society*, 2nd edn. London: Routledge.
Film. (1965). Film. Directed by Alan Schneider. [DVD]. USA: Milestone.
From Here to Eternity. (1953). Film. Directed by Fred Zinnemann. [DVD]. USA: Sony Pictures.
Grace of Monaco. (2014). Film. Directed by Olivier Dahan. [DVD]. USA: Warner Home Video.
Grumpier Old Men. (1995). Film. Directed by Howard Deutch. [DVD]. USA: Warner Bros.
High Society. (1956). Film. Directed by Charles Walters [DVD]. US: MGM.
Jermyn, D., ed. 2013. *Female celebrity and ageing: Back in the spotlight*. London: Routledge.
Jermyn, D., and S. Holmes, eds. 2015. *Women, celebrity and cultures of ageing: Freeze Frame*. Basingstoke: Palgrave Macmillan.
On Her Majesty's Secret Service. (1969). Film. Directed by Peter Hunt. [DVD]. USA: MGM Home Entertainment.
Shingler, M. 2012. *Star studies: A critical guide*. London: British Film Institute.
The Buster Keaton Story. (1957). Film. Directed by Sidney Sheldon. [Streaming]. USA: Paramount.
Walsh, K. 2014. *Mickey Rourke*. Basingstoke: Palgrave Macmillan.
Whelehan, I., and J. Gwynne, eds. 2014. *Ageing, popular culture and contemporary feminism: Harleys and hormones*. Basingstoke: Palgrave Macmillan.

SECTION 1

Lasting Stardom

CHAPTER 2

From Angry Young Man to Icon of Neo-liberal India: Extra-cinematic Strategies that Make Amitabh Bachchan India's Lasting Super-Star

Aparna Sharma

In 1999, Amitabh Bachchan was voted the 'Greatest Super-Star of the Millennium' by a BBC online viewer poll, surpassing such luminaries as Lawrence Olivier and Marilyn Monroe. Starring in over 180 films since his career began in the late 1960s, Amitabh Bachchan epitomises the quintessence of stardom in India. His domination of Hindi cinema from the 1970s to the 1990s and his extra-cinematic media undertakings since then have ensured that Bachchan is a persistent presence in India's public imagination. He is both a media participant—that is, a vehicle of media messages—and a subject of media attention, spanning news media and fanzines that have persistently followed his work as well as his political and personal life for decades. A vast and highly evolved fan culture exists around him, made up of the usual items, such as posters, T-shirts, calendars, and mugs with Bachchan motifs, but also the actor's memorabilia, and dedicated shrines where fans worship and perform rituals before iconic objects including

A. Sharma
Department of World Arts and Cultures/Dance,
University of California Los Angeles, Los Angeles, UK

photographs and the star's film costumes. This means that Amitabh Bachchan has a quite material and iconic presence across India.

Between 1984 and 1987, Amitabh Bachchan had a brief stint in national politics and his family continues to be politically active. His styling in the political arena compares with that of former US President Ronald Regan, who was also an actor turned politician. Bachchan has been embroiled in political scandals such as the Bofors Gun Scandal, has suffered health and economic setbacks, and has had a love-hate relationship with the press.[1] Given these factors, the singularity and persistence of Bachchan's popularity in the public realm constitutes a unique phenomenon in India that is linked to, but clearly exceeds, his cinematic performances. In this chapter, I will focus on extra-cinematic factors, particularly Bachchan's consistent use of mass media other than cinema to illustrate how the actor has maintained his star image. I take my cue here from Janet Staiger's new historicist move to examine 'adjacent facts' or 'related histories' through which an area of focus related to stars can be studied and complicated (qtd. in Staiger, 1991, p. 3). Star images, as Richard Dyer points out, are 'constructed personages in media texts'. These images are particular and interesting, and can 'be both normative with respect to social types and individuated with respect to the specific realization of those types' (1998, p. 97). In this essay, I will analyse the workings of Bachchan's star image that audiences have identified for decades and that account for Bachchan's longevity as an iconic star.

Since the early 1990s when Bachchan's domination of Hindi cinema started to decline, his non-cinema, media activities proliferated, building on his popularity from his years of active domination of Hindi cinema. I specifically want to probe a disparity between Bachchan's early screen persona as the angry young man and his more recent star image that mobilises and endorses the values of India's neo-liberal economic agendas. It appears that the contemporary Bachchan star image lacks the anti-establishment force of the earlier, angry young man, but this seeming disparity can be contested if we closely analyse how the recent Bachchan star image coincides with, and galvanises, the appeal of the angry young man. For this analysis, it is pertinent to begin by understanding the angry

---

[1] Amitabh Bachchan's relationship with the press has been marked by fractures throughout his career. Numerous media reports reference this. See, for example, http://gulfnews.com/arts-entertainment/film/amitabh-bachchan-s-love-hate-relationship-with-rann-1.575972. Also, see Mishra (2002).

young man persona with which Amitabh Bachchan came to be associated in his reigning years.

Exploding the Screen: Bachchan as the Angry Young Man

Amitabh Bachchan started his film career in 1969. He debuted in the moderately successful, *Saat Hindustani* (*Seven Indians*) by Khwaja Abbas Ali, a film on the liberation of Goa from Portuguese colonial rule. The same year, he voiced parallel cinema director[2] Mrinal Sen's highly acclaimed *Bhuvan Shome*, a satirical take on a civil servant's encounters in the countryside. Bachchan continued in a number of films until his 'big break', the 1973 hit *Zanjeer* (*Chain*), a revenge action thriller directed by Prakash Mehra. Though Bachchan had already been noted for his remarkable performance in earlier films such as *Anand* (1971), it was *Zanjeer* and the hits that followed, like *Sholay* (1975) and *Deewar* (1975), that established him as the ruling star of Hindi cinema.

Bachchan has been understood as an all-round entertainer whose performance style has seamlessly met the needs of the dominant *masala* and melodramatic genres of Hindi cinema. He has, at once, been able to deliver a serious, comedic, romantic, heroic and cynical performance all peppered with accomplished song and dance presentations. In the period of his singular domination of Hindi cinema, Bachchan principally performed as an urban and industrial subject either fully situated in the urban landscape or making a transition from the rural to the urban. Many of his performances are set against urban landscapes, towering cityscapes, and specifically, in industrial locations such as railway stations, docks, five-star hotels, and industries. The narratives of these films are closely tied to the economic and social life of these settings. Their themes include displacement, loss, poverty, crime, and the values associated with these: victimhood, deceit, and revenge. Situating Bachchan in the urban context was semiotically significant for it brought him into conversation with progressive national discourse in which industrialisation and urbanism had been reified as the routes and symptoms of modernised development.

---

[2] Parallel cinema is a term used to refer to India's art-house, non-commercial cinema. Acclaimed parallel cinema directors include Satyajit Ray, Ritwik Ghatak, Aparna Sen, Mrinal Sen, Mani Kaul, and Kumar Shahani, among others.

Through the 1970s and 1980s, Bachchan assumed the screen persona of the angry young man, the rebel, the anti-hero who contests dominant powers and the established order (Fig. 2.1). In much Indian film scholarship Bachchan's donning of the 'angry young man' persona is tied to the rising social and political unrest in India during the 1970s (see Virdi, 2003; Mazumdar, 2007; Prasad, 1998). A political crisis of the 1970s had culminated in the watershed Emergency of 1975–1977, when Prime Minister Indira Gandhi suspended the democratic apparatus, imposing military rule to combat what her government projected as nationwide anarchy. The socio-political crisis of this time can be contextualised in relation to the broader public sentiments of the preceding decades in India. Following India's independence in 1947, a sense of euphoria, hope, and idealism swept public imagination. The birth of a new nation free from colonial domination fostered social and political self-confidence on which converged aspirations for political, economic, and social progress. The euphoria and idealism of the early decades after independence started to

Fig. 2.1 Amitabh Bachchan as the angry young man Jai in *Sholay* (1975) (courtesy of the Kobal Collection at Art Resource, New York)

dwindle by the late 1960s and early 1970s, being replaced by a sense of disillusionment with the political, social, and economic orders. Against this backdrop, Bachchan's angry-young-man persona offered a kind of articulation of the general sense of despair in India, forming an outlet for the Indian people's loss of faith in the socio-political establishment.

As an angry young man, Bachchan performed what can be loosely termed as proletarian roles, figures who were situated at the fringes of society, members of the working classes, and small-time crooks or criminals. The angry young man embodied deep senses of loss, anger, dissent, and rebelliousness that were often tied to a disturbed past and formed the basis for a desired future, evidenced in films including *Coolie* (1983), *Namak Halal* (1982), *Sholay* (1975), *Main Azaad Hoon* (1989), and *Hum* (1991). Situating the angry young man on the fringes of society socialised his anger, rebelliousness, and anti-heroism. Commenting on the links of Bachchan's angry-young-man persona with working-class consciousness, Jyotika Virdi states:

> In the body politic of the nation, these films showcase working class disenchantment. Always a subaltern figure—coal miner, dock worker, factory worker, porter, slum dweller—the Bachchan figure challenged employers, factory owners, mafia men, and capitalist bosses either from his underdog position, or by rising to the top to vindicate past (inevitably familial) humiliation. In the process he exposed the machinations of the system. (2003, p. 107)

A number of film scholars have further illustrated that the rebelliousness and dissatisfaction at the heart of the angry young man finds precedents in India's epic literatures (see Mishra, 2002, p. 128; Mazumdar, 2007, pp. 11–13). The angry young man rebelled against the established order of things and, through this, he challenged the figure of the noble, transcendent *dharmik* hero, who had dominated Indian cinema in the preceding decades. The *dharmik* hero was a virtuous figure who was aligned with tradition and occupied a dominant, socially sanctioned position, one that enforced existing social hierarchies. The angry young man, on the other hand, was closer to the complex figure of Karna, the anti-hero from the epic *Mahabharata*.[3] Karna was the eldest of the Pandavas, whose parentage

---

[3] The *Mahabharata* is one of the two Sanskrit epics of ancient Indian literature. It focuses on the great war between the Kauravas and the Pandavas. A part of the *Mahabharata* is Krishna's discourse of the *Bhagvad Gita*.

was withheld from him and, in rebellion, he sided with the Kauravas, enemies of the Pandavas, during the Great War, the *Mahabharata*. Karna was thus an anti-hero and a rebel. Bachchan, as the angry young man, contested the virtuous and *dharmik* hero, and this served a dual purpose for Bachchan, the star. First, it gave his screen persona a cultural sanction and mythic symbolism linking Bachchan with India's classical traditions. This is in keeping with Richard Dyer's reasoning that in evaluating a star's roles it is pertinent to examine them in regard to a culture's precursor texts (1998).[4] Second, aligning Bachchan with the epic anti-hero infused the star with a radical drive, opening him up for wide and popular appeal, cutting across class lines.

Bachchan's angry-young-man persona rested on a distinct performance style that was evident early in his career, in films such as *Anand* (1971) and *Guddi* (1971). The key feature of this performance style has been a clear, often quiet communication of raging dissent simmering beneath a very commanding, self-assured and, on occasion, melancholic exterior. Ranjani Mazumdar has noted that Bachchan's acting is based on a 'brooding, inward-looking yet outwardly searching' screen presence that efficaciously touched upon the vulnerable anger that was the symptom of the 1970s and 1980s. She adds, 'Bachchan's ability to absorb and transmit both the "modern" and the "traditional", the Eastern and the Western, through a novel body language, is perhaps the single most important reason for his unmatched status in the history of Bombay cinema' (2007, p. 10). Commenting on Bachchan's appeal, Vijay Mishra notes that he was the first post-partition star who came from the Hindi-speaking heartland and was thoroughly conversant with standard Hindi and a number of its dialects, a major factor that contributed to the star's mass appeal. Mishra adds that Bachchan was also the last pan-Indian hero, given that most contemporary Bollywood film stars command audiences in particular linguistic and cultural constituencies across India (Mishra, 2002, p. 128).

While the angry young man was often a proletarian figure, the values of the films themselves were not necessarily proletarian. The melodramatic form of the films Bachchan starred in often styled him as a sort of 'superhero', avenging himself and making a desirable transition from poverty-stricken and disadvantaged fringes to positions of power and affluence in society. Narratives of revenge, retribution, and the rags-to-riches journey

---

[4] For detailed discussion of Bachchan's alignment with Karna, see Mishra (2002) and Mazumdar (2007).

offered an imaginary fulfilment of the fantasies of the urban poor and slum dwellers, and this elevated the star above the masses he was supposedly representing. This elevation is at the heart of an ambiguity in relation to stars generally: they have to be identifiable with the masses they represent and yet their star appeal rests on qualities that distinguish them from the masses—the stars-as-ordinary and stars-as-exceptional dynamic that Dyer points out (1998). So while the angry young man might have started as a proletarian figure, he did not form the basis of a proletarian cinema, advancing proletarian values or approaches to social and economic issues. Madhava Prasad has described these as middle-class films that adopted a code of ordinariness and excluded both the 'splendour of the aristocracy'—thereby contesting the established social hierarchies—and the political passions and approaches to social change of the proletariat. Specifically commenting on Bachchan, Prasad elaborates:

> the star became a mobilizer, demonstrating superhuman qualities and assuming a power that transformed the others who occupied the same terrain into *spectators*. As the auratic power of the represented social order diminished, there was a compensating increase in the aura of the star as public persona. (Prasad, 1998, p. 134)

In relation to Bachchan, it can then be argued that an uncanny identification occurred in which audiences could identify with the actor and yet there was a separation, an aura, that distinguished him from his fans, thus intensifying the liminality of the cinematic experience. Nandini Bhattacharya comments on this:

> To retain iconic, talismanic charisma, the star and the fan must not become undifferentiated, indistinguishable, etc. The star, in representing fans, must not lose his defining otherness, and become fully present without absence, or fully representative and inclusive. Indeed, his presence must rather always gesture toward a return from that utter abyss of the liminal and the void, which the incommensurable hoi polloi represent with their cargo of excess and difference; the invocation of that eternal return as also an eternal separation must never be done away with. (2013, p. 154)

The angry young man was a macho super-hero and, as the principal driving agent for the film narrative, eclipsed women's roles. This had a negative fall-out for Hindi cinema because it resulted in a lack of women-centered narratives. Reduced to limited roles, often a romantic sub-plot in the film, women, as Jyotika Virdi points out, were turned into 'liminal figures in narratives centered on a newfound masculinity' (2003, p. 178). While the angry young man revealed corruption and anti-national elements, such as smugglers and racketeers, the women's functions in these films were often reduced to spectacular display offering temporary relief from a hyper-masculinised aggressive plot led by a super-macho figure. Hindi cinema, through a figure such as Bachchan, thus regurgitated exactly the kind of heterosexual division of labour that Laura Mulvey describes in *Visual Pleasure and Narrative Cinema* in relation to the classical Hollywood genre (Mulvey, 2008, pp. 202–212). Bachchan clearly dominated most of his films including *Satte Pe Satta* (1982), *Shakti* (1982), *Sharaabi* (1984), *Shehanshah* (1988) and *Agneepath* (1990).

Following the 'Angry Young Man': Bachchan and Neo-liberalism in India

From the 1990s, Bachchan's dominance started to decline as younger stars came to the fore and the film genres based on the persona of the angry young man receded. Instead, predominantly romantic and familial films that constitute the bulk of what is today known as Bollywood gained popularity. Bachchan has continued to work in films, on occasion, in a leading role, and at other times, as a guest or supporting actor. His roles are more diversified and the anchorage of film narratives is now often shared between him and other stars. In a number of films, Bachchan has performed what can be loosely described as experimental roles, in that he takes on the role of a social misfit who is at odds with the socially sanctioned order. While this may resonate with his angry-young-man persona of earlier years, the difference is that the misfits he portrays are often from society's well-heeled sections and not the proletariat. For instance, in *Cheeni Kum* (2007), he performs as an eccentric head chef at an upmarket London restaurant while, in *Nishabd* (2007), he plays a well-to-do senior photographer.

Bachchan has adapted his performance style to meet the needs of contemporary film aesthetics that have acquired particular definition with the explosion of Bollywood on the global arena.[5] Ravi Vasudevan notes that

---

[5] The global popularity of Bollywood is due to the growing visibility of Bollywood films at international film festivals and the constitution of Indian diasporic audiences as defined exhibition and distribution territories for films.

the style of contemporary Bollywood cinema has developed largely in response to a growing external market, involving export of 'the elaborate staging of Indianness through the rituals of the so-called traditional family' (2011, p. 304). In this scenario Bachchan has increasingly donned the role of a patriarch, a seat of familial and/or institutional values, and on occasion, a disciplinarian, as seen in films such as *Kabhie Khushi Kabhie Gham* (2001), *Mohabattein* (2000), and the *Sarkar* series (2005, 2008). Bachchan's performances in the last decade and a half appear diametrically opposed to the angry young man who came from the peripheries and disadvantaged sections of urban and industrial society. How can we contextualise and appreciate this visible shift from the periphery to the centre? If the angry young man articulated a backlash against the order of the day, then we have to now ask how Bachchan's contemporary persona relates to the socio-political and economic currents in India since the 1990s.

In order to undertake this we have to start by following the particular trajectory of Indian society since the 1990s. In 1991 the Indian economy was liberalised, ushering in a period of sharp economic growth and the expansion of India's middle classes. The start of the 1990s was the time when Bachchan was shifting from the cinematic centre-stage and his star image called for a rearticulation that would allow him to maintain his public presence. In the 1990s he made large investments in film and entertainment productions, and event management. His enterprises were not very successful and public enthusiasm around him dwindled. But Bachchan swung back to popularity in 2000, when he hosted the popular quiz game show, *Kaun Banega Crorepati* (*KBC*, translated as *Who Wants to Be a Millionaire?*). Bachchan has also gone on to undertake many product endorsements, appearing in televisual and print advertisements for products and services as diverse as chocolate, fast food, jewellery, clothes, cement, and public services. He has made numerous television appearances on chat and game shows, and lent his voice to a number of films.

Bachchan's proliferation into other media clearly reflects the avenues available to a star beyond his prime years. This proliferation is very closely styled and builds on Bachchan's popularity, advancing it by increasingly situating the star as an accessible figure in the public arena. In contrast to the angry young man who was palpably visible against urban vistas and who embodied the proletariat's senses of displacement and loss in its encounters with modernity, the older Bachchan is more mellow and appears almost co-extensive with the urban vista, aligned with the values underpinning the contemporary urban dweller. The angry young man's visual persona had built on Bachchan's particular physique—that is, his tall figure (by Indian standards), standing at over six feet. Commenting on this, Ravi Vasudevan notes that from the 1970s onwards, the urban vista and its associations with modernity had increasingly come under a critical lens. Icons of modernisation of a Nehruvian persuasion were rendered dark provocateurs of mayhem and destruction. The body's relationship to industry, and the urban vista more broadly, were unsettled, 'bound up with involuntary industrial rhythms' (2011, p. 308). Bachchan's tall figure, Vasudevan notes, in films such as *Muqqaddar ka Sikandar*, *Coolie*, and *Trishul*, 'appears almost architecturally of a piece with the vertical lines of the Bombay cityscape' (2011, p. 309).

The older Bachchan (Fig. 2.2) aligns with the urban vista (which, after economic liberalisation, is increasingly metropolitan), less through anger or rebellion and instead, more affirmatively. In the contemporary context, Bachchan is often framed against metropolitan vistas as a warm and inviting figure, leading India towards the global arena. This warm and mellow Bachchan persona follows the very modes of interaction from programmes, including *KBC*, that inaugurated a direct and intimate mode of

Fig. 2.2 Older Bachchan as Samarjeet or Sam in *Kabhi Alvida Naa Kehna* (2006) (courtesy of the Kobal Collection at Art Resource, New York)

address towards audiences. *KBC* was the first show that brought the star in face-to-face contact with his audiences as they played a quiz game that he anchored.[6] Dealing with fortunes of money, Bachchan created a very sensitive place for the game show participants, a place that was upheld by his warm, jovial, and supportive demeanour. Following *KBC*, many advertising campaigns, including public service advertising, built on this warm, intimate, and commanding persona—for example, the 2005 advertisement campaign run by the Ministry of Health and Family Welfare in collaboration with UNICEF that sought to encourage mass participation in a programme for polio eradication. Bachchan appeared in a series of television advertisements for this programme and in these, he exhibits a diverse repertoire of address modes towards the public. Principally conversational, on occasion, he is comedic and challenging to others, elderly and giving advice, and, at all points, he speaks directly into the camera, thereby breaking the invisible wall that divides the star and his audience. In a few advertisements he is even accompanied by family members, heightening the senses of informality and intimacy with his audiences.

In yet another public interest campaign, Bachchan almost constitutes a stand-in for India's accelerating economic profile. In the *India Poised: Our Time Is Now* campaign devised by the Times Media Group, we see Bachchan touting the span of India's unfolding economic miracle. The advertisement is shot in both Hindi and English, to reach wide audiences. The site for enacting this testimonial is symbolically charged: a metropolitan vista, including an under-construction road that connects an industrial installation out in the vast sea, is geared to reflect India as a landscape on the march, increasingly making her global presence felt. India is represented as a landscape going through a profound transition. The metropolitan vista is visibly unpeopled, with no traces of labour at this industrial site, which is still under construction. This gives us a sanitised view that erases the disparities of class that such a site necessarily implies. Directly addressing the audience, Bachchan charts a rhetorical divide between one India that *wants and leads* and another that *hopes and follows*. He says,

> There are two Indias in this country. One India is straining at the leash, eager to spring forth and live up to all the adjectives that the world has recently

---

[6] Many participants have expressed that their reason for participating in the show was not the prospect of winning it as much as that it offered them a chance to get face-to-face with the star.

been showering upon us. The other India is the leash. One India says give me the chance and I'll prove myself. The other India says prove yourself first and maybe then you'll have a chance. One India lives in the optimism of our hearts. The other India lurks in the scepticism of our minds.

As Bachchan's commentary proceeds, India is presented as passing through a transition where the older view of things is being replaced by a new, more emphatic and assertive view. This narrative of transition is directed towards a decisively favourable conclusion, a happy ending much like those of many of Bachchan's mainstream films.[7] A deep sense of affirmation underlies the narrative of this advertisement and the whole scenario lends itself seamlessly to the euphoric discourses on India's economic progress that have proliferated since the liberalisation of the economy. The India that is poised to be a key global player is diametrically disparate from the India of the Emergency years, when the angry young man had mobilised a deep sense of disillusionment and despair against the established socio-economic orders.

Both the advertisements discussed above use very specific camera vocabulary that successively takes the viewer closer to Bachchan, magnifying his figure and complementing his direct and intimate address to the audience. A camera choreography that finely mixes mid shots and close-up shots is deployed for this. In keeping with his cinematic persona, Bachchan delivers a commanding performance that is restrained and builds on the emotional identification audiences feel towards him. His age is barely concealed and actually bolsters a sense of authority complementing his overall persona.

Conclusion

It is clear that Bachchan's screen persona has undergone a massive shift through the two broad periods of his film career. The first, when his presence was principally tied to cinema, and the second, when he had become

---

[7] Writer and activist Arundhati Roy has commented on the India Poised campaign, noting that Bachchan's commentary in the advertisement divides India into the rich and the poor. According to Roy, the campaign presents the poor as having a choice to 'become rich'. The campaign asserts, she adds, that if the poor choose not to 'become rich', 'it's because they are choosing pessimism over optimism, hesitation over confidence, want over hope'. Roy's analysis of the campaign reflects Bachchan as aligning with a neo-liberal agenda in India (Roy, 2009, p. 166).

a prominent figure who easily migrated across media. Over the last few years, Bachchan's social media presence has also increased, offering him a new platform through which to exert his presence in the public sphere. Regular tweets either by or on behalf of the actor include memories of working in films, reminiscences of colleagues, family news, and private photographs. Bachchan's tone in the social media builds on the intimacy that has defined his televisual presence. His tweets are personal, emotional, and on occasion, poetic, positioning the star as a reflective people's person—as, for instance, when he composed a poem in memory of Delhi's rape victim in 2013. Social media offers a more ready avenue for insight into the personal life of the star, which was only partially revealed through other media.

Social media also enables the star to monitor and respond to the parallel texts surrounding him. In this regard, Martin Shingler notes that Bachchan's Internet presence has enabled him 'to exercise a greater degree of control over his image, forge more direct links with his audience, while providing his fans with more immediate, extensive and direct information about the star and enabling them to contribute to the Bachchan discourses in public circulation around the world' (2012, p. 136). Whereas, in the 1980s and 1990s, the parallel texts around Bachchan reported on dimensions of his personal life, like a near-fatal accident and his involvement in the Bofors gun scandal, through social media, Bachchan appears as the direct source of information and minutiae about his life. There is thus a greater element of authenticity to his social media profile than that which has been constructed by print media, particularly fanzines. This sense of authenticity serves to enhance a feeling of direct access to the star.

Bachchan has persisted in India's public imagination for over four decades. This is on account of his ease of migration across media, which is partly facilitated by the way film actors in India pursue lucrative parallel careers through television. For Bachchan, however, his migration to other media rests, in large part, on his phenomenal success as the angry young man, the persona which shot him to pan-Indian stardom. The space within the public imagination that he was able to secure has so persisted that it has facilitated the appeal of his more recent star image. There is a seeming contrast between the angry young man who started as a proletarian figure and the recent Bachchan who very explicitly aligns with India's neo-liberal agenda, becoming, in turn, a brand himself. But if we follow Madhava Prasad's argument of the angry young man as the basis of middle-class films—namely, that even though he hailed from the proletariat, the angry young man's films upheld middle-class values—then it stands to reason that Amitabh Bachchan's star persona would lend itself favourably to the socio-economic changes that have occurred in India over the last two-and-a-half decades. The desire for mobility that was at the heart of the angry young man narratives has found realisation in the socio-economic milieu that has evolved in India following economic liberalisation. Bachchan's explicit alignment with the neo-liberal worldview also marks what Richard Dyer has termed *transcendence*: 'when a great star transcends the [social] type to which they belong and become utterly individual' (1998, p. 99). This transcendence, in the case of Bachchan, pertains both to his screen persona and his broader star image. He can reach vast audiences as someone close and in touch with their moods, and yet he is no longer one of them. The moment that exemplifies this is in Danny Boyle's *Slumdog Millionaire* (2009) is when Bachchan is seen giving his autograph to a child from the slums. This scene marks Bachchan's transcendence of the social type the angry young man was associated with: the urban poor, the slum dwellers. In the act of giving his autograph to the slum child, the Bachchan star text marks the full transcendence of the star from the social class he *represented* and for which he has become a demi-god, a brand himself.

References

Anand. (1971). Film. Directed by Hrishikesh Mukherjee. [DVD]. India: Shemaroo.
Bhattacharya, N. 2013. *Hindi cinema: Repeating the subject*. London: Routledge.
Bhuvan Shome. (1969). Film. Directed by Mrinal Sen. [DVD]. India: Ultra Distributors Pvt. Ltd..
Cheeni Kum. (2007). Film. Directed by R. Balki. India: MAD Entertainment Ltd.
Coolie. (1983). Film. Directed by Manmohan Desai. India: Aasia Films Pvt. Ltd. and M. K. D. Films Combine.
Deewar. (1975). Film. Directed by Yash Chopra. [DVD]. India: Eros Entertainment.
Dyer, R. 1998. *Stars*. London: BFI Publishing.
Guddi. (1971). Film. Directed by Hrishikesh Mukherjee. [DVD]. USA: Bollywood Entertainment.
Hum. (1991). Film. Directed by Mukul Anand. India: Dharma Productions.
Kabhi Alvida Na Kehna. (2006). Film. Directed by Karan Johar. [DVD]. India: Dharma Productions and Yash Raj Films.

Kabhi Khushi Kabhi Gham. (2001). Film. Directed by Karan Johar. [DVD]. India: Yash Raj Films.
Main Azaad Hoon. (1989). Film. Directed by Tinnu Anand. India: Nadiadwala Sons.
Mazumdar, R. 2007. *Bombay cinema: An archive of the City.* Minneapolis: University of Minnesota Press.
Mishra, V. 2002. *Bollywood cinema: Temples of desire.* London: Routledge.
Mohabbatein. (2000). Film. Directed by Aditya Chopra. [DVD]. India: Yash Raj Films.
Mulvey, L. 2008. Visual pleasure and narrative cinema. In *The Routledge critical and cultural theory reader*, eds. N. Badmington, and J. Thomas. London: Routledge.
Muqaddar ka Sikandar. (1978). Film. Directed by Prakash Mehra. India: Prakash Mehra Productions.
Namak Halal. (1982). Film. Directed by Prakash Mehra. [DVD]. USA and Canada: Video Sound.
Nishabd. (2007). Film. Directed by Ram Gopal Varma. India: Reliance Mediaworks and Eros International.
Prasad, M.M. 1998. *Ideology of the Hindi film: A historical construction*, 6th edn. New Delhi: OUP.
Roy, A. 2009. *Field notes on democracy: Listening to grasshoppers.* Chicago, IL: Haymarket Books.
Sarkar. (2005). Film. Directed by Ram Gopal Varma. India: K Sera Sera & Sahara One.
Sarkar Raj. (2008). Film. Directed by Ram Gopal Varma. India: Showman Pictures & Balaji Motion Pictures.
Shingler, M. 2012. *Star studies: A critical guide.* Basingstoke: BFI and Palgrave Macmillan.
Sholay. (1975). Film. Directed by Ramesh Sippy. [DVD]. India: Eros Entertainment.
Slumdog Millionaire. (2009). Film. Directed by Danny Boyle. India & UK: Fox Searchlight Pictures and Warner Brothers Pictures.
Staiger, J. 1991. Seeing stars. In *Stardom: Industry of desire*, ed. C. Gledhill. London: Routledge.
Trishul. (1978). Film. Directed by Yash Chopra. India: Yash Raj Films & Trimurti Films.
Vasudevan, R. 2011. *The melodramatic public: Film form and spectatorship in Indian cinema.* New York: Palgrave Macmillan.
Virdi, J. 2003. *The cinematic imagination: Indian popular films as social history.* Permanent Black: New Delhi.
Zanjeer. (1973). Film. Directed by Prakash Mehra. [DVD]. India: Eros Entertainment.

CHAPTER 3

Sophia Loren and the Healing Power of Female Italian Ethnicity in *Grumpier Old Men*

Antonella Palmieri

Pauline Small observes that 'Loren is generally thought of as a star well known to her public' (2009, p. 9). She contends that from the earliest years there has been great media coverage of Loren's public persona, featuring reviews of the films she has starred in, interviews with the star, articles on her appearances at film festivals and award ceremonies, and material related to the books she has authored on beauty, cooking and fashion, and the products she has endorsed, such as perfumes and *haute couture*. Media interest in the circumstances of Loren's 'private' life has been equally consistent over the decades, with reportage covering her modest origins as an illegitimate child in Italy, her marriage to film producer Carlo Ponti, a brief stint in an Italian jail in 1982 for tax evasion, and her struggle to become a mother (2009, p. 9).

An article published in the January 1991 issue of *Vanity Fair* (Collins) features a photograph of Loren looking sultry and alluring in diamond jewellery and a black evening gown that exposes her ample bosom and

---

A. Palmieri
School of Film and Media, University of Lincoln, Lincoln, UK

© The Editor(s) (if applicable) and The Author(s) 2016
L. Bolton, J.L. Wright (eds.), *Lasting Screen Stars*,
DOI 10.1057/978-1-137-40733-7_3

long legs. Loren, then 57, is visually constructed in an image that presents her as the embodiment of smouldering sensuality. Meanwhile, writing in the *Orange County Register* at the time of the release of *Grumpier Old Men* (1995), Barry Koltnow (1995) first reminds his readers that Loren, aged 60, performed a bedtime striptease for Marcello Mastroianni in Robert Altman's *Prêt-à-Porter* (1994). He then suggests that in playing Italian- American Maria-Sophia Coletta Ragetti in *Grumpier Old Men* (hereinafter *Grumpier*) 61-year-old Loren, '[who] helped to define cinematic sexiness in the 1950s and 1960s, is helping to redefine it in the 1990s' (Koltnow, 1995). Along the same lines, in 'Still Sexy after 60', Henry Fenwick claims that what gives Sophia Loren her staying power is 'a potent combination of sex appeal, humour and inner warmth' (1999, p. 17). These and similar pieces function as a testament to the staying power of Loren's star image in American popular culture of the 1990s, as the star was positively connoted as an age-defying sex symbol who, well into her sixties, was still capable of stirring passions with her lasting sensuality. This chapter focuses on Loren's role in *Grumpier*[1] along with the promotional, publicity and critical texts circulating around the film and star. Taking into consideration the discursive elements around Loren's off-screen persona in American popular culture of the time, I discuss how, in *Grumpier,* Loren is presented as highly sexualised within a narrative where the character she plays is connoted, as soon as she enters the story, as a strongly determined, sexy, hard-working, and self-sufficient second-generation Italian American. In turn, Loren's character's ethnicity, legitimated by the casting of Loren, is marked as a sign of authenticity and shown to be a way of injecting a new sense of enjoyment and rejuvenation into a life of exhausted whiteness. In this light I locate my reading of Loren's image as aligned with a specific social climate of the time, one marked by a cultural rethinking of the meanings of whiteness and by the re-evaluation of one's ethnic heritage as a key element in one's individual identity project. I therefore argue that Loren's enduring image at the end of the twentieth century, and her Italian identity, were made meaningful within the production and consumption of 'authentic' Italianness

[1] The sequel of the 1993 *Grumpy Old Men*, *Grumpier,* is set in Wabasha (Minnesota). Neighbours Max (Walter Matthau) and John (Jack Lemmon) still compete with each other to catch the Catfish Hunter, the legendary, local, lake fish. When Italian American Maria Sophia Coletta Ragetti arrives in town, they go to great lengths to sabotage her plan to turn their beloved bait shop into an Italian restaurant. Despite the rocky start, however, Max and Maria-Sophia eventually fall in love and get married.

in the USA, and functioned as a literal and metaphorical incarnation of a specific dimension of ethnicity in American culture of the late twentieth century—namely, the fantasy of de-assimilation.

Signifying Function and National Iconicity of Film Stars

As Richard Dyer suggests, film stars have a 'signification' (1998, p. 1) outside a particular film text that is only partly incorporated into that film. Dyer argues that the construction within culture of a film star's image, and therefore the star's signifying function, incorporates representations of the star within a wide range of media texts beyond films, including newspaper and magazine stories, fan magazines, publicity material, television programmes, press interviews, personal appearances and promotional material. It follows, according to Graeme Turner, that since 'stars are "signs" not necessarily or entirely subsumed within the character they are asked to play [...] the casting of a particular star has important repercussions on the effect the characterisation will have' (1999, p. 120). Turner then refers to John Wayne, suggesting that his casting 'was always determined by what *he* signified, the inscription of a particular version of Americanism. His later roles (in *The Shootist* and *True Grit*) were self-reflexive in that they commented upon this signifying function by parodying it or self-consciously mythologizing it' (1999, p. 120). Building on Turner's argument, I argue that Loren's signifying function is evident in *Grumpier*. The film's narrative plays with Loren's on-screen and off-screen persona: for example, her character is called Maria-Sophia, and three of Maria-Sophia's former husbands are named Carlo, Edoardo, and Marcello—Carlo and Edoardo being the names of Loren's sons, and the names Carlo and Marcello also reminding the audience of Loren's film producer husband Carlo Ponti and the Italian film star Marcello Mastroianni, with whom, as Small observes, Loren formed her most fruitful on-screen partnership (2009, p. 89). However, what is particularly significant in the context of my discussion is that the casting of Loren sanctions *Grumpier*'s projection of ethnic identity.

Loren's representative relationship to Italian culture authenticates her as a 'native informant'[2] on the grounds of her national affiliation. Ginette Vincendeau suggests that French stars of the calibre of Catherine Deneuve

---

[2] Negra (2002, p. 74, note 41).

or Gerard Depardieu carry the 'burden' of national identity and come to be defined by their Frenchness (2000, p. 31). Vincendeau also argues that whereas American stars, given the global nature of the Hollywood system of production and distribution, tend to acquire an international dimension because of the worldwide market to which they are exposed, European-born stars can be regarded as 'more national', because they are exposed to a much smaller market. Building on this, I propose that those Italian film stars who, like Loren, happen to enjoy international popularity are perceived as embodying the nation, and are defined by their national identity. When abroad, actors, whether they are stars or not, also function as 'ambassadors' for their country, and thus also embody a 'fantasised', constructed ethnicity which, as Ian Jarvie claims, can be said to result from the interaction of their 'real' ethnicity (the ethnicity of actors/actresses as it would appear on their census form), their 'perceived' ethnicity (the ethnicity of the stars embodied in those actors/actresses: the off-screen star persona), and their ethnicity on screen (the ethnicity of the role the star plays on the screen: the ethnic content of the role itself) (2004, pp. 168–169).

That national film stars are culturally validated as embodiments of the nation seems to be especially evident in a particular episode Gundle makes reference to in 'Sophia Loren, Italian Icon'. When Loren was voted Italy's national idol (*mito nazionale*) in a poll of several million people in 1989, a proposal to erect a statue of Loren was put forward. This gained strong backing from the local population of Loren's home town, Pozzuoli, which was to be the home of the statue. However, it eventually came to nothing, following a request from Loren that the scheme be abandoned. As Gundle observes, the episode reveals that 'as well as being the best-known and most celebrated Italian actress, [Loren] is seen as a timeless symbol of her country's spirit, someone who stands above fashion and shifts in popular taste' (1995, p. 367). While this shows that national film stars are culturally validated as embodiments of the nation by indigenous audiences, another episode tells how such a perception travels outside national borders. Writing in 1999, Fenwick commented, 'Last year, when [Loren] was awarded a Golden Lion for career achievement at the Venice Film Festival, Italian movie star Vittorio Gassman seemed to be speaking for all Italians when he paid tribute to her as "our constitutional and institutional diva"' (1999, p. 17).

Loren deserves consideration in terms of how American culture has expressed and negotiated ethnic identities. The construction of her American star persona in the late 1950s strongly emphasises the notion of transformation and of ethnic assimilation into whiteness when ethnic assimilation was having a strong impact on immigrant life in America. Her Americanisation, at the time, framed her ethnic identity within a narrative of social progression. This narrative is evident in the overall standing of the characters she played in her American films and in the steady process of glamorisation and refinement applied to Loren's image both on and off the screen. In her first American film, *Boy on a Dolphin* (1957), Loren played a dark-skinned and heavily made-up Greek pearl diver with unkempt hair, dressed in rags; by contrast, in *A Breath of Scandal* (1960), a very refined Loren was cast as a beautifully dressed and impeccably made-up and coiffed patrician of the early twentieth century: the light-skinned and poised Austrian princess Olympia, who is to wed Prince Rupert of Prussia but falls in love with an American engineer. Almost forty years later, the terms in which being Italian American at the turn of the twentieth century are imagined are embodied in the character Loren plays in *Grumpier*, conveying a notion of Italianness in tune with the re-evaluation of ethnic identity in late twentieth-century American culture. In this cultural climate, Italianness, after being stigmatised for decades since the 'new immigration' of the early 1900s as an inferior sub-culture on the margins of whiteness, has come to acquire a particularly high profile.

The Revival of Ethnicity

Grumpier can be said to be part of the ethnic revival whose signs have increasingly emerged over the last decades in American culture and according to which 'ethnic identity is valued for its own sake' (Negra, 2001, p. 4) and is regarded as the best expression of being American. It can be read as an ethnic film narrative that regards European-American identity in general and Italian Americanness in particular as the necessary antidotes to counterbalance a feeling of lack and alienation in late twentieth-century America. As Lester D. Friedman suggests, a revival of the importance of ethnic pride in US culture entered public discourse in the late 1960s and the early 1970s, inspired by the black power movement. He contends that the fact that black people demanded racial recognition helped legitimise the claims of other ethnic groups for their own ethnic individuality. A desire for cultural specificity started to replace the earlier goal of total acculturation and assimilation into the great American melting pot, and ethnic people began to acknowledge and celebrate their cultural heritages. He concludes that being a 'hyphenated' American came to be perceived as a source of pride that would provide Americans of European descent with a feeling of uniqueness (1991, pp. 11–13).³ The reclamation of ethnic identities would question the so-called theory of straight-line assimilation, which assumes the decline in ethnicity for successive generations to be a factor of identity, behaviour, and group life in an upwardly mobile society (Tricarico, 1984, pp. 75–93). While in previous eras the relinquishing of ethnicity was deeply rooted in the structure of American society, over the last few decades an emphasis on the rediscovery of one's ethnic heritage has been witnessed. Such a revaluation expresses a desire to find a sense of place and belonging in an attempt to counterbalance the negative effects of a social life increasingly characterised by ambiguities, crises of value and meaning, fragmentation, homogenisation and incessant change (Halter, 2000, pp. 80–81). As several cultural theorists have recently theorised, whiteness is 'increasingly seen as a "state of incompleteness" that needs to be supplemented by ethnic difference' (Probyn, 2000, p. 81). Therefore, as 'white ethnicity emerges as a trope of empowerment' (Decker, 1997, p. 107), 'ethnicization has itself become normative, a part of the Americanization process. Immigrants no longer simply become Americans; they become *ethnic* Americans so that there is little contradiction between assimilation and ethnic particularity' (Halter, 2000, p. 78).

The ethnic revival has taken many forms, from community cookbooks to a resurgence of interest in tracing genealogies, from creating new ethnic organisations to organising ethnic festivals and tours of ethnic neighbourhoods. The pleasures of ethnic revival have also been staged cinematically in films whose narratives evolve around characters who are Americans of European descent—from *Moonstruck* (1987) and *True Love* (1989) to *A Bronx Tale* (1993), *Big Night* (1996), and *My Big Fat Greek Wedding* (2002). In the films of this category, the ethnic identity of the characters is a key textual element that comes across as empowering rather than diminishing and penalising. Ethnic film narratives trigger, according to Negra, fantasies of de-assimilation in which Americans obtain ethnic identities beyond whiteness based upon nostalgia for a sense of community, closeness, and ethnicity, believed to have existed in the past and powerfully rendered in these films. Thus, ethnicity comes to be 'rhetorically mobilised to assuage the crisis of value and meaning' (Negra, 2002, p. 73) in contemporary American social structures.

---

³ It is worth noting that *Grumpier*'s narrative makes reference to Wabasha's ethnic heritage through the staging of a traditional ethnic festival that is inspired by the German *Octoberfest* and celebrates social bonds based upon community, ethnicity, and intimacy.

Sophia Loren and the Healing Power of Female Italian Ethnicity in *Grumpier Old Men*

It is around Loren's character that *Grumpier*'s narrative develops discourses of food and of places of food consumption as metaphors for ethnic and national identity. The film also employs (albeit indirectly) a notion of food as 'a powerful emotional capital' (Negra, 2002, p. 73), although it does not foreground, unlike the films mentioned above, the preparation and consumption of ethnic food in showcase scenes. Indeed, food has always been a major element in people's sense of identity and roots (Pillsbury, 1998). Within the current cultural rethinking of what it means to be American, ethnic food remains as strong a signifier of ethnic identity as it was in the past. What has changed over the last three decades is the connotation attached to ethnic food in US culture: whereas around the beginning of the twentieth century ethnic foods would be seen as 'suspicious signifiers of an inappropriate attachment to non-U.S. homelands ... [and] of a recalcitrant ethnicity that resisted assimilation' (Negra, 2002, p. 65), they currently hold a high status as a 'proud signifier of ethnic heritage conjoined with American identity' (Negra, 2002, p. 65). They are valued as an outlet for emotional sincerity and as a mark of anti-mass production, standing for the values and customs of a bygone, deeply missed era when families would always have home-made, mother-served meals. Shannon Peckam has observed that 'arguments about a nation's decline and rejuvenation are often reflected in anxieties about the dynamism or health of its culinary culture' (1998, pp. 171–172), whilst Negra, significantly, has linked the relative decline of a monolithic US cuisine in the 1990s to a fracturing of consensus about the meanings of positive Americanism (2002, p. 65), which in turn has triggered a re-evaluation of ethnic identities.

In *Grumpier* this change is made particularly evident via the juxtaposition of convenience food and cheap drink (Max's favoured, ready-made macaroni cheese and the cheap wine he brings Maria-Sophia) and the town-based, chain restaurant Chuck E. Cheese's (a popular US chain of family entertainment centres) with the genuine *vino rosso* (red wine) and freshly made Italian dishes Loren's character will serve at her *ristorante* (restaurant). And although at Ragetti's ethnic food is made and consumed in a public space and in exchange for money, Maria-Sophia's *ristorante* comes across as a cosy Southern Italian American restaurant where food will be prepared according to family recipes. This assumption is validated by the presence of Maria-Sophia's elderly mother as a cook and, more importantly, by the extra-textual reference to Loren's personal expertise with traditional Italian food. Loren has collected her family recipes in popular cookbooks: *Eat with Me* (1980), *In the Kitchen with Love* (1972), and *Sophia Loren's recipes & memories* (1998). All the cookbooks are beautifully illustrated with pictures of Loren at work as well as in her kitchen, making some of the dishes herself. While Max's association, within *Grumpier*'s narrative, to standardised food can be, in turn, linked with feelings of loneliness, alienation, and cultural homogenisation, the film's (re)presentation of Ragetti's as an old-fashioned Southern Italian American restaurant can be regarded as a metaphor for the healing power of ethnicity in general, and of Italianness in particular, via the joyous exuberance, warmth, and vitality of Loren's Maria-Sophia—the ethnic woman who manages to inject a palpable new sense of enjoyment of life into Max. Max's encounter with Italian food can be said to exemplify Elspeth Probyn's suggestion that 'the consumption, the ingestion and incorporation of difference adds life to white consumer subjectivity' (2000, p. 42). We can sense the successful working of ethnic food as the magical agent of 'rejuvenation' because of the transformation Max undergoes after eating Italian at Maria-Sophia's. If, before meeting Maria-Sophia, Max would chew his pre-cooked macaroni cheese directly from the packaging while sitting in his armchair, watching the talk-show *Geraldo*, after a romantic dinner *al fresco* at Maria-Sophia's (and a passionate kiss), Max seems to be reborn to a new life: he sings and dances, strutting down his front lawn.

STILL SEXY IN HER SIXTIES

The centrality of food in Italian culture, and the link between food and the figure of the mother who prepares the food for her family with care and love, day in, day out, has traditionally produced in American popular culture a fantasy of the Italian woman as 'the mamma'. Daniel Golden has argued 'the mamma' is 'the more common vision of the Italian American woman … safely distanced from her sexuality in her middle age, housecoat and hairnet. And, like so many mammas in media, the Italian woman is in the kitchen, brandishing a stirring spoon, and insisting we eat, *mangia*' (1980, pp. 73–97). Despite the link between female Italianness and food, in *Grumpier,* Maria-Sophia's character seems to challenge stereotypical cinematic (re)presentation of the ageing Italian American woman as the domestic figure of the desexualised mamma. Firstly, in *Grumpier*,

Loren is placed within a narrative where old age becomes a sentimental theme. In this respect, the film is in line with a trend of commercial films of the 1980s and 1990s about old people, such as *Cocoon* (1985) and *Grumpy Old Men* (1993), which were produced at the time to cater to the potential market created by an ageing American population (Kaplan, 1997, p. 269). Secondly, Loren's Maria-Sophia is presented as highly sexualised. She stands out in a red dress with matching wrap and shoes while food shopping in a supermarket and is clearly constructed as the object of the male gaze when she crosses the local bar, Slippery's, to speak with Max in an attempt to convince him to stop sabotaging her *ristorante*. Medium shots of her voluptuous figure crossing the venue and close-ups of Loren's cleavage alternate with shots of the reaction of the gasping male patrons mesmerised by Maria-Sophia. While the film's soundtrack plays the classic 1969 hit 'Venus', performed by Shocking Blue, Maria-Sophia comes across as extremely self-confident and fully aware of the reaction she provokes amongst Slippery's patrons: wearing a figure-hugging dress with a deep neckline that enhances her physical and sexual attractiveness, she does not turn away her eyes but quite self-assuredly returns the look. She puts herself on display for her own benefit in an attempt to secure a future for her business by 'seducing' Max: as soon as she enters the bar, she removes a black shawl and then takes some time to adjust her dress's neckline to better display her cleavage, before moving towards the counter where Max is sitting with John, drinking beer. Later on, while sweet-talking enthralled Max into stopping their feud over her *ristorante*, she takes some ice cubes from her drink and provocatively rubs them down her neck and exposed breasts. Here Loren's character seems to challenge traditional cinematic (re)presentations of the ageing woman. Contrary to ageing male stars, whose sexiness 'can be stretched into a fantasy of ageless sexual potency' (Kozlowski, 1993, p. 8), according to Kaplan, writing in 1997, 'women stars are summarily dismissed from sexy roles on the screen after menopause. [...] Popular culture, then, has no category for women between sexy youth or young motherhood, on the one hand, and "old aged women", represented as tired, bitter, evil or jealous, on the other' (1997, p. 270).

Yet, despite such a deliberate sexualisation, Maria-Sophia does not come across as the other stereotypical Italian American woman—the female counterpart of the male mafioso, with big hair, a tough Brooklyn accent, sparkly jewellery, heavy make-up, flashy clothes, and stiletto heels, as seen in Jonathan Demme's *Married to the Mob* (1988) and in *My Cousin Vinny* (1992)

(McDonald, 2002, pp. 155–156). Challenging traditional cultural understandings of the Italian American woman either as 'the mamma' or as the 'dumb bimbo', Maria-Sophia is framed, as soon as she enters the story, as a strongly determined, hard-working and self-sufficient female entrepreneur, a second-generation Italian American who is socially and culturally integrated in the American way of life. Drawing on Halter's contention, I suggest that assimilation and ethnic particularity are not mutually exclusive in Maria-Sophia. This is made evident in two different scenes via the juxtaposition of Maria-Sophia with her Sicilian-born mother, Francesca, who exudes a sense of deep-seated distrust and cynicism regarding American society. In the first scene, Francesca verbally and physically attacks Max, who, she believes, has intruded into their property and is stealing some *vino rosso*. In the second scene, Francesca insults the health inspector, who has ordered the elderly woman to wear a hairnet while cooking for the restaurant's customers. In both cases, Francesca speaks in broken English marked by a thick Italian accent. According to a deeply rooted stereotype, Francesca, as a first-generation immigrant, is imagined not to be able to speak good English. On the contrary, Loren's character, Maria-Sophia, urges her mother to trust people and interacts politely with authority, represented by the health inspector. In addition, despite the fact that Maria-Sophia makes use of the Italian language, her English is fluent and bears no particular accent. While the set of cultural notions of Italianness attached to Francesca are negatively connoted, the ethnic features in Maria-Sophia's characterisation are positively marked. While there are instances where Maria-Sophia speaks Italian, it gives the character a fashionable touch of exoticism validated by Loren's media associations with 'glamour and great elegance' (Small, 2009, p. 9) and in tune with the cultural re-evaluation of individual ethnic identity.

Loren's sexualisation in *Grumpier* did not go unnoticed in the American press coverage of the time. In 'Loren still a sexy knockout', which appeared in *The Los Angeles Times* in December 1995, Liz Smith observes that '*Never*—and we mean *never*—has a 61-year-old woman (or man or vegetable or mineral) looked as divine as Sophia Loren does in "Grumpier Old Men". Talk about still-smouldering sex-appeal, timeless femininity and all that jazz'. Meanwhile, Kevin Thomas describes Loren as 'glowing, eternally gorgeous and witty', and argues that 'in a cast of scene stealers, special note goes to Loren for weathering the passage of time beautifully' (1995). It is interesting to note how comments about Loren still managing to be sexy after 60 intersect with an appreciation of her ability to age gracefully, and to come across as 'an example of serene beauty that defeats the years' (Fenwick, 1999, p. 17), thanks to her self-discipline and a rigorous regime. In a remarkable demonstration of Loren's lasting appeal in American popular culture, a few years after the release of *Grumpier*, Loren is still presented as 'a model of good longevity behaviour' (Lague, 1999b, p. 38) in an article published in *Modern Maturity*, an American magazine covering senior lifestyle. Here, Loren's 'age-defying secrets' are sanctioned by the medical expertise of Isadore Rosenfeld, MD, who is introduced to the readers as Loren's cardiologist as well as the author of *Live Now, Age Later*. Rosenfeld firstly provides general advice about how to make life after 50 worth living. In addition to diet and exercise, people should work on what Rosenfeld calls 'contentment', which has to do with a calm, optimistic, positive attitude, being 'more about finding inner peace than just being happy' (Lague, 1999a, p. 36). Rosenfeld then praises Loren for being 'more beautiful than ever' at 64, thanks to her exemplary lifestyle, as she emphasises that the Italian star's 'glow' is due not just to her impeccable make-up and hair style, tasteful jewellery, and haute-couture wardrobe but also to 'a lifelong devotion to healthy self-care, including what she refers to as "good thoughts"' (Lague, 1999b, p. 37). Rosenfeld goes on to say that Loren's age-defying looks are undoubtedly a result of her unfailing commitment to preserving them.

Conclusion

The popular cultural trope of Italian femininity, as personified by Loren, has generated powerful images within American culture, and these images can be successfully deployed 'in shaping and sustaining cultural debates about ... valued ethnicities' (Negra, 2001, p. 24). Taking as a starting point the recent rediscovery of ethnicity as a solution to the increasingly problematic status of whiteness in late twentieth-century and early twenty-first-century American culture, and with a particular focus on *Grumpier Old Men*, I have explored the enduring power of Loren's star image in American culture of the 1990s, and how Loren's persona was aligned with a cultural context marked by a revival of the importance of ethnic pride in American society. I have argued that as Italianness emerged and was validated as a very marketable form of white ethnicity in late twentieth-century America, Loren's star persona of the time was framed in *Grumpier* within a narrative where ethnicity is positively connoted as a sign of sincerity and authenticity validated by Loren's representative relationship to

Italian culture. Loren's American persona exemplifies how female Italian film stars have functioned from within their embedded position in media texts to consolidate and enhance America's sense of its national identity and place in the world, and in particular, the extent to which such stars are illustrative of a particular stage of ethnic group validation in relation to American society and values.

REFERENCES

Big Night. (1996). Film. Directed by Stanley Tucci. [DVD]. USA: Samuel Goldwyn Company.
Boy on a Dolphin. (1957). Film. Directed by Jean Negulesco. [DVD]. Italy and USA: Twentieth Century-Fox Film Corp.
A Breath of Scandal. (1960). Film. Directed by Michael Curtiz. [DVD]. USA: Paramount Pictures Corp.
A Bronx Tale. (1993). Film. Directed by Robert De Niro. [DVD]. USA: Savoy Pictures.
Cocoon. (1985). Film. Directed by Ron Howard. [DVD]. USA: Twentieth Century-Fox Film Corp.
Collins, N. (1991, January). Sophia. *Vanity Fair*, 82–84, 121–125.
Decker, J.L. 1997. *Self-styled success from Horatio Alger to Oprah Winfrey*. Minneapolis: University of Minnesota Press.
Dyer, R. 1998. *Stars*. London: British Film Institute.
Fenwick, H. (1999, March). Still sexy after 60. *Get Up and Go*, 17–19.
Friedman, L.D. 1991. Celluloid palimpsests: An overview of ethnicity and American film. In *Unspeakable images: Ethnicity and the American cinema*, ed. L.D. Friedman. Urbana: University of Illinois Press.
Golden, D.S. 1980. The fate of La Famiglia: Italian images in American cinema. In *The kaleidoscopic lens: How hollywood views ethnic groups*, ed. R.M. Miller. Englewood, NJ: Jerome S. Ozer.
Grumpier Old Men. (1995). Film. Directed by Howard Deutch. [DVD]. USA: Warner Bros.
Grumpy Old Men. (1993). Film. Directed by Donald Petrie. [DVD]. USA: Warner Bros. Pictures.
Gundle, S. 1995. Sophia Loren, Italian icon. *Historical Journal of Film, Radio and Television*. 15(3): 367–385.
Halter, M. 2000. *Shopping for identity*. New York: Schocken Books.
Jarvie, I.C. 2004. Stars and ethnicity: Hollywood and the United States, 1932–1951. In *Stars: The film reader*, eds. L. Fischer and M. Landy. London: Routledge.

Kaplan, E.A. 1997. *Looking for the other: Feminism, film and the imperial gaze.* London: Routledge.

Koltnow, B. (1995, December). Grump magnet. *The Orange County Register*, 19.

Kozlowski, J. 1993. Women, film and the midlife Sophie's choice: Sink or Sousatzka? In *Menopause: A midlife passage*, ed. J.C. Callahan. Bloomington: Indiana University Press.

Lague, L. (1999a, November–December). The Longevity. *Masters Modern Maturity*, 34–36.

——— (1999b, November–December). Sophia's secrets: The mind-body regimen of the world's most alluring woman. *Modern Maturity*, 37–40, 82.

Loren, S. 1972. *In the kitchen with love.* Garden City, New York: Doubleday & Company.

——— 1980. *Eat with me.* London: Sphere Books.

——— 1998. *Sophia Loren's recipes & memories.* Rome: Gremese.

Married to the Mob. (1988). Film. Directed by Jonathan Demme. [DVD]. USA: MGM.

——— 1988. Film. Directed by Jonathan Demme. [DVD].USA: Orion Pictures.

McDonald, M.A. 2002. Italian American women as comic foils: Exploding the stereotype in *My Cousin Vinny, Moonstruck* and *Married to the Mob*. *Literature Interpretation Theory* 13: 155–166.

My Big Fat Greek Wedding. (2002). Film. Directed by Joel Zwick. [DVD]. Canada and USA: IFC and Gold Circle Films.

My Cousin Vinny. (1992). Film. Directed by Jonathan Lynn. [DVD].USA: Twentieth Century Fox.

Negra, D. 2001. *Off-white hollywood: American culture and ethnic female stardom.* London: Routledge.

——— 2002. Ethnic food fetishism, whiteness and nostalgia in recent film and television. *Velvet Light Trap* 50: 62–76.

Peckam, S. 1998. Consuming nations. In *Consuming passions: Food in the age of anxiety*, eds. S. Griffiths, and J. Wallace. Manchester: Manchester University Press.

Pillsbury, R. 1998. *No foreign food: The American diet in time and place.* Boulder, CO: Westview.

Prêt-à-Porter. (1994). Film. Directed by Robert Altman. [DVD].USA: Miramax Films.

Probyn, E. 2000. *Carnal appetites: Foodsexidentities.* London: Routledge.

Small, P. 2009. *Sophia Loren: Moulding the star.* Bristol: Intellect Books.

Smith, L. (1995, December). Loren still a sexy knockout. *Los Angeles Times*, 9.

The Shootist. (1976). Film. Directed by Don Siegel. [DVD].USA: Paramount Pictures Corp.

Thomas, K. (1995, December). Stars add luster to 'men's' contrived tale. *Los Angeles Times*, 22.

Tricarico, D. 1984. The 'New' Italian-American ethnicity. *Journal of Ethnic Studies* 12(3): 75–93.
True Grit. (1969). Film. Directed by Henry Hathaway. [DVD].USA: Paramount Pictures Corp.
True Love. (1989). Film. Directed by Nancy Savoca. [VHS].USA: United Artists Pictures, Inc.
Turner, G. 1999. *Film as a social practice*. London: Routledge.
Vincendeau, G. 2000. *Stars and stardom in French cinema*. New York: Continuum.

CHAPTER 4

Cutting a Dash in Interwar Hungary: Pál Jávor's Enduring Stardom

Gábor Gergely

With his pencil moustache, strong physical presence, and volatile character, Hungarian film star Pál Jávor rose to fame as a dashing romantic lead in the Clark Gable mould. However, as opposed to Gable, Jávor emerged as a star in a state-controlled film sector, where audience demand was at times overruled by film industry bosses, most notably during the anti-Jewish purge of 1938–1941. While star studies as a field of inquiry focused on Hollywood at the outset (Dyer, 1998) and have since been enriched by explorations of stardom in France (e.g. Vincendeau, 2000; Hayward, 2004), and beyond (e.g. Bandhauer & Royer, 2015), the star systems of pre-1945 undemocratic Europe have received little attention, with the exception of Germany (Ascheid, 2003), and Occupied France (Mayne, 2010). This chapter seeks to address this gap in scholarship by sketching the context of Hungary's interwar and wartime film sector through the star image of Jávor, and by exploring his longevity in an industry which he struggled to fit into, but which, in turn, depended on his box office

It is gratefully acknowledged that this chapter was written as part of a research project into Hungarian cinema in 1931–1944, funded by the Leverhulme Trust under its Early Career Fellowship scheme. I take responsibility for all translations, including Hungarian film titles.

G. Gergely
School of Film and Media, University of Lincoln, Lincoln, UK

draw. This chapter, then, has the dual aim of exploring star studies within a national cinema not usually addressed through its framework and investigating a national cinema little known outside Hungary.[1]

The Hungarian Film Industry

State investment and the advent of talkies helped revitalise a film sector that had gone into decline, alongside the national economy after the First World War (Balogh, Gyürey, & Honffy, 2004, pp. 36–44). The state's establishment of the newsreel maker Magyar Filmiroda in 1924, and of the Film Fund in 1925 were important first steps (p. 36). Corvin Filmgyár, Alexander Korda's old studio, was nationalised in 1928, renamed Hunnia, and refurbished with sound technology at taxpayers' expense (Nemeskürty, 1974, p. 71; Lajta, 2001). Demand for Hungarian talkies grew steadily and, by the end of the 1930s, domestic films accounted for a quarter of all releases. Subsidies funded from import duties and a quota system created room for growth.

The Hungarian film industry sought to achieve the same gloss and profitability as Hollywood while offering audiences authentic national culture on the screen (see Fejős in Kovács, 2001, pp. 296–304). Major differences were the relative lack of private venture capital, and the absence of a studio system built on competition and specialisation. Hungarian films were produced by a constantly changing stream of production companies, with financing secured from creditors rather than capital-rich owners, creating a boom and bust industry that was neither predictable nor codified.

Ultimately, it was state ownership of Hunnia, the only viable production facility, that gave the Hungarian sector a degree of uniformity. Producers operated on a tight budget of up to 160,000 *pengős* (Lohr, 1941, p. 3),[2] and it was not in their interest to step outside the state-approved institutional framework, which would have made their productions ineligible for state subsidies. Relying on a limited pool of technical crew, Hungarian

---

[1] Nemeskürty (1974) and Cunningham (2004) are the only two book-length studies of Hungarian cinema in the English language. The former was published in the Communist period and is both outdated and factually unreliable, while the latter draws heavily on the former.

[2] Lohr compares this to the 525,000 *pengős* (USD 150,000) spent on low-budget films in Hollywood (1941, p. 2).

films are instantly recognisable from the distinctive architecture of the Hunnia sets, and stock solutions that varied little from film to film.[3]

The Hungarian star system was characterised by a hybridity that came from state control applied alongside limited market competition. It lacked the minutely regimented nature of the Hollywood model, or the fluidity of the French system (Vincendeau, 2000, pp. 10–14). There was central organisation, in particular from 1938 onwards, when the ostensibly democratic Film Chamber was established,[4] allowing the state to assume total control of the industry while continuing to feed the perception of exercising delicate oversight at arm's length.

The other important aspect of this hybrid model was the need to cater to audience demand. Vincendeau notes that the audience had a relatively great role in bestowing stardom upon certain actors in France (pp. 10–14). This was also true, although with restrictions, in Hungary. Here audiences occasionally found their choice overruled. The anti-Jewish acts of 1938–1941, passed as the culmination of two decades of anti-Semitic state policy and practice,[5] removed dozens of stars from Hungarian screens, irrespective of their popularity. As a consequence, Hungary's star system was one that was distorted by the ideological goals of the state which subsidised it but still exposed to the tastes of the audience. It was this duality that gave Jávor's stardom longevity, and an undercurrent of conflict.

Jávor's Home-Grown Stardom

Pál Jávor was one of the first homegrown Hungarian film stars. Following the era's dominant trend, he 'Hungarianised' his surname from the German-sounding Jermann. He made his screen debut in a 1929 silent melodrama after an undistinguished stage apprenticeship. His next film was Hungary's first talkie, *The Blue Idol* (1931), a relative flop. However, his supporting role in *Hyppolit, the Butler*, in the same year, was a huge success. In his entertaining memoirs, Székely wrote, 'We all agreed on [casting] Pali Jávor. But during the shoot I realised that [he] was not a

---

[3] Hunnia sound engineer Ferenc Lohr had 97 credits in 1931–1944. Cinematographers István Eiben and Rezső Icsey made 178 films between them. Zoltán Farkas and Zoltán Kerényi edited 47 and 42 films respectively. Márton Vincze designed 69 sets, and István Básthy 44.

[4] The Film Chamber was set up by an act of the Hungarian Parliament in 1938 at the same time as Jewish Hungarians were banished from above-the-line roles.

[5] See Kovács (1994), Pelle (2004), Gyurgyák (2007), and Ungváry (2012).

good actor. If he had to say, "I was there", he would surely say, "there I was"' (Székely, 1978, p. 86). Székely is a mischievous chronicler, but his remarks indicate that it was Jávor's looks and pleasant voice that made him a star, rather than any acting talent.

A string of hits followed, including *Romance of Ida* (1934), *Salary: 200 per Month* (1936), and *Deadly Spring* (1939). Although his roles varied, pride was a key component of his characterisations and became an important aspect of his stardom. As I explain later, volatility, excess pride, and the resultant inability to compromise were seen as quintessential Hungarian characteristics. By embodying these, he projected a version of the typical Hungarian male that was less than flattering, but was clearly appealing to the audience. He achieved unprecedented box office success with his star turn in the first Hungarian colour film, *The Talking Robe* (1941), which took a record 38,963.30 *pengős* in its first week on release in one Budapest cinema alone (*Magyar Film*, 10 March 1942, back cover).

Starring in seventy-three films between 1931 and 1944, including two Italian and three German productions, Jávor was unrivalled as a romantic lead. He was voted the country's most popular leading man four times by the readers of *Sztár* between November 1937 and April 1938 (Skaper, 2008),[6] featuring on no fewer than fourteen covers of the trade paper *Magyar Film* between 1939 and 1943. In an industry under minute state control, and dedicated to the dissemination of an officially approved discourse of Hungarianness, his stardom endured in a traumatic period of radicalisation and war. This has to be seen as remarkable longevity. Star systems are not wholly top-down in organisation. Thus, as Alberoni argues [cited by Dyer (1998, p. 19)], stars are offered to the movie-going audiences who confirm their stardom by consuming their films, or reject it by staying away. Therefore, the audience has some agency in 'electing' film stars.

It is important to note here that Hungarian audiences had an opportunity to vote with their feet as the domestic industry fell short of achieving its ambition of 'film self-sufficiency' (see, for instance, *Magyar Film*, 1 June 1940, p. 1 and 27 September 1941, p. 1). The Hungarian output peaked in 1943, accounting for just under a third of films released that year. Audiences continued to choose Jávor's films, and his popularity endured even after his 1943 suspension from the Film Chamber for speaking out against its president. His special status as a star, reinforced by

---

[6] Jávor topped the poll of readers in December 1937, February, March, and May 1938 and was the runner-up in November, January, and April.

unwavering popular appeal, gave him a degree of autonomy, and allowed him to offer a more complex and contradictory image of Hungarianness than the official ideal.

Jávor's Star Body and Persona

A key element of Jávor's enduring stardom was his physique. He was styled 'the Hungarian Clark Gable' (Bános, 1978, p. 152)[7], with one critic describing him as 'a youthful tiger-man of feverish temper, tousled hair and flaming eyes' (p. 216). His solid frame (he was six feet tall, and slightly heavy set) suggested power, and his high forehead gave him an air of intelligence. His voice was deep, and he spoke in a slow and instantly recognisable tone. His hair was dark, dense, and wavy. He wore it fashionably slicked back, and in moments of extreme passion, a strand would come loose and fall into his eyes, giving him a wild look of despair more typically associated with the period's go-to villain, Zoltán Greguss.

Jávor's characters were always physical. He used his body to convey the sense of great physical power contained with difficulty. He played proud men easily aroused to passion but also capable of tenderness. Whether a peasant or nobleman, his characters displayed the same volatility, oscillating between eruptions of rage, or joy, and moments of paralysing sorrow. This volatility motivates the narratives of both *Salary: 200 a Month* and *From among the Waves* (1943). In the former, he plays Gábor Kórody, an engineer who struggles to settle into a job as his pride and quick temper lead him into unsought conflicts with his new boss. In the latter he plays a married man who, despite himself, begins a tempestuous affair with a suicide survivor. Both films display his inability to control himself: in the former, a romantic comedy, the series of conflicts are exploited for humour; in the latter, a stifling melodrama, János's emotional instability is used for dramatic effect.

The Jávor temper is a motivating force of any narrative in which he appears. Volatility was also a major component of Jávor's off-screen image as an actor known for his lightning temper and inclination to violence (Jávor, 1987, p. 121). He had a conviction for assault after a violent confrontation with a horse trainer who accused him of overusing the whip in an equestrian number (Bános, 1978, pp. 99–104; Skaper, 2008). The

---

[7] This label was used as recently as 1998 in the film magazine *Kardos Piece* 1998 (16), p. 58.

film that, perhaps, makes the most of his star persona is *I Cannot Live without Music* (1935). Here he plays Balázs, a country squire whose hard partying lifestyle puts a strain on his marriage. When his best friend, the explorer Viktor (Ferenc Delly) visits, the marriage nearly breaks down. Viktor, who had been engaged to Balázs's wife, Pólika (Erzsi Somogyi), tries to rekindle their relationship. At first, she waivers, but her passion for her intemperate husband wins out. The basic plot relies almost solely on Jávor's star persona, tellingly displayed in the scene where he seeks to mollify his wife after yet another drunken fight. When Pólika seeks refuge with her aunts, Balázs serenades her with a song about his need for music, moving between sorrowful lament and repressed fury. Accompanied by the musicians from the previous night's party, and with total confidence in his charm, Balázs sings, 'I Cannot Live without Music' over and over again. This assertion of the importance of music in his life is not a roundabout expression of his all-consuming love for his wife. It serves, instead, to assert the unchangeable truth about Balázs/Jávor's character that his is an addictive and volatile personality that craves excess but also yearns for settled domesticity. It explicitly states Balázs's need for music (and the drinking that goes with it), while acknowledging his reliance on the wife that his addictions drive away. All this can be read in light of Mayne's summation of Dyer's condition of stardom: 'the negotiation of contradictions through the actor's charismatic appeal' (Mayne, 2010, p. 170). We might conclude that it is his complexity of character that makes Balázs attractive to his wife, and possibly, what made Jávor, the star, attractive to his audience.

Performance of Stardom

Significantly, the gap between Jávor's star persona and off-screen life was blurred. This is displayed clearly in press reports, in which he was ever-present due to the notoriety he acquired for violent confrontations (see Bános, 1978, p. 94, 102). A report on Jávor's police interview after an assault shows how a discourse of stardom had come to dominate the news coverage: Jávor 'was summoned to police headquarters for 10 am [...] He wore a Burberry coat with its collar turned up, his hand was bandaged, and he had on horn-rimmed glasses and full make-up. [He] came from the film set.'[8] The reference to the star's expensive jacket, and the way he wore it, and the fact that he had come from a shoot shows how, even in

---

[8] Printed in *Az Est* on 29 August 1934. Cited in Bános (1978, p. 100).

the context of criminal proceedings against him, Jávor was presented as a movie star and a focus of consumption.

Hungarian audiences expected stars to live up to the Hollywood standard of stardom. This is evident in this typical fan response: 'a star must always shine. They should embody for the audience a remote world beyond reach. They must be able to cope with being a star in real life, as well as on the stage' (Skaper, 2008). Jávor's off-screen life displayed the escapism and fantasy audiences craved through his luxurious lifestyle that combined conspicuous consumption with demonstrations of bourgeois discernment (Dyer, 1998, p. 38).[9]

The Hungarian industry also emulated Hollywood by making use of narratives of social mobility. These were not as prevalent as in Hollywood and, as I note below, social class was an important element in Hungarian constructions of stardom. When asked to comment on his road to stardom, Jávor supplied a poem which shows that a rags-to-riches story was mobilised in order to present Jávor as an ordinary member of the public plucked from obscurity. It is hard to attribute authorship beyond doubt, but the Hungarian industry lacked the capital to match the complexity and sophistication of the Hollywood publicity machine, and we can therefore speculate that Jávor may have had a hand in writing it. The awkward verse goes:

I arrived from Arad, travelling light

my cup overflowed with trouble and strife

I slept under underpasses dreary

my shoulders heavy with want and misery

I traipsed the streets of Pest aimlessly

wondered at the sights with melancholy.

Woe was plenty and joy was rare;

in fact, this is how I still often fare.

I'm turning the corner into easy street

but my youth is all but gone with the wind.[10]

---

[9] He was often presented in fan magazines as a man of culture. See, for example, the piece by his friend Lajos Gogolák in *Film Színház Irodalom* 12–18 March 1943, p. 16.

[10] The poem is reprinted in the Hungarian by Bános in his biography of Jávor (1978, p. 6). I am grateful to my friend the translator and poet Balázs Bujna for the wonderful translation.

This curious poem framed Jávor as coming from a disadvantaged background and rising to fame due to a lucky break. This breaching of class boundaries and rising from hardship to luxury, thanks to good fortune, hard work, and established social and economic structures, is an essential component of the star system (Dyer, 1998, p. 42). It is also a total fantasy in the context of interwar Hungary, a country where education beyond the elementary school was effectively barred to those from underprivileged backgrounds, while systemic nepotism coupled with anti-Jewish legislation protected the vested interests of the racist nationalist elite.

The effort to portray Jávor as a crosser of class boundaries gains significance when set against other stars of the era. Male romantic leads such as Tivadar Uray and Andor Ajtay were generally presented as aristocratic and wealthy by birth. Much of their romantic appeal derived from their high social status. To be sure, some male stars were used to communicate the concept of social mobility. For instance, János Sárdy, a trained opera singer, starred in numerous films about searing talent (musical or otherwise) lifting a deserving youth out of poverty and into the limelight. Antal Páger was another star whose films focused on his humble origins in narratives about the just reward for hard work. Sárdy and Páger were used to celebrate the virtues of the ordinary Hungarian. They succeeded because they had the common sense and natural wit of the mythical Hungarian peasant. Theirs were not so much rags-to-riches stories but, rather, stories about the non-material richness hidden under the peasant's rags. Jávor is set apart from other romantic leads because his own success story is not mirrored in his film roles. He stands alone as a complexly constructed star persona who has romantic appeal but no innate nobility and has the promise of social mobility without being explicitly linked to the radical nationalist ideology served by the Sárdy and Páger films.

Furthermore, the above poem's reference to Jávor's arrival from Arad roots him in a part of Hungary that had been annexed to Romania under the Trianon Treaty in 1920. This placed Jávor in a region that by virtue of its occupation by Romanian forces and the national obsession with its recovery was seen as a site of true Hungarianness. The key to Jávor's appeal, then—the contradictions that his charisma helped resolve (Mayne, 2010, p. 170)—can be rooted in the tensions of his persona's simultaneous occupation of a privileged position within the film industry and the narrative, and his self-declared status of the outsider who nonetheless came from a city that was seen as quintessentially Hungarian while being, literally, outside the country's borders.

The complexity of the Jávor star persona was a major part of his appeal, achieved through his chief trait of volatility, which allowed him to reconcile dramatically different and sometimes mutually exclusive characteristics. This complexity ran counter to the official narrative of Hungarian national identity as a single-race nation-state of Catholic Hungarians battling a destructive alien minority: 'the Jews'.[11] The false binary of 'the Jews' against Hungarians gained virtually undisputed credence in the aftermath of the Trianon Treaty, which left Hungary with a population consisting of 90% ethnic Hungarians. But while no longer multi-ethnic, Hungary's population remained diverse in other ways: it consisted of rural peasantry, landed gentry, urban middle classes, and a sizable aristocratic class. The religious landscape was also varied with Catholic, Protestant, and Jewish communities and significant ethnic German and Roma populations. Jávor's star persona disturbed the misrepresentation of Hungary as a homogenous nation and acted to fragment the unproblematic and coherent national identity that emerged from official narratives of nationhood.

His temperamental characters struggled to fit into the grand scheme of the national project: they were outsiders, individualists, and rebels.[12] Where his contemporary Antal Páger embodied the rightwing myth of the peasant as the wellspring of national virtues, Jávor was a man apart: he did not fit in, due to his maverick status, as seen, for example, in *Emmy* (1934), *Late* (1943), and *Little Mary* (1937). Ultimately, his flaring temper and his uncompromising individualism fragmented the illusory national homogeneity and pointed to the possibility of difference from the putative norm. This complexity of character offered a rare relief from the blandness of the new guard of youthful, vigorous leading men, such as László Szilassy and Gyula Benkő, who had their breaks after the anti-Jewish purge of the industry.

By drawing equally on Hollywood glamour and Hungarian archetypes, embracing fallibility by constantly teetering on the brink of disaster brought on by his violent temper, and by reconciling seemingly irreconcilable extremes, thanks to his character trait of volatility, Jávor offered something unique to the Hungarian movie-going public. He performed potentiality within an industry that specialised in iterating an inflexible

---

[11] See Gyurgyák (2007).

[12] For example, he was banned from acting for six months after speaking out against, and smashing a bust of, Film Chamber president Ferenc Kiss (*Magyar Film* 20 April 1944, p. 11).

national character. In embodying a lovable and fallible Hungarian, the ideal and the potential for failure, Jávor destabilised the national homogeneity narrative. In doing so, his character put into question one component of the binary that cast Jewish Hungarians as possessed of all the negative characters determined by the Hungarian ideal's catalogue of virtues. He offered audiences a relief from the comparative predictability of the period's other stars.

It is worth comparing Jávor, and his contemporary Páger, to get a sense of this attractively disruptive complexity. The dance hall scene in *Emmy* is especially illustrative as the two play hussar lieutenants who both court and dance with the titular Emmy (Irén Ágay). Jávor's Korponay dances a basic 'slow' dance with Emmy in a tight hold, bodies close together. He extends his leading arm downward, holding it rigidly at waist height, pulling her close so that her face is just inches from his. This is a modern dance for the 1930s, with a strong erotic charge. Just as the film's star does, so does his dance draw on and evoke a multitude of discourses by bringing together Western cultural motifs with strong indicators of Hungarianness. When Páger's Pálóczy and Emmy dance next, they dance a traditional Hungarian *csárdás*: they stand apart, each dancer's arms outstretched, the man's on the woman's hips, the woman's on the man's shoulders. This is a rigid dance that communicates a respect for customs, and promotes the 'healthy eroticism' of reproduction, as opposed to the obscenity of recreational sex. The differences between the two star personas are neatly expressed in this scene: Páger is traditionalist, duty-bound, and disciplined; Jávor is sensuous, sophisticated, but also instinctual and therefore ultimately apolitical.

This apolitical persona explains why Jávor was targeted by the anti-Semitic press. The far right commentator Pálóczy-Horváth, in a review of Jávor's *Dankó Pista* (1940), condemns the entire output of the past decade of Hungarian cinema, reserving special contempt for Jávor, whom he describes as possessed of a nose like a cudgel, and a rheumatically rigid gait (quoted in Sándor, 1992, p. 148). Giving evidence of the significance of dance in constructions of masculinity and nationality, he scoffs at how Jávor dances, calling it sweat-soaked, contrived, incredibly rigid and 'angular as a puppet show Punch' (p. 151). This is blunt criticism that denies those very qualities—the actor's grace, good looks, strong physical presence—that had made him a star. The fact that such a popular star was now openly targeted by the radical publications of the rightwing press, which, by this time, had come to occupy the mainstream, gave clear evidence that for the radical elite, Jávor did not embody the 'new' Hungarian masculine ideal. Páger, whom Jávor regularly bettered in romantic films in the 1930s, was now emerging as the ideal for a 'new Hungary'.[13]

Conclusion: Career's End, Enduring Stardom

Jávor's career ended suddenly, although his stardom, his fame, and the meanings associated with his star body, have endured. He was arrested in the chaotic days that followed the Nazi-backed Arrow Cross coup that unseated Admiral Horthy in October 1944.[14] Almost uniquely among actors who were not Jews under Hungary's anti-Jewish laws, Jávor was singled out for arrest and deportation. According to his memoirs, he was held alongside the chief of the general staff, the foreign secretary, and the defence minister of the fallen regime, among others (Jávor, 1987, p. 31).[15] The ferocity of the Arrow Cross's hatred for an actor with so little political clout is hard to explain, with even the star bewildered by his arrest. Jávor speculated in his memoir, 'I feel this was how it had to be'. He went on to suggest that he had come to internalise his own publicity, 'I played so many heroes in my life. Why couldn't I be a real hero for once?' (p. 33).

The same thing that had made him a star now ensured his fall. He successfully embodied a kind of Hungarian masculinity that was seen as typical but that the radical right rejected, favouring, instead, an explicitly political ideal as embodied by Páger. Jávor's character was inflexibly proud, short-tempered, and violent but rigidly honourable. It was also indolent and indulgent, prone to rebellion and disobedience, especially where honour was concerned, and was therefore apolitical. These qualities gave him a degree of complexity that his contemporaries could not match. He was both archetypal and unique, a contradiction he resolved through volatility and violence. Above all else, Jávor was individual and therefore strained against a state-controlled system that sought uniformity and expected obedience from subordinates who were to understand that their duty was first to the nation (state), and only second to the audience.

---

[13] 'New Hungary' referred to a rebirth brought about by anti-Jewish legislation. The phrase occurs most notably in the anti-Semitic problem film *Dr. Kovács István* (Bánky, 1941) starring Páger.

[14] For English-language accounts, see Kenez (2006) and Braham (2000).

[15] The historian Kovács confirms Jávor's account (2006, p. 90).

Jávor returned from a displaced persons camp in late 1945. An August 1945 issue of the new, popular culture magazine, *Fényszóró*, reported that he was back at work (19 August 1945, p. 17). This would become the first post-war film, *The Tutoress* (1945). Jávor, a staunch anti-Communist, emigrated to the USA as the Soviet-backed Hungarian workers' party MDP seized power. He appeared in just two Hollywood films in ten years. He joined a touring company with Hungarian expatriate Mihály Szüle, playing stage revivals of his old successes and putting on poetry recitals (Szüle, 1982). A 1948 poetry festival to mark the centenary of Hungary's national poet Sándor Petőfi attracted a 4,000-strong audience in New York, which featured a speech by the mayor (Szüle, 1982, p. 58). Jávor quit the touring company and returned to Hungary in 1957, but the post-1956 Hungarian film industry had no use for a ghost of cinema past. Jávor's health declined rapidly and he died in 1959, aged just 57.

What this too-too brief study of Jávor's stardom has sought to show is that despite the relative lack of capital and sophistication, the Hungarian film industry of the 1930s and 1940s made use of a star system in order to sell its films and communicate ideas about national identity. Jávor played a major role in the emergence of this star system but also strained against it. His destabilising power threatened the narrative of national cohesion and homogeneity, which earned him the enmity of the era's dominant radical right. His continuing popularity with audiences notwithstanding, Jávor's career came to an end in 1944. His stardom, however, endures as his films are regularly broadcast on Hungarian TV and screened at clubs and cinemas that specialise in Hungary's 'golden age' of film comedy. His appeal reaches through to the present, and his name still denotes a Hungarian masculinity of exuberance and despair, and what is in between: volatility.

References

Ascheid, A. 2003. *Hitler's heroines: Stardom and womanhood in Nazi cinema*. Philadelphia: Temple University Press.
Balogh, Gy., V. Gyürey, and P. Honffy. 2004. *A magyar játékfilm története a kezdetektől 1990-ig*. Budapest: Műszaki Könyvkiadó.
Bandhauer, A., and M. Royer. 2015. *Stars in world cinema: Screen icons and star systems across cultures*. London: I.B. Tauris.
Bános, T. 1978. *Jávor Pál*. Budapest: Gondolat.
A beszélő köntös/The Talking Robe. (1941). Film. Directed by Géza Radványi. Hungary: Erdélyi.

Braham, R.L. 2000. *The politics of genocide: The holocaust in Hungary.* Detroit: Wayne State University Press.
Cunningham, J. 2004. *Hungarian Cinema: From coffee house to multiplex.* London: Wallflower.
Dankó Pista. (1940). Film. Directed by László Kalmár. Hungary: Mester Film.
Dr. Kovács István. (1941). Film. Directed by Viktor Bánky. Hungary: Magyar Film Iroda.
Dyer, R. 1998. *Stars.* London: BFI Publishing.
Emmy. (1934). Film. Directed by István Székely. Hungary: Művész Film.
Fényszóró. (1945, August 19). A magyar film a szellemi újjáépítés eszköze lesz. p. 17.
Gogolák, L. (1943, March 12–18). Irodalmi estén Jávor Pálnál *Film Színház Irodalom.* p. 16.
Gyurgyák, J. 2007. *Ezzé lett magyar hazátok: A magyar nemzeteszme és nacionalizmus története.* Budapest: Osiris.
Halálos tavasz/Deadly Spring. (1939). Film. Directed by László Kalmár. Hungary: Pegazus Film.
Havi 200 fix/Salary: 200 per Month. (1936). Film. Directed by Béla Balogh. Hungary: Mozgóképipari.
Hayward, S. 2004. *Simone Signoret: The Star as cultural sign.* London: Continuum.
Hyppolit, a lakáj/Hyppolit, the Butler. (1931). Film. Directed by István Székely. Hungary: Kovács Emil és Társa.
Ida regénye/Romance of Ida. (1934). Film. Directed by István Székely. Hungary: Thália Film.
Jávor, P. 1987. *Egy színész elmondja....* Budapest: Akadémiai Kiadó.
Kardos, I. (1998, August). A magyar Clark Gable. *Vox,* p. 58.
Kenez, P. 2006. *Hungary from the Nazis to the Soviets: The establishment of the Communist regime in Hungary, 1944–1948.* Cambridge: Cambridge University Press.
A kék bálvány/The Blue Idol. (1931). Film. Directed by Lajos Lázár. Hungary: Palatinus.
Kovács, M.M. 1994. *Liberal professions and illiberal politics: Hungary from the Habsburgs to the Holocaust.* Oxford: Oxford University Press.
Kovács, T. 2006. A Nemzeti Számonkérő Különítmény. *Múltunk.* 3: 71–100.
Késő/Late. (1943). Film. Directed by József Daróczy. Hungary: Hajdu Film.
Kovács, Zs. 2001. *A magyar film olvasókönyve (1908–1943).* Budapest: Magyar Nemzeti Filmarchívum.
Lajta, A. (2001). A magyar filmlaboratóriumok története 1901–1961. *Filmspirál.* [Online] Available from: http://www.filmintezet.hu/magyar/filmint/filmspir/27/lajta.htm [Accessed: 21 July 2014], pp. 25–27.
Lohr, F. 1941. *A filmszalag útja.* Budapest: Királyi Magyar Természettudományi Társulat.

Magyar Film. (1940, June 1). Filmönellátás felé. p. 1.
———. (1941, September 27). Európai filmönellátás. p. 1.
———. (1942, March 10). *A Beszélő köntös* első hetének rekordbevételei a Royal Appolóban, back cover.
———. (1944, April 20). Fél évre eltiltották Jávor Pált a színpadi és filmszerepléstől. p. 11.
Marika/Little Mary. (1937). Film. Directed by Viktor Gertler. Hungary: Budapest Film.
Mayne, J. 2010. Danielle Darrieux, French female stardom, and the occupation. *Studies in French Cinema.* 10(2): 169–187.
Nemeskürty, I. (1974). *Word and Image: History of the Hungarian cinema* (2nd ed., Z. Horn & F. Trans.). Budapest: Corvina Press.
Ném élhetek muzsikaszó nélkül/I Cannot Live without Music. (1935). Film. Directed by Alfréd Deésy. Hungary: Kino.
Pelle, J. (2004). *Sowing the seeds of hatred: Anti-Jewish laws and Hungarian public opinion 1938–1944* (J. Held, Trans.). Boulder: East European Monographs.
Sándor, T. 1992. *Őrségváltás: A magyar film és a szélsőjobboldal a harmincas-negyvenes években.* Budapest: Magyar Filmintézet.
Skaper, B. (2008). Magyar filmsztárok a két világháború közötti Magyarországon. [Online]. *Médiakutató.* Available from: http://www.mediakutato.hu/cikk/2008_03_osz/08_regi_magyar_filmsztarok [Accessed: 26 August 2014].
Székely, I. 1978. *Hyppolittól a Lila akácig.* Budapest: Gondolat.
Szüle, M. 1982. *Miszter Jávor.* New York: Püski-Corvin.
A tanítónő/The Tutoress. (1945). Film. Directed by Márton Keleti. Hungary: Hunnia.
Ungváry, K.. 2012. *A Horthy-rendszer mérlege: Diszkrimináció, szociálpolitika és antiszemitizmus Magyarországon, 1919–1944.* Budapest: Jelenkor Kiadó.
Valamit visz a víz/From mong the Waves. (1943). Film. Directed by Lajos Zilahy. Hungary: Pegazus Film.
Vincendeau, G. 2000. *Stars and Stardom in French Cinema.* London: Continuum.

CHAPTER 5

From Boy N the Hood to Hollywood Mogul: Ice Cube's Lasting Stardom in Contemporary Hollywood

Julie Lobalzo Wright

Popular music stars have been a mainstay of Hollywood since the advent of sound and the popularity of the musical in the classical era. However, the longevity of these stars, as film stars, is variable. In the early 1990s a new wave of popular music stars broke into Hollywood, appearing in films that reflected their music and took place within the environments from which they originated. Hip hop stars including Ice-T, Tupac Shakur, and Ice Cube were able to make a seamless transition to cinema through the hip hop, 'ghetto action' (Watkins, 1998, p. 175) or 'hood' cycle of films that were released in the aftermath of gangster rap, the genre of music these stars helped to invent.

Although hip hop stars like Ice-T and LL Cool J have been successful on American television in long-running American television series, few rappers have had the success or, indeed, the lasting stardom of Ice Cube. In fact, his only true comparison may be Will Smith, who emerged at a similar time but possessed a more family-friendly image that was easier to incorporate within, first, television and later, film. Cube's longevity is

J.L. Wright
School of English and Languages, University of Surrey, Guildford, UK

© The Editor(s) (if applicable) and The Author(s) 2016
L. Bolton, J.L. Wright (eds.), *Lasting Screen Stars*,
DOI 10.1057/978-1-137-40733-7_5

remarkable due to the extreme nature of his ganger rap image, which was defined as part of the seminal rap group, NWA (Niggaz Wit Attitude). This image developed further after he left the group and began his solo career, with the release of *AmeriKKKa's Most Wanted* in 1990, featuring the controversial song, 'The Nigga You Love to Hate' and his cinematic debut as Doughboy in *Boyz N the Hood* (1991). The importance of authenticity to hip hop through the oft-quoted phrase, 'keepin' it real' (which generally means a desire to stay true to one's origins) suggests that alterations to an artist's hip hop image are unwelcome. Cube has been able to 'keep it real' by maturing and developing his younger gangster rap image through projects he has a fundamental role in producing. Thus, Cube has navigated the ideological limitations of his transgressive image through his own star agency within the industry by directing, writing, starring in, and producing many of his films.

This chapter will explore Ice Cube's unique star trajectory from controversial gangster rapper to Hollywood mogul as the co-founder of Cube Vision productions (with partner Matt Alvarez), producing more than half of the thirty films he has appeared in since 1991. Cube's longevity can be directly linked to the changing structure of Hollywood since the early 1990s, especially the conglomerate nature of Hollywood studios and their impetus to produce specialty or niche films under studio subsidiaries. This success, however, is limited by the same industry, due to the industry's perception of black-oriented films as 'niche'.

'Gangsta' Rap

Before examining Ice Cube's work in Hollywood, it is important to define gangster (or 'gangsta') rap, the music genre he helped to invent and which defined his early star image. Rap music was part of the larger culture of hip hop, which included rap music, graffiti, and breakdancing, with its influence slowly extending from New York to the rest of America in the 1980s. The commercialisation of rap music, beginning in the late 1980s, led to a divide between pop rap, which celebrated having a good time (Smith's DJ Jazzy Jeff and the Fresh Prince belonged to this strand) and rap music made by more politically minded artists, such as Public Enemy.

Gangster rap was a socially and politically conscious music whose 'primary thematic concerns' were 'identity and location' (Rose, 1994, p. 10). The identity was black, young and, mainly, male, and the location was various 'hoods' (short for neighbourhood) in South Central Los

Angeles, most notably, Compton,[1] made famous by NWA and Ice Cube. The lyrics were extremely controversial due to its emphasis on violence, especially through first-hand representations of gang violence, misogyny, and aggressive macho posturing. Gangster rap gave voice to young men who lived in environments where violence (gang and police) and death defined their everyday lives, addressing, as Todd Boyd (1997) suggested, 'the worldview of the truly disadvantaged' (p. 34). The irony of this, S. Craig Watkins (2005) argues, was that the ability to sell death through 'the embrace of guns, gangsterism, and ghetto authenticity brought an aura of celebrity and glamour to the grim yet fabulously hyped portraits of ghetto life' (p. 2). This tension between the authentic, truthful representations of hood life and the overly performed 'gangsta' image extended from the music to the rap stars themselves, especially Ice Cube. Many have argued, including Eithne Quinn (2005), that Cube engages in role-playing and assumes 'many faces' throughout his music (p. 126). His music often moves between 'the general and the specific, simultaneously analyzing individual actions as well as societal oppression' (Boyd, 1997, p. 51), allowing the star to 'portray' various characters within his music, with a primary mode of address in an aggressive style that presents him as 'the angry Black man, the enraged lyricist' (Boyd, 1997, p. 52).

Transition to Cinema

Boyz N the Hood was not only a seminal film for the hip hop cycle but also for Cube, as it was his first film role and one that director John Singleton wrote for the star. In the film, Cube portrays Doughboy, the brother of college-bound athlete Ricky and friend of Trey, whose strict father, Furious, ensures Trey doesn't get mixed up with gangs, or wind up in jail or dead (the eventual fate of Doughboy and Ricky). The film was critically and commercially successful, and following Spike Lee's influential *Do the Right Thing* (1989), signaled a new wave of black filmmaking, all due to the rise of rap, and even more so, 'gangsta' rap, which first shed light on the plight of young black men in urban Los Angeles. Watkins (1998) notes the central role location has within the narrative, exploring 'how urban space shapes post-industrial ghetto life', developing the theme of entrapment for the three primary characters and how each character

---

[1] As Todd Boyd has argued, Compton became synonymous with gangster rap even though few knew the specifics of the area (p. 68).

experiences 'social isolation differently' (p. 213). Doughboy is the listless, jobless, directionless opposite of his brother (Ricky), who will secure a college education through his athletic prowess, and Trey, who has been raised to work hard and pursue a profession. Doughboy is the embodiment of what Ice Cube had been rapping about: the young black male engaged in gangs and criminal activity, the poverty and desperation of being socially marginalised in the hood, the absent father, lack of educational opportunities, and the propensity to end up in jail (Perry, 2004, p. 108). In other words, the character and the film were a 'perfect fit' (Dyer, 2004, p. 129) between Cube's music star image and the character he portrayed on-screen.

Four years after *Boyz N the Hood*, and following major roles in *Trespass* (1992), *The Glass Shield* (1994), and *Higher Learning* (1995), Cube appeared in *Friday* (1995), a turning point in his film career as the first film he co-wrote (with DJ Pooh) and produced through his Cube Vision production company. *Friday* acts as a spiritual, but comedic, sequel to *Boyz N the Hood* with its similar attention to the South Central hood location and Ice Cube portraying a less tragic version of Doughboy, a young man listlessly spending his days sitting on his front porch with no sense of direction. Many have noted the importance of location to hip hop music, including Tricia Rose (1994) who states, 'Life on the margins of post-industrial urban America is inscribed in hip hop style, sound, lyrics, and thematics' (p. 21), replicating and reimagining the experiences of urban life (p. 22). The post-industrial urban environment forms a significant part of the identity of hip hop artists (noted above) who, in turn, produce music that is

> deeply rooted in the specific, the local experience, and one's attachment to and status in a local group or alternative family. These crews are new kinds of families forged with intercultural bonds that, like the social formation of gangs, provide insulation and support in a complex and unyielding environment and may serve as the basis for new social movement. (Rose, 1994, p. 34)

It is not surprising, then, that NWA referred to themselves as a gang, with their music rooted in the 'local experience' of living in Compton and the bonds between these 'alternative families'. These locations were, as Eithne Quinn (2005) notes, 'imagined communities' (p. 75) with Compton becoming 'a symbol of [...] brand identity and differentiation' (p. 76), leading to an increased ability to cross-promote their place-based image through, most notably, music, film, music videos, and film soundtracks

(p. 87). *Friday* and its sequels *Next Friday* (2000) and *Friday after Next* (2002) is an example of what Quinn (2005) defines as 'marketable expressions of authentic place-bound identity' ("life from the ghetto") (p. 67). In *Friday*, Ice Cube portrays Craig, a man in his early twenties, who still lives in his childhood home and, having been fired from his job, spends his days sitting on his front porch with his best friend, Smokey (Chris Tucker), watching what goes on in his hood. *Friday* takes place over one day,[2] and features many comedic situations, but ultimately, as Craig's voiceover notes at the beginning, 'after this Friday, neighbourhood ain't never gonna be the same'. From the opening crane shot that descends to show the neighbourhood street where most of the action will take place, *Friday* uses many of the same locations featured in *Boyz N the Hood* (and other hip hop films): the front porch, the liquor store, the ice cream van, and various homes. Thus, the film maintains its authenticity to the West Coast hood location while also exposing the potential comedy within these tight communities.

COMMUNITY

Murray Forman (2002) argues that a shared sense of community exists in many 'hood communities' where an interest in localised issues and a collective sense of place and common causes survives (p. 29). Beginning with *Boyz N the Hood*, but more so since he began producing films, Ice Cube has emphasised community in his many of films, creating a direct link from the locale-specific 'gangsta' music he is known for to his film stardom. He has referred to these films, which include the *Friday* series—*Barbershop* (2002); *Barbershop 2: Back in Business* (2004); *First Sunday* (2008); *The Longshots* (2008); and *Lottery Ticket* (2010)—as 'neighborhood classics', claiming they are films that 'don't get recognized by the Oscars, but are recognized by the neighborhood as movies you want to see' (Swanson, 2003, p. 82). While these films, which connect with the 'imagined communities' Cube first rapped about, generally still take place within the hood, they are devoid of the aggressive posturing and violence that defined his early image. This is not to suggest the films are uncontroversial. In fact, *Barbershop* has received criticism for many of the

---

[2] Jodi Brooks (2001) notes the importance of time in many 'gangsta' films, including *Friday*, which, through the marijuana consumption of Craig and Smokey, oscillates between 'real time' and 'dope time' (p. 370).

off-handed comments Cedric the Entertainer's character, Eddie, makes about various black politicians and entertainers. These films, however, promote a sense of community within black communal spaces, such as the barbershop (the prominent environment in the *Barbershop* series) and the church (featured in *First Sunday*), often suggesting that individualism and materialism is not as valuable as the family or community (Golphin, 2004, p. 7). The films correspond to Rose's (1994) notion of 'alternative families' that provide 'insulation and support in a complex and unyielding environment' (p. 34). In *First Sunday*, a group of parishioners held hostage by Durell (Cube) and Lee John (Tracy Morgan) eventually convince the robbers to change the direction of their lives and become upstanding citizens in the community. In *The Longshots*, the success of the local school-aged American football team, coached by Curtis (Cube), inspires the downtrodden town to physically clean itself up. *Barbershop 2: Back in Business* reaches its climax in a speech by Calvin (Cube), who emphasises the importance of the people who live in the neighbourhood, as opposed to selling the barbershop and giving in to gentrification. Thus, the locations have not altered from 'gangsta' rap, but the focus and tone have—from storylines that concentrate almost exclusively on the social and economic hardship of the young black male to films that 'deliver uplifting messages about the value of self-respect, personal responsibility, entrepreneurship, community, family and diversity' (Leonard, 2006, p. 141).

This has led many to suggest that Cube has 'sold out', producing films that may make money but that are not 'true' to his hip hop past. As noted earlier, authenticity pervades all aspects of hip hop with a localised perception of the world having an impact on the audience's reception of the music. Perry describes it thus:

> The rapper or MC is both subject and artist in much hip hop composition; who he or she is, constitutes a direct part of our experience of the music, and often the artist is imagined in the popular realm as doing nothing more than verbally expressing his or her experiences, self, and ideas. The MC usually occupies a self-proclaimed location as representative of his or her hood. As a representative, he or she encourages a kind of sociological interpretation of the music, best expressed by the concept of 'the real'. 'This is the documentary story of my world', we are told. (2004, p. 38)

Perry pinpoints how the self, whether genuine or imagined, becomes the representative of a specific place, encouraging the audience to view their music and their star image as a document of the rapper's real life.

The 'keepin' it real' mantra applies here, as representing where one comes from becomes vitally important when success, especially mainstream success, beckons. As Todd Boyd (1997) puts it, 'not only must one exist in a hostile world, but as the lure of financial success becomes real and the temptation to assimilate becomes stronger, it is necessary to remain true to one's cultural identity while existing in the mainstream' (p. 14). Cube has been able to remain true to his cultural identity, altered over time through financial success and ageing, by making films that align him with places and communities that defined his younger rap image.

Industry versus Ideology

The 'crossover' potential of rap stars has been utilised since the early 1990s through cinematic appearances and the release of hip hop based soundtracks. This was not limited to just selling products, but, as Boyd suggests above, the ideology of rap music and the notion of 'going mainstream' meant these stars, as Keith Harris (2012) has argued, sought to maintain their 'grounding in a particular tradition and retaining the original audience, while [also] gaining a wider audience moving from one market to another' (p. 255). Hip hop stars, including Ice Cube, sought to retain the ideology of their stardom as black American rappers while also appealing to a more mainstream (often white) audience through various products (film, music and television, mainly). I have discussed elsewhere (Lobalzo Wright, 2015) the difficulty of music stars, due to their already established stardom in another medium, transitioning to the cinema, but the crossover of hip hop stars was more straightforward and uncomplicated due to the hip hop genre of films being made in the early 1990s.[3] What has not been as effortless is the longevity of hip hop stars in Hollywood cinema with Cube as one of the few stars to find a way to 'keep it real' by connecting to his roots ideologically and industrially. Quite simply, Cube has become a significant black presence within Hollywood as a 'small scale movie mogul' (Prescod, 2004), by focusing on commercial imperatives as an independent within mainstream Hollywood. His ability to develop and produce films is often acknowledged as encouraging within an industry that is still dominated by white men, but his films are not without criticism, and it is the industrial context and ideology of these films that I wish to now discuss.

---

[3] See Jonathan Munby (2007) for an analysis of the connection between gangster rap and the gangster film genre.

Patrick Goldstein wrote in the *Los Angeles Times* that Hollywood is 'one of the most minority free industries in America,' with 'barely any people of color in any high-level positions at any major studio, talent agency or management firm' (qtd. in Quinn, 2013, p. 196). Many have noted (Green, 1994; Coker, 2000) the wave of independent black comedies being made in Hollywood since the 1990s, including films produced through Cube Vision Productions. Tyler Perry, one of the most successful black filmmakers in history,[4] has spoken about the invisibility of his core audience in mainstream Hollywood, quoting executives who, when Perry first approached them to fund his projects, stated, 'Black people who go to church don't go see movies' (Lynskey, 2010, p. 104). Perry's films (including the Madea franchise), which have been described as 'part-gospel revival, part medieval morality play, part vaudeville slapstick, part four-hanky romance, and part bathroom humour' (Donahue, 2005, p. 48), inhabit the space between what Geoff King (2009) calls the 'shades of difference', the 'globally dominant Hollywood blockbuster' and the 'low-budget independent or "indie" feature' (2009, p. 1). Cube's films function similarly, developed and produced through Cube Vision and distributed through specialty divisions of larger studios and conglomerates or through existing corporate partnerships. For example, Cube's films have been released through Screen Gems (Sony), Dimension (Weinstein Company), New Line (Warner Brothers) and Revolution (formally Sony). Cube Vision films, however, are compromised by the financial ceiling imposed on these 'niche' films through the studio's 'unwritten rules for making 'black films': cap budgets at around £30 million; cut a killer soundtrack; and limit the number of gross players (directors or actors who get a share of the total revenues)' (Coker, p. 29).[5] This last part is key because Cube's involvement in a film limits the 'gross players' due to his multifaceted stardom as producer, actor, and (sometimes) writer. He stated in 2005, 'Sometimes people look at me as a package: "Get Cube to be in it, and his company can produce it, and we'll make sure it comes out right to his audience"' (Donahue, p. 88). These films

---

[4] Perry, a director, writer, producer, and actor, became the first African American to own a studio and earned more than $130 million in 2011 alone (Quinn, 2013, p. 197). See Quinn (2013) for a sustained analysis of Perry's success in Hollywood.

[5] See also Guerrero (1993), who wrote about the $30 million dollar budget ceiling for black films in Hollywood in the early 1990s (pp. 166–168). This budgetary limit appears to have not altered in over twenty-five years.

generally double or triple their investment—only *Janky Promoters* (2009) and *Lottery Ticket* did not, at least, double the budget[6]—keep budgets to a reasonable figure under £20 million—only the *Barbershop* films and *Ride Along* (2014) have budgets above—and limit marketing, allowing a higher profit-to-cost ratio, generally 5–1, than mainstream Hollywood pictures (Guerrero, 1998, p. 296).

While these films are profitable, some have argued they are 'emptied of their social and political meanings' (Guerrero, 1998, p. 291) with many of the black comedies Cube has produced criticised for 'erasing any connections to hip hop and minimising displays of sexuality', creating characters that are 'non-threatening, modernized, hipper Uncle Tom [s]' (Leonard, p. 143).[7] Some critics, however, choose not to recognise the social contexts and communal values put forth in these films and, instead, focus on possibly stereotyped characterisations or the lightness in tone.[8] Catherine A. John (2013) argues that contemporary black comedies (including Cube's *Barbershop*) need to be reassessed to expose their 'euphoric and rejuvenating element of African American ethnic humor' as films that use 'ingroup' and 'outgroup codes' of interpretation and meaning (p. 343). Thus, these films should be celebrated for their specific black aesthetics consumed by black audiences and, as John suggests, the industrial position of the filmmakers, like Ice Cube, who are infiltrating white mainstream industries with films that encompass high and low culture but are decidedly black American products (from development to production to reception). The reception of these films, critically, suggests an uneasy relationship between the politics of representation and the politics of production, with Cube a central figure in the industry of black filmmaking.

Conclusion

In 2010 Cube stated that Cube Vision specialises in the 'upbeat neighborhood comedy' because the production company is 'one of the best out there that do this kind of movie' and because 'it's smart business' (Rabin). These quotes illustrate the aesthetic and financial imperatives that drive

---

[6] All budget and box office figures are from boxofficemojo.com.

[7] Criticisms have also been leveled against the *Barbershop* franchise for its promotion of middle-class values and conspicuous commodity consumption. See Mukherjee (2006).

[8] See Aftab (2008) for an example of a review that focuses on the social and political context one of Ice Cube's comedies, *First Sunday*.

Cube's auterism in contemporary Hollywood as a film star with great control[9] over his filmic products and a desire to 'keep it real' by producing films that come 'from the street'.

Cube is part of a group of black filmmakers who have shifted popular representations of blackness and black life 'to higher levels in terms of funding, production standards and perhaps more importantly the broad circulation of their films among popular audiences' (Guerrero, 2000, p. 37). Even with the supposedly 'niche' position of these films in Hollywood, Cube has, so far, created franchise properties—the *Friday* and *Barbershop* series; sequels—*Are We Done Yet?* (2007), which was the sequel to *Are We There Yet?* (2005), and *Ride Along 2*, scheduled for release in 2016; and television series based on his films—*Friday*, *Barbershop*, and *Are We There Yet?*—all became television series. Within the contemporary media industry, sequels, franchises, and spin-offs into other media not only benefit the star and producer but also many of the large media conglomerates. The success of a film like *Ride Along* is especially significant: produced by Cube Vision, starring two black leads (Ice Cube and Kevin Hart), budgeted at over $40 million, with a domestic box office of over $134 million. Ice Cube's largest box office success outside his co-starring role in *21 Jump Street* (2012) and *22 Jump Street* (2014), *Ride Along* may represent a breaking of the ceiling and Cube's future ability to produce films with bigger budgets and production values while continuing to utilise 'ingroup' and 'outgroup' cultural codes to appeal to a wider audience. In a similar way to Will Smith and Tyler Perry, Cube has been able reach the top 'against the racial odds but also ironically because of [his] hard-won experience of those racial odds' (Quinn, 2013, p. 208).

His career appears to have come full circle through his Hollywood industry clout, which has led to the development, production, and release of *Straight outta Compton* (2015), a biopic about NWA, with his son, O'Shea Jackson, Jr., portraying him. The longevity Cube has achieved is remarkable in light of his gangster origins and within an industry that is still viewed as 'one of the most racially exclusionary cultural industries' (Quinn, 2013, p. 197). Throughout his career he has kept hold of his cultural identity, becoming an important star who has

---

[9] The only project Cube did not have full control over was *Janky Promoters*, released straight-to-DVD in 2010 by the Weinstein brothers. Due to the Weinsteins' financial problems, Cube was offered the chance to sell the film elsewhere, but, according to Cube, before he finalised an alternative deal, the unfinished film was released (Rabin).

used the system to the best of his ability and thrived when many never imagined that 'the nigga you love to hate' could become such an important Hollywood figure.

References

21 Jump Street. (2012). Film. Directed by Phil Lord and Christopher Miller. [DVD]. USA: Columbia Pictures and MGM.
22 Jump Street. (2014). Film. Directed by Phil Lord and Christopher Miller. [DVD]. USA: Columbia and MGM.
Are We There Yet?. (2005). Film. Directed by Brian Levant. [DVD]. USA: Columbia.
Are We Done Yet?. (2007). Film. Directed by Steve Carr .[DVD]. USA: Columbia.
Aftab, K. 2008. Review of *First Sunday*. *Sight and Sound* 18(6): 56.
Barbershop. (2002). Film. Directed by Tim Story. [DVD]. USA: MGM.
Barbershop 2: Back in Business (2004). Film. Directed by Kevin Rodney Sullivan. [DVD]. USA: MGM.
Boyd, T. 1997. *Am I black enough for you?: Popular culture from the 'hood and beyond*. Bloomington, IN: Indiana University Press.
Boyz N the Hood. (1991). Film. Directed by John Singleton. [DVD]. USA: Columbia.
Brooks, J. 2001. Worrying the note: Mapping time in the Gangsta film. *Screen*. 12(4): 363–381.
Coker, C.H. 2000. Hollywood blackout. *Premiere* 14(2): 29–30.
Cube, I. (1990). *AmeriKKKa's most wanted* [CD]. USA: Priority.
Donahue, A. 2005. The XXX factor. *Premiere* 18(8): 88–90.
Do the Right Thing. (1989). Film. Directed by Spike Lee. [DVD]. USA: Universal.
Dyer, R. 2004. *Stars*, 2nd edn. London: BFI Publishing.
First Sunday. (2008). Film. Directed by David E. Talbert. [DVD]. USA: Screen Gems.
Forman, M. 2002. *The 'hood comes first: Race, space, and place in rap and hip-hop*. Middletown, CN: Wesleyan University Press.
Friday. (1995). Film. Directed by F. Gary Gray. [DVD]. USA: New Line Cinema.
Friday After Next. (2002). Film. Directed by Marcus Raboy. [DVD]. USA: New Line Cinema.
The Glass Shield. (1994). Film. Directed by Charles Burnett. [DVD]. USA: Miramax.
Golphin, V.F.A. 2004. *Barbershop* revisited. *Blackfilmaker* 6: 7.
Green, D. 1994. Tragically hip: Hollywood and African-American cinema. *Cineaste* 20(4): 28–29.
Guerrero, E. 1993. *Framing blackness: The African American image in film*. Philadelphia: Temple University Press.
——— 2000. Be black and buy. *Sight and Sound* 10(12): 34–37.

―― 1998. A circus of dreams and lies: The black film wave at middle age. In *The contemporary Hollywood reader*, ed. T. Miller. London and New York: Routledge.
Harris, K. 2012. Black crossover cinema. In *The Wiley-Blackwell history of American film: Vol. IV, 1976 to the present*, eds. C. Lucia, R. Grundman, and A. Simon. Wiley-Blackwell: Chichester.
Higher Learning. (1995). Film. Directed by John Singleton. [DVD]. USA: Columbia.
Janky Promoters. (2009). Film. Directed by Marcus Raboy. [DVD]. USA: Third Rail Releasing.
John, C.A. 2013. Black comedy as vital edge: A reassessment of the genre. In *A companion to comedy*, eds. A. Horton, and J.E. Rapf. Wiley Blackwell: Chichester.
King, G. 2009. *Indiewood, USA: Where Hollywood meets independent cinema*. New York: IB Taurus.
Leonard, D.J. 2006. *Screens fade to black: Contemporary African American cinema*. Westport, CN: Praeger.
Lobalzo Wright, J. 2015. David Bowie is the extraordinary rock star as film star. In *David Bowie: Critical perspectives*, eds. E. Devereux, A. Dillane, and M.J. Power. London: Routledge.
The Longshots. (2008). Film. Directed by Fred Durst. [DVD]. USA: Dimension.
Lottery Ticket (2010). Film. Directed by Erik White. [DVD]. USA: Warner Brothers.
Lynskey, D. 2010. Who the Hell is…Tyler Perry? *Empire* 255: 102–105.
Mukherjee, R. 2006. The ghetto fabulous aesthetic in contemporary black culture: Class and consumption in the *Barbershop* films. *Critical Studies*. 20(6): 599–629.
Munby, J. 2007. From gangsta to gangster: The Hood film's critical allegiance with Hollywood. In *The new film history: Sources, methods, approaches*, eds. J. Chapman, M. Glancy, and S. Harper. Palgrave: Basingstoke.
Next Friday. (2000). Film. Directed by Steve Carr. [DVD]. USA: New Line Cinema.
Quinn, E. 2005. *Nuthin' but a 'g' thang: The culture and commerce of gangsta rap*. New York: Columbia University Press.
―― 2013. Black talent and conglomerate Hollywood: Will Smith, Tyler Perry, and the continuing significance of race. *Popular Communications* 11: 196–210.
Perry, I. 2004. *Prophets of the Hood: Politics and poetics in hip-hop*. Durham, NC: Duke University Press.
Prescod, M. 2004. Mr. Mogul: The Iceman Cometh. *Black Filmmaker* 6(25): 15–17.
Rabin, N. (2010) *AV Club Interview: Ice Cube* [Online]. 29 August. Available from: http://www.avclub.com/article/ice-cube-44306 [Accessed: 10 June 2015].

Ride Along. (2014). Film. Directed by Tim Story. [Film]. USA: Universal.
Rose, T. 1994. *Black noise: rap music and black culture in contemporary America.* Hanover: Wesleyan University Press.
Straight Outta Compton. (2015). Film. Directed by F. Gary Gray. [Film]. USA: Universal.
Swanson, T. 2003. Next generation of Hollywood's power elite: Ice cube, for brining the Hood to Hollywood. *Premiere* 16(10): 82–84.
Tresspass. (1992). Film. Directed by Walter Hill. [DVD]. USA: Universal.
Watkins, S.C. 1998. *Representing: Hip hop culture and the production of black cinema.* Chicago: University of Chicago Press.

SECTION 2

Faded Stardom

CHAPTER 6

'What Price Widowhood?': The Faded Stardom of Norma Shearer

Lies Lanckman

In July 1934 *Photoplay* magazine featured an article entitled 'The Real First Lady of Film', introducing the piece as follows:

> The First Lady of the Screen—there can be only one—who is she?
> Her name is not Greta Garbo, or Katharine Hepburn, not Joan Crawford, Ruth Chatterton, Janet Gaynor or Ann Harding.
> It's Norma Shearer. (Lee, 1934, p. 28)

Originally from Montréal, Canada, Norma Shearer signed her first Metro-Goldwyn-Mayer (MGM) contract at age twenty. By twenty-five, she had married its most promising producer, Irving Thalberg, and by thirty-five, she had been widowed through the latter's untimely death, ultimately retiring from the screen forever at forty. During the intervening twenty years, Shearer won one Academy Award and was nominated for five more, built up a dedicated, international fan base with an active fan club, was consistently featured in fan magazines, and starred in popular and critically acclaimed films throughout the silent, pre-Code and post-Code eras. Shearer was, at the height of her fame, an institution. Unfortunately, her career is rarely as well remembered as those of her contemporaries—including many of the stars named above. This chapter, then, will attempt

L. Lanckman
School of Arts, University of Kent, Canterbury, UK

© The Editor(s) (if applicable) and The Author(s) 2016
L. Bolton, J.L. Wright (eds.), *Lasting Screen Stars*,
DOI 10.1057/978-1-137-40733-7_6

to provide an explanation for this discrepancy between Shearer's former success and her current relative obscurity.

Rhetoric on Shearer to Date

Scholarly work on Shearer has been relatively scarce, with many early works on stars ignoring her completely. Texts that did mention the star frequently examined her in highly negative terms, with Richard Schickel's 'The Santa Monica Beach House of a Hollywood Genius and his Leading Lady' (1990) a good example. Although this article seemingly focuses on the Shearer-Thalberg home, instead, the author provides an extensive condemnation of Shearer's career, life, and even physical appearance. According to the author, Shearer was the 'Queen of MGM' solely by 'virtue of her husband's decree'. Since she was devoid of any talent or star quality, he explains, 'all of Shearer's star contemporaries at MGM [...] exercise larger claims on film history and our memories' (p. 218).

Other authors have written about Shearer in more sympathetic, but limited, ways. Although Jeanine Basinger's *A Woman's View* (1993), which focuses on women's film from the 1930s to 1960s, includes an appendix on 'Women at the Box Office' citing Shearer as one of the highest-earning female Hollywood stars for four years in the 1930s, Shearer is only mentioned three times throughout the book, solely in a context of 'excessive nobility' (p. 167). The greater accessibility of Shearer's pre-Code films on home video in the 1990s and 2000s led to a further examination of her career, including Mark A. Vieira's *Sin in Soft Focus* (1999), which featured her as a key pre-Code star within a wider discussion on the Production Code. Mick LaSalle's *Complicated Women* (2000) went significantly further by mixing biography and scholarly analysis to examine Shearer's star persona with a focus on her oft-forgotten pre-Code films. LaSalle usefully notes that many of Shearer's earlier films did not fit into the 'excessive nobility' paradigm highlighted by Basinger and is particularly interested in the way her films often embodied elements of feminine modernity, such as sexual independence and female employment. LaSalle highlights these as significantly more interesting than Shearer's comparatively dull later roles, and attributes her fading to this fact, but ignores the development within Shearer's star image that contributed to this evolution. This sentiment is echoed in Basinger's *The Star Machine* (2007), in which the author expands her analysis of Shearer and attributes her fading, in part, to the fact that only her later films are ever revived (p. 357). Basinger also raises the point that 'Shearer's reputation has been given the coup de grâce by a simple biographical fact': her marriage to Irving Thalberg in 1927, which led to the assumption (as reiterated by Schickel) that he 'made her career for her' (p. 358).

These works suggest Shearer's lack of longevity as a star is due to the difference between her earlier (and, it is argued, better) and later (rather dull) films, and to the Thalberg marriage and its negative connotations for Shearer. No scholarly work has, however, analysed either of these factors in detail. This chapter aims to trace the evolution of Shearer's star image throughout her career, allowing for an emphasis on key biographical facts such as the Thalberg marriage but also demonstrating how this evolution may have impacted on the reception of particular films.

In *Stars*, Dyer notes that a star image 'can be found across a range of media texts' (1979, p. 60) and while films remain 'privileged instances of the star's image' (p. 88), it is important to look also at media sources outside the purely filmic or biographical. In this chapter, I focus on the research potential of the fan magazine, which at this time was the primary way, outside the cinema, for many fans to learn more about their idols. Many fan magazines, including publications such as *Photoplay* and *Motion Picture*, were published by independent companies from the early 1910s onward but, to a large extent, 'published and wrote what the studios determined they should publish and write' (Slide, 2010, p. 73).

Fan magazines, therefore, played a crucial part in shaping and communicating a star's studio-sanctioned public image and can be highly useful for research on specific stars. Nonetheless, none of the above authors takes them into consideration when discussing Shearer. I aim to examine the way Shearer's film roles and biographical facts were incorporated by the magazines into a wider star narrative, and how this narrative evolved across months and years. For this purpose, I have divided Shearer's life and career into three distinct phases: from her arrival in Hollywood in 1923 to her marriage to Thalberg in September 1927, from the marriage to Thalberg's death in September 1936, and from his death to her retirement in 1942.

Ingénue (1923–1927)

Shearer signed a contract with MGM in 1923, but mentions of the starlet in fan magazines only became more extensive when she starred in *Lady of the Night* (1925). An examination of magazine (publicity) rhetoric in these early years is particularly fruitful, since it illustrates the formation of Shearer's star image before the Thalberg union.

Interestingly, speculations on Shearer and romance were infrequent during these pre-Thalberg years and remained limited to vague references, such as 'Norma has a number of beaux' in *Photoplay*, November 1926 (Questions and Answers, 1926, p. 106). Instead, Shearer's social class, a key element of her star image, was often discussed. The starlet's very first mention in *Motion Picture* magazine in April 1924 referred to her as 'a trained society girl' (Carr, 1924, p. 63), and this type of coverage continued throughout the years, with a reader's letter in January 1925 describing her as 'aristocratic' and 'like girls of good family are in real life', a 'wholesome, charming, well-bred little thing' (Brickbats and Bouquets, 1925, p. 12). This was rooted in the reality of Shearer's life since, contrary to many contemporary female stars, Shearer hailed from a respectable middle-class family and had started working primarily due to her father's financial problems after the Great War. This was often illustrated through visual means, such as an image published in *Picture Play* in October 1926 of Shearer and her elegantly clad mother seated at a beautifully decorated dinner table (How Do You Take Your Tea?, 1926, p. 73).

Magazine publicity also reflected upon this image as early as 1926. In June of that year, *Motion Picture* published an article entitled 'No Casting Today', which highlights the extent to which Shearer had to struggle to achieve her (ostensibly well-deserved) fame. It refers to the 'social butterfly myth' in which Shearer was universally seen as privileged and wealthy (Thorp, 1926, p. 29) and thus tries to counter the effects of her aristocratic, privileged image. The article recognises her background, while attempting to soften this by fitting the middle-class star into the 'soda fountain girl to star' narrative Daniel Boorstin describes as a 'leitmotif of American democratic folklore' (Boorstin, 1962, p. 162): the belief that a class system does not apply in America (Dyer, 1979, p. 42). A number of articles highlighting Shearer as a 'plucky' and ambitious young woman followed, but the middle-class traces remained alongside these, and the attempt to tie the star completely into established patterns of democratic stardom remained problematic.

Shearer's well-bred public image also impacted on the fan magazine rhetoric on her films, such as *Lady of the Night*. In this film, Shearer played both lead roles, the rich, naïve Florence and the poor and worldly Molly. Although Florence was similar to the ingénue roles Shearer had previously played, Molly was decidedly different. In April 1925, *Photoplay* highlighted that many people initially believed Shearer to be miscast as the 'tough little dance-hall girl', but in the end, she was 'superb' in this role (York, 1925, p. 47). Some readers' letters, however, expressed reservations about this sudden turn; even in January 1926, six months after the film's release, one *Photoplay* reader claimed to still be 'shuddering from [the] shock' of seeing 'the exquisite little Norma Shearer as a "lady of the night"' (Brickbats and Bouquets, 1926, p. 12).

Wife (1927–1936)

During the next phase of Shearer's career, from her marriage to Thalberg in 1927 to his death nine years later, this marriage became increasingly important to her star image. The magazine treatment of the marriage built further on Shearer's upper-class image, since it made her a part of Hollywood's executive elite, with publicity materials presenting the Thalbergs as an aristocratic Hollywood couple. This was a widespread phenomenon as early as 1930: in December of that year, the birth announcement of their son in *Picture Play* called the baby 'the Prince Royal' and 'the crown prince of the Metro-Goldwyn-Mayer establishment' (Schallert & Schallert, 1930, p. 28) with his parents the de facto king and queen. Other articles reiterated this 'royal couple' identity: in March 1935, *Motion Picture* published an article entitled 'Dinner for Eighteen' (Shearer, 1935, p. 45), in which Shearer gave readers tips as to how to act like a successful society hostess. This shows that the representation of Shearer as an aristocrat was incorporated into the public image of her marriage to Thalberg.

Alongside coverage of Shearer's marriage to Thalberg, however, fan magazines also chose to focus on the institution of marriage itself, particularly in terms of its position within the life of a modern, working woman such as Shearer. An early example was published in *Photoplay* in May 1927, four months before their marriage and during speculations about a Shearer-Thalberg engagement. This article was entitled, rather disingenuously, '"I'm Not Going to Marry" Says Norma Shearer' and was an outgrowth of the established commentary on Shearer's pluck and ambition. Although the article echoed previous characterisations which focused on Shearer's wealthy background—comparing her to girls 'just graduated from finishing school' (Rogers St. Johns, 1927, p. 33)—it was also the first article to refer repeatedly to the star as a highly intelligent, ambitious 'modern'.

Its most interesting aspect is an outlining of the sacrifices Shearer had willingly made for stardom, including a decision not to marry. The star states that she believes 'an entirely new marriage relation, in which the husband and wife are equals' will eventually evolve, 'but that hasn't come yet' (p. 121). Thus, she claims she will not yet marry, since she wishes to focus primarily on her career and believes she could not muster the energy or will to care for a husband as wives are still expected to do.

The career-family balance debate for working women was particularly relevant to the social climate of the time. While female employment was on the rise, 'public sentiment in the 1920s was hostile to wives working out of a sense of personal fulfilment, rather than dire need' (Dumenil, 1995, p. 124), and film stars were certainly a part of that group. The phenomenon of working wives had, in fact, been commented on in fan magazines a number of times before. As early as 1922, an article on Gloria Swanson noted that the star did not believe 'that marriage—happy, successful marriage [...]—is possible if a woman insists on following a career', and if a woman wants a career, she 'must leave marriage alone' (Rogers St. Johns, 1922, pp. 21–22). This 1922 article cited careerism as an unnatural state and the main cause of unhappiness for the modern woman, whereas the Shearer article quotes the star as repeatedly saying that personal sacrifices are worth it for a career. This is a first hint, perhaps, that writing on Shearer would move further and further away from Swanson's standpoint throughout the following years.

A mere four months after the publication of the 'I'm Not Going to Marry' article, Shearer married Thalberg and the career-home balance took precedence in her star image, especially in 1930 when she became a mother for the first time, giving birth to Irving Thalberg, Jr. in August—and when at the same time, in November of that year, she won her first and only Academy Award for *The Divorcee* (1930). *The Divorcee* represented a transition within Shearer's film career, since it was the first of a series of films I have titled her 'free soul' films, including such films as *Let Us Be Gay* (1930), *A Free Soul* (1931), *Strangers May Kiss* (1931), and *Riptide* (1934). The 'free soul' films generally feature a main character, played by Shearer, who explores issues of modern femininity, such as the institution of marriage, sexual freedom for women, female employment, and so on, and who remains empowered and sympathetic at the end of the film. *The Divorcee*'s reception in fan magazines is particularly interesting since, rather than representing Shearer as a star portraying a particular role, she is given agency in the choice of this film. *Photoplay* reported in

September 1930 that it was Shearer who recommended the original book, *Ex-Wife* (1929), to the studio, thus emphasising Shearer's support for the messages conveyed in book and film (York, 1930, p. 99).

In *The Divorcee*, Shearer is a young, modern career woman who lives in a companionate,[1] equal union with her husband. They have agreed that, since they are modern people, everything will be 'fifty-fifty', but when he has an affair and tells her such things shouldn't matter in a modern world, she decides to have an affair of her own. After she finds he still believes women are not allowed the same sexual freedom as men, she promptly divorces him and has a string of lovers, as well as a successful career. He, on the other hand, loses his job, and the two are reunited in the end when he asks her to give him another chance.

The film thus highlights multiple themes. Firstly, it focuses strongly on modern, companionate marriage and the place of sexual equality therein. This is broadened to include notions of sexual equality outside marriage, without loss of status for women who choose to experiment. Furthermore, despite the film's focus on the couple's divorce and reunion, the career of the Shearer character is never problematised or blamed for the couple's problems. Considering that at this time, most working women were single and the idea of a wealthy, married woman choosing to have a career was still rare, this filmic depiction was fairly controversial, especially as such wealthy career women were often labeled 'the enemies of society' (Dumenil, 1995, p. 124), and wives who did work very rarely pursued well-paid and fulfilling careers (p. 116).

In August 1930 *Photoplay* addressed this career-home question directly in an article entitled 'Will Norma Shearer Retire?': a question to which the answer was a resounding no. In this article, Shearer not only suggests it is possible to have both a career and a successful marriage but goes further, advising that 'one should take up a career for the sake of love' and that she celebrates 'women who have accomplished things' (Ogden, 1930, p. 47). Her work has strengthened her marriage, because her husband is proud of her accomplishments, and working makes her a more pleasant and interesting person to be married to.

Throughout the next few years, Shearer's magazine coverage consisted of a number of similar items, including a July 1931 article in *Motion*

---

[1] In the context of early twentieth century history, the term 'companionate marriage' indicates a supposedly new type of marriage in which the spouses are friends and equals rather than simply partners for procreative or financial purposes.

Picture, 'Married the Modern Way', in which Shearer described herself as 'the mistress kind of wife' (Manners, 1931, p. 108), proclaiming that a modern wife should be attractive, exciting, and adventurous, but not necessarily tied to domestic life. 'Norma Shearer Tells What a Free Soul Really Means' described, almost a year later, how Shearer believed that a woman should get as much sexual freedom as a man, and while a woman should not take lovers purely for 'transient pleasure' (Hall, 1932, p. 96), experimentation is fine as it makes her a better partner. This sentiment is also advocated in Shearer's films *A Free Soul* and *Strangers May Kiss* (1931), in which she portrays young women who are sexually active without being married. A third article, entitled 'Let's Be Civilized about Sex', published in *Photoplay* in December 1934, had the star defending sex as a part of life which brings 'electricity and vitality' to it, and which must be represented on-screen as well (Rankin, 1934, p. 45). Although these sentiments were still controversial at the time, Shearer and the characters she portrayed on-screen embraced female sexual freedoms but were never condemned for this.

While Shearer remained an aristocratic presence at this time, the star's unusually stable love life allowed her to embrace a particularly progressive view on a happy, companionate, modern marriage between two people with their own careers. This enlightened, yet respectable modernity balanced out the potentially traditionalist or elitist connotations of her aristocratic star image, and in a sense rendered it more relatable and palatable. Her films, which were able to represent an unprecedentedly progressive image of the modern woman during this brief window of time before the enforcement of the Hays Code, aided this balancing act and enhanced it further.

Widow (1936–1942)

After the production of *The Barretts of Wimpole Street* (1934), Shearer did not make any new films for almost two years until *Romeo and Juliet* (1936), due to personal reasons: she gave birth to her second child in June 1935, and her husband suffered a heart attack the same year. In September 1936, Thalberg died of pneumonia aged 37, leaving Shearer a young widow with two small children. This would prove to be a pivotal moment for her career, as Shearer's new tragic widowhood problematised the careful balance between upper-class respectability and the modern freedom her star image had been based on.

Tragedy had never been part of Shearer's star narrative. As noted, her early stardom characterised her as a plucky, ambitious girl, whereas during her marriage, she became 'the one girl in Hollywood who has everything' (Hall, 1931, p. 113). In her pre-Code films, as well, her characters had always emerged romantically triumphant as respectable, free-spirited women with the man of their choice, in part due to the inherently progressive nature of this phase of Hollywood filmmaking. Set in this broader context, the tragic ending of Shearer's real-life love story was jarring.

Additionally, the concept of star-as-widow had few precedents at this time, when most writing on widowhood confined itself to the economic needs of young, impoverished widows (Berardo, 1968, p. 193), a vision incompatible with the financially secure Shearer. Previous examples of young, widowed film stars were scarce. Although Jean Harlow, widowed in 1932 after the supposed suicide of husband Paul Bern, might be the closest precedent, the nature of his death and the short duration of their marriage meant that widowhood never became central to her star persona.

Another trope in regard to widowhood was that of the aristocratic/royal widow, of which the prime example was still Queen Victoria, who had notoriously worn mourning dress for forty years after the death of her husband and who was the subject of the play *Victoria Regina*, a Broadway hit throughout 1936–1937. As such, the widowed Queen was still a common cultural presence at this time, and the connotations of tragic, aristocratic, and conservative widowhood may well have, in some sense, influenced public perceptions of the widowed Queen of MGM.

In the first full-length article on Shearer after Thalberg's death, she was referred to as 'the tragic young star' (Manners, 1936, p. 36) with the remainder of the article illustrating the conservative turn Shearer's image was taking. Firstly, it announces her retirement; while Shearer was too 'modern' to retire for marriage, widowhood apparently easily accomplished this. In a similar way, this article also indicates that a star who tended to steer clear of excessive domesticity now became defined by her position as wife, mother, and homemaker. Her only desire, it states, is 'to carry on the dreams and ideals of Irving Thalberg', and 'her only thought is of her children', whom she wants to 'grow up here in the home their father planned for them' (p. 81). This traditionalist emphasis on devoting herself to Thalberg's legacy and to her children's happiness remained almost unchanged until 1938, when the star finally began production of a new film, *Marie Antoinette* (1938).

This film broadly covered the life of Marie Antoinette from her teenage years to her death, and thus required Shearer to play the tragic queen at different phases of her life. As such, the (fairly complex) film fulfilled different functions within Shearer's evolving star persona. Particular elements of its plot were not wholly different from the earlier 'free soul' films, particularly the middle section of the film which focuses strongly on Marie's exploration of extramarital sexuality before she reclaims her respectability by becoming a happy wife and mother. However, the film's tragic ending overshadows these earlier scenes, with Marie's ultimate widowhood and death re-emphasising the tragic angle that had become an unavoidable part of Shearer's persona. Additionally, Shearer's identity as the dignified and tragic Queen of MGM matched, to a large extent, Marie's royal persona as sketched in the Zweig biography, the film's main source material.

The film was announced in *Photoplay* in July 1938 in an article entitled 'A Queen Comes Back', establishing this parallel between the tragic Queen of France and the tragic Queen of MGM that ran throughout the promotion of the film. In fact, its very production was represented as 'a testimonial to one of the greatest real life loves Hollywood has ever known' (Baskette, 1938, p. 20), and a great deal of emphasis was put on the fact that this film, particularly close to Shearer's heart and personal life, was chosen as her return from retirement. The article ends by reiterating the tragic links, stating that '[Thalberg and Shearer] were the royal couple and she is still queen. As queenly as Toinette herself' (p. 86). Once again, press and film came together to sketch an image for Shearer, but now the aristocratic and tragic elements of the film's plot, rather than the sexually empowered elements, were stressed. Similar stories emerged during the next few years, with Shearer no longer linked with modernity but, instead, with traditionalism, quiet maturity, and tragedy. Articles now focused on her 'handful of memories' (Wilson, 1938, p. 32), or as an 'Open Letter to My Fans', on Shearer giving emotional support and advice to other young widows (Hall, 1940, p. 87).

In 1939 Shearer starred as the central character in *The Women*, a divorce film reminiscent of her 'free soul' films of the early 1930s, re-introducing concepts of progressive femininity into her star image. The restrictions, however, of the 1934 Production Code resulted in a more conservative worldview and collaborated with Shearer's already traditionalised star image; *The Women*'s central divorcée was a 'devoted mother and wife' (Brief Reviews, 1939, p. 92) with none of the formerly typical traces of radical modernity in terms of female employment or sexual liberation. In an article connected to the film, Shearer is described as 'calm, intelligent and reserved' (Hayes, 1939, p. 19), laudable attributes of an aristocratic widow, but a far cry from Shearer's previous star image.

CONCLUSION

In 1956, John Springer, publicist for RKO Pictures, authored the first issue of *Old Hollywood* magazine, a publication focused on 'Movieland's Mad Past'. The front cover of the issue featured such stars as Rudolph Valentino and Greta Garbo, alongside a small portrait of Norma Shearer. The photo used was a publicity image for *The Divorcee*, yet the only mention of Shearer within the magazine was not connected to this film but to the more conservative *The Women* (Springer, 1956, p. 72). This magazine thus neatly illustrates the—particularly post-retirement—development of Shearer's star image and emphasises once more the importance of fan magazines as a methodological tool to trace and analyse the star narratives of faded stars.

These fan magazines illustrate that throughout Shearer's career, the star was identified by her wealthy background and aristocratic demeanour, magnified when she married mogul Irving Thalberg. This chapter, however, has attempted to establish that the contents of both her pre-Code films and fan magazines enabled the star to use this stable home life as a vehicle to articulate a particular brand of modernity, in which women were able to enjoy both a happy, egalitarian marriage and a successful career. Despite what Basinger suggested in *The Star Machine*, therefore, it was not the marriage itself that really problematised Shearer's legacy. As Shearer became a young widow in 1936, however, this progressive emphasis was completely reversed as her star image became rooted in tragedy, and her films, impacted by the more conservative atmosphere of the post-Code era, could no longer assist her in presenting an alternative image. As Springer's magazine demonstrates, even by 1956, Shearer was only casually remembered as a respectable star-as-widow, which remains the case to this day.

REFERENCES

A Free Soul. (1931). Film. Directed by Clarence Brown. [DVD]. USA: Warner Home Video.
Basinger, J. 1993. *A woman's view*. New York: A. A. Knopf.
——— 2007. *The star machine*. New York: A.A. Knopf.
Baskette, K. (1938, July). A Queen comes back. *Photoplay*, pp. 20–22, 85.

Berardo, F. M. (1968, July). Widowhood status in the United States. *The Family Coordinator*.
Boorstin, D. 1962. *The image*. London: Weidenfeld and Nicholson.
Brickbats and Bouquets. (1925, January). *Photoplay*, p. 12.
———. (1926, January). *Photoplay*, p. 12.
Brief Reviews. (1939, December). *Photoplay*, pp. 6, 8, 92.
Carr, H. (1924, April). On the camera coast. *Motion Picture*, pp. 62–63.
Dumenil, L. 1995. *The modern temper*. New York: Hill & Wang.
Dyer, R. 1979. *Stars*. London: BFI Publishing.
Hall, G. (1931, June). The lady who knows it all. *Motion Picture*, pp. 47, 93, 113.
——— (1932, April). Norma Shearer tells what a free soul really means. *Motion Picture*, pp. 48–49, 96.
——— (1940, November). Open letter to My fans—by Norma Shearer. *Modern Screen*, p. 87.
Hayes, B. (1939, November). Hedy Lamarr vs Joan Bennett—and other dangerous Hollywood feuds. *Photoplay*, pp. 18–19.
How Do You Take Your Tea?. (1926, October). *Picture Play*, p. 73.
Lady of the Night. (1925). Film. Directed by Monta Bell. [DVD]. USA: Warner Archive Collection.
LaSalle, M. 2000. *Complicated women*. New York: Thomas Dunne Books/St. Martin's Press.
Lee, B. (1934, July). The real first lady of film. *Photoplay*, pp. 28–29, 96–97.
Let Us Be Gay. (1930). Film. Directed by Robert Z. Leonard. [DVD]. USA: Warner Archive Collection.
Manners, D. (1931, July). Married the modern way. *Motion Picture*, pp. 58–59, 108.
——— (1936, December). How Norma Shearer faces the future. *Photoplay*, pp. 36, 80–81.
Marie Antoinette. (1938). Film. Directed by W. S. Van Dyke. [DVD]. USA: Warner Archive Collection.
Ogden, E. (1930, August). Will Norma Shearer retire? *Photoplay*, pp. 47, 125.
Parrott, U. 1929. *Ex-Wife*. New York: Grosset and Dunlap.
Questions and Answers. (1926, November). *Photoplay*, p. 106.
Rankin, R. (1934, December). Let's be civilised about sex. *Photoplay*, pp. 45, 105.
Riptide. (1934). Film. Directed by Edmund Goulding. [DVD]. USA: Warner Archive Collection.
Rogers St. Johns, A. (1922, February). Confessions of a modern woman—as told by Gloria Swanson. *Photoplay*, pp. 20–22, 114.
——— (1927, May). "I'm not going to marry" says Norma Shearer. *Photoplay*, pp. 33–34, 121.
Romeo and Juliet. (1936). Film. Directed by George Cukor. [DVD]. USA: Warner Archive Collection.

Schallert, E. and Schallert, E. (1930, December). Hollywood high lights. *Picture Play*, p. 28.

Schickel, R. (1990, April). The Santa Monica beach house of a Hollywood genius and his leading lady. *Architectural Digest*, pp. 218–230.

Shearer, N. (1935, March). Dinner for eighteen. *Motion Picture*, pp. 45–46, 72.

Slide, A. 2010. *Inside the Hollywood fan magazine*. Jackson: University Press of Mississippi.

Springer, J. (1956). The good ones never die. *Old Hollywood*, pp. 64–72.

Strangers May Kiss. (1931). Film. Directed by George Fitzmaurice. USA: MGM.

The Barretts of Wimpole Street. (1934). Film. Directed by Sidney Franklin. [DVD]. USA: Warner Archive Collection.

The Divorcee. (1930). Film. Directed by Robert Z. Leonard. [DVD]. USA: Warner Home Video.

The Women. (1939). Film. Directed by George Cukor. [DVD]. USA: Warner Home Video.

Thorp, D. (1926, June). No casting today. *Motion Picture*, p. 29.

Vieira, M.A. 1999. *Sin in soft focus*. New York: Harry N. Abrams.

Wilson, D. (1938, October). Norma Shearer's handful of memories. *Photoplay*, pp. 32–33, 87.

York, C. (1925, April). East and West. *Photoplay*, pp. 46–47, 68.

——— (1930, September). East and West. *Photoplay*, p. 99.

CHAPTER 7

Robert Taylor: The 'Lost' Star with the Long Career

Gillian Kelly

Although Robert Taylor was a high-profile star with a constant presence in Hollywood for almost four decades during his lifetime, he is not well remembered today. He can, in fact, be labelled as a 'lost' or 'forgotten' star of classical Hollywood cinema. He is by no means the only 'lost' star of the era but, given his status as a top box-office attraction, his on-screen diversity, and his sustained audience appeal, he is certainly a noteworthy 'lost' star and therefore one in need of reappraisal. On the rare occasions when Taylor is mentioned in academic literature, it is usually only a passing reference to him co-starring with Greta Garbo in *Camille* (1936) or playing the lead in the grand epic *Quo Vadis* (1951). Given Taylor's longevity as a star, and his substantial film and television output, his 'lost' status is simultaneously noteworthy and peculiar.

This chapter discusses Taylor as a key example of a wider phenomenon important in star and celebrity studies, and his persona can be used as a template to investigate similar stars (both classical and contemporary) who, despite strong initial emphasis on their looks, become respected for their acting ability over time. Taylor's career also brings up questions around the longevity of stars, changes in masculinity and male stars, and

G. Kelly
Department of Theatre, Film and Television Studies, University of Glasgow, Glasgow, UK

the ageing process. Here I look specifically at the construction and subsequent developments of Taylor's star persona over time, the possible reasons why he endured as a star during his lifetime and why the reasons for his longevity when his career was active are, arguably, the same reasons for his being 'lost' today.

When Taylor signed with Metro-Goldwyn-Meyer (MGM) in 1934, he began what would become the longest-running contract in Hollywood history. Following an extremely quick rise to stardom, he appeared consistently as a leading man from 1935 until his death in 1969, never becoming a character actor or bit-part player. Appearing in a diverse range of genres including comedy, drama, war, and Westerns, Taylor left behind a collective legacy of over 200 feature films, shorts, television shows, and radio appearances across his thirty-five-year career. Off-screen he had a high-profile marriage to actress Barbara Stanwyck; has his hand and footprints immortalised in concrete outside Grauman's Chinese Theatre, and has a star on Hollywood's Walk of Fame. Furthermore, a diverse range of extra-filmic merchandise was dedicated to Taylor throughout his career, including jigsaw puzzles, postcards, comic books of his films and even a promotional coin, featuring his face in profile, released by MGM.

In order to present a case study of a star whose image endured during his lifetime but not after it ended, we might first identify examples of star images that *have* endured, and the means by which this has been achieved, in order to understand the context of the image of a 'lost' star. An enduring star is not necessarily one who enjoys a long or varied career, for example, Marilyn Monroe and James Dean. The (now iconic) images of a select few stars continue to appear on high-street merchandise, such as posters, clothing, and mugs, which results in their omnipresence in the public's consciousness after their screen careers (and lives) have long ended. Those who have never seen a classical Hollywood film will no doubt still recognise Monroe's white dress from *The Seven Year Itch* (1955) or Judy Garland's gingham dress from *The Wizard of Oz* (1939) as a result of this continued presence. Stars' longevity may also be due to their association with a particular film (James Stewart with *It's a Wonderful Life* (1946)) or screen role (Clark Gable as Rhett Butler in *Gone with the Wind* (1939)) which become, and continue to be, recognisable over time. This allows certain stars to remain extra-textually active through the generation of new merchandise, but not new images, while the stars themselves are textually, and physically, inactive. Other areas which may ensure enduring stardom are scandalous private lives and tragically early deaths.

Unlike his contemporaries Stewart and Gable, there is no specific film or definitive role that Taylor is associated with and, although he died at the relatively young age of 57, it was not tragically young like Dean (aged 24), Jean Harlow (aged 26) or Monroe (aged 36). Additionally, the only potential 'scandals' in Taylor's life stem from his marriage to the slightly older Barbara Stanwyck and his testimony at the House Un-American Activities Committee hearings, neither of which had a negative impact on his career. Although 'Robert Taylor' was a constructed persona, as are all star images, this persona was created around an everyday person with an accessible off-screen life. Thus, by weighing the aspects of Taylor's private life against the lives of stars who become notorious through associations with the likes of murder, drug abuse, or multiple marriages, Taylor's extremely tame and, by all accounts, largely uneventful private life may be a key contributing factor to his 'lost' status.

Furthermore, having built an image around the four most conventional and dominant social norms in Western society: his whiteness, heterosexuality, Americanness and maleness, the ideological conservatism of Taylor's star persona may have resulted in his being considered *too* normal, and therefore an uninteresting figure for academic study. Taylor's type of stardom is akin to the cliché of Hollywood's conventional 'happy ending' which, despite its traditional and successful function, is, as James MacDowell suggests, academically overlooked because of its conventional nature (2013, p. 1). Just as MacDowell notes that the 'happy ending' is usually discussed in derogatory terms such as 'standard', 'predictable', or 'typical', a similar argument can be made for actors like Taylor who embodied typical, dominant, Western norms and, thereby, almost became clichés of Hollywood stardom, resulting in their becoming almost invisible within cinema history. However, just as the 'happy ending' tells us much about the industry and how it worked because of its very dominance and typicality, so too can 'typical' stars. Scholarly accounts of stars still tend to focus on more unusual stars, such as Marlon Brando or Montgomery Clift, who did not conform to Hollywood's standards or sit comfortably within trends and industry expectations. However, a 'cookie cutter' star like Taylor, who appeared to seamlessly fit Hollywood's studio system and trends, can tell us much more about how the industry worked as a direct consequence of this fit than stars who did not conform.

As can be expected for a star whose career spanned four decades, several social, political, cultural, and industrial changes affected the construction and development of Taylor's star persona. I will now discuss Taylor's star persona throughout his career, identifying shifts which occurred and reading his image across the decades in which he worked. Taylor's career began in 1934, the same year in which Hollywood started to recover from the devastation that the Great Depression had caused (Balio, 1993, p. 30), and as Gregory Paul Williams suggests, 'the public became movie mad again [and] Hollywood made a comeback' (2011, p. 201). Hollywood's comeback meant a fresh start, and new faces on the screen were vital to this process. Additionally, as Richard Maltby notes, the Motion Picture Production Code was enforced in 1934 in a bid to 'clean up' Hollywood and sanitise its film content (1995, p. 61). Studios would, therefore, not only want to clean up their films, but also the off-screen lives of the stars they had under contract. While films appear an easier area to manage, a star's publicity (defined by Dyer as what the press finds out or what a star 'lets slip' in an interview; 1998, p. 61) would be more challenging. In attempting to 'sell' a star to audiences, studios created a 'fit' between the star's on- and off-screen lives in order to convince audiences that stars consistently acted the same (Balio, 1993, p. 165). Thus, studios might gravitate towards promoting stars who posed less of a moral threat than those who were perhaps more interesting and exciting but were a bigger risk to the studio's principles.

The most effective way for studios to 'sell' stars was to have them appear in film fan magazines, which Tino Balio calls 'the most voracious consumers of publicity' (1993, p. 170). These magazines were extremely important for studios since, as Tamar Jeffers McDonald puts it, they 'worked to foster reader awareness of stars in the run-up to new releases' (2013, p. 35). Since historical audiences could only see films through theatrical releases, fan magazines allowed them prolonged access to the stars and their films. Consequently, by appearing in fan magazines, stars could reach a wider audience, build up a fan base and create excitement around future theatrical releases (McDonald, 2013, p. 35). Within film studies, fan magazines are increasingly perceived as important sources for determining how stars were presented to audiences outside their films. As Anthony Slide suggests, fan magazines may appear 'seemingly worthless object[s]', but they are of interest and value for film scholars and sociologists (2010, p. 3). However, from the mid 1930s onwards, fan magazines were almost fully controlled by Hollywood's major studios; stories had to be submitted for studio approval, editing and rewriting before publication, a practice which greatly benefited the industry (Barbas, 2001, p. 99; Slide, 2010, p. 8).

Publicity material on Taylor began to appear extremely early in his career and had a clear emphasis on informing (predominantly female) readers about his off-screen life, particularly his status as perpetual bachelor. Discussing Gable's 'irresistible' persona, Deborah Nadoolman Landis suggests that MGM's publicity department 'captured [the] mystique in its famous ad line about Clark Gable: "Men want to be him, women want to be with him"' (2007, p. xxii). Although there is a lack of evidence to suggest that men wanted to *be* Taylor, there is a definite sense that women and girls wanted to be with him, and article titles such as 'Why Girls Fall in Love with Robert Taylor' (Levin, 1970) illustrate that Taylor's early appeal was much more wholesome than Gable's overt eroticism. In relation to their looks, Taylor's symmetrical, precision-made face also contrasted with Gable's looks, which were more uneven and irregular but sexy. Mick LaSalle calls Gable 'the most sexually dangerous of the dangerous men of the pre-Code' (2002, p. 132), and although Gable straddled the pre-Code and Code eras, most of his performances are erotically charged. For example, in *It Happened One Night* (1934), Gable and Claudette Colbert's unwed characters sleep in the same room, with only a blanket over a rope separating them, while he sings *Whose Afraid of the Big Bad Wolf?* to her, with a profound sense of naughtiness. Although Taylor was presented as a rival for Gable, he was marketed as more of an all-American romantic ideal and poster boy for the new 'clean' Code era; his persona strongly linked to his wholesome small-town background.

Born Spangler Arlington Burgh in Filley in Nebraska on 5 August 1911, Taylor was the only child of a grain merchant who trained as a doctor to cure his ailing wife. It appears that Taylor also intended becoming a doctor, something which publicity material consistently made reference to.[1] When his father died in 1933, Taylor relocated to Hollywood with his mother, and early fan magazine articles greatly emphasised their closeness and his college education. This allowed Taylor's initial star persona to effortlessly fit the new image MGM was creating for itself, while also setting him up as both doting son and eligible bachelor who might hold appeal to female readers and audience members of all ages.

---

[1] The Nebraska Historical Society holds personal letters written by Taylor whilst at college. These letters note his plans to become a doctor and never mention acting or Hollywood.

The 1930s

In the 1930s, MGM was particularly noted for its glamorous female stars and, as a result of his undeniable good looks, Taylor was initially marketed as a male pin-up and 'romantic foil' for some of the studio's top actresses including Garbo, Harlow, and Joan Crawford. Marketed as 'the man with the perfect profile', Taylor was repeatedly shot in profile, in both publicity stills and on screen, in order to highlight his famous attribute (Fig. 7.1). In addition, his jet-black hair with widow's peak, blue eyes, full lips, and large, but not exaggerated, frame allowed Taylor to be simultaneously pretty and manly.

Taylor averaged 3.5 films a year throughout the decade and his final film of 1935, the melodrama *Magnificent Obsession*, was his breakthrough film and turned him into a major box-office star.[2] The film's plot appears intrinsically linked to publicity surrounding Taylor's family

Fig. 7.1 Taylor's Celebrated Profile, with Janet Gaynor in *Small Time Girl* (1936)

[2] The character of Merrick was also Rock Hudson's breakthrough role when Douglas Sirk remade *Magnificent Obsession* in 1954. Hudson is, arguably, a very similar type of star to Taylor.

background since his character, Robert Merrick, becomes a doctor in hopes of restoring the eyesight of the woman he loves (Irene Dunne). Perhaps the film's plot fitted a little too well with studio publicity and fan magazines articles recounting Taylor's late father's work, but it cemented Taylor's stardom and ensured him leading-man roles from that point forward. As well as blurring the lines between his professional and private lives, *Magnificent Obsession* established the three most persistent themes of Taylor's persona: irresistibility to women, Americanness and good looks.

In an attempt to 'beef up' Taylor's image, MGM cast him in the two sports-themed films: *A Yank at Oxford* (1938) and *The Crowd Roars* (1938). The former not only added elements of athleticism and virility to Taylor's image but also built up a stronger sense of his Americanness since Taylor plays the 'Yank' in a film dealing primarily with Anglo-American conflict. In line with Taylor's prettiness, even in this more masculine context, he is repeatedly put on display. However, for the first time, more emphasis is placed on his body than on his face. Although repeatedly dressed in revealing sports gear, Taylor is nevertheless 'safely' shown to be actively engaged in sports, even if this stretches narrative economy at times. For example, before running a race in *A Yank at Oxford,* he holds up a telephone with separate mouth and ear pieces, helping to emphasise his muscular arms and well-developed chest in a tight vest. While in the centre of the frame, he then removes his sweat pants to reveal shorts, before stopping to turn and face the camera in a full body shot highlighting his exposed body and impressive physique which had been concealed in previous screen roles.

Although depicted as an active man, Taylor continued to be spectacularised through his tight-fitting sporting gear and interactions with female characters. In *A Yank at Oxford* we are introduced to Elsa Craddock (Vivien Leigh) when she first notices Taylor. Glancing towards him, she does a double-take before her eyes bulge. She then looks him up and down, smiles approvingly, and moves towards him. Similarly, in *The Crowd Roars,* Taylor plays a boxer, and for the majority of the film, he is dressed only in satin shorts or wrapped in a towel; the erotic display of his body being both justified by his role and aiding the advancement of his tougher persona. However, romance is still allowed to be at the centre of the film in order to avoid alienating his strong, established (female) fan base.

The 1940s

The tougher Taylor who emerged at the end of the 1930s consequently prepared him for more brutal roles while World War II raged in Europe and the threat of conflict hung over America. As the atmosphere in America darkened, so did Taylor's roles, and in 1940 he grew a moustache in what appears to have been another way of progressing his tougher image along and a further attempt to escape the pretty-boy label placed on him. Alongside a number of other dark roles, Taylor played a credible gangster in *Johnny Eager* (1941) and a convincing, hardened sergeant in the brutal World War II combat film *Bataan* (1943). Off screen, Taylor ultimately became a lieutenant in the US Naval Air Corps during his real-life active war duty between 1943 and 1946.

After the war ended, Taylor returned to the screen in even darker roles, playing a number of psychologically disturbed (potential) killers in the likes of *Undercurrent* (1946) and *Conspirator* (1949). Although an extremely dark period for Taylor's star persona, the post-war years allowed him to display a much wider acting range and created a sense of danger in his image, which brought him closer to the character Gable had always displayed. In the uncertain environment of 1940s America, it appears that it was no longer enough for Taylor to be the cocky all-American he had been in the 1930s; he was now required to display a mature, solid, and patriotic Americanness, which he successfully did both on- and off-screen. This advancement in Taylor's image also meant that he continued to fit changes within Hollywood, and America more generally, and his ability to adjust to technical, social, and economic changes added to his longevity as a performer who was able to work across a range of genres and who could, ultimately, appeal to a wide audience.

The 1950s

Hollywood faced some serious challenges in the 1950s, including the decline of the studio system and the rise of television (Lev, 2003, pp. 1–3). In the words of Robert Dance, the 1950s was a decade of glamour which provided 'a spectacular final chapter' for Hollywood (2012, p. 9). It was also a spectacular final chapter for many long-established male stars including Taylor, James Stewart, Cary Grant, and Gary Cooper, who enjoyed continued success even as new, younger stars came along. In a bid to get audiences back into theatres, the studios released several big budget epics, with Taylor again at the centre of the trend. He played the lead role in MGM's first epic of the decade, *Quo Vadis*, which went on to become the studio's biggest money maker at the time. He also starred in the highly successful 'unofficial medieval British trilogy' directed by Richard Thorpe, consisting of *Ivanhoe* (1952), *Knights of the Round Table* (1953), and *The Adventures of Quentin Durward* (1955). While these historical costume epics advanced Taylor's tougher masculinity and romantic appeal (Fig. 7.2), his extensive work in Westerns during this decade further developed his tough screen presence and Americanness.

In 1956, twenty-three years into Taylor's career, *Picturegoer* magazine ran an article called 'Robert Taylor—the Perfect Star', which presented stardom as something of a checklist. Dividing the article into six subheadings, Margaret Hinxman (1956) outlines the qualities required for true stardom before concluding that Taylor meets all of the criteria needed to become, and remain, a star in the traditional sense of the word. We can only assume that Hinxman is using Taylor as a unisex model for stardom and, that if he is indeed the blueprint or the 'norm' for perfect stardom, it follows that many other stars do not fit the rigid criteria established here. The subheadings used to prove that Taylor is the 'perfect' star are: He Began the Right Way, He Gets the Right Publicity, He Does the Right

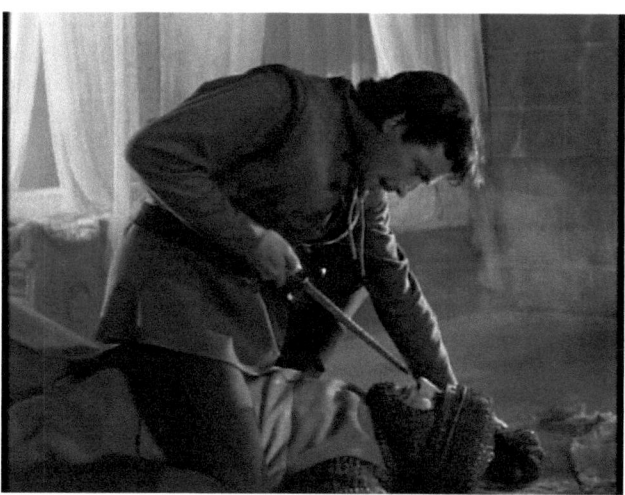

Fig. 7.2 Taylor in action, and in profile, in *Ivanhoe* (1952)

Thing, He Looks Right, He Toes the Right Line, and He Says the Right Things. Although covering a range of areas, this generally proposes obedience (the repetition of 'right'), and suggests that stardom is both positive and conventional (and even conservative), since 'right' also appears to mean that he *fits* well. Hinxman invites the reader to 'study [Taylor's] record [...] and see just how perfect a paragon star can be', before proposing a list of 'wrong' things which other (presumably 'non-perfect') stars have done. This is conveyed through what Taylor has *not* done: he has never 'given an indiscreet interview', 'been caught [...] in an indiscreet act', or 'been suspended' by his studio. Ironically or not, by the end of the decade, MGM had lost all of its stars from the 'golden age', with Taylor being the last to exit in 1958. Taylor's departure ended the longest running contract in Hollywood history and also signalled the demise of Hollywood's classical era. The descent of the industry and its 'golden age' stars continued throughout the next decade.

THE 1960s

Paul Monaco calls the 1960s a decade where Hollywood struggled to hold on to its audience, and 1960 the year that the American film industry was 'in the midst of a transition that was proving to be long and difficult' (2001, p. 1). Biographer Linda Alexander quotes Taylor as saying that at this time, Hollywood was in 'one helluva condition [and] I don't see the end of the dilemma' (2008, p. 197). After the breakdown of the studio system, Taylor, like many of his contemporaries, made a handful of low-budget and made-for-television films. However, again demonstrating an ability to adapt to the industry, he moved into television, where he worked regularly for the rest of his career. In the years prior to his death, Taylor hosted (and occasionally starred in) eighty-four episodes of the Western series *Death Valley Days* (1952–1970) and starred in all ninety-seven episodes of the weekly crime series *The Detectives* (1959–1962). Fans who had grown up with Taylor and were familiar with his 'matinee idol' past, would see new developments of authority in Taylor's star persona, while younger viewers would be introduced to Taylor as a more mature patriarchal figure. Based on Taylor's star power, *The Detectives* was renamed *Robert Taylor's Detectives*, and the show also helped launch the careers of younger actors starting out in television, including Mark Goddard, who went on to appear in *Lost in Space* (1965–1968), and Adam West, who starred as *Batman* (1966–1968).

The 1960s was a decade of loss and violence, including the Vietnam War and the assassinations of John and Robert Kennedy, Martin Luther King, and Malcolm X. Several classical-era stars died (including Gable, Cooper, and Spencer Tracy), as did a number of younger stars such as Monroe, Garland, and Montgomery Clift. As Taylor's career, and life, were coming to an end, so too was the style of filmmaking which had become associated with Hollywood, and MGM's time as a leading studio was over. Monaco suggests that the release of *The Wild Bunch* (1969) firmly established a new aesthetic of sensation (2001, p. 2). Accordingly, if 1969 marked the birth of New Hollywood, it also marked the death of a key product of Old Hollywood with Taylor's death on 8 June, only ten days before *The Wild Bunch* was released. That same year, Las Vegas real-estate dealer Kirk Kerkorian acquired a controlling interest in MGM and used the studio's name for a hotel he was building. James Monaco suggests Kerkorian's only concern was with MGM's brand name and its connotations as the 'most powerful and prestigious' studio in Hollywood (2009, p. 275). Although MGM continued to release films, they were mostly low-budget and generally unsuccessful productions which stood in direct contrast to the studio's past glamour, affluence, and star power (Monaco, 2009, p. 275).

Conclusion

Taylor appeared on numerous magazine covers throughout his career, including film fan magazines and, later, television listings magazines. While many stars from the classical era still feature heavily on magazine covers today, again they tend to be enduring stars who are instantly recognisable to readers.[3] Despite an enduring presence during his lifetime, I have only been able to source three recent publications featuring Taylor as cover star: 1994's *Nebraska History* (which mentions him as a famous person from Nebraska) and *Now Playing* (2001, 2010), the listings magazine from Turner Classic Movies, which owns MGM's archives and, therefore, most of Taylor's films.

---

[3] Elizabeth Taylor and Grace Kelly are other enduring stars who have featured on modern magazine covers. However, they also fit the model of scandal (Taylor) and short career and early death (Kelly). Furthermore, *Vanity Fair* recently featured cover images of Nicole Kidman and Lindsay Lohan styled as Kelly.

Taylor's long and successful career and his ability to fit changes and trends in the industry enabled him to be presented as the 'perfect' star for demonstrating how the industry worked in the classical era. From an early persona based on his remarkable looks and ordinary all-Americanness, Taylor progressed into a solid and masculine actor whose work crossed several genres, four decades, and both film and television. His 'lost' status appears particularly unusual given his vast and varied output of work, a high-profile marriage, and sustained popularity throughout his lifetime. Since Taylor did not have a tragic private life, had a happy marriage, and died as a result of smoking too much,[4] it is obvious that he does not fit with academia's continued desire to promote 'maverick' stars or to read against the grain of conventional Hollywood. However, Taylor's capacity to adapt and grow at, sometimes, difficult points in his career should not be understated, and his ability to inform us about both stardom and the industrial processes of Hollywood studios in the classical era makes him an important figure of Hollywood history.

REFERENCES

A Yank at Oxford. (1938). Film. Directed by Jack Conway. USA: Metro-Goldywn-Mayer.

Alexander, L.J. 2008. *Reluctant witness: Robert Taylor, Hollywood and communism*. North Carolina: Tease Publishing LLC.

Balio, T. 1993. *Grand design: Hollywood as a modern business enterprise, 1930–1939*. New York: Charles Scribner's Sons.

Barbas, S. 2001. *Movie crazy: Fans, stars, and the cult of celebrity*. New York: Palgrave.

Bataan. (1943). Film. Directed by Tay Garnett. [DVD]. USA: Metro-Goldwyn-Mayer.

Batman. (1966–1968). ABC.

Camille. (1936). Film. Directed by George Cukor. [DVD]. USA: Metro-Goldwyn-Mayer.

Conspirator. (1949). Film. Directed by Victor Saville. [DVD]. USA: Metro-Goldwyn-Mayer.

Dance, R. 2012. Introduction. In *Hollywood unseen*, ed. Gareth Abbott. ACC Editions: Suffolk.

Death Valley Days. (1952–1970). CBS.

---

[4]The happy marriage I refer to was Taylor's second marriage to actress Ursula Thiess, which produced two children and lasted until Taylor's death.

Dyer, R. 1998. *Stars*, 2nd edn. London: British Film Institute.
Gone with the Wind. (1939). Film. Directed by Victor Fleming. [DVD]. USA: Metro-Goldwyn-Mayer.
Hinxman, M. (1956, 4 February). Robert Taylor—The perfect star. *Picturegoer*, pp. 10–11.
It Happened One Night. (1934). Film. Directed by Frank Capra. [DVD]. USA: Columbia Pictures.
It's a Wonderful Life. (1946). Film. Directed by Frank Capra. [DVD]. USA: RKO Radio.
Ivanhoe. (1952). Film. Directed by Richard Thorpe. [DVD]. USA: Metro-Goldwyn-Mayer.
Johnny Eager. (1941). Film. Directed by Mervyn LeRoy. [DVD]. USA: Metro-Goldwyn-Mayer.
Knights of the Round Table. (1953). Film. Directed by Richard Thorpe. [DVD]. USA: Metro-Goldwyn-Mayer.
Landis, D.N. 2007. *Dressed: A century of Hollywood costume*. New York: HarperCollins Publishers.
LaSalle, M. 2002. *Dangerous men: Pre-code Hollywood and the birth of the modern man*. New York: Thomas Dunne Books/St Martin's Press.
Lev, P. 2003. *Transforming the screen, 1950–1959*. New York: Charles Scribner's Sons.
Levin, M. 1970. *Hollywood and the great fan magazines*. New York: Arbor House Publishing.
Lost in Space. (1965–1968). CBS.
MacDowell, J. 2013. *Happy endings in Hollywood cinema: Cliché, convention and the final couple*. Edinburgh: Edinburgh University Press.
Magnificent Obsession. (1935). Film. Directed by John Stahl. [DVD]. USA: Universal Pictures.
Maltby, R. 1995. *Hollywood cinema: An introduction*. Oxford: Blackwell Publishers Ltd.
McDonald, T.J. 2013. *Doris day confidential: Hollywood, sex and stardom*. London: I. B. Tauris.
Monaco, P. 2001. The sixties: 1960–1969. New York: Charles Scribner's Sons.
Monaco, J. 2009. *How to read a film: Movies, media, and beyond*, 4th edn. Oxford: Oxford University Press.
Nebraska History. (1994). 75 (4).
Now Playing. (2001). September.
———. (2010). April.
Quo Vadis. (1951). Film. Directed by Mervyn LeRoy. [DVD]. USA: Metro-Goldwyn-Mayer.
Slide, A. 2010. *Inside the Hollywood fan magazine: A history of star makers, fabricators and gossip mongers*. Mississippi: University Press of Mississippi.

Small Time Girl. (1936). Film. Directed by William A. Wellman. USA: Metro-Goldwyn-Mayer.
The Adventures of Quentin Durward. (1955). Film. Directed by Richard Thorpe. [DVD]. USA: Metro-Goldwyn-Mayer.
The Crowd Roars. (1938). Film. Directed by Richard Thorpe. [DVD]. USA: Metro-Goldwyn-Mayer.
The Detectives. (1959–1962). ABC/NBC.
The Seven Year Itch. (1955). Film. Directed by Billy Wilder. [DVD]. USA: 20th Century Fox.
The Wild Bunch. (1969). Film. Directed by Sam Peckinpah. [DVD]. USA: Warner Brothers/Seven Arts.
The Wizard of Oz. (1939). Film. Directed by Victor Fleming. [DVD]. USA: Metro-Goldwyn-Mayer.
Undercurrent. (1946). Film. Directed by Vincente Minnelli. USA: MGM.
Williams, G.P. 2011. *The story of Hollywood*. Austin, Texas: BL Press LLC.

CHAPTER 8

Melanie Griffith: Wild Girl and Working Woman

Lucy Bolton

At the heart of the star image of Melanie Griffith is a bewildering array of contradictions, which carve out a particular place for her as an ageing female star in Hollywood. A large part of her image has been centred on vulgarity and excess, created by her film roles in the 1980s, elements of her physicality, and her off-screen persona, leading to connotations of cheapness, artifice, and ageing disgracefully. Another side of her persona is founded on a unique Hollywood female genealogy and familial loyalty, imbuing Griffith with a security and stability in the Hollywood firmament that others are only able to dream of. Griffith's persona and career are more complex than first appears, and revealing of both the Hollywood film industry's treatment of ageing actresses and popular culture's prurient obsessions with the appearance and behaviour of ageing women. In this chapter, I will argue that Griffith's film career may have faltered, but her star image endures, standing for defiance and irrepressibility in surprising and significant ways.

Herstory

Famously, the daughter of Hitchcock heroine Tippi Hedren, Melanie was introduced to acting as a child. Griffith's first significant film role was as teenage temptress Delly in Arthur Penn's bleak neo-noir *Night Moves*

L. Bolton
School of Languages, Linguistics and Film,
Queen Mary University of London, London, UK

© The Editor(s) (if applicable) and The Author(s) 2016
L. Bolton, J.L. Wright (eds.), *Lasting Screen Stars*,
DOI 10.1057/978-1-137-40733-7_8

(1975). In this film she plays a sexually promiscuous, drug-taking teenager, whose disappearance sparks detective Harry Moseby's descent into a maelstrom of duplicity and murder. Roger Ebert described how Delly 'has a disconcerting way of taking off her clothes' (2006), and this observation is also insightful into Griffith's on-screen persona from this point onward. She *disconcerts* with her bodily exhibitionism, her vocal range and mode of delivery, and also her usually unshakeable sexual confidence.

At the age of 14 she starred in *Roar* (1981) with her mother,[1] and her screen persona was established with *Body Double* (1984) in which she played porn actress Holly Body. This excessive and parodic film set the scene for several of Griffith's roles over the next decade: sexually provocative, dangerous, and vulnerable characters, stripping, dancing, and teasing their way through the eighties. In films such as *Fear City* (1984), *Stormy Monday* (1988), and *The Bonfire of the Vanities* (1990), Griffith played prostitutes, mistresses, and molls, and her combination of baby voice and voluptuous body helped to create a persona focussed on bawdy sex and dangerous eroticism. Integral to this image was the visual excess of the decade, with all its garish colour and exaggerated proportions, reflected in the bold and attention-grabbing colours of Griffith's hair and clothes. These were era-definingly evident in Griffith's starring performance as career woman Tess McGill in *Working Girl* (1988). As the secretary who wanted to work her way into a serious career in acquisitions and mergers, Tess learnt that she had to tame her look, consisting of monumental hair and shoulder pads, if she wanted to succeed. As she observes to best friend Cynthia, 'If you want to be taken seriously, you need serious hair'. Tess cuts her hair, lowers her voice, and refines the clothes and make-up, thereby winning the job and the leading man. In return for this self-taming turn, Griffith was rewarded with an Oscar nomination, a Golden Globe, and widespread critical acclaim.

Despite this starring role in this much loved and lauded film, Griffith's career was not ignited by her awards season in the spotlight. In his 'Notes on Starmaking and Female Stardom in Contemporary Hollywood', Peter Kramer considers the career of Sandra Bullock in the context of the nineties and 2000s. Griffith does not feature in his chapter, although her contemporaries Julia Roberts, Demi Moore, Meg Ryan, Cameron Diaz,

---

[1] This legendary film featuring Hedren and her family being besieged by lions was rereleased in 2015, prompting fresh revelations about the making of the film and the way in which Hedren's family lived with big cats. See Stobezki (2015).

and Jodie Foster do. Kramer discusses the idea of 'the next big thing' in Hollywood, and differentiates between those actresses whom he sees as 'temporarily hyped' (when writing, he predicts Diaz will be this) and those who are building well-established careers, such as Roberts and Bullock (2004, p. 90). Despite some of Kramer's predictions and categorisations seeming rather forced, his comments on 'starmaking' do help understand the particular trajectory of Griffith's image. Kramer describes how 'production decisions [...], the actress's choices, her performance, film marketing [...], critical responses and box-office results interact so as to select a particular performer to become the focus of intense public interest and substantial financial investments on the part of the industry'. This process, Kramer says, 'can work positively to elevate the performer to stardom, if the various factors mentioned above reinforce her unique status, thus differentiating her from other performers. However, it can—and indeed much more frequently does—also work negatively, keeping her in the position of an undistinguished working actress, or relegating her back to that status, once she has achieved stardom' (p. 92). Kramer's analysis rings true in relation to 'temporarily hyped' stars one might think of, such as Heather Graham (*Boogie Nights*, 1997) or Alison Doody (*Indiana Jones and the Last Crusade*, 1989), and his other category of career builders might include Julianne Moore or Kirsten Dunst, but Griffith defies both categorisations.

After Griffith had worked with seminal directors and appeared in significant films in the seventies and eighties, *Working Girl* (1988) was—in professional terms—the most successful role of her career at the age of 31. As the decade progressed, and Griffith headed towards the age of 40, the films she appeared in ranged from unsuccessful to downright bombs, and she garnered six nominations for Worst Actress 'Razzies'.[2] Griffith's star image remained prominent, however, for many complex reasons other than high-profile film performances. Although Griffith has played many dramatic roles over her fifty-year career, the associations of bawdiness, excess, and sexual availability have remained integral parts of her screen persona, as have elements of her personal life and family history. I will now unpack the features of her stardom that together create her unique status as an ageing female star in Hollywood.

---

[2] Griffith has received eight nominations in the Worst Actress category of the Golden Raspberry Awards, and has won the award three times (source www.imdb.com).

THE ELEMENTS OF THE GRIFFITH STAR IMAGE

1. *Physicality*

It could of course be said that physical appearance is the major aspect of every star image, especially female stars in Hollywood. However, Griffith's physical appearance has always been particularly under scrutiny. Firstly, there is the question of whether she resembles her famously beautiful mother: her eyes are possibly similarly shaped, but her chin and face shape was broad around the jaw when she was young, and she is tall, thin limbed and curvaceous, unlike her tiny, bird-like mother. Her face is attractive but unconventional. As mentioned, her nakedness is integral to many of her films. Her breasts have been seen very frequently on-screen, drawing attention to their shape (adolescent, pre- and post-augmentation) and colouring, of her skin and pale nipples as well as the colouring of her body skin, which is pinkish and white with freckles.

I have written elsewhere about the currency of the naked star female body in relation to Meg Ryan, Demi Moore, and Halle Berry (Bolton, 2009). For these three stars, the revelation of their nakedness was a major selling or talking point. Griffith's body is so familiar, however, that there is a somewhat gratuitous tone to images of her naked, and an over-familiarity with her ageing body. The nudity in *Night Moves* has already been mentioned, but it also features prominently in *Joyride* (1977), *Fear City* and *Body Double*, as well as varying degrees of nudity from a glimpse of a breast to full frontal and rear, in *Working Girl*, *Stormy Monday* (1988), *Something Wild* (1986), *Along for the Ride* (2000), and *Nobody's Fool* (1994), when Griffith lifts her jumper to flash her clearly augmented breasts at a bemused Paul Newman. In *Milk Money* (1994) Griffith's body clad in a nude leotard is used to illustrate the female reproductive system to a class full of excited pubescent boys and girls. The femininity and accessibility of her body is a dominant element of her performances.

Not only on-screen, but in press and media images from red-carpet appearances and candid shots, reproduced online and in celebrity magazines, there has been a concentration on Griffith's body, especially as it has been ageing, and subjected to surgical procedures and tattoos. There are close-up images of wrinkling knees accompanied by the classically double-edged criticism of the media in this regard: criticised for having wrinkles and showing them to the world, and yet also criticised for having obvious plastic surgery.[3] Kirsty Fairclough writes that Griffith belongs to a group of celebrity women she classifies as 'the gruesome'; 'positioned as abject freaks, who lie outside the boundaries of appropriate and acceptable feminine selves' (2012, p. 96). The idea that Griffith has rendered herself abject by excessive plastic surgery contributes to the idea that her life is mired in tragedy, or that her appearance reflects that she suffers 'the real price of fame' (Boshoff, 2015).

Her colouring features markedly in her on- and off-screen images. Her hair ranges from natural dark blonde in early films such as *Night Moves*, to bright red in *Cherry 2000* (1987), through various shades of blonde to orange in *Working Girl*, black to peroxide blonde in *Something Wild*, and jet black in *Crazy in Alabama* (1999). The colours of her clothes are often garish and clashing, either as emblematic of the fashions of the decade, the film worlds she is moving in (*Body Double*), or the extreme characters that she plays (*Cecil B Demented*). Her voice is perhaps her most distinguishing physical attribute: breathily babyish and gratingly raucous, and often preceded by a self-conscious clearing of the throat, it is both high pitched and languorous but can turn into a barracking squawk very easily. This last element is put to effect as the loud-mouthed mistress, Maria, in the critically and commercially disastrous *Bonfire of the Vanities*. In the climactic courtroom scene, a recording of Griffith's character saying, 'I'm a sucker for a soft dick' resonates around the courtroom, exposing her lying testimony and sexual voracity. This tendency toward exaggerated screeching and coquetry leads on to the next inescapable element of her persona.

2. Vulgarity

This pejorative word sounds critical and judgemental, but in terms of Griffith's persona, these connotations arose out of her films roles and her voice, and the garish colours adorning her provocative body. Her film roles are frequently associated with professional sex, as a stripper or a prostitute. In *Working Girl* she famously announces that she has a 'head for business and a bod for sin', contrasted with Sigourney Weaver's refined but 'bony ass'. In some ways, the narrative arc of this film was too taming and restrictive for the unruly Griffith image. Elisabeth Traube writes how *Working Girl* 'transposed the joyously sensual and erotic Melanie Griffith into a "good", passively sexual, oedipal daughter' (1992, p. 113).

---

[3] See Fairclough (2012) and Bolton (2015).

Griffith's image is primarily working class, and this is why the aspirational Tess McGill was a perfect fit for her persona more so than the successfully tamed one. Class was also the focus in *Born Yesterday* (1993), in which Griffith reprised the role of the socially embarrassing but clever mistress, played by Judy Holliday in the 1950 original. Comparisons with Holliday were often a feature of Griffith's reception and criticism, arising because of her girlish, squeaky voice and comic roles, but also, I suggest, because of the complexities of her performance style that make her so difficult to categorise. In a newspaper article from 1988, a journalist writes of Griffith's Tess, 'drawing on the '30s, she's the reincarnation of both Jean Harlow's hussy and Jean Arthur's working girl. Drawing on the '50s, she's the reincarnation of Marilyn Monroe's vulnerable, baby-talking seductress, and Judy Holliday's dumb-smart blonde' (Huffhines, 1988). This alignment with a group of actresses from the golden era demonstrates the complex resonances of Griffith's performance style but does not account for it fully.

Discussing Monroe's embodiment of sexuality in the fifties, Richard Dyer writes that Monroe's unabashed attitude to the nude pin-up photographs of her from the days before she was a film star suggests 'guiltless, natural, not prurient' sex: she was a pin-up and 'the girl next-door' (2005, p. 36). Compared to Griffith, however, the girlish Monroe was always legal, not jailbait. As Dyer describes it, Monroe embodied the kind of desirable sexual playmate who became 'the vehicle for securing a male sexuality free of guilt' (p. 39). Griffith more frequently stands for dangerous sex that will lead a man off the straight and narrow, whether she is the teenage temptress of *Night Moves* or the schizophrenic ex-girlfriend of *Along for the Ride*.

Her off-screen life is a similarly complex mixture of contradictory elements. She has been married and divorced four times, and has four children. There was an early marriage and remarriage to Don Johnson (whom she began dating when she was 14); a five-year marriage to actor Steve Bauer, and marriage to Antonio Banderas in 1999, whom she met on the set of *Two Much* (1995). She had a large decorative heart tattooed on her upper arm, featuring the name 'Antonio' in bold ornate font. For a woman in her forties and fifties to display such a baroque statement of her romantic love gave the appearance of brashness and teenage ostentation which contrasted with the refinement and gentility of her mother's image and that expected of Hollywood royalty. During her life, she has battled

Fig. 8.1 Melanie Griffith at Cannes in 2000

addictions to alcohol and painkilling drugs and sought rehabilitation treatment. She and her family talk very openly about this, frequently stating that the whole family have been involved in supporting her.[4] Overall, her personal life has been eventful, but she has maintained a relatively secure family unit. Elements of her own behaviour, however, such as tattoos and addictions, are more usually associated with younger stars and 'wild child' offspring than middle-aged mothers.

In 2014 Griffith and Banderas divorced, and press coverage has concentrated on the Antonio tattoo and whether she will have it removed: also the process of removal, whether it is painful and if it will be successful. I suggest there is an element of prurience and a desire for punishment in this focus, as if she now has to face the consequences of the ostentation and juvenility of the display. She is, after all, the daughter of Melanie Daniels, but she is also now the mother of Anastasia Steele.[5]

---

[4] Griffith often speaks about the support from ex-husbands Steve Bauer and Antonio Banderas, and from her children as well. See Oh (2009).

[5] Melanie Daniels is Tippi Hedren's character's name in *The Birds* (1963) and Anastasia Steele is the name of Dakota Johnson's character in *Fifty Shades of Grey* (2015).

3. Female Genealogy

Griffith's relationship with her mother, Tippi Hedren, is a recurrent element of her press coverage, as it is invariably the opening gambit of any magazine interview, followed by the frequently cited tale of how Alfred Hitchcock presented the six-year-old Melanie with a doll dressed as her mother's character Melanie Daniels in a coffin.[6] Griffith and Hedren have attended each other's red carpet events, and took part in the series of television interviews called *Superstars and their Moms* in 1987. The relationship appears solid, without the rifts that so often beset mothers and daughters in Hollywood. Family photographs of Griffith with her children have been regular occurrences, but in the last three or four years, as Griffith's daughter Dakota Johnson has begun her own acting career, Griffith has appeared at events alone with Dakota, forging a newly focused mother-child relationship with Griffith as the mother.

In a role similar to that which her mother might have played thirty years ago, and possibly the most talked about female role of recent times, Johnson has been the subject of press attention about nudity and explicit content in *Fifty Shades of Grey* (2015). There has also been the question whether or not her parents will see the film, and Griffith has said in interview that it would be too awkward to see (CelluloidVideo, 2014). This places Griffith in the mature parental role of disapproval and potential opprobrium, and clearly marks her out as the older generation in terms of today's media. Griffith and Johnson attended the 2015 Academy Awards together, with Johnson wearing a youthful, one-shouldered, red slip dress and Griffith in a matronly, black, tailored ensemble. Widely reported as having been 'snapped at' by truculent Johnson, Griffith was a refined picture of maternal support, in a display of body language and verbal restraint that suggested the generational baton had been passed.[7]

Elements Have Consequences

Having discussed the elements of Griffith's image, the consequences of these features become evident. The difficulties about accepting her ageing face and body have been cited as the reason for a lack of good roles in her forties and fifties. Disability scholar Sally Chivers compares Griffith

---

[6] There are numerous instances of this, but for one example see Chilton (2015).

[7] Johnson appeared to express irritation at the fact that her mother had not seen *Fifty Shades of Grey*.

with Harrison Ford, her co-star in *Working Girl* in 1988, and assesses their profiles in movies today. Chivers concludes, 'Harrison Ford boldly faces the camera but Melanie Griffith must hide from its ungenerous gaze' (2011, p. 16). Chivers highlights the fact that the ageing male body can take refuge in action, but the ageing female face is not able to disguise itself on-screen, and therefore Griffith can no longer get a decent part (p. 148). Griffith has been working, but not in high-profile commercial cinema. Her role call includes parts in television shows such as *Raising Hope* (2012a, 2012b) and *Hawaii Five-0* (2014a, 2014b, 2014c) and the role of Roxie Hart in the Broadway production of *Chicago* in 2003. This role would seem to be a perfect fit for Griffith. As *Variety* magazine wrote, 'the contours of the character fit Griffith's screen persona like a lace glove: inside this Roxie, a knowing woman playing the little girl lost, is a real little girl lost' (Isherwood, 2003).

Griffith's combinations of class and age, brass and vulnerability, have also been reflected poignantly in some of her film roles. Her portrayal of Lolita's mother Charlotte in Adrian Lyne's 1997 version of the film is imbued with a particular authenticity in light of her star persona. As Humbert first arrives at the house, Charlotte's crudeness, her large underwear on the line, and ostentatious hospitality work to contrast exquisitely with Lolita's natural childlike pleasure and unself-consciousness as she lies in the spray of the garden hose.[8]

In the film about the making of *Citizen Kane* (1941), *RKO281* (1999), Griffith plays the mistress of William Randolph Hearst, who was the inspiration for Susan Kane. Here, her babyish voice, simple taste for jigsaw puzzles, and garish clothing are again imbued with the tenderness and vulnerability of a human being who is in love and in pain, and seen by others as rather ridiculous. These roles reflect how the persona of the ageing sexy girl into a slightly inappropriate older woman has been capitalised on and has enabled Griffith to convince in some really moving and multilayered performances.

As a young actress, Griffith embodied a very particular set of contradictions: refined pedigree, slutty films; baby voice, statuesque physique; old-school Hollywood, contemporary and risqué. These contradictions

---

[8] In a comment that reveals the lack of respect that the writer has for Griffith, and also for Shelley Winters who played Charlotte in the Stanley Kubrick version (1962), Richard Corliss says of Charlotte, 'Can she really be that crude—a cow who deserves to be drugged into a more profound stupor? Must she be Shelley Winters, Melanie Griffith?' (1998).

enabled her to carve a particular path in 1980s Hollywood, carrying the constant connotation of the wild child. As she has aged, however, these contradictions have become more marked and disconcerting: baby voice, woman in her 50s; sexual availability, family stability; ageing face and body, youthful clothes and behaviour. Some of her less successful films, such as *Shining Through* and *A Stranger among Us* (1992) fail to utilise these contrasts and jar because they deny the specificity of her image and performance style.

Unsurprisingly, some of Griffith's most enjoyable characters play with these elements. In *Something Wild*, Griffith is both demonic Lulu and angelic Audrey, as her raven-haired, dominant, sexual predator is actually revealed to be a blonde, vulnerable girl going to her school reunion. As Cameron Bailey writes, 'Lulu is primarily *about* sex (from the position of active subject), while the Audrey to which she reverts is a victim, inscribed and proscribed by sex, but hardly sexual' (1988). By the end of the film, her costume and car more resemble a 1930s 'old style' movie actress than a 1980s wild child, thereby incorporating many aspects of the Griffith persona and enabling her to convince in them all.

As Aunt Lucille in *Crazy in Alabama*, Griffith plays a beautiful woman who kills her abusive husband and carries his head around in a hatbox. Lucille's aim is to be a movie star, and she travels to Hollywood to pursue her dream. Ultimately put on trial for the murder, she manages to persuade the judge (Roy Steiger) that her actions were justifiable and that he should suspend her sentence, although how she does this remains a mystery as it happens 'in his chambers'. Her name is Lucille Fleur, extremely similar to Joan Crawford's real name Lucille Le Seur, and places her firmly in the trajectory of the damaged, vulnerable, working-class woman, who will make her way to where she wants to be in Hollywood, using surprising grit and unbridled sex.

Conclusion

Griffith has lived her last five decades at the coalface of ageing in public: from a Hitchcock heroine's daughter, through a teen marriage, battles with addiction, remarriage, and going down the plastic surgery route. She has also been simply working away as a fairly regularly employed actress, in over seventy-five films and television series since 1969. The classic star studies' dichotomy of ordinary and extraordinary form a peculiar combination in Griffith's case. Although her family heritage, voice, and appearance could be painted as extraordinary, there is also something very down-to-earth and ordinary about Griffith, such as her willingness to discuss her family and her devotion to her children. As Pam Cook explains when writing about Nicole Kidman, the star name 'indicates that the star exists as an individual person despite the conflicting accounts of her. A personal history is made available via various sources that provides a backstory for a character we follow through a series of life events' (2012, p. 9). This backstory is perhaps now coming to the fore: as she balances her roles as famous daughter and mother, paradoxically, her individuality is becoming more notable.

In some ways, Melanie Griffith's on-screen persona was crystallised by the 1980s and all the colour, brashness, and garishness that went with that decade. Peter Kramer's analysis of star making in this era cannot account for Griffith's trajectory, in particular, her continued star status despite her diminished or variable on-screen presence. Upon further consideration, it is Griffith's combination of physical characteristics, roles and off-screen life that see her in the position she is now, and this actually invites some rather more laudatory terms than usually describe her. Perhaps she can be seen as standing for dignity and strength of character in the face of a viciously ageist and sexist press and society, having engaged with issues that all ageing actors face but keeping a consistent and solid presence and personal story.

Thinking about Melanie Griffith leads on to thinking about what an ageing star has to do to be a *surviving* star. Like all stars, Melanie Griffith is unique, but she is a remarkably strong and challenging persona to think about. In an online interview as part of the *Radical Living* series, Griffith is described by the interviewer as a 'totally radical girl' (2013). The idea of Griffith's life consisting of motherhood and resilience is stressed as being 'the real Melanie' that the press and *People* magazine do not let us know about: there is a real woman at the centre of the Melanie Griffith persona, who survives as many other women do.

Ultimately, Melanie Griffith contains but does not resolve the uneasy contradiction between wild child and working woman: the Hollywood daughter with the baby voice, addictions, plastic surgery and tattoos, alongside the hardworking actress in her fifties with four children. In interview at the Locarno film festival in 2014, Griffith describes how

> when you hit forty in Hollywood it's a little bit iffy and you go through a certain period when you're not getting the roles that you used to, and I did take a lot of time to raise my kids, and now I am doing a lot of work and I've

got a couple of movies to shoot very soon and then I'm gonna do Pippin on Broadway in January. I can do whatever I want to now; I only have one child left with one senior year of high school and it's the time for going to colleges, and then I'm free, so I'm gonna do whatever the fuck I wanna do. (ExtraTV, 2014)

Announcing her freedom in this way suggests that Melanie Griffith is still a figure of defiance and resistance. The girlish connotations may make her particularly public ageing even more commercially difficult than with other ageing women in Hollywood, but they also certainly make her a star whose image defies reduction to stereotype.

References

Along for the Ride (aka *Forever Lulu*). (2000). Film. Directed by John Kaye. [DVD]. Germany, USA: Cinelulu Internationale.
Bailey, C. 1988. Nigger/lover: The thin sheen of race in *Something Wild*. Screen 29(4): 28–43.
Body Double. (1984). Film. Directed by Brian De Palma. [DVD]. USA: Columbia.
Bolton, L. 2009. Meg gets naked! Exposing the female star in Jane Campion's *In the Cut*. In *Feminism and the Body*, ed. C. Kevin. Cambridge: Cambridge Scholars Press.
——— 2015. Winslet, Dench, Murdoch and Alzheimer's disease: Intertextual stardom in *Iris*. In *Feminisms: Diversity, difference and multiplicity in contemporary film cultures*, eds. L. Mulvey, and A. Backman Rogers. Amsterdam: University of Amsterdam Press.
Boogie Nights. (1997). Film. Directed by Paul Thomas Anderson. [DVD]. USA: New Line Cinema.
Born Yesterday. (1993). Film. Directed by Luis Mandoki. [DVD]. USA: Hollywood Pictures.
Boshoff, A. (2015, July 2). In one face, the real price of fame: As Melanie Griffith is pictured looking eerily smooth-skinned at 56, how her face charts the highs and lows of a troubled life. [Online] *Mail Online*. Available from: http://www.dailymail.co.uk/femail/article-2482446/Melanie-Griffiths-face-charts-highs-lows-troubled-life.html [Accessed: 1 December 2015].
CelluloidVideo. (2014, August 7). Melanie Griffith on ageing in Hollywood, and her future plans. [Online]. Available from: https://www.youtube.com/watch?v=F52IFsoYJnc. [Accessed: 1 December 2015].
Cherry 2000. (1987). Film. Directed by Steve De Jarnatt. [DVD]. USA: Orion Pictures.

Chilton, M. (2015, April 29). Alfred Hitchcock: A Sadistic Prankster. [Online]. *The Telegraph*. Available from: http://www.telegraph.co.uk/culture/film/film-news/9470343/Alfred-Hitchcock-a-sadistic-prankster.html [Accessed: 1 December 2015].
Chivers, S. 2011. *The Silvering Screen*. Toronto: University of Toronto Press.
Citizen Kane. (1941). Film. Directed by Orson Welles. [DVD]. USA: RKO Radio Pictures.
Corliss, R. 1998. Lolita: From Lyon to Lyne. *Film Comment* 34(5): 34–39.
Crazy in Alabama. (1999). Film. Directed by Antonio Banderas. [DVD]. USA: Columbia.
Dyer, R. 2005. *Heavenly bodies: Film stars and society*, 2nd edn. London: Routledge.
Ebert, R. (2006). *Night Moves*. [Online]. Available from: http://www.rogerebert.com/reviews/great-movie-night-moves-1975 [Accessed: 1 December 2015].
ExtraTV. (2014). *Melanie Griffith: It will be too awkward to see daughter in Fifty Shades of Grey*. [Online]. Available from: https://www.youtube.com/watch?v=MXWAtFZdknU Accessed: 1 December 2015].
Fairclough, K. 2012. Nothing less than perfect: female celebrity, ageing and hyper-scrutiny in the gossip industry. *Celebrity Studies* 3(1): 90–103.
Fear City. (1984). Film. Directed by Abel Ferrara. [DVD]. USA: Twentieth Century Fox.
Fifty Shades of Grey. (2015). Film. Directed by Sam Taylor-Johnson. [DVD]. USA: Focus Features.
Hawaii Five-0. (2014a, March 7). TV Series. Season 4, Episode 16. Hoku welow-elo. CBS.
Hawaii Five-0. (2014b, March 14). TV Series. Season 4, Episode 17. Ma lalo o ka 'ili. CBS.
Hawaii Five-0. (2014c, February 28). TV Series. Season 4, Episode 15. Pale 'la. CBS.
Huffhines, K. (1988, December 30). Melanie Griffith: the Judy Holliday of the '80s?. [Online]. *Freelance Star*. Available from: https://news.google.com/newspapers?nid=1298&dat=19881230&id=9QJOAAAAIBAJ&sjid=JIwDAAAAIBAJ&pg=3340,5729372&hl=en [Accessed: 1 December 2015].
Indiana Jones and the Last Crusade. (1989). Film. Directed by Steven Spielberg. [DVD]. USA: Paramount.
Isherwood, C. (2003, August 3). *Chicago* Review. *Variety*. Available from: http://variety.com/2003/legit/reviews/chicago-16-1200540147/ [Accessed: 14 December 2015].
Joyride. (1977). Film. Directed by Joseph Ruben. [DVD]. USA: MGM/UA.
Kramer, P. 2004. The rise and fall of Sandra Bullock: Notes on starmaking and female stardom in contemporary Hollywood. In *Film stars: Hollywood and beyond*, ed. A. Willis. Manchester: Manchester University Press.

Milk Money. (1994). Film. Directed by Richard Benjamin. [DVD]. USA: Paramount.
Night Moves. (1975). Film. Directed by Arthur Penn. [DVD]. USA: Warner Bros.
Nobody's Fool. (1994). Film. Directed by Robert Benton. [DVD]. USA: Paramount.
Oh, E. (2009, August 26). Inside Story: Melanie Griffith's Struggle with Addiction. [Online]. *People.* Available from: http://www.people.com/people/article/0,,20300441,00.html [Accessed: 1 December 2015].
Radical Skincare. (2013). Melanie Griffith: A radical story. [Online]. Available from: https://www.youtube.com/watch?v=uBLBLfLUddQ [Accessed: 1 December 2015].
Raising Hope. (2012a, October 2). TV Series. Season 3, Episode 1. Not Indecent but Not Quite Decent Enough Proposal. Fox.
———. (2012b, October 23). TV Series. Season 3, Episode 4. If a Ham Falls in the Woods. Fox.
RKO 281. (1999). Film. Directed by Benjamin Ross. [DVD]. USA: HBO Pictures.
Roar. (1981). Film. Directed by Noel Marshall. [DVD]. USA: American Filmworks.
Shining Through. (1992). Film. Directed by David Seltzer. [DVD]. USA: Twentieth Century Fox.
Something Wild. (1986). Film. Directed by Jonathan Demme. [DVD]. USA: Orion.
Stobezki, J. (2015, February 19). Utterly Terrifying ROAR, Starring Tippi Hedren & Melanie Griffith, joins pride of Drafthouse films. [Online]. *Drafthouse Films.* Available from: http://drafthousefilms.com/blog/entry/utterly-brainsick-roar-starring-tippi-hedren-melanie-griffith-joins-pride-o [Accessed 1 December 2015].
Stormy Monday. (1988). Film. Directed by Mike Figgis. [DVD]. UK/USA: Warner.
Superstars and their Moms: Melanie Griffith. (1987). Film. Directed by Jeff Margolis and Al Schwarz. [TV]. Dick Clark Productions.
The Birds. (1963). Film. Directed by Alfred Hitchcock. [DVD]. US: Universal.
The Bonfire of the Vanities. (1990). Film. Directed by Brian DePalma. [DVD]. US: Warner.
Traube, E.G. 1992. *Dreaming identities: Class, gender and generation in 1980s Hollywood movies.* Boulder: Westview Press.
Two Much. (1995). Film. Directed by Fernando Trueba. [DVD]. USA and Spain: Divisa.
Working Girl. (1988). Film. Directed by Mike Nichols. [DVD]. USA: Twentieth Century Fox.

SECTION 3

Ageing

CHAPTER 9

The Ageing Stars of European Art-House Cinema: Jean-Louis Trintignant and Emmanuelle Riva in *Amour*

Fiona Handyside

Are stars human? Do they age? Analysing the deeply felt, popular, and emotional appeal of the cinema star, Richard Dyer argues that part of the seductiveness of stars is that they are not only screen gods and goddesses but also flesh-and-blood individuals. Their humanity, he argues, the fact that they are, on some level, 'real people', is what allows them to perform the ideological work of making the myths they support and 'act out' seem plausible (Dyer, 1979). At least part of stars' appeal, then, is based on their ability to negotiate between a 'real' human self and a mythical 'other' being, to authenticate as well as to glamorise the human condition.

When it comes to the process of ageing, however, mainstream cinema, whether produced in Hollywood or Europe, tends toward what the French sociologist Edgar Morin called the mythological and Olympian aspects of stardom rather than its quotidian and human qualities. As cinema itself has aged, it has become a repository, an archive, a mausoleum, preserving forever the youthful glamour of its iconic stars in images that don't age and that dominate our thoughts of them. As Laura Mulvey explains,

F. Handyside
Department of Modern Languages, University of Exeter, Exeter, UK

more and more cinema has come to be a memorial to those who personified its modernity, its glamour, its triumph as both a popular form and art form [...] To see the star in the retrospectives that follow his or her death is to see the cinema's uncertain relation to life and death. Just as the cinema animates its still frames, it brings back to life, in perfect fossil form, anyone it has ever recorded, from great star to fleeting extra. (Mulvey, 2006, p. 17)

Mulvey's comments suggest that the cinema operates above all, in the case of the classical Hollywood era and the polished, studio stars associated with it, as a shrine to youth. When these films do show us ageing, it is often in the mode of horror or the grotesque, with female stars driven mad precisely by the contrast between their past celluloid selves and their current aged bodies, such as in *Whatever Happened to Baby Jane?* (1962) and *Sunset Boulevard* (1950).

It is this that makes Michael Haneke's 2012 film *Amour* such a striking and unusual film through which to consider ageing stars. Starring two of the most canonical stars from European art cinema, Jean-Louis Trintignant and Emmanuelle Riva, Haneke's film presents us with an unflinching view of the ageing process, in a style typical of this cinema's realist aesthetic codes (long takes, sequence shots, muted colour palette, restrained mise-en-scène) and declaration of authorial agency, here via the device of giving his characters the same names, Georges and Anne Laurent, as in the vast majority of his films.[1] *Amour* is far from the grotesque, supernatural, noir presentation of Hollywood ageing. Yet Haneke, in line with the films I mention above, does choose to inflict this ageing most violently and graphically upon a female star body, and in such a way that his film too offers us insights into the reliance of stardom on cinematic technology. He links the deconstruction of the star body via ageing to a deconstruction of the cinematic apparatus itself, continuing his authorial project of undermining and unsettling our relationship with image-based media, which includes society's fascination with stardom and celebrity.

In her discussion of Michael Haneke as the paradigmatic filmmaker of the new European art cinema, Libby Saxton argues that his films offer a compelling exploration of 'the liquid ethical bonds which survive in a diegetic reality where intersubjective relations are increasingly mediated

---

[1] In eight of his eleven feature films, Haneke has named his male lead Georg, George, or Georges, and his female lead Anne. In seven of these films, the characters also have the same surname, Laurent.

by technology' (Saxton, 2008, p. 86). In earlier works, Haneke has placed this investigation of ethics and the role of image-making technology in mediating our relations into an explicitly political terrain, through figures such as a war photographer documenting the collapse of the former Yugoslavia into the chaos of civil war in *Code Unknown* (2000), or an upper-class, television chat show host associated with the October 1961 massacre of Algerians in Paris in *Hidden* (2005). In contrast, *Amour* is in an intimate mode, entirely focused on a Parisian haute-bourgeoisie couple, and would thus seem a more solipsistic exercise. There is no consideration of the outside world, and the inward, intimate nature of the film is reinforced both by its title and its setting entirely within the Laurents' apartment, other than one trip, right at the start of the film, to a concert recital. Furthermore, while several earlier Haneke films foreground image technology, with characters' living rooms dominated by television screens, this particular incarnation of the Laurents appear to live without a television, and their living room contains, instead, a grand piano, an index of their cultured lifestyle and the importance and significance of music.

However, *Amour* is absolutely a continuation of the Haneke authorial project identified by Saxton, precisely because of its investigation of an ageing European female star body. He continues in this film to investigate how ethical bonds remain where intersubjective relations are mediated by technology and is still very much engaged in a cinema that aims to investigate the possibilities and boundaries of a European identity. My arguments rest on four intertwined points on the nature of cinematic stardom and ageing within the European art-house context that I will treat in turn. First, I will discuss how Haneke's film theorises the ageing process itself as a kind of becoming-other. Second, I will argue that this interplay of self and other, familiarity and difference, is more marked in the case of the European star, as their previous cinematic 'selves' are available for both the star and the trained cinéphile audience to identify. Third, I will discuss this process as a complex drama of (mis)identification that depends upon cinematic technology for its existence, and draws on our memories of earlier performances. Lastly, drawing on Mulvey's theory of the relation between female stardom and technology, I shall suggest that Haneke's decision to depict the ageing process of the female star body is part of a broader questioning of the very viability of a European cinematic project.

The otherness Haneke is addressing here is that of the aged body to earlier incarnations of itself; the foreigner within, according to Simone de Beauvoir, who wrote that 'old age is particularly difficult to assume because we have always regarded it as something alien, a foreign species'. As she tellingly wrote, 'Can I have become a different being while still remaining myself?' (de Beauvoir, 1972, p. 3). This recognition of the ageing body as other to itself is exacerbated in a culture that enables us to preserve images of our previous bodily selves through photography and cinema. Theorisations of the relationship between the photographic image and death by André Bazin and Roland Barthes are now classics of film theory, but we must also acknowledge that by their very nature, photographic images also demonstrate the ageing process, as they document individuals becoming-other to themselves.[2]

Intriguingly, although previous work on *Amour* has discussed its depiction of death, so far I have been unable to find any accounts of its engagement with the process of ageing, echoing the critical tendency to privilege the relation between the image and mortality than between the image and the ageing *process*.[3] This is rather a strange discrepancy, for, as Asbørn Grønstad explains, 'in order to understand better the meaning of mortality in cinema, we need to turn away from the narrative moment of death itself and focus instead on the *anticipation* of death and how this sense of anticipation permeates the work on a global, rather than just a local level' (Grønstad, 2013, pp. 185–186 [italics in original]). According to Grønstad, Haneke removes suspense from his film through his decision to show us the final outcome of Anne's illness in the prologue, which shows us events that occur after the end of the narrative outcome of the main film. We see Anne's decayed corpse, laid out on a bed, bedecked with flowers, as firefighters break into the apartment in which her dead body has been left. Grønstad continues that this lack of suspense leaves Haneke 'free to focus fully on life as it is lived with the *awareness of death* fast approaching [my italics]' (p. 188). With the molar process of ageing speeded up to molecular level, I would add to Grønstad's discussion of awareness of death that *ageing* itself becomes visible and shocking, via the cinematic technique Haneke deploys to show us Anne's decline. While Anne's decline may, overall, be gradual, we are presented it in a series of shocking stages. In several cases, we witness it alongside her daughter,

---

[2] See Bazin (1960) and Barthes (1993).
[3] For discussion of *Amour*'s relation to death, see Grønstad (2013), Grundmann (2012), and Dima (2015). Ironically, the only reference to *Amour* as a study of ageing I have come across is Elaine Showalter's comment that 'laughter, rather than another documentary on Alzheimer's or a night out to see Michael Haneke's *Amour*, is among the truest pleasures and consolations of ageing' (Showalter, 2013, p. 4).

Eve (Isabelle Huppert), who, like us, is an outside observer, held at arm's length, startled and distraught by her mother's physical changes. Through his deployment of ellipsis followed by lengthy sequence shots that allow for real-time depictions of the process of Anne's nursing (most notably a harrowing scene where she refuses to drink water from the beaker Georges holds to her lips), Haneke both withholds knowledge so as to shock us and offers us almost too much information for it to be bearable, showing us an account not of death but the journey to it—that is, the ageing process in its terminal stages.

Anne has her first attack over morning breakfast, failing to respond to Georges when he asks her to pass the salt. Increasingly frantic, he tries to catch her attention, finally getting up from the table, running the kitchen tap over a tea towel, and placing the damp cloth to her face. When she still fails to respond, he makes his way to the bedroom to get dressed to go and summon help. The camera follows him from the kitchen to the bedroom. In his agitation, he has forgotten to turn off the tap, and his actions are accompanied throughout by the sound of running water. Suddenly, the sound of water stops. Georges is shocked by the abrupt silence, as is the audience. When the film returns to the kitchen, Anne is unaware that anything has happened, and her distress in the face of Georges' explanation is palpable. We cut to a series of images of the rooms of their apartment, devoid of human presence, before we have a close-up of Eve chatting to her father about her husband and her son, and then they finally discuss the outcome of Anne's operation. It is through this dialogue we learn that the operation has failed, and Anne is paralysed. This establishes a typical pattern, where Anne declines off-screen in an ellipsis, and we only see the impact of her subsequent strokes, rather than witnessing the attacks themselves. A similar example occurs 1 hour and 7 minutes into the film, when we cut from an angry and humiliated Anne, who has just wet herself in bed but who is still able to communicate and move herself in her electronic wheelchair, to a quasi-comatose figure in bed, her daughter sitting next to her, talking about property prices. Anne struggles to speak through a mouth contorted by the effects of a stroke. As Vlad Dima explains,

> Anne suffers both an emotional and physical decay *before* her actual death [...] the film captures beautifully the slow decomposition of its characters through its own cinematic composition, which acts as a durational parallel to the slow change of form signalled by decay. (Dima, 2015, p. 6, italics in original)

Dima is referring to Haneke's predilection for fixed camera positions and long, static tableaux with only slight panning. To this, I would add the effect of ellipsis and shock I discuss above to argue that Haneke's film form here is one of ageing: slow, relentless change in form, accompanied by sudden, dramatic bodily failures. By this I mean not simply that Haneke shows us ageing but that his film gives us the affective experience of ageing as we are sutured into its complex form. Yet Dima still aligns this process as an investigation of death rather than that of ageing, a strange denial which echoes that of Grønstad. The process of decay before death is clearly ageing, and yet there seems to be a critical reluctance to name it as such. Both Dima and Grønstad argue, then, for Hanake's film as considering death, whereas, ironically, I would see the very point Haneke's film is making is that death will not come quickly enough. Haneke's film foregrounds processes of bodily decomposition and decay in *living* bodies through the cinematic techniques discussed above, and throws light not so much on death as on the indignities of, and moral dilemmas associated with, the ageing process.

Furthermore, the body whose decomposition and decay our attention is being brought to is a star body. Haneke's decision to cast two of the most iconic stars of European art-house cinema, Jean-Louis Trintignant and Emmanuelle Riva, means *Amour* becomes a meditation on stardom and its play of becoming-other, so that stardom and ageing can be seen as in a metaphorical relation. Audience recognition of the star, and thus their association with previous roles, is obviously key to how stardom works, for its function within the industrialised marketplace of cinema is to generate audience appeal via a play of repetition and difference. However, this takes on a very particular form in Haneke's casting of Trintignant and Riva, both of whom starred in some of the most significant films of the European art-house cinema that Haneke deliberately recalls here. In the case of Jean-Louis Trintignant, the key reference is *Ma nuit chez Maud* (1969) and for Emmanuelle Riva *Hiroshima mon amour* (1959) and *Three Colours: Blue* (1993). All three of these films cover similar thematic and conceptual ground to Haneke's film, treating issues of love, loss, trauma, and grief, especially the latter two. Roy Grundmann argues that *Amour* invites us 'to take a detour through French film history' and he further connects Anne and Georges to 'the French New Wave's tales of romantic love because there is still a spark—and a little bit of mystery—between them' (Grundmann, 2012). He explains how Trintignant is effectively recast by Haneke as Rohmer's timid libertine, caught in debates about the nature of love and fidelity in a manner that harks back to the tradition of *amour courtoise* (courtly love). He comments that, unlike the ardent courtier of Andrew Marvell's *To His Coy Mistress,* 'for Georges time's winged chariot is not hurrying nearly enough', a reference to courtly and libertine musings on love enabled through a consideration of Trintignant's star persona.

However, I want especially here to concentrate on the connotations of casting Riva. It is to her star body that Haneke applies his most insistent treatment of ageing and degradation. Furthermore, her star persona is intimately tied to questions of recognition and remembrance pertinent to more general discussions of stardom and ageing. Her face is seen so frequently in close-up in *Hiroshima mon amour* as to become intimately identified with it. It remains entirely recognisable in both *Blue* and *Amour.* Emma Wilson argues that Kieślowski's decision to use Riva in *Blue* 'allows [him] to signal [...] how far *Bleu* will pursue the examination of memory, and specifically memory loss, undertaken by Resnais and Duras in *Hiroshima mon amour.*' (Wilson, 2000, p. 33).

Wilson discusses how *Blue* 'remembers' *Hiroshima mon amour* as 'the film is recalled literally and visually at several junctures' (Wilson, 2000, p. 34). *Blue* and *Hiroshima mon amour* form a complex set of intertextual meanings: whereas Riva in *Hiroshima mon amour* plays a woman who bemoans the necessity of forgetting in order to survive, in *Blue* she plays a woman who is amnesiac, unable to recognise her own daughter and who seems to be locked in her own world. *Amour* extends and enriches the dialogue between these two explorations of memory and trauma, and invites further reflection on how film itself depends partially on recognition and remembrance of stars from one text to another, and how the ageing process intervenes in and reshapes the cultural and industrial roles stars play.

In *Blue*, there is a scene of chilling misrecognition between Riva, playing Julie's mother, and Julie. The scene begins when Julie visits the *maison de retraite* that houses her mother: its calming atmosphere and the dominance of natural greens and whites contrasts to the saturated blue colour that marks Julie's grief. The camera pans over photographs, including one of a younger Julie. As we are looking at these photographs, we see another image reflected: that of Julie's mother. The camera pulls the reflection, rather than the photo, into focus, so that both images (of mother and daughter) are caught in a circuit of virtual images—photographs and reflections—that anticipates the confusions of mother and daughter later in the same sequence. The mother misrecognises her daughter as her sister, Marie-France, adding in understandable confusion, 'They told me you were dead. You seem well'. Julie corrects her mother, 'I'm not your sister, Mum. I'm your daughter', but her identity seems to perpetually slide away from her mother.

While Wilson goes on to discuss the Deleuzian repercussions of Kieślowski's series of repetitions and displacements of *Hiroshima mon amour* in *Blue*, she does not return to her initial point of departure: that Resnais's film is, above all, recalled through the casting of Riva, and the powerful connotations of her performance in a classic of European art-house cinema. The scene discussed above self-consciously suggests how recognition depends on remembrance, and on past knowledge, but also it tell us that memory is faulty and vulnerable. The drama of misrecognition played out in *Blue* haunts *Amour* as Riva's character once again slips into dementia. Yet, ironically, the full meaning of this sequence comes only from the recognition of the star performance. While all claims to stardom depend on recognition, particularly of the face, this finds a particular nuance in the European art-house context. As David Bordwell explains, European art-cinema constructs its narratives and characterisations differently from those of Hollywood, partly depending on a 'competent viewer' to interpret authorial signatures and stylistic motifs (Bordwell, 1979, p. 61). Such viewing strategies, built on cinéphile audience knowledge, are being drawn upon by Haneke, as his film remembers a European model of stardom which depends on recognising the appearance of performing bodies across films rather than on the classical, studio-driven model of a polysemic on-screen and off-screen star image only partially located in film.

The casting of Trintignant and Riva goes beyond thematic/conceptual motifs on the ideas of love, death, and loss discussed by Grundmann and also by Dima, significant though these are. Rather, Haneke's film shows us how stardom is the meeting point of technology and the body, or, to put it more precisely, the site where technology and the body (potentially) become visible and experienced as one. We recognise performances across film texts thanks to the technology that preserves them, and a system that encourages us to remember and seek out star performers both in and outside the film texts. It is worth recalling at this point Christine Gledhill's observation that stars reach us via their bodies (Gledhill, 1991, p. 210). That is to say, they reach us via their *appearance*: through an illusion of presence dependent on technology and ever vulnerable to misrecognition and displacement in the way *Blue* hints at in its display of virtual images and drama of shifting and uncertain identities. Susan Hayward claims that depending on whether they are a male or female star, this reaching—us—with—their—body changes as they age. Not for nothing do so many female stars decry the lack of roles for mature, older, even old women. For male stars, ageing is not (or is less of) an issue where their appearance is concerned […] the female star has trouble ageing not just for herself […] but for her audience. On the whole, her fans do not like her to age. (Hayward, 1996, p. 357)

As stars reach us via their bodies, via technology, both bodies and cinema become part of a gendered discourse, for, as Hayward suggests, male and female ageing signifies differently.

It is necessary here to acknowledge that it is Riva's body that we see undergo the most dramatic changes and decay (despite the fact that, statistically, women are more likely to outlive men). It is central to Haneke's film's musing on stardom that it is the female star body we see ageing, when it is precisely that body which is more likely to remain hidden, to withdraw its appearance from the cinematic apparatus. To explain this, it is useful to make a detour to Mulvey's work on the female star body. The female star within classical Hollywood cinema, according to Mulvey, who takes as her paradigmatic example Marilyn Monroe, iconic image of that very star system and its potentially objectifying/dehumanising tendencies, functions to hide the operations of technology through becoming a fetish. In both Marxist and Freudian theorisations of the fetish, the spectacle works to distract the eye (and thus the mind) from the traumatic reality of a situation (in the former case, exploitation of labour; in the latter, anxieties over sexuality and individuation from the parent). The star as fetish is particularly complex, because she is both a product of what Karl Marx would call the 'congealed labour' her image works to hide (from cinematographers to make-up artists, investment in her body as commercial product is naturalised as 'innate' beauty) and a Freudian fetish, her body cut up into close-ups that allow fixation on one body part, halting narrative and offering up static contemplation/absorption in a part standing for a whole.

The female star as fetish offers herself up for sale in a market place, using her appearance (meaning both her presence and her attractiveness) to sell her products, including films, and by extension, herself. But, as Mulvey comments, the seductive surface she creates implies something hidden: the more glossy and attractive the image, the more it suggests a secret underneath. This structure of the alluring surface covering the real aims of the woman, associated above all with the femme fatale, can be applied to the cinematic apparatus as well, as it conceals its mechanisms of production underneath the glossy surfaces of its beautiful alluring stars. Cinema is also another commodity that circulates successfully through its seductive power, and its seductiveness is encapsulated by the presence of the eroticised female body on the screen. The female star body thus become analogous with the production of cinema itself. Both attract audiences through a play of seductive surfaces and beautiful appearances which mask over other processes. The fetishised female star is held still and hides the ugly reality of cinematic production and circulation of images in a capitalist system. The de-fetishisation of the woman allows the beginning of the de-fetishisation of the cinematic form, or, to quote Mulvey,

> the dichotomy between surface and secret, artifice and truth is paradoxical. The artificial surface of feminine beauty may disguise an inside that can only be unveiled to reveal the danger of the *femme fatale*. But the artificial surface of cinematic illusion may disguise an inside that can be unveiled to reveal the true beauty of its materiality and its potential to analyse political reality. (Mulvey, 1996, p. 77)

Haneke's attention to the disintegration and degradation of the ageing female star body, its loss of appearance in one sense of the word, can thus be seen to be intimately linked to his broader authorial project of questioning image-making technology and the habitual forms that cinema takes. To expose a star body as friable, faulty, and in need of care, can be in some ways be seen as a way of revealing 'the true beauty' of cinema's materiality, to use Mulvey's phrase. Technology in Haneke's films is usually used to communicate to us the pain and suffering of others: we have war photography in *Code Unknown*, and the relentless pace of twenty-four-hour rolling news in *Hidden*. This echoes Susan Sontag's discussion of how photographic and film technology introduces us to 'the suffering of others'. She comments on the 'innumerable opportunities a modern life supplies for regarding—at a distance, through the medium of photography—another person's pain' (Sontag, 2004, p. 11). Here, Anne's pain, following her seizure and devastating series of strokes, is not mediated to Georges at all, but felt, lived, sensed. His utter closeness to Anne means her pain is not held at any kind of mediated remove but experienced by Georges's body, as is indicated to us in the scene where Georges dreams that he is suffocating (an event that cruelly anticipates his decision to smother Anne with a pillow).

In this situation, then, Haneke's attention to the role of technology is mediating relations between individuals and our awareness of another's suffering is clearly different from in his previous films. As the star body itself is subjected to the ageing process, and close-ups reveal anxiety and suffering rather than fetishising beauty, it is cinematic technology and stardom itself that comes under pressure. Haneke's own technology brings us face to face with pain and suffering, and the relationship that is being mediated and whose ethical bonds are being stretched is not between the fictional Georges and Anne but between the star bodies of Trintignant and Riva. Their past representations echo through and expose the film's constructedness and materiality by drawing our attention to layered circuits of images. If the classic female cinema stars hides the reality of her dependence on cinematic technology for her appearance, the film here brings together technology and bodies repeatedly, only to expose the gap between them, the moments when the star body can no longer hide technology, or when the connections between technology and the star body sever.

Consider the complex scene where Georges listens to Anne playing the piano. This is filmed in a conventional shot/reverse-shot sequence of a close-up on Georges in an attitude of intense concentration, and a long shot of Anne at the piano. George reaches behind and switches off a CD player. The music stops. The levels of representation and mediation are complex here. Anne playing at the piano was a figment of Georges's imagination, a reverie, or an intense recall of the past. But the music was really playing, although its source was a CD recording rather than a person sitting at a piano. For a brief moment, the audience is fooled into thinking that the source of the music is Anne. When Haneke reveals that Georges has been listening to a CD recording, he demonstrates our inability to distinguish between different layers of mediation in the cinematic transcription of experience. Rather than the body masking the artifice of cinematic technology bringing us into contact with stars, here the imagined appearance and actual absence of Anne's body demonstrates how we rely on technology to have any contact at all with stars, a reliance that is usually hidden.

In *Amour*, Haneke subjects his stars of European art-house cinema to a story that depicts their bodies as vulnerable, abject, and ageing, and questions the star's ability to cover up the very mechanisms by which cinema functions. If the title of this book posits stars as caught between 'enduring personas' and 'fading images', Haneke's film deftly returns us to the corporeal, reminding us that stars are also bodies that age. Stars, female stars in particular, become part of the very production of cinema itself, incorporated into its technology even as they hide it through such varied devices of glamour, naturalness, and skill. When we see their bodies as faulty, breaking down, beyond repair, Haneke takes us to the vulnerability of cinema itself, never in the end able to halt the process of ageing, however perfect its technological resurrection of these bodies may *appear* to be.

References

Amour. (2012). Film. Directed by Michael Haneke. [DVD]. UK: Artificial Eye.
Barthes, R. 1993. *Camera Lucida: Reflections on photography*. London: Vintage.
Bazin, A. 1960. The ontology of the photographic image. *Film Quarterly* 13(4): 4–9.
Bordwell, B. 1979. The art cinema as mode of film practice. *Film Criticism* 4(1): 56–63.
Code Unknown. (2000). Film. Directed by Michael Haneke. [DVD]. UK: Artificial Eye.
de Beauvoir, S. (1972). *Old age* (P. O'Brien, Trans.). Harmondsworth: Penguin.
Dima, V. 2015. Sound, death and *amour*. *Studies in French Cinema* 15(2): 1–12.
Dyer, R. 1979. *Stars*. London: BFI.
Gledhill, C. 1991. Signs of melodrama. In *Stardom: Industry of desire*, ed. C. Gledhill. London: Routledge.
Grønstad, A. 2013. Haneke's *amour* and the ethics of dying. In *Death in classic and contemporary film: Fade to black*, eds. D. Sullivan, and J. Greenberg, 2013. New York: Palgrave.
Grundmann, R. (2012, December) Love, death, truth—amour. Senses of cinema. [Online]. Available from: http://sensesofcinema.com/2012/feature-articles/love-death-truth-amour/[Accessed 10 September 2014].
Hayward, S. 1996. *Key concepts in cinema studies*. London: Routledge.
Hiroshima mon amour. (1959). Film. Directed by Alain Resnais. [DVD]. UK: Optimum Home Entertainment.
Ma nuit chez Maud. (1969). Film. Directed by Eric Rohmer. [DVD]. UK: Artificial Eye.
Mulvey, L. 1996. *Fetishism and curiosity*. Bloomington: Indiana University Press.
——— (2006) Death 24× a second. London: Reaktion.
Saxton, L. 2008. Close encounters with distant suffering. In *Five directors: Auteurism from Asseyas to Ozon*, ed. K. Ince. Manchester: Manchester University Press.
Showalter, E. 2013. Introduction. In *Out of time: The perils and pleasures of ageing*, ed. L. Segal. London: Verso.
Sontag, S. 2004. *Regarding the pain of others*. London: Penguin.
Sunset Boulevard. (1950). Film. Directed by Billy Wilder. [DVD]. UK: Paramount.
Three Colours: Blue. (1993). Film. Directed by Krzysztof Kieslowski. [DVD]. UK: Artificial Eye.
Whatever Happened to Baby Jane? (1962). Film. Directed by Robert Aldrich. [DVD]. UK: Warner Home Video.
Wilson, E. 2000. *Memory and survival: The French cinema of Krysztof Kieślowski*. Oxford: Legenda.

CHAPTER 10

The Great Stoneface Ruined: From *The Buster Keaton Story* to *Film*

Paul Flaig

Among the 'waxworks' playing bridge in Norma Desmond's mansion, Buster Keaton utters only one word in *Sunset Boulevard* (1950): 'Pass'. He says it twice, the first time, his eyes darting at his table mates until forced to pass one final time, his face shifting from anxious activity to the melancholic frieze for which Keaton was once famous. This cameo gives viewers a glimpse of the Buster they once knew but also suggests a desperation on the part of the actor, both on-screen and off, to maintain his career. For those familiar only with Keaton's silent masterworks, hearing the former star croak out this repeated single line is the most damning sign of failure, not to mention the sight of a receding hairline, weathered face, and alcohol-ravaged eyes upon a visage once praised the world over for its statuesque beauty. Indeed, Keaton had once posed in a well-known publicity still as the paragon of the Greek physical ideal, renamed 'Buster de Milo.'

Keaton's tragic-comic cameo recites an oft told tale of the silent actor ruined by sound, and of cinema's infancy ruined by time itself (Cavell, 1979, p. 74). This tale is usually told by Hollywood, and there is no shortage of examples that suggest the wide span between the immortal silent

P. Flaig
Department of Film & Visual Culture,
University of Aberdeen, Aberdeen, UK

film idol and the ruined statue. As if in reply to Wilder's film, *Singin' in the Rain* (1952) would disjoin the tragic from the comic, with its story of a silent idol who manages this transition while offering up the comic instance of his on-screen partner's squawky voice and vulgar speech. That *Singin' in the Rain*'s premise would be regurgitated in *The Artist* (2011) suggests the trope of the fallen silent star has an intense staying power, colouring popular perceptions of American film history.

In contrast with such late career cameos, Buster Keaton would receive title credit in a Hollywood movie of the fifties far less admired than *Singin' in the Rain*. Featuring one of the latter's stars, Donald O'Connor, in the title role, *The Buster Keaton Story* (1957) would put Keaton's career at centre-stage while keeping the former star's ruined face off-screen. Acting as a technical consultant, Keaton accepted money from Paramount for this position as well as for the rights to his life's story. For Keaton as well as his fans, the film was an abysmal failure, not only inert in terms of its simulated slapstick and melodramatic arc but greatly removed from Keaton's actual career. Today the film is largely remembered as a footnote to the footnote of Keaton's sorry career in the sound era (Neibauer, 2010, p. 180; Dardis, 1979, pp. 264–265).

In this essay, I argue that *The Buster Keaton Story*'s lapses in form and fidelity reveal how classical Hollywood cinema, approaching its own obsolescence, delineates the history of its former silent stars. Keaton's fading stardom becomes a way of simultaneously acknowledging and repressing media crises, an allegorical venue for melodramatic rise and fall in which Hollywood history is a justification of the present, past epochs, like past stars, respectfully put out to pasture through false homage. To contrast with *The Buster Keaton Story* another of Keaton's later collaborations, his performance in Alan Schneider and Samuel Beckett's *Film* (1965), will be my concluding focus. Keaton's performance suggests a different allegory of faded stardom, one not nearly as transparent as *The Buster Keaton Story* but nonetheless concerned with the perceptual and temporal dynamics of film fame. *Film* casts Keaton's ruined statue as a figure fleeing the central pillar of stardom itself, that of an existence produced only by perception, a being defined entirely as image. To be is to be a faded star, one never ready for a close-up.

Mortals of the Silver Screen

Before *Sunset Boulevard, Singin' in the Rain,* and *The Artist* there was *Hollywood Cavalcade* (1939). Its hero is a director who refuses to accept the approaching trend of talking pictures, exclaiming to his studio bosses,

'People don't want to hear their idols talk. Takes away all the mystery and the glamour. Makes them ordinary and commonplace'. After stumbling into a screening of *The Jazz Singer* (1927), the director describes to his leading lady a conversion to the gospel of sound as introduced by Al Jolson (who here re-performs a scene from this supposedly first of talking pictures), promising to alter his most recent film to a part talkie and reassuring her, 'Oh honey, your career's only just begun'. Shot in the new Technicolor process, the film was one of the first of Hollywood's forays into its own past, a past only visible because the American film industry now seemed to have a history marked by changes in technology as much as in style, genre, and stardom. *Hollywood Cavalcade*'s original title, *Falling Star*, suggests how stardom and the story of its rise or fall are related to the possibility of the new as much as the possibility of the obsolescent.

Anticipating his cameo in *Sunset Boulevard*, Buster Keaton would also appear in *Hollywood Cavalcade*, associated with the good old days of slapstick. While Keaton's appearance in the film can be opposed to Jolson's singing and the future history it was thought to have announced, *The Buster Keaton Story* would turn to Jolson as a model for converting Buster's inability to star in that history into profit, appealing to the proven formula of entertainer biopics, its publicity listing *The Jolson Story* (1946) as precedent (*Motion Picture Daily*, 1957, pp. 4–5). Yet the film would be received as one of the worst iterations of the entertainer biopic, failing with critics and audiences alike (*Film Bulletin*, 1957). The film, however, allows us to grasp Hollywood's vision of its fallen silent stars as it approached its own crisis during the final years of the classic studio system. It also suggests how and why Keaton was so often deployed as shorthand for the antiquity of cinema, he too an object lesson on the necessary mortality of the movie star. If the biopic is the genre by which Hollywood understands history, then the entertainer biopic, and in particular the movie star biopic, is the subgenre in which Hollywood constructs its own history (Custen, 1992, p. 4; Bingham, 2010, pp. 3–30).

Filmed in black and white VistaVision, *The Buster Keaton Story* begins with a pre-credit text: 'This is the sad, happy, loving story of one of the immortals of the silent screen'. The film, however, will go on to emphasize how finite stardom is and how the mortality of stars is tied to the reasons Keaton's story is simultaneously 'sad, happy, loving'. Far from emphasizing the mythic nature of Keaton's antique fame, the film fulfils the fears of Norma Desmond or the director in *Hollywood Cavalcade*, dissolving Keaton's former 'mystery' and 'glamour' and transforming his divine deadpan into the 'ordinary and commonplace'. This is made clear in the film's opening, a prologue focusing on Keaton's rough childhood. After a depiction of his family's bottom-of-the-bill vaudeville routine, a dissolve from one stage bill in 1904 to another in 1920 reveals that 'The Three Keatons' remain far from the top.

This relationship between the mortality of the film star and of film itself is made clear in *The Buster Keaton Story*'s transition from 'The Three Keatons' to Buster Keaton, the 1920 playbill giving way to the first of a series of newspaper headline montages that integrate Keaton's story within film history: 'Movies Kill Vaudeville/Standard Acts Splitting Up/Many Try Hollywood'. O'Connor is introduced as Buster walking into the studio, chatting up his future love interest, a studio casting director named Gloria Brent (Anne Blythe). After Gloria and the studio's boss offer him a small role, Buster will negotiate himself into starring in and directing his own features, and for the film's middle act, *The Buster Keaton Story* justifies the comedian's expertise through its first full pastiche, a short entitled *The Criminal*. This is an abbreviation of *Cops* (1922), right up to that film's final credit of 'The End' inscribed on a grave, Buster's hat sitting atop. If *The Criminal* ends with Buster's death, it will herald his proclaimed status as 'one of the immortals of the silent screen', as this credit gives way to *Variety*'s top story: 'Keaton New Box Office Smash'. For *The Buster Keaton Story*'s critics, these brief pastiches were the film's highpoints (Weiler, 1957; *Film Bulletin*, 1957, p. 14).

Unfortunately, as one critic noted, 'the admittedly "freely fictionalized" facets of [Keaton's] career […] are timeworn and as obvious and dated as a 1910 tear-jerker' (Weiler). Ignoring the varied successes of 'The Three Keatons', not to mention Keaton's first film roles as an apprentice of another fallen star, Fatty Arbuckle, the film invents a romantic triangle between Keaton, Blythe's steadfast casting director, and a pneumatic movie siren, Peggy Courtney (Rhonda Fleming). Transforming Keaton's first and second marriages, the film positions Gloria against Peggy and, more broadly, the narcissism of movie stardom against the virtues of loyalty. Each of O'Connor's comedy impersonations is framed by this struggle, the parodic interplay between both gag and plot crucial to slapstick here overwhelmed by the tired psychological causalities of the 'tear-jerker'. Buster hopes to impress Peggy with a party and proposal only to discover that she is marrying a European aristocrat. Justifying her self-interest, she explains, 'I'm a business, Peggy Courtney, Inc.' In response, Buster flees his guests, grabbing two bottles of whiskey along the way. The refusal to smile that made Keaton a star here becomes a symptom of a selfish desire for fame rooted in insecurities wrought by a rough and tumble childhood. Dismissing the 'passing fad' of sound cinema drawing crowds for *The Jazz Singer*, Buster's all too familiar last words are followed by career collapse, his willingness to stake his fortune on what will be his final film leading to bankruptcy. After a disastrous try at sound film, Buster is inexplicably saved by Gloria, who marries him after a drunken spree.

The Buster Keaton Story concludes with Buster giving up booze and giving in to Gloria's devotion, but more importantly, it involves a deeper commitment to making people laugh beyond the ego-massaging bounds of fame. Buster returns to the stages where he started, coming full circle to his and the film's beginning, with the blessings of the paternal studio boss and the recommitment of the maternal Gloria, who will join him in a stage routine faithful to the act Keaton performed throughout the forties and fifties: Buster awkwardly fumbles a comatose wife to bed. In the film, however, this routine functions as a reversal of an earlier incident, when Gloria carried a drunken Buster to bed. Comedy sublimates and has its explanation in tragedy while the devoted wife transforms from maternal figure to comic prop the husband is now fit to command. A happy ending makes this return to a pre-star past explicit as Gloria announces that she is pregnant: there will once again be 'The Three Keatons'.

Sunset Boulevard lampoons grotesque attempts to regain the divinity of former stardom. *Hollywood Cavalcade*, *Singin' in the Rain*, and *The Artist* all suggest the ways stars might enrich their fame by adapting to a dominant trend in Hollywood rather than selfishly refusing it. *The Buster Keaton Story* moves between these poles, wringing melodrama out of a silent star's resistance to be contemporary to his times while suggesting that adaptation might require giving up stardom itself. The film's deviations from the star's history expose its own allegory all too clearly. If, according to Jerome Christensen, *Singin' in the Rain* was a 'star punishment picture', *The Buster Keaton Story* is a star retirement picture (Christensen, 2012, p. 170). Hailing Keaton as one of the 'screen's immortals', the film's opening sequence immediately suggests the mortality of that screen's predecessor, vaudeville having been 'kill[ed]' by the movies. The ending, in turn, suggests Keaton's acceptance of his screen mortality while vaudeville has been miraculously resurrected, a hospice for fallen stars accepting themselves as such.

Among its many factual travesties, *The Buster Keaton Story*'s most telling omission is any mention of Keaton's actual career after sound, which featured dozens of film roles, in major and supporting roles throughout the thirties and forties. Vaudeville was attenuated as a popular entertainment and though Keaton did occasionally perform onstage, his primary source of income in the fifties was from television, which here goes symptomatically unmentioned (Becker, 2008). The film's omission of his post-star career on screens both cinematic and televisual is a double denial of the way studios manage their stars as 'business' and of the studio's own finitude. The fear that television itself inspired in Hollywood was based on the mortality it suggested for movies and the studio system (Stokes, 1999; Young, 2006, pp. 137–192). Like *Hollywood Cavalcade* before it or *The Artist* after it, *The Buster Keaton Story* speaks the anxieties of media transformation, using the entertainer biopic as a way to immunize the shift from one media regime to another, from silence to sound, black and white to colour, cinematic to televisual, or analogue to digital.

Deadpans Never Die

Perhaps the best-known work in Keaton's post-silent filmography, *Film* has attracted a good deal of scholarly attention largely because it brings together Buster Keaton with Samuel Beckett for the latter's only text for the cinema. Made eight years after *The Buster Keaton Story*, *Film* is in every way that film's other, adapted from a series of notes by Beckett, inspired by the Irish idealist philosopher Bishop Berkeley, and filmed far from the confines of a Hollywood studio, on the streets of New York City in the summer of 1965. *Film*'s use of Keaton recalls an entirely different aspect of the comedian's stardom, far from the self-justifying teleologies disavowed in *The Buster Keaton Story*.

Film, according to Beckett's notes, is set in the year 1929, a backward turning of the clock further echoed by the film's near-total silence and casting of an ancient Keaton. Recounting his visit to Keaton's California home, director Alan Schneider's description of Keaton playing an 'imaginary' poker game with the long-deceased Irving Thalberg and Nicholas Schenk—'everything in the room harked back to circa 1927 or earlier'—cannot help but recall the grotesqueries of Norma Desmond's bridge game or the primordial trauma of *The Jazz Singer* (Schneider, 1969, p. 67). Beckett, it seems, knew better, speaking reverentially of Keaton and transforming Schneider's poker game into a different image: '[Keaton] had a poker mind as well as a poker face' (quoted in Rossett, 2010, p. 54).

Film, however, refuses its viewers this face, which Beckett calls, extending his metaphor, Keaton's 'trump card' (quoted Rossett, 2010, p. 54).

By doing so, it submits Keaton's stardom to Berkeley's dictum, '*Esse est percipi*' (to be is to be perceived), and to film's unique ability to confer existence upon that at which it gazes. Proving this dictum through a protagonist who refuses to be seen, Schneider reveals the implicit connection between *Film*'s philosophical concern, its precise staging of this concern, and the necessity of having a movie star as this protagonist. He does so by asking, 'What actor of star stature would be willing to play a part in which we would almost never see his face?' (Schneider, p. 66).[1] Schneider's question betrays the importance of stardom and of Keaton's own particular kind of ruined stardom to *Film*'s design and effect.

A little less than a half hour in length, *Film* is divided into three sections. Each of these is devoted to an increasingly enclosed space and all are traversed by two central figures, O, an object played by a scampering Keaton, and E, an unseen eye, conveyed by point-of-view shot, chasing O across these locations. After a brief, extreme close-up of an eyelid opening, Keaton's O scurries along a brick wall as the camera tracks him at a 45-degree angle, which Beckett's notes dictate as 'the angle of immunity' (Beckett, 1969, p. 11). This angle demarcates, for the perceived object, the border between what Beckett calls the 'anguish' or 'agony' of 'perceivedness' and the implied relief of not being seen and therefore not, following Berkeley, existing (Beckett, 1969, p. 11). Something of this comedy is suggested twice in this opening sequence, the camera's E driving O to stumble amidst the detritus and ruins between wall and street, the latter 'storm[ing] along in comic foundered precipitancy' (Beckett, 1969, p. 12). Something of this agony is indicated when O crashes through an 'elderly couple of shabby genteel aspect' reading a newspaper, not having seen them for fear of being seen (Beckett, 1969, p. 12). In the first of several shots from O's perspective, the camera moves between husband and wife, a gauze over the lens distorting the image and distinguishing it from the intense clarity of E's regard. For Beckett, E's gaze should be 'acute and penetrating' while O's vision should be of 'a different world. Everything becomes slower, softer' (quoted in Gontarski, 1985, p. 191). While O flees from the 'agony of perceivedness', we see something of that agony when E confronts the elderly couple, their mouths opening wide,

---

[1] Keaton was not Schneider or Beckett's first choice for *Film*, other older comic stars (Charlie Chaplin, Zero Mostel) being considered as well as Jack MacGowran. Keaton, however, would come to be seen by both the film's makers and critics as the ideal, retroactively perfect choice.

eyes closing in revulsion before they blindly flee. This play of avoidance and agony recurs in a second section, which takes place in a vestibule beneath a staircase, after O has entered a building. Caught between E and an old woman descending the stairs, O hides while the woman collapses in fright after making eye contact with E. Finally, O reaches his destination, which Beckett's script suggests may be the apartment of O's hospital-bound mother (p. 59). Here *Film* spends the rest of its time, O increasingly caught between the insistent E and a range of other eyes, which proliferate to effects both comical, when seen through E's perspective, and anxiety-inducing, when seen in O's 'different world': three animals (cat, dog, and fish), a mirror, a portrait of 'God the Father', two circles on a folder, two holes in the headpiece of a rocking chair and, finally, a series of photographs of O being looked at. O progressively excludes all these sources of vision, exiling the animals, covering over mirrors, and tearing up portraits of both God and self, all the while checking his pulse to see whether existence will stop once perception does. Sitting sleepily on his rocking chair, O is forced to recognize the futility of escaping perception as E circles, like the letter designating his object's name, away from O only to return right back to him. O is revealed to be an ancient Buster Keaton, one eye covered by a black patch, and his reaction to E follows those before him, mouth open wide in agony. O's reveal also reveals E, who turns out to be none other than O—that is, none other than a monocular, ancient Buster Keaton. Yet in contrast to the anguished O, E is imperious, his cyclopean vision the very figure of what Beckett describes as an 'absolute steadiness of vision' (quoted in Gontarski, 1985, p. 191). A second exchange of shots, now much closer, shows O's gauzy look at E's eye, glassy but unblinking, before concluding *Film* with O closing his eye and covering his entire face with both hands. The film fades to black and then returns to its initial image of an extreme close-up of Keaton's wrinkled eyelid opening.

Like *The Buster Keaton Story*, *Film* has often been viewed as a failure, though in an entirely different vein from the all-too-average Hollywood biopic. It is precisely because of it being exceptional, a decrepit former slapstick star and Beckett's only attempt at film, its title and philosophical basis in Berkeley's dictum suggesting metaphysical ambitions, all undermined by Schneider's amateur direction. This was exceptional not because it brought together two entirely opposed figures but, rather, because across the cultural, historical, and aesthetic gaps between Keaton's slapstick and Beckett's literary and theatrical practice there are striking affinities (North, 2009, pp. 141–162). Although Keaton would publically state that he thought *Film* 'didn't mean a damn thing', he was willing to offer up an interpretation to his biographer: 'What I think it means is that a man can keep away from everybody, but he can't get away from himself' (Brownlow, 2007, p. 215; Dardis, p. 270).

While *Film* has generated a range of scholarly responses, this interpretation brings us specifically back to Schneider's question: 'What actor of star stature would be willing to play a part in which we would almost never see his face?' (Deleuze, 1997, pp. 23–26; Critchley, 2007, pp. 108–121). *Film* is, as its title indicates, an allegory of cinema's own perceptual dynamics, one with essential ramifications for the figure at its centre, the former movie star. Keaton's casting is uniquely relevant to this, not simply because of his recognizable if aged face and the effect its revelation has in *Film*'s climax but also in the way it taps into his particular fading stardom. Amenable to any role on nearly any kind of stage or screen, Keaton had played parts, supporting and bit, in Europe and North America, ceaselessly chasing cameras, audiences, and paychecks. *Film* reverses this sad chase, his O fleeing from others and from himself, trapped between his existence as an object and his status as a perceiver of himself as object. Caught between existence and perception in a loop, one suggested by the literally eye-opening image that starts and ends *Film*, Keaton's O refuses being seen as a means to the end of refusing existence, chasing after his mortality but failing to die. A star's contract with its audience has the very same conditions, embodying, more than any other kind of object captured on film, something that exists only by virtue of being seen. Above all, it is the star's face that has to express this stardom, seen and accepted by all as the very emblem of stardom, this especially true of the silent film star. Keaton's O refuses, over the course of *Film*, every possibility of being seen so as to escape not simply perception but also the panoptic existence that perception brings. The implicit contract between a star and its viewers, from studio heads to filmmakers to audiences, is a voluntary submission to exist only according to the terms of how and why these others look upon it. Existing only through this submission, the star's identity can therefore never be entirely reduced to either the specific roles played or to the actor/actress playing them. Rather, the stars are forced to be only as they are seen, always, in Edgar Morin's (2005) words, 'faithful to their image' (p. 61). While *The Buster Keaton Story* dramatized the desire for its title character to become precisely this, *Film* reverses this quest, taking as its object someone who refuses to exist altogether if existence means being an image for others and for one's self. By casting Keaton, this also reverses the story of his own career, which required fitting his face into a deadpan in every role he played.

The most important contrast between *The Buster Keaton Story* and *Film* as allegories of stardom is the casting of Keaton himself, as opposed to a younger impersonation of a slapstick star. An older Keaton, one year before his actual death, is sent back to the time when he was at the height of his vitality and fame—the film's setting of 1929—but also, tellingly, the last year he could be considered contemporary with silent stardom's agelessness. Even more than the claustrophobia perception implies through its angles and agonies, it is this specifically temporal aspect that is crucial for understanding *Film*'s use of Keaton's fading stardom. It is not simply that O is perceived but that he *was* perceived. Considering Keaton's age, the film's time period, its ruinous evocations of slapstick, and its final revelation of O and E, *Film* offers an allegory of not just the perceptual dynamics at the core of stardom but also the temporal dynamics at work in faded stardom. Stars cannot escape themselves because they—and this paradox holds, above all, for the silent stars—were once immortal.

Thus, *Film* exhausts all the trappings of Keaton's slapstick. *Film* takes the two essential aspects of the chase film, the chaser and the chased, and applies them to the very terms of cinematic perception, between camera and object. Exhaustion here implies extension as much as it does finitude, a living on, by which the past preserves, but always in an attenuated, feeble manner. This is quite different from the historiography underlying *The Buster Keaton Story*, where firm divisions in time and medium easily separate one era from another just as much as they consign one mode of entertainment to retirement. In *Film*, everything, including film itself, is caught up in an ongoing ruination, never non-existent—the pulse still beats, the chair still rocks—but never fully present either, always somehow out of time. To exist is not merely to be seen but to *have been seen,* and it is this temporal aspect that Beckett supplements to Berkeley's equation, especially in the sequence of O tearing up photographs of his life's history (Critchley, pp. 119–120). The interval between being and perception is not merely spatial but also durational, with a measure of time interceding above all in those cases of seeing one's self as one was. If the casting of a star and of Keaton's unique version of the faded star was essential to *Film*, this was because such a figure best dramatizes the agonizing dynamics of a life become image. The sadness of Keaton's interpretation of *Film* comes from the double alienation the fading star undergoes: alienation from what one is as well as from what one was, an immortal mortality that lives on even after stardom seems over.

The ruining of time in *Film* opposes the neat nostalgia of *The Buster Keaton Story*, which uses the faded star to brush up and define strata in a media archaeology *avant la lettre*. In its penultimate turn to photography, *Film* refuses this stratification, assimilating film to a broader sense of media that includes not only film's precondition and predecessor but all manner of objects that might perceive or be perceived. For Donald O'Connor's Buster, stardom becomes a narcissistic trap. But behind the poorly staged trappings of this entertainer bio-pic lie a whole range of anxieties around which the career of a fallen comedy star become transparent. The fantasy of Hollywood's forward historical march was as much a response to anxiety-inducing obsolescence among careers, industries, and media as it was a fuel to further anxiety about where one fell according to dividing lines between past and present, mortal and immortal. For Beckett's O, Keaton's stardom is not an explicit concern but, rather, the necessary form through which the split between self as object and self as perceiver plays out. *The Buster Keaton Story* reflects a far less immediately discernible transformation in the history of American cinema, its turn to a supposedly vibrant Hollywood of yore a reflection of a disavowed fifties present. For its part, *Film* points both backward and forward to the avant-garde's engagement with other fallen, inflated, or otherwise alienated stars, from Jack Smith's fondness for Maria Montez to the star factory of Andy Warhol to Joseph Cornell's *Rose Hobart* (1936). According to Deleuze, *Film*'s traversal of film history suggested a condition for the 'experimental cinema' and its 'general tendency' towards an 'acentred' and luminous 'world before man' (Deleuze, 1986, p. 68). In its movement towards an ever-anachronistic past defined by silent cinema and the ruined great stone face, *Film* suggests another version of this 'world before man', one where film history does not move according to some fabricated telos, a story of rise, fall, and retirement. 'Before' Hollywood is not a primal or pure past but, rather, an ageless ruination of stars engulfing audience eyes and memorial media alike.

References

Becker, C. 2008. *It's the pictures that got small: Hollywood film stars on 1950s television*. Middletown: Wesleyan University Press.

Beckett, S. 1969. *Film*. New York: Grove.

Bingham, D. 2010. *Whose lives are they anyway?: The biopic as contemporary genre.* New Brunswick, NJ: Rutgers University Press.
Brownlow, K. 2007. Buster Keaton. In *Buster Keaton interview*, ed. K. Sweeney. Jackson, MI: University Press of Mississippi.
Cavell, S. 1979. *The world viewed: Reflections on the ontology of film.* Cambridge: Harvard University Press.
Christensen, J. 2012. *America's corporate art: The studio authorship of Hollywood motion pictures.* Palo Alto, CA: Stanford University Press.
Cops. (1922). Film. Directed by Edward Cline and Buster Keaton. [DVD]. USA: First National.
Critchley, S. 2007. To be or not to be is not the question: On Beckett's *Film*. *Film-Philosophy* 11(2): 108–121.
Custen, G. 1992. *Bio/pics: How Hollywood constructed public history.* New Brunswick, NJ: Rutgers University Press.
Dardis, S. 1979. *Keaton: The man who wouldn't Lie down.* New York: Scribner.
Deleuze, G. (1986). *Cinema 1: The movement-image* (H. Tomlinson and B. Habberjam, Trans.). Minneapolis: University of Minnesota Press.
——— (1997). The greatest Irish film. In *Essays critical and clinical* (pp. 23–26, D. W. Smith and M. A. Greco, Trans.). Minneapolis: University of Minnesota Press.
Film. (1965). Film. Directed by Alan Schneider. [DVD]. USA: Milestone.
Film Bulletin. (1957, April 15). Vol. 25, p. 14.
Gontarski, S.E. 1985. Appendix A: Beckett on *Film*. In *The intent of undoing in Samuel Beckett's Dramatic texts.* Bloomington: Indiana University Press.
Hollywood Cavalcade. (1939). Film. Directed by Irving Cummings and Malcolm St. Clair. [DVD]. USA: 20th Century Fox.
Morin, E. 2005. *The Stars.* Minneapolis: University of Minnesota Press.
Motion Picture Daily. (1957, April 2). Vol. 81, No. 63, pp. 4–5.
Neibauer, J. 2010. *The fall of Buster Keaton: His films for MGM, Educational Pictures, and Columbia.* Lanham: Scarecrow Press.
North, M. 2009. *Machine-age comedy.* Oxford: Oxford University Press.
Rose Hobart. (1936). Film. Directed by Joseph Cornell. [DVD]. USA.
Rossett, B. 2010. Beginning to end: Publishing and producing Beckett. In *A companion to Samuel Beckett*, ed. S.E. Gontarski. Chichester: Blackwell.
Schneider, A. 1969. On directing film. In *Film.* New York: Grove Press.
Singin' in the Rain. (1952). Film. Directed by Gene Kelly and Stanley Donen. [DVD]. USA: Metro-Goldwyn-Mayer.
Stokes, J. 1999. *On screen rivals: Cinema and television in the United States and Britain.* London: MacMillan.
Sunset Boulevard. (1950). Film. Directed by Billy Wilder. [DVD]. USA: Paramount.
The Artist. (2011). Film. Directed by Michel Hazanavicius. [DVD]. USA: Warners Brothers and the Weinstein Company.

The Buster Keaton Story. (1957). Film. Directed by Sidney Sheldon. [Streaming]. USA: Paramount.
The Jazz Singer. (1927). Film. Directed by Alan Crosland. [DVD]. USA: Warner Brothers.
The Jolson Story. (1946). Film. Directed by Alfred E. Green. [DVD]. USA: Columbia Pictures.
Weiler, A.H. (1957, April 4). The Buster Keaton story. *New York Times.*
Young, P. 2006. *Cinema dreams its rivals: Media fantasy films from radio to the internet.* Minneapolis: University of Minnesota Press.

CHAPTER 11

Ageing Masculinity in the Films of James Mason

Adrian Garvey

James Mason's death at the age of 75, on 27 July 1984, prompted many tributes and appraisals of his life and work, with widespread acknowledgement of his achievements as a film actor in a career that spanned nearly fifty years. In Britain, *The Times* described Mason as 'a highly intelligent and creative performer' (1984), while *The Observer* argued that he was 'one of the four or five best film actors this country has produced' (French, 1984). The American press responded similarly, with *The New York Times* describing Mason as 'the actor with a resonant touch-of-Yorkshire voice', and 'a self-critical craftsman' who was 'noted for portraying suave and cerebral aristocrats and scoundrels' (Flint, 1984), and he was characterised by *Variety* as 'the darkly handsome, brooding actor' who 'created a gallery of memorable portraits in more than 100 pictures' (McCarthy, 1988).

The dominant narrative of Mason's career which emerges through these testimonials can be divided into three distinct periods: his years of British stardom in the mid 1940s, when he appeared 'often as a romantic villain who brutalizes the leading lady' (Flint, 1984); an erratic, somewhat inconsistent Hollywood career during the following decade, when 'although he appeared in some notable American films … a reputation for arrogance, combined with a caustic tongue made him few lasting friends' (Weatherby, 1984); then, from the early 1960s, when he was no longer a major star,

A. Garvey
Department of History, Queen Mary, University of London, London, UK

'there was still however much to relish' (*The Times*, 1984) in the twenty years spent as an exceptional and versatile character actor.

The general high regard for Mason as an actor, both for his past work and more recent achievements, is evident throughout this coverage. All commentators stress his consummate acting skills, as displayed in several iconic roles in both Britain and America, with *Odd Man Out* (1947) and *A Star is Born* (1954) as the most frequently cited films. These abilities are also seen to have been demonstrated—and even enhanced—in supporting roles after the end of his star career.

The actor's talent for playing charismatic brutes in such films as *The Seventh Veil* (1945) is especially highlighted in Britain, where this persona was first established, and a consonance is suggested between his habitual screen persona and his own combative, intransigent personality. Along with references to his abrasive off-screen persona, another common theme amidst the praise is the suggestion of unfulfilled promise during his time in Hollywood.

Further tributes were later prompted by Mason's posthumous appearance in his last two major projects: the prestigious television adaptation of Graham Greene's *Dr. Fischer of Geneva*, which was broadcast by BBC2 in October 1984; and the heritage film *The Shooting Party*, which was released in Britain and America in 1985. *Fischer* received mixed reviews, but many praised Mason's contribution, with Greene himself saying, 'I was delighted to see him in the part … His eyes conveyed simultaneously enormous pride and profound sadness, which is exactly what I wanted' (Greene, 1995, p. 547). Peter Waymark in *The Times*, noting 'the current estimate of Mason as one of our most gifted and sensitive screen actors', suggested that 'his last two performances will rank among his finest' (Waymark, 1985).

This third, final phase of Mason's career, which began uncertainly in the early 1960s, and culminated in such elegiac tributes, will be the main focus of this chapter. The overall trajectory of his career is an unusual one, with some marked shifts in image and performance style, and in status and reputation, as Mason moved between Britain, America and Europe, from star to character actor and supporting player, and from playing barnstorming villains to wise elder statesmen. These later years provide much more than a footnote to his star career: between 1935 and 1985 he appeared in 113 films, with around fifty of these made during the last two decades. In focussing on this final period, I wish to consider how the actor's image and performance style developed and changed, the critical reception of his work at this time, and what his late career might reveal about the evolution of star personae, about film acting styles and representations of ageing masculinity. A discussion of his work in *Fischer* and *The Shooting Party* will also consider these two acclaimed roles as contrasting and highly apposite summations of his late career.

THE PERVERSE PATRIARCH

Mason's core screen persona, a deeply transgressive authority figure, can be understood as the perverse patriarch. With power conferred variously by gender, class, and age, this is generally a charismatic, but also dangerous or malign character, and one often associated with predatory and violent sexual behaviour. While this archetype is not applicable to all the actor's work, it is an enduring career trope, first established by key star-making roles at Gainsborough Studios, in *The Man in Grey* (1943), *The Wicked Lady* (1945), and *They Were Sisters* (1945), then nuanced in the film which launched his international career, *The Seventh Veil*. Numerous later variants can be found in such widely diverse examples as *North by Northwest* (1959), *Lolita* (1962), *Georgy Girl* (1966), *Age Of Consent* (1969), *Mandingo* (1975), and *Dr. Fischer of Geneva*.

Parallel, and in some ways complementary to this persona is a contrasting image of vulnerability and, suffering, as seen in such films as *Odd Man Out* and *The Reckless Moment* (1949). These highly polarised depictions of masculinity are then also occasionally fused, as in two key 1950s films, *A Star is Born* and *Bigger Than Life* (1956), in both of which his character's destructive violent behavior is pathologised, and he shifts between the role of aggressor and victim.

Such a dark, dissonant, persona was not amenable to the demands of mainstream star narratives during the studio era. Untypically for a star, Mason frequently played villains rather than heroes, or even anti-heroes. The key imperative to 'create the couple' was confounded by this image, and, rather than share a happy ending, his character dies in many of his major films. Where romantic fulfilment is achieved, it is most commonly in the form of an *amour fou*, as in *The Seventh Veil* or *Pandora and the Flying Dutchman* (1951).

Frustrated by the limitations of this image as he tried to establish an international career at the end of the 1940s, Mason had sought to reposition himself as a more conventional hero. In *Caught* (1949), his first American film, he rejected the characteristic—and more colourful—role of a disturbed Howard Hughes-like millionaire, which he was first offered, and chose instead to play a dedicated, unassuming doctor. 'I was determined', he records in his autobiography, 'to smash my villainous image, and offer myself in the guise of a sympathetic leading man' (Mason, p. 202). The commercial failures of both this film and *The Reckless Moment*, made soon after, and also directed by Max Ophuls, immediately damaged Mason's prospects in Hollywood and limited his choice of roles.

A *Daily Mirror* report on *The Desert Fox* (1951), his sixth film in America, noted that

> This is the best role Mason has had since coming to Hollywood and it may have proved something of a life-saver to his career. He has said that until this Rommel role came along he was beginning to worry about getting a start in Hollywood, for up to now he has done nothing important here. (Jones, 1951)

This popular and critical success provided a complex leading role for Mason, as the masterful German commander who was also portrayed as a principled opponent, and victim, of Nazism. However, less nuanced, unsympathetic roles in such films as *The Prisoner of Zenda* (1952), *Botany Bay* (1953), and *Prince Valiant* (1954) followed.

Despite appearing in some prestigious films, such as *Julius Caesar* (1953), and some very successful ones, notably *20,000 Leagues under the Sea* (1954), Mason failed to become a star of the first rank during the 1950s. *Leagues* was primarily a Disney film rather than a star vehicle, and his role as Captain Nemo was that of another European villain. While many stars were increasingly producing their own projects during this period, Mason's attempts, as in *Lady Possessed* (1952) and *Bigger Than Life*, were not great commercial successes.

Mason's Hollywood film career has, in retrospect, often been framed as a failure. There was a perception, expressed at times by the actor himself, that failure to escape typecasting, and a combination of mismanagement and arrogance had denied him the international stardom which had seemed attainable when he left Britain. He was also the subject of largely unsympathetic press coverage in both countries, first regarded as having abandoned Britain, and then as being insufficiently respectful to Hollywood. In 1955 the *Saturday Evening Post* noted that 'hardly anyone is more unpopular among film people than this talentless, tactless man' (Hubler, 1955), while in 1957 the British fan magazine *Picturegoer* asked, 'Are you tired of Mason?' (Moore, 1957).

Adapting to Ageing: *North by Northwest* and *Lolita*

Difficulties in sustaining a star career in Hollywood increasingly encouraged Mason towards character parts and supporting work from the late 1950s onward. Entering his fifties, and with his leading man status less secure, ageing also dictated some changes to his career and image. His work in two key films from this period, *North by Northwest* and *Lolita*, illustrate how he negotiated these transitions. In their variations upon elegant and world-weary perversity, the two roles draw on his existing star persona, but themes of age and ageing are also evident in both.

North by Northwest is now probably Mason's most widely known film. Released in 1959, it also marks the midpoint of his screen career and usefully illustrates his standing at the time. It is a highly prestigious film, with the status and gloss of an MGM-produced Hitchcock vehicle, and the star power of Cary Grant, and it was one of the top commercial successes of the year. However, Mason's role as Phillip Vandamm, though integral, is undeniably a subsidiary one. Vandamm is a winning, sardonic figure, presented with the humour and warmth Hitchcock often accorded to his villains—as with Claude Rains's Alex Sebastian in *Notorious* (1946)—but he is not the film's protagonist. In addition, the character typifies the villainous roles which Mason had become overly identified with in Britain and then failed to escape in Hollywood. Once a candidate for leading roles in Hitchcock films, such as *The Paradine Case* (1947) and *Rope* (1948), his reduced industry stature is now evident.

If appearing opposite his British-born contemporary Cary Grant, then at the height of his popularity, underlines Mason's reduced star status, it also highlights the issue of age. Born in 1909, Mason was four years younger than Grant, but he appears to be playing an older man. Though the two men vie as sexual rivals for Eve (Eva Marie Saint), the film also suggests parallels between Vandamm and 'The Professor' played by Leo G. Carroll (born in 1886), as competing good/bad father figures for Grant's Roger Thornhill.

The Grant of this period, with his image of 'a worldly, sophisticated man who has become more attractive with the years (Kael, 1994, p. 645), represents an extreme ideal of ageing masculinity, yet his subsequent career was brief, and he retired from acting, after only five further films, in 1965. However, Mason's gradual transition into middle-aged, supporting roles can be seen to have revived and extended his career. Character parts were less age-restrictive and also allowed him to play a far wider range of roles in his later career. By contrast, surviving studio era stars were often used iconically in this period, with James Stewart, Spencer Tracy, Barbara Stanwyck, and Bette Davis, for example, generally cast in roles which drew on their long-established and quite strictly defined personae. Even occasional examples of 'off-casting', as with Henry Fonda as the murderous villain in *Once Upon A Time in the West* (1968), or John Wayne as a drunken incompetent sheriff in *True Grit* (1969) relied for their effect on the essential continuity of star images.

Mason had not achieved stardom until his mid thirties and was almost invariably cast as a mature authority figure. His image was thus never linked with youthfulness, and so the feminised beauty of 'a dark young god' (Powell, 1987, p. 474), evident in some of his pre-stardom films of the 1930s, seems alien to his star persona. Indeed, issues of ageing and mortality are evident in Mason's films as early as *A Star Is Born*, made when he was in his mid forties, in which, as the fading star Norman Maine, he commits suicide when convinced that his self-destructive alcoholism has made him a burden to his wife.

Mason had been cast in *A Star is Born* only after Grant, and then several other actors, refused the part of Norman Maine, and he was not the first choice for many of his key film roles. Grant may have been briefly considered for the role of Humbert Humbert in *Lolita* (as he was for most leading roles in the period), but it was certainly rejected by Laurence Olivier and David Niven, who are both thought to have been concerned about the notoriety of the project (Mann, 1960). This heavily publicised, controversial, and very successful film was Mason's last as a major international leading man. He would have further leading roles, and also top billing, at times, but was a supporting actor in subsequent films of this stature.

Kubrick's adaptation negotiates some of the transgressive aspects of the story by emphasising its comic elements. Like Vandamm, Humbert's sophistication is also cynical and corrupt, and this film plays on the clash between cultured European manners and American popular culture. Mason's age is associated with exhausted old-world values, as he is suddenly confronted with the era of the teenager and the transistor radio (Fig. 11.1).

His performance successfully combines elements of comedy with the darker themes of the story, and the predatory, obsessive nature of his characterisation of Humbert is made clear. The perverse aspects of his image,

Fig. 11.1 James Mason in *Lolita* (1962)

implicit in *North by Northwest*, are central here, with some additional thematic echoes of earlier films: of the tormented central relationship in *The Seventh Veil*, which begins when the schoolgirl Francesca is sent to live with her stern guardian Nicholas, played by Mason; and also of *They Were Sisters* (1945), which implies that the domestic tyrant Geoffrey, played by Mason, has incestuous feelings for his teenage daughter, Margaret (who is played by Mason's wife, Pamela Kellino).

The 'May-November' romance, which pairs middle-aged male actors with much younger female co-stars, proliferated in the 1950s and early 1960s, with Gary Cooper, Fred Astaire, Clark Gable, and others paired with such stars as Audrey Hepburn, Grace Kelly, and Leslie Caron. This enduring convention, which excludes mature femininity, seemed especially acute in this period when male stars who had emerged in the early sound era were concluding their careers as the studio system itself declined. In addition, a number of female stars of the period, notably Hepburn, were associated with a girlish femininity.

However, Mason's darker image, and the youth-oriented, liberalised cinema of the 1960s, could more strongly convey the inappropriate and problematic nature of such representations. In *Georgy Girl*, Mason's character, James, a lonely middle-aged businessman drawn to the much younger Georgy, is described simply as 'that dirty old man'. As if proposing a business deal, he suggests setting up Georgy, the innocent, gauche daughter of his servants, as his mistress. Their relationship is full of awkwardness and miscommunication, and his predatory interest in Georgy is made uncomfortably clear in a scene where he manhandles her on the pretext of some fashion advice, suggesting that she wears a 'jersey a couple of sizes smaller', in order to 'give the boys a treat'. The film ends with their unlikely marriage, and the suggestion that Georgy has opted for security for the child she is raising.

A Star Is Reborn

Mason continued to play the malevolent roles he became identified with for the remainder of his career, and some of his most commercially successful late films rely on this archetype, notably *Mandingo*, in which, as a depraved Southern plantation owner, his frock-coated appearance even echoes his Gainsborough roles, and *The Verdict* (1982), in which his ruthless lawyer character is described by a rival as 'The Prince of Fucking Darkness'.

However, there was a concomitant broadening of the actor's screen image from the 1960s onwards as he also began to play more benign, gentle characters. These might be elder statesmen, associated with wisdom and benevolence, as in *The Fall of the Roman Empire* (1964), or identified more with passivity and failure, as in *The Sea Gull* (1968). His acting technique also adjusted in these roles: partly in line with a general trend towards greater naturalism, his style became more restrained and less marked by the signs of 'ostensive' performance. In reviews from this period, critics began to identify the subtlety and restraint of Mason's contributions to his films. Judith Crist describes him as 'expertly underplaying both the ludicrousness and pathos of his part' in *Georgy Girl* (Sweeney, 1999, p. 161), while Pauline Kael, reviewing *The Sea Gull*, called Mason 'a quiet, almost passive actor' (1970, p. 235).

Mason's off-screen image also began to change from the 1960s onwards. Upon achieving stardom in the 1940s he had become a notoriously outspoken critic of British cinema, which he regarded as a parochial and poorly run industry, capable of producing only a few good films per year. His dismissive views were aired extensively in interviews and authored articles. 'When I see a film of my own on the screen', he told the *Daily Express*, 'I am pleased when I see myself, but bored with the rest of it' (Betts, 1946). Such criticisms created widespread controversy, and the Association of

Cine-Technicians union attempted to bar him from working in British studios. He remained an outspoken and volatile figure during his time in Hollywood: a 1957 *Daily Sketch* profile was entitled 'The Rudest Man in America', and he and his wife Pamela were often in litigation with producers, journalists, and others over contracts and perceived inaccuracies in press reporting. His association with playing violent characters was also sustained off-screen: he is said to have punched the Gainsborough director Leslie Arliss on the set of *The Wicked Lady* (MacNab, 2003), and, in a widely publicised incident in 1952, he slapped the writer William Saroyan during an altercation over noise in a Hollywood cinema (Mason, 220).

However, interviews and profiles from the 1960s onwards, especially after the conclusion of Mason's acrimonious divorce in 1964 and subsequent move from Hollywood to Switzerland, constructed the image of a much calmer and more amenable figure. 'It's more fun now than in the early years', he told the *Observer* in 1969 (Mace, Dawson, & Pritchett, 1969), and in a *Guardian* profile of the same year, tellingly entitled 'The Rebirth of James Mason', said that 'Act three of my life is much the best act and I now regard myself as a happy and well-adjusted man. Perhaps it has something to do with age, but I'm enjoying life so much more'. In the same article, Mason also professes to be rueful rather than resentful about the trajectory of his career, and there is a note of atonement over his perceived defection to America at the height of his success in the late 1940s: 'I now feel that those 20 years in Hollywood were entirely wasted. From a professional point of view they rendered nothing' (Stott, 1969). By the 1980s, Mason was ruminative and self-critical about his career in his restrained autobiography, *Before I Forget* (1981). Of his Hollywood ambitions, he says in a *Desert Island Discs* appearance at the time that 'If you wanted to be an international star, which I'm ashamed to say I did want to be at that time, that was the place to be' (1981).

SWAN SONGS: *DR. FISCHER* AND *THE SHOOTING PARTY*

Dr. Fischer of Geneva should have been Mason's last major project. As happened so often in his career, he was not the first choice for *The Shooting Party*, the film which fortuitously followed *Dr. Fischer*; in this case he was not taking a role rejected by others but replacing an injured actor, Paul Scofield, who was hurt in a carriage accident on the first day of filming. These two roles are the culmination of a late career renaissance—marked also by the Academy Award nomination Mason received for *The Verdict*—and they also suggest both continuity and change in his screen image.

Doctor Fischer, a cold, wealthy megalomaniac, is the last of Mason's perverse patriarchs. Claiming an interest in 'studying the greed of the rich', he enjoys tormenting his 'toads', the weak sycophants who surround him, by hosting dinner parties where they are mocked and humiliated (choking on cold porridge at one event, while he enjoys caviar), in exchange for gifts. Fischer's authority is eventually challenged by Alfred Jones, who marries his estranged daughter, Anna-Louise, and his misanthropy is revealed as a response to his late wife's infidelity. He tells Jones that 'one has to take one's revenge while there's still time. When the person that inflicted the wound is dead, one has to strike back at others.'

Sir Randolph Nettleby, Mason's role in *The Shooting Party*, is, by contrast, a benign, almost saintly patriarch. The film takes place at a weekend shoot at his country estate in 1913, during which he is shown to sense, and ruefully accept, the imminent passing of the old order which he represents. 'Life is so extraordinarily pleasant for those of us who are fortunate enough have been born in the right place', he says in the introductory voiceover. 'Ought it to be so pleasant, and for so few of us?' Anticipating the First World War, he asks, 'And supposing it did come, some great trial? Might it not cleanse us of our materialism, our cynicism, our lax, lazy hypocrisies?'

Fischer and Nettleby are both emphasised as the presiding figures in their narratives, with recurrent shots of them shown seated at table and overseeing their guests, with a particular weight given to cutaways to a reflective Nettleby, which occur throughout *The Shooting Party*. Mason underplays the two roles, with a constrained physicality, minimal gestures and a controlled vocal style, all appropriate for both the quiet, reserved Nettleby and for Fischer, who, despite his extravagant villainy, is a banal, unremarkable character with the air of a seedy bureaucrat, 'a man much like any other man', as he is described by Greene (1984, p. 25). Fischer mostly wears black, stressing his formal severity, and is often in evening dress. Nettleby is also seen in evening dress but is more identified with well-worn tweed, which links him to aristocratic rural ease.

Physically, Fischer seems shrunken in comparison to Nettleby, who appears solid, despite his evident frailty. Mason is clean-shaven in *The Shooting Party*, his open, exposed face conveying innocence as well as gravity. For Fischer, he adopts a slightly tinted moustache, and his face appears sallow. The actor was clean-shaven or very occasionally bearded for much of his star career, and the tidy moustache he adopted frequently in the 1960s, as in *The Pumpkin Eater* (1964), *Georgy Girl* and *The Deadly Affair* (1966), often seemed a marker for the middle-aged despair of the characters he played. Here it adds to the sense of Fischer as a petty, bureaucratic figure.

If *Fischer* completes Mason's long tradition of perverse villainy, played this time at a lower register, his role in *The Shooting Party* represents the culmination of his late career image transformation into a respected character actor, associated with performances of subtlety and restraint (Fig. 11.2). The film's own elegiac tone was matched by many reviews in their posthumous tributes to Mason. *The Guardian's* Derek Malcolm wrote that 'I don't say this just because he is no longer with us—it is James Mason's film' (1985), while the *New York Times* argued that 'Mr. Mason's secure, wise and utterly relaxed performance here ranks with the best work of his long, rich, increasingly productive film career' (Canby, 1985).

These judgments are demonstrated in two important scenes in the film that match Mason with another older actor and emphasise *The Shooting Party's* importance within his late career. His encounter with John Gielgud, as the anti-hunt protester Cornelius Cardew, is a beautifully performed

Fig. 11.2 Mason in *The Shooting Party* (1985)

comic interplay of Cardew's intense sincerity and Nettleby's dreamy concern, and also of the two actors' rich expressive voices.

Extra-textually, this scene also conveys Mason's improved standing as a distinguished character actor, one now approaching Gielgud's elder statesman rank. As a film star he had once lacked the cultural respectability of his contemporaries Gielgud, Richardson, and Olivier, but now rivalled them in the field of supporting roles and cameos in which they all specialised. A greater parity had certainly been achieved with Gielgud since their joint appearance in *Julius Caesar*, for the read-through of which, according to the producer John Houseman, Gielgud 'just sailed through the part of Cassius with terrifying bravura', while 'Mason, both depressed and embarrassed by the brilliance of his compatriot, chose to read the entire role of Brutus with a pipe clenched firmly in between his front teeth' (Morley, 1989, p. 100).

In a climactic scene, Nettleby tends to the dying beater Tom Harker (Gordon Jackson), who has been accidentally injured by an overly competitive shooter. As Nettleby offers the comforts of alcohol, a cigarette, and some prayers, and then weeps over the man, the film's tone of elegy combines with themes of ageing and mortality, and Mason's own physical fragility and simple, naturalistic rendering of emotion is extremely powerful.

The film's evocation of First World War imagery is completed by the depiction of Harker's death, and the group's subsequent slow procession home, silhouetted against the sky, in a repeat of the film's monochrome opening shot, though now in colour. A report from the front is heard in voiceover, with one of the guests recalling 'that shooting party at Nettleby', and a series of titles explains the future fate of some of the film's (fictional) characters, several of whom will die in the war.

The film ends, as it began, with Mason as Nettleby at the rear of the parade. He pauses, allowing the group to disappear screen left, leaving him alone in the middle distance for almost a full minute before following on. This scene is strongly echoed in the melancholic final shot of *Fischer*, which shows the defeated doctor retreating into the distance as he heads home through snow (the suicidal gunshot which then concludes the novel is omitted). Fortuitously, these scenes together also constitute a striking elegy for the actor.

Mason's long and productive career was partly a privilege of gender, as the lengthy careers of male film stars are often denied to women performers. Notoriously, the male star is permitted to age, while his female co-stars are replaced by newer generations, and this is clearly evident with Mason, whose earlier colleagues, such as Margaret Lockwood and Ann Todd had mostly retired from the screen long before his renaissance in the 1980s (only Deborah Kerr from this period, who was twelve years younger than Mason, enjoyed any kind of extended star career after the 1950s).

An extensive *New York Times* appreciation in 1973 declared Mason capable of lending 'unexpected dimension' to mediocre films by 'creating characters which command attention', and judged him 'one of the most consistently interesting actors working today' (Canby, 1973, p. 3). The actor's transition to supporting roles, and to a more modest, self-effacing demeanour—both on- and off-screen—undoubtedly both prolonged and enriched his later career, as well as encouraging more appreciation of his performances. This new perspective on the actor also seems to have fostered a narrative of redemption, in which he was seen to atone for earlier arrogance and truculence. Together, the surprisingly rich 'third act' of his long career, and the critical responses to it, offer a complex account of late stardom and ageing masculinity on screen.

References

20,000 Leagues Under the Sea. (1954). Film. Directed by Richard Fleischer. [DVD]. USA: Buena Vista.
A Star is Born. (1954). Film. Directed by George Cukor. [DVD]. USA: Warner Bros.
Age of Consent. (1969). Film. Directed by Michael Powell. [DVD]. Australia: Columbia.
Betts, E. (1946, January 4). 'I am sick of films' says James Mason. *Daily Express*, p. 3.
Bigger Than Life. (1956). Film. Directed by Nicholas Ray. [DVD]. USA: Twentieth Century-Fox.
Botany Bay. (1953). Film. Directed by John Farrow. [DVD]. USA: Paramount.
Canby, V. (1973, July 29). James Mason: Is he better than ever?. *New York Times: Arts and Leisure*, pp. 1–3.
——— (1985, May 24). Film: Shooting party, end of an era. *New York Times: Weekend*, p. 8.
Caught. (1949). Film. Directed by Max Ophuls. [DVD]. USA: Enterprise.
Desert Island Discs. (1981, January 2). James Mason. *BBC Radio 4.*
Dr. Fischer of Geneva. (1984, October 1). BBC2, 21.30.
Flint, P.B. (1984, July 28). James Mason, 75, Dead: Suave Star of 100 Films. *New York Times*, p. 8.

French, P. (1984, July 29). A fine actor. *Observer*, p. 19.
Georgy Girl. (1966). Film. Directed by Silvio Narizzano. [DVD]. UK: Columbia.
Greene, G. 1984. *Dr Fischer of Geneva, or the bomb party*. London: Vintage.
—— 1995. The John Player film lecture. In *Mornings in the dark: The Graham Greene film reader*, ed. D. Parkinson. London: Penguin.
Hubler, R.G. (1955, June 25). He makes Hollywood mad. *Saturday Evening Post*, p. 32.
Jones, L. (1951, May 24). What has happened to Jimmy's hair? *Daily Mirror*, p. 4.
Julius Caesar. (1953). Film. Directed by Joseph L. Mankiewicz. [DVD]. USA: MGM.
Kael, P. 1970. *Going Steady*. London: Temple Smith.
—— 1994. *For keeps: Thirty years at the movies*. London: Dutton.
Lady Possessed. (1952). Film. Directed by William Spier and Roy Kellino. USA: Republic.
Lolita. (1962). Film. Directed by Stanley Kubrick. [DVD]. UK/USA: MGM.
Mace, E, Dawson, H. & Pritchett, O. (1969, November 12). Briefing: The masonic touch. *Observer*, p. 23.
MacNab, G. (2003, October 30). Odd man out. *The Guardian*, p. 10.
Malcolm, D. (1985, January 31). The double-barrelled bang show. *The Guardian*, p. 23.
Mandingo. (1975). Film. Directed by Richard Fleischer. [DVD]. USA: Paramount.
Mann, R. (1960, August 21). Mason says Yes—and Lolita gets a leading man. *Sunday Express*, p. 16.
Mason, J. 1981. *Before I forget*. London: Sphere.
McCarthy, T. 1988. Actor James Mason, 75, dies in Switzerland; made over 100 pics. In *Variety obituaries, 1984–1986*, vol 10. New York: Garland.
Moore, R. (1957, February 16). Are you tired of Mason? *Picturegoer*, p. 21.
Morley, S. 1989. *James Mason: Odd man out*. New York: Harper & Row.
North by Northwest. (1959). Film. Directed by Alfred Hitchcock. [DVD]. USA: MGM.
Notorious. (1946). Film. Directed by Alfred Hitchcock. [DVD]. USA: RKO.
Odd Man Out. (1947). Film. Directed by Carol Reed. [DVD]. UK: Two Cities.
Once Upon a Time in the West. (1968). Film. Directed by Sergio Leone. [DVD]. Italy/Spain/USA: Paramount.
Pandora And the Flying Dutchman. (1951). Film. Directed by Albert Lewin. [DVD]. UK: Romulus.
Powell, M. 1987. *A life in movies*. London: Methuen.
Prince Valiant. (1954). Film. Directed by Henry Hathaway. [DVD]. USA: 20th Century-Fox.
Rope. (1948). Film. Directed by Alfred Hitchcock. [DVD]. USA: Warner Bros.
Stott, C. (1969, November 26). The rebirth of James Mason. *The Guardian*, p. 7.

Sweeney, K. 1999. *James Mason: A bio-bibliography*. Westport, Connecticut: Greenwood Press.
The Deadly Affair. (1966). Film. Directed by Sidney Lumet. [DVD]. UK: Columbia.
The Desert Fox. (1951). Film. Directed by Henry Hathaway. [DVD]. USA: Twentieth Century-Fox.
The Fall of the Roman Empire. (1964). Film. Directed by Anthony Mann. [DVD]. USA: Paramount.
The Man in Grey. (1943). Film. Directed by Leslie Arliss. [DVD]. UK: Gainsborough.
The Paradine Case. (1947). Film. Directed by Alfred Hitchcock. [DVD]. USA: Selznick International.
The Prisoner of Zenda. (1952). Film. Directed by Richard Thorpe. [DVD]. USA: MGM.
The Pumpkin Eater. (1964). Film. Directed by Jack Clayton. [DVD]. UK: Columbia.
The Reckless Moment. (1949). Film. Directed by Max Ophuls. [DVD]. USA: Columbia.
The Sea Gull. (1968). Film. Directed by Sidney Lumet. [DVD]. USA: Warner Bros.
The Seventh Veil. (1945). Film. Directed by Compton Bennett. [DVD]. UK: Sydney Box Productions.
The Shooting Party. (1985). Film. Directed by Alan Bridges. [DVD]. UK: Geoffrey Reeve.
The Times. (1984, July 28). Mr. James Mason: Versatile cinema talent, p. 10.
The Verdict. (1982). Film. Directed by Sidney Lumet. [DVD]. USA: 20th Century-Fox.
The Wicked Lady. (1945). Film. Directed by George Arliss. [DVD]. UK: Gainsborough.
They Were Sisters. (1945). Film. Directed by Arthur Crabtree. [DVD]. UK: Gainsborough.
True Grit. (1969). Film. Directed by Henry Hathaway. [DVD]. USA: Paramount.
Waymark, P. (1985, January 26). Shooting pains. *Times*, p. 19.
Weatherby, W.J. (1984, July 28). The Cad who came good in Hollywood. *The Guardian*, p. 10.

SECTION 4

Posthumous Stardom

CHAPTER 12

The Afterlives of Rudolph Valentino and Wallace Reid in the 1920s and 1930s

Lisa Bode

In the 1920s two screen idols, both aged 31, died suddenly at the peak of their fame: Wallace Reid, Anglo-American, cheerful, sporting, and dubbed 'the screen's most perfect lover', and Rudolph Valentino, the exotic, androgynous yet dominating 'Latin lover'. News of their passing (Reid in early 1923 of morphine withdrawal, Valentino in 1926 of peritonitis) dominated the front pages of all North-American newspapers, with cries that they were 'never to be forgotten'. Certainly, 'Valentino's recognition factor remains surprisingly high' (Koszarski, 1990, p. 299): numerous online shrines are dedicated to his image; *Son of the Sheik* (1926) is still screened annually at revival theatres; and scholars have analysed the alluring threat of his ethnic masculinity.[1] Reid, though, is 'one of Hollywood's most

---

[1] See for instance: Hansen, M. (1991) *Babel & Babylon: Spectatorship in American Silent Film*. Cambridge MA and London: Harvard University Press; Studlar, G. (1996) *This Mad Masquerade: Stardom and Masculinity in the Jazz Age*. New York: Columbia University Press; Studlar, G. (2004) Valentino and Ethnic Masculinity in the 1920s. In: L. Grieveson & P. Kramer (Eds.), *The silent cinema reader*. London: Routledge; Lawrence, A. (2010). Rudolph Valentino: Italian American. In: P. Petro (Ed.), *Idols of modernity: Movie stars of the 1920s*. New Brunswick: Rutgers University Press.

L. Bode
School of Communication and Arts, University of Queensland,
Brisbane, Australia

forgotten stars' (Fleming, 2007, p. 1) and apart from scattered mentions in accounts of 1920s Hollywood scandals, and Mark Lynn Anderson's (2011) work examining how his fall came to serve public understandings of drug addiction in the 1920s, he has been reduced to a footnote on Hollywood's dark tourism trail. How and why did one endure while the other faded from cultural memory?

The answer lies partly in the fact that Valentino's *Son of the Sheik* (1926) has played intermittently for decades in revival theatres, whereas Reid's films have been largely lost and never rescreened. The fate of their films, however, is tangled up in their divergent posthumous narratives, which I chart here over the 1920s and 1930s through North American newspapers and fan magazines of the era. Fan magazines provide us with the means to track posthumous fame over time, due to their focus on stars and star making, and their temporality, which, focused on the past as well as the present, tends to be more expansive than that of newspapers. At the same time, they can be used as 'a crucial index of the ideological and historical dimensions of the cinematic field of the 1920s' (Studlar, 1996, p. 264). In their relationship to the studios—independent, but also desirous of keeping good relations in order to maintain access to stars—fan magazines tended to draw rather conservative boundaries around what could or could not be discussed (Slide, 2010). While newspapers reported the star scandals of the day, sometimes in salacious detail, the majority of magazines did not, only alluding to them long after they had occurred. More sentimental than sensational, fan magazines were the venues in which posthumous stardom was nourished or left to wither. In the likes of *Photoplay* and *Picture-Play* we find interviews in which the dead idol is filtered through the memories of often famous family and friends. We also find columnists dissecting the nature of the star's legacy, and lingering fan feeling for the dead star leaking into the letters pages. Below, I trace Reid and Valentino's respective posthumous trajectories through three stages: death reportage, recuperation and memorialisation in the fan magazines, and the revival (or not) of their images in the 1930s. These stages help explain the respective longevity or otherwise of their images.

REID'S DEATH, ADDICTION, AND QUESTIONS OF CHARACTER

Before his morphine addiction became public knowledge, Reid was seen as jolly, strapping, 'big Wally', an ideal of young American manhood both on-screen and off, with a twinkle of mischief in his blue eyes, always ready to protect his sweetheart, but also one of the boys. Known for dashing auto racing pictures and romantic comedies, he had also been lauded for his role as Peter Ibbetson in *Forever* (1921), in which he had demonstrated dramatic potential as a more serious actor. Possibly because of his cross-genre stardom, as well as his wholesomeness and humour, he appealed to both men and women and had a large cross-generational following including teenage boys and elderly people (Studlar, 1996, p. 289; *Picture-Play*, April 1923a, p. 8).

This public image cracked after he was admitted into a sanatorium in late 1922 to withdraw from the grip of morphine addiction, and his wife, Dorothy, confessed the truth to the *Los Angeles Times*, leaving his audience bewildered as to how they could have been so misled. E. J. Fleming argues that his death 'rocked Hollywood to its foundations' (p. 2) not simply because it drew unwanted attention to the lifestyles of Hollywood's elite but also because of the chasm it revealed between star persona and private man. As the *Washington Post* declared: 'His frank smile and straight-looking eyes were irreconcilable with thought of him as a slave to the needle' (19 January 1923, p. 6).

The Reid scandal broke in the midst of a panic about 'the drug menace', one that Dorothy Reid subsequently addressed (or exploited, depending on your point of view) with her morality tale film *Human Wreckage* (1923). The deviant image of the junkie had only crawled into public consciousness during the previous two decades. Various narcotics, previously legal, had come to be seen as laying waste to the health of a cross section of the public who could not discipline their appetites. Still, the North American newspapers, perhaps desirous of reconciling the star image with the private man, worked hard to generate sympathy for Reid. They painted him in heroic martyr terms as a victim of his own generous spirit, rallying valiantly to fight his addiction, and finally succeeding in purifying his soul but, in the process, sacrificing his body. As the *Washington Post* put it, this story was in keeping with 'the Reid of the screens' being a 'triumph over self, but it cost him his life' (19 January 1923, p. 6).

Reid's death narrative was nevertheless complicated and riddled with awkward tensions and silences around how he came to be addicted in the first place, posing a challenge to his recuperation. Fleming argues that the studio was actually to blame: Reid became addicted to morphine onset after being forced to work through pain from injuries sustained in a train crash (2007, pp. 142–145). However, studio culpability was, at the time of his death and for decades afterward, largely omitted from the explanation, pointing to a wider institutional problem that did not serve the Hollywood 'housecleaning' narrative, which had emerged in response to the scandal cluster of the very early 1920s.[2] Instead, the focus turned to questions of individual character. As Anderson notes, the dominant news narrative had Reid involved with 'the wrong element' in his leisure time, a story that neatly dovetailed into popular fears and fantasies of Hollywood's wild parties. This cautionary tale had him repent his ways before his death and welcomed back into the wholesome bosom of family and longstanding friends. The nature of his death and the questions it raised around his 'true' character continued, as we shall see below, to present a nagging friction with his normative screen image, but one that could only be addressed in veiled terms within fan magazines.

Valentino's Death, Feminine Desire, and the Immortal Spirit

If Reid had exemplified the ideal American male, Valentino posed a 'pernicious challenge' to normative models of Anglo-American masculinity in the 1920s, during that decade's heated debates about immigration (Lawrence, 2010, p. 89). An Italian immigrant who played dangerously attractive foreign lovers, his threat lay not just in his foreignness but also in that he personified the 'woman-made' star (Studlar, 1996, pp. 286–287). The fan magazines exploited but also attempted to manage or undercut his intense appeal to women by framing it as a hysterical fantasy without substance. While continuity had been stressed across Reid's on- and off-screen personas, the Valentino threat required dilution by highlighting a gap between the romantic screen idol and the 'childlike' or 'ordinary young man' real life person (Studlar, 1996, p. 289).

The effete image immediately dissolved as he was portrayed in the newspapers as having engaged in a 'brave struggle' against the sepsis

---

[2] I refer here to the poisoning death of young rising starlet Olive Thomas in 1920; the trials of 1921 and 1922 of film comedian star Fatty Arbuckle for the rape and manslaughter of Virginia Rappe at a party; and the 1922 unsolved murder of director William Desmond Taylor, in which a couple of young female stars were implicated. These widely reported scandals, and the damage they did to Hollywood's reputation, spurring stronger calls for government censorship, have been commonly understood by film historians such as Douglas Gomery as a key catalyst for the formation of the Motion Picture Producers and Distributors of America, in 1922, headed by Will Hays. Under this organization the studios developed morality clauses for star contracts and in 1930, the Production Code, which used moral guidelines to shape screen content.

that had invaded his organs. His obituaries remade the Latin threat into a humble immigrant and American success story, and the fantasy into a man of substance who had longed to become a serious actor and to move beyond the shallow matinee idol position he feared would not last. Nevertheless, although posthumously masculinised and Americanised, it is largely female-led hysteria and erotic longing that have become the key frames through which he is recalled. Focus quickly shifted to the women—fans and stars—who mourned him, and '[s]tories of the riot of the Frank Campbell Funeral Home and newsreels of the endless procession of black limousines have become a standard reference point in any cultural history of the twenties' (Koszarski, p. 299). Another dominant news image featured screen star Pola Negri swooning theatrically, 'overcome beside the coffin of her dead fiancée' (*New York Times*, 30 August 1926, p. 3). In addition, there were stories of grief-stricken women attempting suicide in London and Paris, and the mysterious Lady in Black, with her annual visit to his mausoleum at the Hollywood Forever cemetery on the anniversary of his death. While memorial profiles in the fan magazines sought at first to deepen and substantiate Valentino's image, the dominant meaning associated with him became that of a powerful, torrid, feminine desire that death could not cool. His relationships with exotic female stars who, by association, further emphasised his romantic otherness, also proclaimed the continuity of his presence in spiritual terms.

Actresses Negri and Natacha Rambova—the former his fiancée, the latter his ex-wife—competed for proximity to both his legacy and his immortal spirit in their respective interviews with the fan magazines. Rambova claimed to have received, via a medium, messages from Valentino who 'was just as alive, but in a different vibration' (Smith, 1927, p. 38). Much skepticism greeted her claims, however, as the evident desire to believe in Valentino's spiritual presence, or to profit from it, triggered a rash of stories of ghostly visitations to the point where *Photoplay*'s editor asked, 'Will these hokus-pokus spiritualists, psychic investigators, and mediums ever let poor Valentino rest in peace?' (Quirk, 1931, p. 25). Negri continued the talk of his immortality but in terms of public memory rather than ghost: 'He is less a shadow, even though he is gone, than men who live in the world as flesh and blood, because he was all things to all women' (Hall, 1935, pp. 46–47). The association of his spiritual or mnemonic continuity with exotic female stars fed into what became known as the cult of Valentino in the 1930s but was also buoyed by the persistence of his image on screen.

Reid's Domestic Recuperation and Film Revival

Unlike Valentino, no stories of hauntings or messages from beyond accompanied Reid, and he was more or less absent from the screen. Due to the efforts of his family and friends to recuperate his image, it was the benign associations of domesticity and friendship that clung to his memory in the obituaries, memorial statements, and interviews that appeared in the fan magazines. In the fan magazine context, the franker newspaper discussions of narcotics, dope rings, and addiction were silenced, or alluded to only obliquely in terms that mostly sought to reconcile his scandal with the image his fans knew and loved.

For instance, *Picture-Play*'s 'Some Memories of Wallace Reid' brimmed with anecdotes from his friends picturing a fun-loving character, full of 'restless energy' and 'always trying something new', while being too generous to others (May, 1923b, pp. 26–29). Elsewhere, his best friend characterized Reid as a 'big wholesome kind-hearted boy' who loved his family, learned and mastered new skills, and, by being generous and fun-loving to a fault, had 'killed himself with kindness to others' (Post, 1924, pp. 20–21). Most articles on Reid from this time featured family portraits of the Reids at home with their son and adopted daughter, in images of saintly domestic contentment.

This domestication narrative, however, was not entirely uniform. *Motion Picture Classic*, for instance, was notable for its refusal to fully sanctify Reid's memory or shy away completely from association with addiction. Its references to him were largely about his mourning widow who 'carries on' with a brave heart and courage, a gallant crusader against the evil thing that cost Wallace Reid his life, with her production of the anti-narcotics film, *Human Wreckage* (June 1923, p. 36). There was no attempt to associate him with terms like 'wholesome', but instead, the magazine stressed character weakness and the devastation he had wrought on his family.

Nevertheless, through the 1920s, Dorothy, her mother-in-law, Bertha, and Reid's fans persisted in their efforts to sanctify his memory, largely with reference to his wholesome screen image, in attempts to push the studio to reissue his films. In the pages of *Photoplay*, for instance, Dorothy shared some of the 'hundreds of letters' still sent to 'dear Wally', claiming that the volume alone proved 'how deeply the people of this and every other country love the clean, wholesome type of picture and the clean, wholesome type of young, strong, red-blooded American that Wally typified' (Reid, 1924, p. 81). Bertha lauded the 'clean joy' he gave his fans, even declaring 'what a brave effort it must have been to remain true to the clean and wholesome in this decadent age of fleshpots in literature, screen and stage' (Westbrook, 1926, p. 3). Until the end of the decade, fan letters continued to appear in *Photoplay* and *Motion Picture Magazine*, requesting the reissue of his films, even in heavily redacted forms, just so they could have some form of 'reunion with Wallace Reid's shadow self' (Boyer, 1926). Another pleaded, 'We want Wallace Reid to smile at us again from the screen so we can have again that part of him that we used to have and that is still left to us' (Riqueur, 1926, p. 5). His fans felt that his films would provide flickering evidence for why they had been so beguiled in the first place by the screen persona of a man who had, privately, fatally, turned out so very flawed.

'The Answer Man' section in *Motion Picture Magazine* repeatedly informed readers, with no reason given, that it was highly unlikely that they would see Reid's pictures again. According to Fleming, Will Hays had tried to convince Lasky to withdraw all Reid's pictures from circulation as soon as his illness became known around Hollywood (p. 213). Anderson explains that North American exhibitors in the early 1920s led the charge against showing films featuring performers who were deemed to be immoral. The basis for such denial was the idea that immoral people made immoral art and such performers should not benefit financially from their notoriety, but also that they should not be seen by young impressionable audiences to gain from immoral behaviour. Another problem, besides the reluctance of the industry to risk being tainted by Reid's disgrace, was that the strain of his malady was all too visible in the films he had made in the two years up to his death. As the *Los Angeles Times* pointed out, Reid became 'a pitiful shadow' of his youthful 'zest' and 'a painted smirk replaced the quick and ready smile of other days', while make-up could not 'conceal the fatigue' (1923, p. I3).

After a decade, with the emergence of the1930s, sound-era, Hollywood nostalgia for 1920s silent filmmaking, a few short film clips in which Reid made an appearance *did* eventually make their way into a few theatres, in nostalgia reels. *Motion Picture Magazine* reported in 1932 the release of *The Movie Album* featuring short clips of Charlie Chaplin, Clara Kimball Young, and Wallace Reid, sliced from dusty reels in studio storerooms to 'amuse' audiences with a glimpse of what 'movies were like when they were young and crude' (J.E.R., 1932). This reduced his work to serving a narrative of Hollywood's aesthetic progression, just as his name, during the 1930s, came to serve a narrative of Hollywood's moral supersession. While Reid's rather normative and wholesome screen image had nothing to offer 1930s audiences, and his films were perceived as stylistically and technologically inferior to current films but not sufficiently other in their content, Valentino's screen image helped to define a 1930s view of 1920s cinema as erotic, exotic, and morally colourful.

The Various 'Lives' of the Sheik

As Valentino's death had no moral import, his posthumously released film, *The Son of the Sheik*, was allowed to run as long as it drew an audience. In September 1926 newspapers were reporting that his final film had proved to be his most popular, making '$30,000 a day for his heirs' and continuing to play in theatres in '50 American cities' due to public demand (*Washington Post*, 1 September 1926, p. 1). It was also suggested that other Valentino films, such as *The Four Horsemen of the Apocalypse* (1921) might be posthumously reissued. By the late 1920s, screenings of *The Sheik* (1921) and *Son of The Sheik* had become an annual rite in various North American revival theatres, playing on August 23rd, the anniversary of his death. But viewing these films was not an entirely reverent ritual, as even the fan magazines that every year featured breathless stories of commemoration, last interviews, or hypothetical 'if he were alive today' stories, revealed the growing coexistence with reverence of a reception we would label 'camp': gaining enjoyment from an excessive theatricality, marked as dated. For instance, in an article otherwise assuring the longevity of Valentino's stardom: 'The other day an audience [...] shrieked with hysterical mirth at the revival of 'The Sheik,' [... for ...] the melodramatic gestures and cave-man love-making were ridiculous to a sophisticated movie audience twelve years later.' Doubtless they were referring to Vilma Banky's anguished chest clutching, and repeated shots of Valentino glowering while ripping open his own shirt to bare his smooth chest. The author goes on to assure us that Rudy, if he had lived, was talented enough to have transformed his style from 'Latin love-making to the new vogue for restraint and under-emphasis' (Nicholai, 1934, p. 31).

In 1938 *The Sheik* and *Son of the Sheik* had been revived to play in New York to 'tremendous business' but, as Bell noted, 'to be sure, they are looked upon more or less as comic museum pieces and their most serious moments are hilariously laughed at by audiences that are preponderantly feminine'. He did observe a mix of original older fans, reliving their first swooning encounter with the film, and a 'newer crop of film-goers to whom the name Valentino is scarcely more than a nebulous sort of legend' (Bell, 1938, p. X18). However, much to the annoyance of fans, the love scenes—such as the infamous tent scene, which implies an impending rape—had been sliced under the Production Code to remove any hint of dangerously stirred passions. This is evidenced in a letter to *Motion Picture Magazine* criticising how *The Son of the Sheik* had been mutilated by 'Will Hays and his bureau of censors'. For 'It was hardly a tribute to the "great lover" to deprive the public of the very thing for which he was famous' (Ratcliff, 1939, p. 14).

Nevertheless, while at least some of Valentino's films continued to be 'revived', and audiences could be enthralled, or amused, or both by his smouldering, kohl-lined, brutal grace, the star remained present, almost as if alive, in the public consciousness. That said, as the aesthetic and moral norms of the motion picture and its performance styles changed in the wake of sound and the Hays code, the reception for Valentino shifted, and his image ossified into an enduringly seductive glittering ghost from an era of silent Hollywood and performance that was either mourned as more colourful and erotic than the present, or mocked for its overt theatricality. In the final section we shall see how Valentino became a central figure in Hollywood's past-present relationship during the nostalgia and self-historicising of the 1930s, while Reid largely receded from view.

Reid's and Valentino's Fates through Institutional Nostalgia in the 1930s Fan Magazines

Between 1931 and 1935 *Photoplay* and *Motion Picture Magazine* published monthly 'Ten Years Ago' columns, celebrating the longevity of Hollywood cinema and feeding the nostalgia of fans that may have grown up with it. Valentino was largely discussed as a figure from a more opulent time, deploying an outdated but alluring performance style. At the same time, he maintained a contemporary relevance as a benchmark for masculine sex appeal against which all new leading male stars were measured. A parade of dark-haired and charismatic leading men such as Clark Gable, George Raft, Richard Dix, and Cary Grant were declared 'the new Valentino': more evidence that the 'Latin' connotations of his stardom were now dissolved in favour of a generic Hollywood 'great lover' (Pryor, 1933, pp. 30–31). He appeared in all surveys of great screen lovers, and Mae West proclaimed him 'the most romantic man of all time' (West, 1935, p. 32). *Photoplay* in October 1938 reported the release of a new book *Remember Valentino: Remembrances of the World's Greatest Lover*, which purportedly covered all his famous romances (June Acker, Natacha Rambova, Pola Negri) and friendships with Gloria Swanson and Vilma Banky (p. 96). These associations persisted to the point where his name alone had become shorthand for a powerfully marketable dark and sensual masculine appeal, used in sentences such as 'a touch of the Valentino' and 'Valentino heartthrobs' with no further explanation required.

While Valentino became boldly outlined, Reid faded away, his name mentioned less as the decade progressed. In *Movie Classic* (previously titled—until 1931—*Motion Picture Classic*) he is entirely absent. *Photoplay*, however, because of its longer publication history stretching into the 1910s, and therefore its longer and closer association with Hollywood, performed the bulk of Hollywood historicising and nostalgia, and so in these pages, Reid took almost the rest of the decade to disappear. At the beginning of the 1930s in *Photoplay*'s 'Screen Memories' columns, Reid is an innocuous, light-hearted, romping figure without a solid outline. His name is dutifully recited whenever another star dies, one of a litany of the biggest names of the screen that had passed, used to anoint the newly dead into their company. As the years pass, his outline grows fainter. By the late 1930s he occasionally appears, painted in benign affectionate terms, just one of a list of names, within memories of film going in the late 1910s. For instance:

> My mother and I went often at night to the snug neighbourhood theaters where those talented pioneers of pantomime—Mary Pickford, Douglas Fairbanks, Marguerite Clark, Wallace Reid, Charles Ray, and all the rest—made us forget the heaviness of our hearts. (Bailey, 1938, p. 19)

Reid is, by this time, formless, undifferentiated and nonspecific.

There is one exception. He is given specific associations within the context of scandal, and we see this a decade after his death: 'Last rumbles of the parting storm about "movie morals" … an editorial speaking our mind about the handling of the Arbuckle case. And a melancholy after-note to the period of trouble … a two-page notice and farewell tribute occasioned by the tragic death of Wally Reid' (*Photoplay*, 1933, p. 121). While the terms 'addiction' and 'narcotics' were unmentioned, he was explicitly associated here with Arbuckle and the moral scandals that had earlier tainted the industry, whereas in 1920s fan magazines, these scandals had been unmentionable. Later in the decade, his frank association with scandal was further consolidated in a lengthy article historicising Hollywood: 'Then came a series of unfortunate events which gave Hollywood the reputation of being "The modern Babylon"' and it lists Olive Thomas's suicide, the Fatty Arbuckle scandal, the William Desmond Taylor murder, and the death of Wallace Reid. This was a narrative of moral progress that marked Reid and the others as a catalyst for change, with the formation of the Hays Office and moral contracts for stars. *Photoplay* proclaimed '[T]hus public confidence was restored in its stars' before placing Valentino in this next category: morally clean, and yet so erotically compelling on-screen as 'the screen's topmost matinee idol' (*Photoplay*, 1939, p. 82).

Conclusion

The moral questions sparked by the nature of Reid's death meant that the rupture in Reid's image between screen persona and private man was never truly healed despite the best efforts of his wife, friends, and fans. This is evidenced by the fact that his films were withheld from revival during an era of moral panic about narcotic addiction and Hollywood's moral decay. Without the films to keep his screen presence in circulation, he could not retain a prominent position in the personal memories of viewers. Moreover under the Production Code of the 1930s his film image, so wholesome, was not sufficiently exotic to prompt nostalgia. At the same time as 1930s Hollywood looked back at the 1920s, Reid's image shifted from the domestic realm into the category of scandal firmly placed in the past. This, consequently, is how, if at all, he has been half-remembered: a tragic catalyst for moral housecleaning. Valentino's presence, however, was sustained after his death, both on-screen, in revivals of his films, and in a feminised, cultish spiritualism led by his ex-wife, Rambova. The latter, as it gained a hysterical traction, served to further assert his extraordinariness. Meanwhile, his screen image gained in erotic power even as his performance style came to accrue camp value in a mid 1930s context in which film lovemaking was, due to the Production Code, by comparison rather more chaste and low-key. While Reid came to serve Hollywood's narrative of moral progress, Valentino was associated with aesthetic progress, while also remade as an enduring 'great lover' figure, cleansed of his threatening ethnicity and effeminacy, and used to anoint and measure the sex appeal of all new American leading men with dark hair and bedroom eyes. By the end of the 1930s the respective legacies of Valentino and Reid had become sedimented as forms that remained more or less stable for decades to come.

References

Anderson, M.L. 2011. *Twilight of the idols: Hollywood and the Human sciences in 1920s America.* Los Angeles & Berkeley: University of California Press.

Bailey, T. (1938, June). Escape into enchantment. *Photoplay*, p. 19.

Bell N.B. (1938, June). Reissue of many old film hits planned. *Washington Post*, p. X18.

Boyer, M. (1926, April). Concerning Wallace Reid's pictures. *Picture-Play*, p. 112.

Fleming, E.J. 2007. *Wallace Reid: The life and death of a Hollywood idol.* Jefferson, NC: McFarland.

Forever. (1921). Film. Directed by George Fitzmaurice. USA: Famous Players-Lasky Corporation.

Gomery, D. 1986. *The Hollywood studio system.* New York: St Martins Press.

Hall, G. (1935, January). Valentino Still Lives—For Pola Negri. *Motion Picture Magazine*, pp. 46–47.

Hansen, M. 1991. *Babel & Babylon: Spectatorship in American silent film.* Cambridge, MA and London: Harvard University Press.

Human Wreckage. (1923). Film. Directed by John Griffith Wray. USA: Film Booking Offices of America.

J.E.R. (1932, June). Featured Shorts. *Motion Picture Magazine*, p. 68.

Koszarski, R. 1990. *An evening's entertainment: The age of the silent picture feature.* Los Angeles & Berkeley: University of California Press.

Lawrence, A. 2010. Rudolph Valentino: Italian American. In *Idols of Modernity: Movie Stars of the 1920s*, ed. P. Petro. New Brunswick: Rutgers University Press.

Los Angeles Times. (1923, January 19). Wallace Reid dies fighting, p. I3.

Motion Picture Classic. (1923, June). Hollywood homes No. XI, p. 36.

New York Times. (1926, August 30). Miss Negri Swoons at Valentino Bier, p. 3.

Nicholai, B. (1934, September). Would Valentino be a star today?' *Motion picture magazine*, p. 41.

Photoplay. (1933, March). Screen Memories from Photoplay, p. 121.

———. (1938,October).Remember Valentino, p.96.

———. (1939,October).Photoplay's Cavalcade of Hollywood.October, p.82.

Picture-Play. (1923a, April). What the fans think, p. 8.

———. (1923b, May 26–29).Some memories of Wallace Reid, p.90.

Post, C. (1924, January). Wally Reid, my friend. *Motion Picture Magazine*, pp. 20–21.

Pryor, N. (1933, July). Clark, George and Gary—How do they rate with men? *Movie Classic*, pp. 30–31.
Quirk, J. (1931, April). Close-ups and long-shots. *Photoplay*, p. 25.
Ratcliff, D. (1939, January). Hay's cut-ups. *Motion Picture Magazine*, p. 14.
Reid, D. (1924, March). Letters to Wally Reid's memory. *Photoplay*, p. 81.
Riqueur C. (1926, May). *Bulletin of the Wallace Reid Memorial Club.* 1 (1), p. 5.
Slide, A. 2010. *Inside the Hollywood Fan magazine: A history of the star makers, fabricators, and gossip mongers.* Jackson, MI: University of Mississippi Press.
Smith, F. (1927, February). Does Valentino Speak from the Beyond? *Photoplay*, p. 38.
Son of the Sheik. (1926). Film. Directed by George Fitzmaurice. USA: United Artists.
Studlar, G. 1996. The Perils of pleasure? Fan magazine discourse as women's commodified culture in the 1920s. In *Silent film*, ed. R. Abel. New Brunswick, NJ: Rutgers University Press.
——— 2004. Valentino and ethnic masculinity in the 1920s. In *The silent cinema reader*, eds. L. Grieveson, and P. Kramer. London: Routledge.
The Four Horsemen of the Apocalypse. (1921). Film. Directed by Rex Ingram. USA: Metro Pictures Corporation.
The Sheik. (1921). Film. Directed by George Melford. USA: Paramount Pictures.
Washington Post. (1923, January 19). Wallace Reid, p. 6.
Washington Post. (1926, September 1). Valentino Film Earning $30,000 Daily for Heirs, p. 1.
West, M. (1935, June). The six most romantic men. *Movie Classic*, p. 32.
Westbrook, B. (1926, May). *Bulletin of the Wallace Reid Memorial Club.* 1(1), p. 3.

CHAPTER 13

Beyond the Bounds of Criticism: Preserving Spencer Tracy as a Liberal Hero

Hannah Graves

In his obituary of Spencer Tracy, Bosley Crowther, the long-serving film critic for the *New York Times*, lamented, 'They aren't writing so many stories these days about Mr. Tracy's kind of man' and 'even if they were, there aren't many actors who could play them'. Tracy's death on 10 June 1967 was viewed as symbolic, representing another 'strong vibrant cable' severed 'in the slowly crumbling bridge between the motion pictures of this generation and the great ones of the past' (Crowther, 1967, p. 2). Crowther's reverence for Tracy's star persona was echoed across the obituaries and retrospectives that celebrated the actor's thirty-seven-year career after his death which came shortly after production concluded on his final film, *Guess Who's Coming to Dinner* (1967). In his recent study of the Best Picture Academy Award nominees of 1967, which included *Guess Who's Coming to Dinner*, Mark Harris has argued that the year served as a turning point for the industry during which 'the dominance of the studio system was challenged by the modes, mores and morals of a new generation of filmmakers and audiences' (Harris, 2008, p. 417). Tracy's passing seemed a death knell for the very system that had created him and, consequently, he became inexorably linked to debates about these changes by virtue of his enduring stardom, the nature of his star persona, and the controversy surrounding his final posthumously released film.

H. Graves
Department of History, University of Warwick, Coventry, UK

As Lisa Bode observes, 'Reviewers tend to characterise a dead actor's final screen appearance as an epitaph or memorial image' (Bode, 2010, p. 61). However, *Guess Who's Coming to Dinner* is particularly ripe for analysis as a career culmination because it was developed, specifically, for Tracy. Produced and directed by independent filmmaker Stanley Kramer, *Guess Who's Coming to Dinner* examines the prejudices within America's well-meaning liberal elite through Matt and Christina Drayton, an aging progressive newspaper publisher and an avant-garde gallery owner. The film depicts Matt and Christina's (Spencer Tracy and Katharine Hepburn) reactions to the announcement that their daughter, Joey (Katharine Houghton, Hepburn's own niece), intends to move to Switzerland and marry a black doctor, John Prentice (Sidney Poitier). By the close of the evening, the Draytons must bless the interracial union or, unbeknownst to Joey, John will end the engagement. While Christina quickly softens to the idea, the suspense rests on whether Matt will live up to his espoused principles. The film culminates in Matt's pre-dinner speech in which he explains his reasons for blessing their marriage to the young couple, John's parents, and Tilly, the Draytons' black maid.

While not the first Hollywood film about a black-white interracial romance, *Guess Who's Coming to Dinner*, with the tagline 'a love story of today', was the first of its calibre: filmed in Technicolor with a large budget and an all-star cast. The Supreme Court's *Loving vs. Virginia* decision of 1967, overturning barriers to interracial marriage, and the announcement that Secretary of State Dean Rusk's daughter was to marry a black National Aeronautics and Space Administration employee, pointed towards the film's timeliness. However, premiering in New York and Los Angeles six months after Tracy's death, *Guess Who's Coming to Dinner* was widely received as an artistically and ideologically flawed film. A complex dialogue emerged because of Tracy's death, as critics sought to preserve his heroic image while still engaging critically with what they perceived as the film's paternalistic approach to its subject matter.

With particular focus on Tracy's final film, this chapter considers how his star image was utilised and, ultimately, influenced by his late-in-life collaborations with Stanley Kramer. Viewing Tracy as his muse, Kramer shaped the latter stage of the actor's career, casting him as the liberal hero of his 'message movies'.[1] Examining the ways critics attempted to preserve Tracy's image within the negative reception of *Guess Who's Coming*

---

[1] Cripps (1993) outlines the emergence and characteristics of 'message movies'.

to *Dinner*, this chapter argues Tracy's final film provides a compelling example of the ways star images are able to stretch and bend when tested, a luxury Kramer was not afforded.

Becoming 'Mr. Tracy's Kind of Man'

Today, Spencer Tracy is predominately remembered for his romantic comedy pairings with Katharine Hepburn and the discrete open secret of their long-term affair.[2] Starting in 1941 and culminating with *Guess Who's Coming to Diner*, Tracy and Hepburn made nine films together, in which Hepburn played 'free-spirited, rebellious, liberal and assertive women' (Nochimson, 2002, p. 189) who find their politics and personalities softened by Tracy's down-to-earth persona. During his lifetime, Tracy was a lauded dramatic actor, famed for his naturalistic performances.

Arriving in Hollywood in 1930, Tracy was initially cast as what Robert Sklar (1992) termed 'city boy' characters. His screen image, however, was able to mature beyond this limited type. After signing with Metro-Goldwyn-Mayer (MGM) in 1935, Tracy won two consecutive Academy Awards, portraying a Portuguese fisherman who helps a young aristocrat come of age in *Captains Courageous* (1937), and Father Flanagan in the biopic *Boys Town* (1938) about the founder of a home for orphaned children. These roles helped establish Tracy as America's most celebrated film actor and, in the words of one biographer, 'the screen's humanitarian conscience' (Swindell, 1973, p. 12). In some of his most popular roles, he was cast as an idealised paternal figure with a stoic, unmoveable but, ultimately, gentle and progressive masculinity. Dedicating and then giving his Academy Award to the real Father Flanagan, Tracy transitioned in the popular imagination (as demonstrated in the pages of *Photoplay*) from a street-smart 'gum-chewing lad' (Biery, 1932, p. 97) to a contemplative family man 'facing forty' (Martin, 1938, p. 30), a transition embraced by MGM's publicity department for its ability to obscure the jarring realities of his off-screen alcoholism and infidelity from the public.

In 1955, at 55 years old, Spencer Tracy ended his contract with MGM and began intermittently freelancing as Hollywood's elder statesman. As

---

[2] Spencer and Louise Tracy, married in 1921, never divorced, because of their Catholicism. Tracy had affairs with other women, but he was with Hepburn from 1941 to his death in 1967. A 1962 *Look* article revealed to the public Tracy's battle with alcoholism and strained marriage. See Curtis (2012, pp. 800–803) for the article's effect.

he explained, 'When you get my age you want to do a picture that's about something' (Alpbert, 1962, p. A10) and Stanley Kramer provided him with the opportunity, keeping the reclusive Tracy in the public eye. Of the eight feature films that Tracy made after leaving MGM, four were produced and directed by Kramer: *Inherit the Wind* (1960), *Judgment at Nuremberg* (1961), *It's a Mad, Mad, Mad, Mad World* (1963), and *Guess Who's Coming to Dinner*.

STANLEY KRAMER'S 'MATURE PICTURES WITH SUBSTANCE'

Stanley Kramer's films crossed a range of genres and were produced over the years with vastly different budgets, but they were all, as Kramer would characterise them, 'mature pictures with substance' (Kramer, 1951, p. X5). After World War II, he established himself as an independent producer who operated outside the restrictions of the studio system, although catering to a shared middlebrow audience. *Home of the Brave* (1949), one of the first films to deal seriously with racism by examining the psychological toll it enacted on a young soldier, fully launched Kramer as an important voice in Hollywood. The film also established Kramer's 'brand' of message film making and his reputation as a pioneering producer within the industry.[3]

With publicist George Glass, Kramer aggressively promoted his type of film making as a heroic feat to a receptive press, rhetorically twinning his bravery in bringing liberal, message-driven films to the screen with the crusading masculine heroism depicted within them. As Kramer moved into directing in the mid 1950s, a consensus began to form among some critics that he was a better producer than director but, first and foremost, a self-publicist.[4] Still, segments of the middlebrow and mass-market press were supportive of Kramer's intentions when he addressed taboo topics. As the *Saturday Review*'s Arthur Knight noted, 'One could often admire the courage of a Kramer picture while finding fault with its execution' (Knight, 1961a, p. 45). Kramer regularly cast actors, built by the studio system, as characters that embodied socially responsible masculinity. However, Kramer's use of Tracy's image differed from his casting of, for

---

[3] Cripps (1993) details the production and widespread praise of *Home of the Brave* as a landmark film, although it was criticised by segments of the political left (pp. 221–226).

[4] Kramer was accused of overly aggressive publicity campaigns by Goodman (1961), pp. 147–149, pp. 189–190) and Kael (1970, pp. 203–214).

example, Gary Cooper in *High Noon* (1952) and Gregory Peck in *On the Beach* (1959) because, through repeat casting and exclusive association, Kramer was able to enrich and extend Tracy's star image.

'THE MOUTHPIECE FOR STANLEY KRAMER'

Redefining each other's late careers, Stanley Kramer and Spencer Tracy entered into a mutually beneficial partnership: Kramer offered Tracy projects tailored to the star's heroic image that showcased his talents as a golden age veteran, while Tracy's image lent Kramer's films a beloved persona with nostalgic connotations, as well as artistic prestige and symbolic capital. Despite his autonomy as an independent producer-director, Kramer was never considered to have the artistic vision of an auteur. However, the collaborations in the Kramer-Tracy partnership are an example of the ways both films and star images can be enriched by 'the star and the director mutually bringing something out in each other', an idea that 'informs much of auteurist criticism' (Dyer, 1998, p. 155).

In the early 1960s Tracy starred in two courtroom dramas for Kramer. Both roles were dependent upon, just as they enhanced, Tracy's image as a crusading 'humanitarian conscience' figure and Kramer's message movie brand. In *Inherit the Wind*, Tracy played Henry Drummond, a fictionalised version of the real life lawyer, Clarence Darrow, who argued for the defence in the 1925 Scopes 'Monkey' Trial, in which a Tennessee school-teacher was accused of violating local anti-evolution laws. Tracy next portrayed the fictional Judge Hayward in *Judgement at Nuremberg*, presiding over a trial of Nazi judges, notable also for being the first commercial feature to show documentary footage of the concentration camps on American screens. As testament to Tracy's own investment in liberal hero roles, it was Tracy, via Hepburn, who suggested the latter as a project Kramer should pursue.[5] Each film offered Tracy a climatic legal summation, in which he articulated the ethos of both his character and the film: in *Inherit the Wind*, on the freedom of expression and in *Judgement at Nuremberg*, on social responsibility. Knight wrote in his review of *Judgement at Nuremberg*, it was a 'measure of Kramer's achievement' that the messages 'emerge from Spencer Tracy's lips not as slippery and shopworn abstractions, but as hard, solid, immutable, and highly specific realities' (Knight, 1961b, p. 45), an early indication of how Tracy's talent was recognised as elevating Kramer's material.

---

[5] See Curtis (2012), p. 756.

While Tracy's performance as Drummond was brasher than his solemn interpretation of Hayward, with more physicality through his sweating and lumbering movements around the courtroom and a louder and more aggressive snarl to his speech, both films were remarkably similar for the way they positioned Tracy as the voice of reason. Although they both revealed, in close-up, Tracy's rapid ageing, they also exhibited his continued vitality through his ability to deliver eloquent, grandstanding, single-take speeches. Celebrating his endurance, the press affectionately described Tracy as a 'caustic, cryptic, crusty white haired acting veteran' (Alpert, 1962, p. A10), characterising his shunning of make-up and willingness to reveal his ageing as evidence of his unpretentious honesty. Kramer encouraged the reception of Tracy's roles as an example of 'perfect fit' casting (Dyer, 1998, p. 129). The press book for *Inherit the Wind* claimed Tracy was 'perfect casting': 'thoughtful, incisive, sardonic, he is beautifully suited' (*Inherit the Wind* Pressbook, 1960, p. 7). Likewise, a press release for *Judgment at Nuremberg* noted that Tracy's role as 'a man of fierce integrity' was 'Tracy as he is in real life' (Untitled Press Release of 24th March, 1961).

Ironically, although Kramer's films privileged the authority of white male liberals and the 'real' Tracy was often compared to the crusading masculine heroes he played, the women in his life better fit the mould. While Tracy portrayed Father Flanagan on screen, it was his wife, Louise Tracy, who received the first Boy's Town award in 1975 for her work establishing the John Tracy Clinic, named for their son, which provided educational opportunities for deaf children. Similarly, during the politically divisive years of the blacklist, Tracy, unlike Hepburn, remained discreet and inactive in politics.[6] Tracy's lack of real-life crusading was advantageous to Kramer, dampening controversy and neither upstaging Kramer's liberal reputation nor prejudicing his potential audience.

Although Kramer often cast Sidney Poitier—in *The Defiant Ones* (1958), *Pressure Point* (1962), and *Guess Who's Coming to Dinner*—Tracy was the liberal hero the producer viewed as a reflection of himself. Pauline Kael even noted with derision that Kramer's new favourite star 'looked startlingly like an aged Stanley Kramer' (Kael, 1970, p. 207). As Donald

---

[6] For a discussion of Louise Tracy's work for the John Tracy Clinic, see Mahon (2012). For Hepburn's political activism, see Edwards (1986, pp. 226–227, 236–237). Although Tracy was private in his politics, biographers have noted Tracy's admiration of President Franklin D. Roosevelt, see Curtis (2012, p. 407).

Spoto astutely observed, Kramer wanted Tracy 'to play his other self on the screen' and he used Tracy as 'the mouthpiece for the struggles, hopes and beliefs of Stanley Kramer' (Spoto, 1990, p. 280). For his part, echoing the language used by reviewers to describe him, Tracy credited Kramer with 'the courage of his convictions at a time when few of us have courage and fewer of us have convictions' (in Newquist, 1972, p. 153). Through each man's public praise of the other, Kramer and Tracy's images conflated and Tracy became a key part of Kramer's brand across the 1960s.

Inherit the Wind and *Judgement at Nuremberg* were not box-office successes. However, Tracy was nominated for an Academy Award for each performance and Kramer, largely indebted to the sense of quality and legitimacy that Tracy's repeated presence accorded his productions, became the sixteenth recipient of the Irving Thalberg Award for consistently high quality production in 1962. As Tracy's health declined, Kramer sought out opportunities to continue to work with the actor, casting him in a comedy caper, *It's a Mad, Mad, Mad, Mad World*, in a small but pivotal role as a detective; Tracy's persona lent the film gravitas as 'the guardian of sane morality' (Crowther, 1963, p. 46) amongst the unruly cast of comics. When Tracy's heart condition, kidney trouble, and diabetes worsened, Kramer decided to produce and direct a final collaboration. Securing Tracy, Hepburn, and box-office-draw Poitier, Kramer sold the controversial idea to Columbia before William Rose's screenplay was completed, with Matt Drayton developed with Tracy expressly in mind.[7]

'A Love Story of Today'

From *Guess Who's Coming to Dinner*'s first announcement, the press celebrated the anticipated reunion of Tracy and Hepburn following their office romance *Desk Set* (1957). However, Kramer's topical comedy of manners structurally differs from the their earlier romantic comedies as it pairs Hepburn and Tracy with a younger couple.

It also, as Nochimson (2002) argues, lacks the dynamic synergy of their earlier screen roles. The doting Christina barely resembles the firebrand liberal characters that built Hepburn's star image. Just as Hepburn became, in effect, Tracy's 'wife, secretary, companion, chauffer, nurse' as his health declined (Edwards, 1986, p. 214), her presence on-screen in

---

[7] See Curtis (2012) on *Guess Who's Coming to Dinner*'s development (pp. 830–842).

Guess Who's Coming to Dinner is to enrich Tracy's last screen appearance, while her role off-screen was to assist Tracy through the rigours of production. Despite being the final Tracy-Hepburn film, *Guess Who's Coming to Dinner* is more closely aligned with Tracy's earlier collaborations with Kramer.

Kramer saw the central conflict of *Guess Who's Coming to Dinner*, in effect, as a wrestling between two elements of Tracy's star persona. For Kramer, the film rested on whether Matt's 'instincts as a father' will 'outweigh his liberal conscience' (Kramer and Coffey, 1997, pp. 226–227). Even before Tracy appears on screen, the two photographs on Matt's office desk embody this conflict: one is a framed picture of Christina holding Joey, and the other, larger photograph, a picture of President Franklin D. Roosevelt (Fig. 13.1) which, in Rose's screenplay, was intended to be 'of FDR standing in the doorway of [the Drayton's] house' (Rose, 1967, p. 12). Although a head shot, the size of Roosevelt's image compared to the family portrait makes plain a close connection and confirms, explicitly, Matt's status as a New Deal liberal.

Throughout the film, Tracy's performance reflects this internal conflict, as he tussles between the articulate composure of his recent performances as Drummond in *Inherit the Wind* and Haywood in *Judgement at Nuremberg* and the exasperation of earlier comedic roles, such as the

Fig. 13.1 John searches for clues as to Matt Drayton's 'kind of man'

flummoxed father Stanley Banks in *Father of the Bride* (1950). At the start, Tracy's expressions and movements are muted as he takes on what Joey called his 'American eagle face': the straight and still mouth, lowered head, and distant gaze Tracy often adopted to signal the thoughtful intelligence of his characters. The confident and composed virility is undone as Matt begins to feel overwhelmed and Tracy's performance becomes more mannered. Just as Matt's black suit and thick-rimmed glasses are removed, revealing an increasingly unkempt white shirt, Tracy exaggerates Matt's inelegance as he frustrates himself with his inability to drive, shave, and dress with ease, becoming emasculated by the situation.

Order is only restored during Matt's final speech. Assembling his dinner guests, Matt asks them to 'indulge […] an old man's eccentricity' as he begins his 'long climatic aria' (Rose, 1967, p. 109). Although divorced of their courtroom contexts and transposed onto a familial setting, the scene evokes the legal summations of *Inherit the Wind* and *Judgment at Nuremberg*. Positioned 'not simply as the object of all lights and looks but as the commanding subject out from whom everything else would appear to radiate' (Courtney, 2005, p. 289), Tracy holds the full attention of both the room and the camera which circles around his body and fixes the actor in close-up, his ageing face evoking both pathos and nostalgia (Fig. 13.2).

Fig. 13.2 Matt offers his controversial final speech

After earlier being accused, by John's mother, of disapproving of the marriage because of his own diminished passions, Matt stands to explain to his seated audience that he now realises, despite the couple's 'pigmentation problem', 'the only thing that really matters is what they feel, and how they feel, for each other'. Speaking of Christina, he adds, never quite allowing his voice to crack or tears to form, 'If it is even half of what we felt, then that is everything'. Despite the 'arguments that are so obvious' for not getting married, he urges the couple to 'cling tight to each other'. As Rose's screenplay directs, by the close of the speech, Matt again 'puts on his American eagle face' (Rose, 1967, p. 109), restoring equilibrium to the performance and returning to his authoritative, masculine composure. A point of fusion between Tracy's image as Hepburn's partner and Kramer's hero, romantic love becomes the agent of Matt's liberal heroics.

'An Artist's Epitaph'

Tracy's obituaries anticipated *Guess Who's Coming to Dinner* as an appropriate end to his career, believing it would be 'both bold and honest, modern yet reflective of the past' (Crowther, 1967, p. A2). However, the affection held for the liberal, paternal Tracy persona was tested once *Guess Who's Coming to Dinner* was screened for the press. The wealthy family, the infallible black suitor, the naïve, giggling bride-to-be, a marriage off-screen and outside the United States, the liberal patriarch, the prejudiced but attendant maid, and the colour-blind claims, at best, irked and, at worst, angered critics. Pauline Kael, Joe Morgenstern, and Richard Schickel, who founded the breakaway National Society of Film Critics in 1966 to challenge the authority of journalism's own aging patriarch (Bosley Crowther), all disliked the film. Many moderate publications also echoed their sentiments, finding Kramer's drawing room approach to racism outmoded by the Civil Rights Era's gains and the emergence of New Hollywood. Little wonder Columbia's guide for exhibitors topped its scant list of praiseworthy quotes to use in exploitation campaigns with the female-oriented *Seventeen* and *Redbook,* a far cry from the taste-maker periodicals Kramer long courted.[8]

---

[8] See Promotion Screening Manual for *Guess Who's Coming to Dinner*, undated, 7 pp., box 82, 'Robert Ferguson' folder, Stanley Kramer Papers, UCLA: 2–3.

The film's most challenging part for reviewers of *Guess Who's Coming to Dinner* was Matt Drayton's final speech. It was, at once, both Tracy's climactic moment on screen and the embodiment the film's reverence for the white, male liberal. A testament to the way the film unquestioningly endows Matt's class, race, and gender privilege, he tells Joey to 'shut up' when she tries to speak and confirms he is finished by gruffly asking Tilly, 'When the hell are we going to get some dinner?' Schickel of *Life* argued Tracy's speech was a rather shocking tirade but believed 'only Spencer Tracy could deliver [it] without making you run from the theatre with your hand clapped over your mouth'. His performance, along with Hepburn's, was, as a consequence, 'beyond the bounds of criticism' (Shickel, 1967, p. 16). Terry Clifford of the *Chicago Tribune* felt the final summation would have been 'nauseatingly sickening if attempted by someone else' but worked 'because of the marvel of the man' (Terry, 1968, p. C1). Likewise, Robert Kotlowitz felt Tracy's skill as a performer elevated the film, writing Tracy's 'forthrightness and spunky conviction almost made me believe at moments in the Draytons' agony' (Kotlowiz, 1968, p. 33). If this invested Tracy with unique abilities, it divested him of any relationship to the story, its development or its politics. In turn, reviewers overlooked the ways in which *Guess Who's Coming to Dinner* was anticipated and promoted as a 'gesture' of Tracy and Hepburn's 'personal idealism' (Champlin, 1967, p. D2).

As the speech culminates in an acknowledgement of his love for Christina, reviewers found it impossible not to read Tracy and Hepburn's subtly acknowledged relationship onto their characters. Contradictorily, the speech was deemed truthful in this regard and, as Susan Courtney observed, reviewers so tightly joined Tracy, his performance, and his role 'that sometimes it becomes impossible to pry them apart (Courtney, 2005, p. 288). In saccharine and hagiographic prose, Joe Morgenstern went the furthest, claiming that the 'melodrama's climax' became 'an artist's epitaph' and, when Matt admits his love for Christina, 'everything wrong with the film was right and we can see, through our tears, that the hero we worshipped was just what we always knew he was, an authentically heroic man' (Morgenstern, 1967, p. 71). Revealing his assumptions about the 'real' Tracy, Morgenstern felt, through Tracy's presence, Matt Drayton became a 'sincere, concentrated, honest man who might as well have been Spencer Tracy' (*Time*, 1967, p. 122). Thus, the nostalgia for Tracy transformed potential readings of the film in ways critics both acknowledged and denied.

The full extent to which critics engaged in a preservation project for Tracy only emerges in comparison to their derision of Kramer. With a general desire among critics to avoid criticising Tracy's character, and by extension, the recently deceased star, Kramer was exposed to criticism for his self-promotion as a liberal crusader akin to Rose's fictional creation. *Time* magazine felt that Kramer 'once again' proved his 'ability to put together cinematic bouquets of platitudes' (*Time*, 1967, p. 122), while *Life* felt *Dinner* was an 'antique' with Kramer 'earnestly preaching away on matters that have ceased to be relevant' (Shickel, 1967, p. 16). Quite simply, Kramer's reputation never recovered.

In their celebration of Tracy and dismissal of Kramer, critics failed to consider the extent to which Kramer's productions reinforced Tracy's heroic image; Tracy's final 'tirade' was in perfect harmony with his post-MGM work with Kramer. While reviewers celebrated Tracy's typecasting as a liberal hero, Kramer's depiction of John as a paragon of virtue came in for derision. Unconscious of the double standard that ran through their reviews, several critics celebrated Tracy's ability to transcend a problematic character type while, at the same time, criticising both Kramer and Poitier for the latter's continual appearance in 'show window Negro assignments' (Terry, 1968, p. C1).[9] This unequal treatment, however, was merely one of many contradictions within *Guess Who's Coming to Dinner*'s reception.

Conclusion

Writing in 1968, Robert Kotlowitz argued *Guess Who's Coming to Dinner* evoked the spirit of the 1930s, 'When we liked our drama cut like crystal, with no edges left unhoned to disturb us', concluding, 'We must have believed then that we could cure the world by making it tidy' (Kotlowiz, 1968, p. 33). Yet, later in his review, and, as I have demonstrated, in others, critics displayed their desire to tidy away some of the troubling implications of Tracy's final film. While a new generation of film critics were seeking to separate themselves from the tastes of Crowther and his peers, many echoed his sentiments. Although disparaging Kramer's 'antique' style of film making, it was clear they were not fully ready to question the deceased and, therefore, now-sacred star image of Tracy's golden-age masculinity or participate further in cutting the ties that bridged classic Hollywood

---

[9] Adler (1968), Hunt (1968), and Terry (1968) all critiqued Poitier's typecasting. Harris (2008) outlines the criticism Poitier's image faced across 1967.

and the emergent New Hollywood. Neither were the initial audiences: *Guess Who's Coming to Dinner* became the greatest commercial success of both Kramer's and Tracy's careers, exceeding $22 million during two years of domestic rentals.

Contemporary readings of *Guess Who's Coming to Dinner* recognise it as 'a film whose project is to maintain the white self in a time of racial struggle and change' (Vera and Gordon, 2003, p. 94). Still, a nostalgia continues to inform readings of the film because Tracy's presence lends it an 'added poignance' (Vera and Gordon, 2003, p. 87). Although Kramer enabled the endurance of Tracy's stardom towards the end of his life, consistently designing projects to emphasise his ageing image as a liberal hero, Tracy's status as a lasting star was, ultimately and ironically, secured through his ability to withstand his association with Kramer. We can only hypothesise whether critics would have been so willing to preserve Tracy's image had he lived longer. Still, *Guess Who's Coming to Dinner* remains a testament to the ways some star images are able to transcend associations and even certain texts, demonstrating how critics privilege certain stars and participate in enabling the endurance of their star images.

References

Adler, R. (1968, March 3). The Negro that movies overlook. *New York Times*, p. D1.
Alpert, D. (1962, November 18). Tracy: There are no kicks in acting. *Los Angeles Times*, p. A10.
Biery, R. (1932, December). 'Worry! who—me? say'. *Photoplay*, pp. 60, 97.
Bode, L. 2010. No longer themselves? Framing digitally enabled posthumous performance. *Cinema Journal* 49(4): 46–70.
Boys Town. (1938). Film. Directed by Norman Taurog. [DVD]. USA: Warner Home Video.
Captains Courageous. (1937). Film. Directed by Victor Fleming. [DVD]. USA: Warner Home Video.
Champlin, C. (1967, June 12). Final Scene for a Great Actor. *Los Angles Times*, p. D23.
Courtney, S. 2005. *Hollywood fantasies of miscegenation: spectacular narratives of gender and race, 1903–1967*. Princeton: Oxford University Press.
Cripps, T. 1993. *Making movies black: The Hollywood message movie from World War II to the Civil Rights Era*. London: Oxford University Press.
Crowther, B. (1963, November 19). Wild comedy about the pursuit of money. *New York Times*, p. 46.

———— (1967, June 19). A captain courageous. *New York Times.* Sect. 2, p. 2.
Curtis, J. 2012. *Spencer Tracy.* London: Arrow Books.
Desk Set. (1957). Film. Directed by Walter Lang. [DVD]. UK: 20th Century-Fox Home Entertainment.
Dyer, R. 1998. *Stars,* 2nd edn. London: BFI.
Edwards, A. 1986. *A remarkable woman: A biography of Katherine Hepburn.* New York: Pocket Books.
Father of the Bride. (1950). Film. Directed by Vincente Minnelli. [DVD]. UK: Warner Home Video.
Goodman, E. 1961. *The fifty-year decline and fall of Hollywood.* New York: Simon and Schuster.
Guess Who's Coming to Dinner. (1967). Film. Directed by Stanley Kramer. [DVD]. UK: Sony Pictures.
Harris, M. 2008. *Pictures at a revolution: Five movies and the birth of the new Hollywood.* London: Penguin.
High Noon. (1952). Film. Directed by Fred Zinnemann. [DVD]. UK: Universal Pictures.
Home of the Brave. (1949). Film. Directed by Mark Robson. [VHS]. USA: Republic Pictures.
Hunt, D. 1968. Guess who's coming to dinner. *Film Quarterly* 21(4): 58.
Inherit the Wind. (1960). Film. Directed by Stanley Kramer. [DVD]. UK: MGM Home Entertainment.
Inherit the Wind Pressbook. (1960) [Pressbook]. Stanley Kramer Papers. Collection 161, Box 32. UCLA, Los Angeles.
It's a Mad, Mad, Mad, Mad World. (1963). Film. Directed by Stanley Kramer. [DVD]. UK: MGM Home Entertainment.
Judgment at Nuremberg. (1961). Film. Directed by Stanley Kramer. [DVD]. UK: MGM Home Entertainment.
Kael, P. 1970. *Kiss kiss, bang bang.* London: Calder & Boyars.
Knight A. (1961a, October 24). Not with a bang or a whimper. *Saturday Review,* pp. 32–33.
———— (1961b, December 2). The producer-director at work. *Saturday Review,* p. 45.
Kotlowiz R. (1968, January). Films: The bigger they come. *Harper's,* p. 33.
Kramer S. (1951, May 13). Kramer analyzes the movie business. *New York Times,* p. X5.
Kramer, S., and T.M. Coffey. 1997. *A mad, mad, mad, mad world: A life in Hollywood.* London: Aurum Press.
Mahon, P. 2012. *Mrs. Spencer Tracy and the John Tracy clinic: A tireless drive to educate deaf children.* Jefferson, North Carolina: McFarland & Company, Inc.
Martin G.H. (1938, March). Spencer Tracy faces forty. *Photoplay.* pp. 30–31, 91–92.

Morgenstern, J. (1967, December 25). Spence and the supergirl. *Newsweek*, pp. 70–71
Newquist, R. 1972. *A special kind of magic*. New York: Pyramid Books.
Nochimson, M.P. 2002. *Screen couple chemistry: The power of 2*. Austin, Texas: Texas University Press.
On the Beach. (1959). Film. Directed by Stanley Kramer. [DVD]. UK: MGM Home Entertainment.
Pressure Point. (1962). Film. Directed by Hubert Cornfield. [DVD]. USA: MGM Home Entertainment.
Rose, W. (1967). *Guess Who's Coming to Dinner* [Script] Stanley Kramer Papers. Collection 161, Box 82. UCLA, Los Angeles.
Schickel, R. (1967, December 15). Sorry stage for Tracy's last bow. *Life*, p. 16.
Sklar, R. 1992. *City boys*. Princeton, NJ: Princeton University Press.
Spoto, D. 1990. *Stanley Kramer: Film maker*, 2nd edn. New York: Samuel French.
Swindell, L. 1973. *Spencer Tracy: A biography*. London: Coronet Books.
Terry, C. (1968, January 25). Sentiment of the '30s comes to dinner. *Chicago Tribune*, p. C1.
The Defiant Ones. (1958). Film. Directed by Stanley Kramer. [DVD]. UK: MGM Home Entertainment.
Promotional Screening Manual for 'Guess Who's Coming to Dinner' [Screening Manual] (n.d.) Stanley Kramer Papers. Collection 161, Box 82. UCLA, Los Angeles.
Time. (1967, December 15). Integrated hearts and flowers, p. 122.
Untitled Press Release of March 24th 1961. (1961). [Press Release] Stanley Kramer Papers. Collection 161, Box 38. UCLA, Los Angeles.
Vera, H., and A.M. Gordon. 2003. *Screen saviours: Hollywood fictions of whiteness*. Lanham: Rowman and Littlefield Publishers.

CHAPTER 14

Everybody's All-American: The Posthumous Rebranding of Marlon Brando

Lisa Patti

In 2015 Coca-Cola celebrated the hundredth anniversary of the Coke bottle by launching the 'Kissed By' campaign, featuring images of Elvis Presley, Ray Charles, and Marilyn Monroe drinking from Coke bottles and pairing the images with the tagline 'I've Kissed Marilyn' and similar captions. Coca-Cola is not the first brand to use posthumous star images in advertising campaigns, but its curation of these star images to demonstrate that 'Coca-Cola connects us across generations and across the globe through the simple act of drinking an icy cold Coca-Cola from the iconic glass bottle', as the Coca-Cola website announced (Pop Icon, 2015), points to the cultural and commercial value of posthumous star images. Brands may establish their relevance by invoking both their longevity and their (existing or invented) ties to legendary celebrities.

Posthumous branding serves as a critical entry point for the discussion of enduring star images because it allows advertisers to curate iconic images of stars and to juxtapose the star as icon with the advertised product. This attempt to create a visual connection between iconic forms is less stable when featuring the images of living stars whose future actions might undermine the value of their endorsement. Paul McDonald (2013)

L. Patti
Media and Society Program, Hobart and William Smith Colleges, Geneva, NY, US

explains the more durable realm of posthumous branding as an 'after-market' for celebrity imagery: 'With posthumous stars, the cultural historical value of legendary status finds an "after-life", or more appropriately an "after-market", as the dead star becomes the subject, or correctly the object, of enduring merchandising lines and other commercial opportunities' (p. 36). Select images of a star may be reproduced to market various brands approved by the star's estate and bolster the popularity of the star's own enduring image. In this chapter, I analyse one example of this phenomenon: Mastercard's posthumous use of Marlon Brando's image, among others, in their 2009 'Priceless' campaign. My analysis seeks to uncover both the ways in which commercials package and transform posthumous star images, and the ways in which star images circulate in tandem or in tension with these commercials, operating as independent brands. McDonald notes that for posthumous stars, 'of the hundreds if not thousands of images generated during the period of their lives, their visibility is largely limited to the reproduction of a small repertoire of key iconic images' (p. 37). This focus on a restricted number of the many available images of a star positions Marlon Brando as an exemplary case study because his long life generated such a vast archive of conflicting images while his commercial 'afterlife' circulates only a few.

The posthumous circulation of Brando images includes the cover photograph for the 2014 biography of Brando by Susan L. Mizruchi, *Brando's Smile*. The photograph, a 1952 studio portrait by Virgil Apger, shows the young Brando clad in a black short-sleeve shirt and black trousers, smirking as he reclines against a wall with his hands in his pockets. The selection of this photograph for the cover along with the selection of a photograph of Brando from the same period for the poster and other marketing materials promoting the 2015 documentary *Listen to Me Marlon* work to secure his status as a legendary star by suppressing the physical, artistic, and political elements of his on-screen and off-screen biographies that weaken the visual and discursive coherence of his star image. Images of Brando that capture his early beauty, his on-screen representations of working-class American masculinity, and his emotionally charged performance style proliferate, particularly those images culled from his films and public appearances during the 1950s. The later Brando recedes, dimming not only the public memory of his weight gain, his awkward and, at times, aggressive behavior during interviews, and his appearance in a string of notable flops, but also, and no less egregiously, his roles in international co-productions, his multilingualism, and his political activism. In other words, the endurance of Brando's celebrity today relies on the cultural interdependence of his physical beauty as a young man, his recognition as an early proponent and practitioner of 'the method' acting style, and his affiliation with characters and films that shaped the popular imaginary of 1950s American masculinity. My analysis of the posthumous rebranding of Brando begins by reviewing the critical assessments of his star image immediately after his death before turning to a close reading of the Mastercard commercial that presents a single image of Brando as a branding tool.

THE CRITICAL RECEPTION OF BRANDO

When he died in 2004 at the age of 80, Brando was canonised in a series of prominent obituaries as the greatest American actor or, at the very least, as one of the greatest American actors. Jack Nicholson's essay in *Rolling Stone* (2004) captures the reverence for Brando among actors: 'Marlon Brando is one of the great men of the twentieth and twenty-first centuries. [...] The impact of movies is enormous, and his impact in the movies was bigger than anybody else's—ever.' Other critical reflections present a more ambivalent assessment of Brando's professional legacy, veering from breathless recitals of the method-informed triumphs of his early films such as *A Streetcar Named Desire* (1951) and *On the Waterfront* (1954) to exhaustive catalogues of his critical and commercial flops like *Morituri* (1965) and *Christopher Columbus* (1992). One example of this tendency toward canonisation with caveats is David Thomson's essay in *The Guardian* in which he refers to Brando as 'the American actor of modern times' before noting that 'most of the film work he did was shameful junk, ill-chosen, slapdash and devoid of soul' and listing sixteen films that qualify as 'a lot of rubbish to clean out in the search for gold' (Thomson, 2004). These mixed reviews of Brando's career extend to the evaluations of his star image and its vicissitudes, tracking the fluctuations of his career and his body; as Thomson (2004) laments, '[H]e was a hulk, a wreck of obesity and self-indulgence, a hideously fat man—he who once had been so beautiful he altered our idea of maleness.' Thomson observes the centrality of Brando's physical appearance not only to his star image but also to shifting cultural 'ideas of maleness'. This link informs Brando's star image during both the early peak of his acting career and its posthumous renovation.

Read as a critical corpus, the obituaries capture a consistent sense of betrayal, with critics lamenting Brando's professional and physical decline as unruly expressions of his discomfort with fame and the industry that supported it. For example, Daphne Merkin's reflection on Brando's stardom in the *New York Times* describes her first glimpse of him as a moment of 'libidinal lightning': 'He suggested that it was possible for an image of male beauty to arouse the female gaze solely on the basis of the aesthetics of desire. Brando was more than a male pinup, of course, but in some ways his complex emotional articulation—his eloquently tongue-tied mixture of truculence and sensitivity—was icing on the beefcake' (2004). Merkin's description of Brando transposes the language of the 'pin-up' and the 'gaze'—terms most frequently invoked to describe female film stars—in order to emphasise the way in which his presence on screen commanded the viewer's attention while evoking desire. The sensitivity and virtuosity of Brando's performances in films such as *A Streetcar Named Desire* allowed the star to be more than just a pinup, shaping his star image with as much force as the publicity stills of Brando in jeans and a T-shirt as Stanley Kowalski.

The performances most frequently invoked by Merkin's reminiscence and other discussions of Brando's complicated sensuality—Brando's roles in *A Streetcar Named Desire*, *The Wild One* (1953), and *On the Waterfront*—form a charismatic trilogy that collaboratively define Brando's star image as anti-glamorous, reflecting a working-class white American masculinity operating in strategic tension with other representations of Hollywood celebrity as elite, detached, or decadent. While the characters of Stanley Kowalski, Johnny Strabler, and Terry Malloy travel in different cultural spheres, they share both a working-class social position and visual appeal presented, most notably, in their sartorial riffs on the uniform of blue jeans and a tight white T-shirt. Anne Helen Petersen (2014) notes that class and its representation through fashion were key elements of the version of masculinity that energised Brando's star image:

> The excitement concerning Brando's maleness was, in truth, over the working-class maleness he seemed to embody. This was due in part because the roles that would make him famous were so clearly marked as such (Stanley Kowalski; road biker; longshoreman), but also because the way he comported himself off the screen so precisely matched that image, all dirty dungarees and T-shirts rolled over the biceps. (p. 222).

She cites a *Photoplay* article that 'scornfully described his "habitual costume of Levi's, a T-shirt, and moccasins without socks"' (Petersen, 2014, p. 223). The consistency of Brando's on-screen and off-screen images in this phase of his career intensified the cultural impact of his star image, generating both the critical admiration of generations of actors such as Nicholson and the adoration and longing of fans such as Merkin. Brando became a repository for a set of intersecting romantic and artistic ideals, identified by James Naremore (1988) in his analysis of Brando's performance in *On the Waterfront*: 'He is a decisive moment in American cinema, one of those actors who represents a type so forcefully that it becomes a persistent feature of the culture. In effect, Brando gives his working-class character a sex appeal based on the same fantasy that would later make James Dean the hero of a young cult' (p. 205). By describing the intensity of Brando's representation of a type and defining Brando himself as a 'moment', Naremore suggests the difficulty of extending that working-class sex appeal beyond the moment.

Brando, of course, could not sustain that allure, and Merkin, like many critics who eulogised Brando in print, dwells on the transformations of his body as an unfortunate, extended coda to his cinematic prime: 'Toward the end, he seemed lost behind his bulk bewildered by the brutal turns his casually improvised life had taken, easily reduced to tears.' Most posthumous references to Brando's early appeal provoke a reference to his eventual decline in a call and response pattern that juxtaposes multiple irreconcilable images of the star. While the headline of Thomson's article proclaims that Brando was an 'icon of 20th-century cinema', the descriptions of Brando's appearance and performances in obituaries present an unstable iconicity, accumulating so many conflicting images that they challenge the idea of iconicity, not only for its clichéd overuse in relation to celebrities but also for its misleading suggestion of visual coherence and reproducibility. Unlike James Dean, who modeled many elements of his acting style and public persona on Brando and whose tragic early death permitted his star image—consolidated in relation to his role in *Rebel Without a Cause* (1955)—to remain a fixed image within popular culture through the present day, Brando lived a long and, arguably, messy life, filled with personal and professional disappointments that tarnished his initial star image. The image of Brando clad in leather jacket and jeans circa *The Wild One* would have been difficult to maintain through the decades even in the absence of Brando's weight gain, uninspired performances, and mercurial behavior.

The Perfect Pair of Jeans: Priceless

A 2009 commercial for the MasterCard 'Priceless' campaign resurrects footage of Brando from *The Wild One* as the visual complement to the tagline, 'The perfect pair of jeans—priceless'.[1] The thirty-second commercial combines the actor Billy Crudup's ubiquitous voiceover, David Bowie's song 'The Jean Genie', and archival images of an eclectic set of jean-clad stars (in order of appearance): Brando, Carlos Santana, John Wayne, Marilyn Monroe, the Ramones, and—once again—Brando. The commercial's voiceover ties the images together (although its application to Monroe is especially tenuous): 'One pair of pleated slacks: I don't think so./A pair of capri pants: Never in a million years./One pair of khaki shorts: Ain't gonna happen./The perfect pair of jeans: Priceless.' The shots of each star appear one at a time in a series, allowing each image to represent momentarily the individualism that the voiceover emphasises.

Footage from *The Wild One* both opens and closes this thirty-second commercial, while also becoming the most resonant image in the 'Priceless' 'Break in Your Jeans' campaign, a promotional contest announced in the commercial. Brando portrays Johnny Strabler, the leader of the Black Rebel Motorcycle Club in *The Wild One*, featuring one of the actor's most famous scenes, utilised in the Mastercard commercial. In the film, after Strabler storms into a small California town with his fellow bikers and they overtake a local bar, Brando leans against a jukebox, striking one of the male pin-up poses that Merkin describes so lavishly. Brando responds to a female character's playful inquiry, 'What are you rebelling against?' with the oft-quoted line, 'Whaddya got?' The line and the pose are central to the image appropriated by MasterCard. In the commercial, Brando appears as Strabler on his motorcycle, with the opening line of the voiceover narration printed across the frame, 'One pair of pleated slacks: I don't think so'. This line echoes the rebelliousness of Strabler, fusing his natural resistance to authority with fashion. Marlon Brando/Johnny Strabler—two figures known for wearing leather jackets and jeans—would not wear pleated slacks. Brando/Strabler would also have rejected the general celebration of consumerism advocated by Mastercard, but the commercial effectively tethers their rebellion to a rejection of conservative clothing rather than a rejection of consumerism itself. The commercial

---

[1] For a related discussion of Brando's stardom in relation to media archives, see Patti, L. (2010).

thus successfully rebrands Brando as an image of American masculinity and rebellion, circulating archival footage of the 'classical Brando' (the lean, reticent rebel) and muting the memory of the 'post-classical Brando' (the fat, irascible expatriate). The repetition of the footage of Brando as the opening and closing shots for the commercial insists on the image of Brando as Johnny Strabler as *the* image of Brando, a visual refrain that points to the broader recirculation of the image beyond the commercial.

The commercial's inter-generational appeal relies on the audience's ability to recognise if not each individual star within the commercial, then the cumulative cool of their combined star images. Brando's star image in this commercial functions both as a specific image (for those viewers who can access memories of Brando's performance in *The Wild One* and his other early expressions of cinematic rebellion) and as a generic image (for those viewers who may not be able to identify Brando or the film but who can identify the brand of masculinity MasterCard is marketing). MasterCard's 'Priceless Jeans' campaign offers consumers the reassurance that adventure and cool do not come with a high price tag, and the perfect pair of jeans is more essential to the visual construction of American masculinity than any luxury item. The constellation of associations that gather around Brando's star image in the commercial—American/white/working-class/masculine/rebellious—is particularly apt for an advertising campaign premiering during the early months of a global economic recession, when many viewers/consumers would have been hesitant to use their Mastercard.

The print version of the commercial features only Brando (officially consigning the other stars to supporting roles in the campaign) as he leans against his motorcycle in a still from *The Wild One*.[2] A bright navy-blue hue has been added to Brando's jeans in the original black and white image, amid a red and white background with splashes of yellow, fusing the red and yellow of the MasterCard logo with the red, white, and blue of the American flag. By importing this image of Brando into an aggressively modern graphic design, the print advertisement transports the young Brando into the present. Brando becomes a graphic emblem of cross-generational American masculinity, working-class consumerism, and corporate-mediated rebellion available to everyone, unburdened by the possibility of Brando's own critique of the ad campaign had he been alive to witness it.

---

[2] To view a color version of this image, see Young (2009).

The commercial's emphatic Americanisation of Brando, enforced by the juxtaposition of Brando and John Wayne, overrides the presence of star images whose identities complicate the reading of the commercial in relation to nationality and masculinity. David Bowie, Carlos Santana, and Marilyn Monroe each signify different modes of cultural rebellion. Despite his long residence as an expatriate in Tahiti, his multilingual forays into European co-production, and his outspoken critiques of American domestic and international policies, Brando emerges in the commercial as a symbol of sanctioned American defiance rather than international decadence. By detaching this footage from the ample evidence of Brando's commercially destructive nonconformity, MasterCard adapts the archival strategies of fan videos and other found footage films—namely, the construction of a digital argument through editing and sound design—in order to re-present the reluctant star as an image of American masculinity through consumerism.[3]

The MasterCard commercial's incorporation of found footage locates Brando at the intersection of two opposed styles of performance—personification and impersonation—and two distinct (yet increasingly imbricated) media forms—Hollywood films and television commercials. Barry King distinguishes between stars associated with personification—defined most succinctly as the overlap between star images and the performances that define them, resulting in the reception of those performances as versions of the star—and impersonation—linked particularly to method-based performances in which the star disappears into each role through radical bodily, linguistic, and affective transformations. King (1991) posits a line of influence from advertising to film that has an impact on the distinction between personification and impersonation:

> In contemporary times, the tendency towards personification may have increased with the advent of advertising as a field of employment, which combines naturalism with the sedulous cultivation of personal charm as an ingredient in the sales pitch. On the other hand, the self-referentiality of Method acting—the so-called personal expressive realism of Brando, for example—rather than representing the triumph of the actor as impersonator can be seen as a successful adaptation of impersonation to the pressures of personification, deploying impersonation to refer back to the person of the actor, the consistent entity underlying each of his or her roles. (p. 179)

[3] For an extended discussion of remix video in relation to the production of 'digital arguments', see Kuhn, V. (2012).

The MasterCard commercial places archival film footage within a commercial, blurring the vectors of influence that King describes, but his theorisation of the fusion of personification and impersonation holds. Brando is frequently cited as a star whose career exemplified impersonation, but the commercial harnesses that citation (and its accompanying implication of Brando's performative virtuosity) to a classic instance of personification in which Brando as star image functions as an immediately accessible visual signifier, suitable for mass reproduction and circulation. The MasterCard commercial selects one of the most potentially threatening images of Brando from the vantage point of the 1950s and chastens it through the transformations of the original film into a commercial, while also transforming Brando into a spokesman, and his style into a branding tool.

Conclusion

MasterCard's rebranding strategy counters Brando's outspoken resistance to the commercial exploitation of star images. While Brando discussed his uneasiness with the institutions of celebrity in multiple venues, interview footage from the 1966 Albert Maysles and David Maysles documentary *Meet Marlon Brando* reveals the depth of his ambivalence about the centrality of promotion, in all its forms, to the film industry. In interviews with journalists to promote the film *Morituri*, Brando makes little effort to conceal his ambivalence about the film, choosing instead to use the occasion to lampoon the ways in which film stars are expected to sell a variety of products, including themselves: 'I think we ought to say we're here as hucksters [...] People don't realize that a press item, a news item is money, and that news is hawked in the same way that shoes are or toothpaste or lipstick or hair tonic or anything else'—such as jeans. Using his signature coquettish charm, Brando criticises the conversion of actors into 'sellable items.' At every turn, Brando refuses the invitation to plug *Morituri*, discussing instead a range of unrelated topics—from the public ignorance of the obstacles facing Native Americans to the beauty of his female interviewers. Moving comfortably if not expertly from English to French to German during the series of interviews, Brando communicates his discomfort with celebrity without alienating those reporters who seek to mine it. The interviews are by any measure (other than the studio's) a success, failing to promote *Morituri* but managing, instead, to promote its star.

Brando's apprehensiveness about the commercialisation of celebrity poses a challenge for the managers of his posthumous star image. The trustees of his estate, working under the auspices of Brando Enterprises, recognize the difficulty of leveraging his star image as a marketable brand. In a *New York Times* interview (Ciepley, 2009), one of his trustees, Mike Medavoy, notes, 'He represents the traditional male, in some ways rebellious, but not all the way. [...] In Marlon Brando's life he always took pride in the idea that he didn't commercialize himself.' The article cites the opening of the Brando, an exclusive eco-tourism resort on Tetiaroa, the island that Brando owned, as one effort to capitalise on Brando's star image while investing in the places and causes that he most valued, a commitment that he nurtured until the end of his life. Fans may also visit the *Official Marlon Brando Website* where film screenings, awards, and other events related to Brando's career are announced, and, notably, where an image of the young Brando's face, transformed into a star logo, is available for sale on tote bags, buttons, and T-shirts.[4] Thus, although the site's store does not sell jeans, it markets the same star image that Mastercard mobilised in the 'Priceless' commercial. The efforts by Brando Enterprises to enshrine this posthumous star image reveal the difficulty of assigning posthumous authorship when analysing stars due to the status of the posthumous star image as both an extension of the star's performances and personas and the collaborative creation of the people and corporations who own the rights to them.

References

A Streetcar Named Desire. (1951). Film. Directed by Elia Kazan. [DVD]. USA: Warner Bros.

Christopher Columbus: The Discovery. (1992). Film. Directed by John Glen. USA: Warner Bros.

Ciepley, M. (2009, April 19). Protecting Brando legacy, trustees you can't refuse. *The New York Times* [Online]. Available from: http://www.nytimes.com/2009/04/20/movies/20brando.html?_r=0 [Accessed: 20 June 2015].

King, B. 1991. Articulating stardom. In *Stardom: Industry of desire*, ed. C. Gledhill. New York: Routledge.

Kuhn, V. (2012). The rhetoric of remix. *Journal of Transformative Works and Cultures*. [Online] 9. Available from: http://journal.transformativeworks.org/index.php/twc/article/view/358/279 [Accessed: 10 November 2014].

---

[4] The site is accessible at: http://marlonbrando.com.

Listen to Me Marlon. (2015). Film. Directed by Stevan Riley. UK/USA: Showtime, Passion Pictures, Universal.
McDonald, P. 2013. *Hollywood stardom*. Chichester: Wiley-Blackwell.
Meet Marlon Brando. (1966). Film. Directed by Albert Maysles and David Maysles. USA: Maysles Films.
Merkin, D. (2004, December 26). Wild one. *The New York Times* [Online]. Available from: http://www.nytimes.com/2004/12/26/magazine/26BRANDO.html?pagewanted=print&position=&_r=0 [Accessed: 10 November 2014].
Mizruchi, S. 2014. *Brando's smile: His life, thought, and work*. New York: W.W. Norton and Company.
Morituri. (1965). Film. Directed by Bernhard Wicki. [DVD]. USA: Twentieth Century Fox.
Naremore, J. 1988. *Acting in the cinema*. Berkeley: University of California Press.
Nicholson, J. (2004, August 19). Remembering Marlon Brando. *Rolling Stone*. [Online]. Available from: http://www.rollingstone.com/music/news/remembering-marlon-brando-by-jack-nicholson-20040819 [Accessed: 10 November 2014].
On the Waterfront. (1954). Film. Directed by Elia Kazan. [DVD]. USA: Sony Pictures Home Entertainment.
Patti, L. (2010) Husker, Huckster: The Archival Brando. *Flow*. [Online] 11 (14). Available from: http://flowtv.org/2010/05/husker-huckster-the-archival-brando-lisa-patti-cornell-university/ [Accessed: 10 November 2014].
Petersen, A. 2014. *Scandals of classic Hollywood: Sex, deviance, and drama from the golden age of American cinema*. New York: Plume.
Pop Icon: Elvis, Marilyn and Icons 'Kissed By' The Coke Bottle. (2015). The Coca-Cola Company. [Online]. Available from: http://www.coca-colacompany.com/pop-culture-elvis-marilyn-and-icons-were-kissed-by-the-coke-bottle [Accessed: 20 June 2015.]
Rebel Without a Cause. (1955). Film. Directed by Nicholas Ray. [DVD]. USA: Warner Bros.
The Wild One. (1953). Film. Directed by Laslo Benedek. [DVD]. USA: Columbia.
Thomson, D. (2004, July 2). Marlon Brando. *The Guardian*. [Online]. Available from: http://www.theguardian.com/news/2004/jul/03/guardianobituaries.artsobituaries [Accessed: 10 November 2014].
Young, A. (2009). Visa vs. MasterCard: Who's on the money? *Ad Age*. [Online] 2 December. Available from: http://adage.com/article/media/advertising-analyzing-visa-s-mastercard-s-media-strategies/140788/ [Accessed: 3 March 2015.]

SECTION 5

Characters, Series and Types

CHAPTER 15

Mrs John Bull: The Later Life Stardom of Margaret Rutherford

Claire Mortimer

Margaret Rutherford's film career was remarkable for her later life stardom. Whereas it is commonplace for ageing actresses to bemoan the shortage of substantial parts, Margaret Rutherford found that the reverse was true; as she aged her career prospered, making the transition from supporting character actor to international star. Rutherford's star appeal was based on the tradition of the comic grotesque, both in terms of roles which challenge normative conceptions of female ageing, and in terms of her physical presence. Indeed it was her physicality in terms of her bodily presence, performance style, and idiosyncratic facial mannerisms which lay at the heart of her enduring appeal as a comedy actor, evoking mythic figurations of the ageing female as godmother to the nation during a time of transition from empire to austerity. This chapter will examine Rutherford's persona within the context of discourses regarding ageing, femininity, class, and national identity, with reference to key roles in the course of her career.

Rutherford's Film Career

Rutherford was 44 at the time of her film debut in *Dusty Ermine* (1936), having established a reputation as a character actress in the West End. The late 1930s and early 1940s saw Rutherford in demand as a supporting

C. Mortimer
School of Art, Media and American Studies, University of East Anglia, Norwich, UK

character, with a tendency to steal scenes, before her breakthrough role as Madame Arcati in *Blithe Spirit* (1945). She became a familiar face in British comedies of the late 1940s and 1950s, before being contracted in her late sixties to Metro-Goldwyn-Mayer (MGM) Britain for four films as Miss Marple. Her international profile led to further Hollywood roles, including her Academy Award-winning performance in *The VIPs* (1963). She became a box-office draw in the United States, with *Variety* magazine welcoming the release of *Murder Ahoy* in 1964, noting that 'Good box office anticipated [...] The Rutherford name and series itself had developed fans. Result should be ready-made audiences' (Variety, 1964). American cinemas launched 'Margaret Rutherford weeks' to publicise some of her later films 'with hot milk and buttered biscuits available at her personal appearances', the accoutrements of old age, in contrast to the customary conflation of stardom with youthful glamour (Zec, 1972).

Many of Rutherford's roles were departures in defying normative expectations of the ageing female, and were characterised by expertise, resilience, and leadership, as well as being dynamic and distinctive characters in her guise as 'the eccentric'. Imelda Whelehan notes that the film roles available to mature women tend to be 'narrative function' rather than 'narrative fulcrum' with 'little engagement with representations of women who are beyond child-bearing years'. It was rare for ageing characters to have a role that is more than merely functional within a narrative, more so for the ageing *female* character (Whelehan, 2010, p. 171). Rutherford's career as an actress centred on performing old age. Indeed, many of her early roles were to cast her as older than her years. Her cousin Tony Benn was to note her talent for 'an affectation of senility' in contrast to the predominant 'affectation of youth when [most people] are past their best' (Macnab, 2000). With regards to Hollywood cinema, Anne Morey suggests that the female grotesque demonstrates a 'willingness to let the disguise of youth and beauty slip, to acknowledge difficulty and discomfort', arguing that such roles would therefore appeal to 'performers with feminist impulses' (Morey, 2011, p. 108). Contrary to the belief that such roles were demeaning for ageing Hollywood actresses 'presentation as grotesque was often an acknowledgement of an actress's artistic effort and ability to perform at the margins of conventional femininity' (Morey, 2011, p. 104). True to her persona as an eccentric, Rutherford performed at the margins of conventional figurations of female ageing, liberated and yet circumscribed by the codes of the comic grotesque.[1]

THE ROLE OF RUTHERFORD'S PHYSICALITY

Rutherford's appearance was a far cry from the glamour one typically equates with stardom, her features drawing attention to her age, and to an asexual persona. The importance of her looks is foregrounded in a 1964 BBC radio interview when she was asked, 'Although you have never tried to be a glamour girl, would you say that your face is your fortune?' Rutherford's answer is explicit as to how age and the grotesque informs her appeal: '[...]I have to admit that my five chins have something to do with it, and all the wrinkles I have.'[2] She was to find success in playing older parts, her physical appearance and performance style denying her the substantial roles written with a younger actress in mind. Critics and interviews highlighted the grotesque aspects of her looks: 'Her snow-white hair is cotton candy. Her bulbous eyes swivel in a deep pouch. The nose is impertinent, and her great fierce jaw is pillowed in an accordion of jowls. She has been called a "splendidly padded windmill"' (Time, 1963). Such descriptions accentuate the comic value of her appearance, although many of these features might be considered to be signs of ageing, such as her 'chin wagging like a windsock on an airfield'.[3]

Her comic appearance was further enhanced by her clothing, both in and out of role, which cultivated a period feel to her roles, verging on caricature of the ageing female, resplendent in tweeds and silks, cloaks, and voluminous bags. Her attitude to fashion demonstrates a dismissive attitude towards social expectations of age-appropriate dress: 'Who would have thought that a woman of 79 could wear a pink and orange patterned

---

[1] Mikhail Bakhtin identifies the grotesque body as being at the heart of the carnival spirit of Renaissance popular culture. He illustrates the grotesque with the terracotta figures of 'senile pregnant hags', who are laughing (Bakhtin, 1984, p. 25). They are grotesque in defying categorisation, in being both birth and death, 'on the threshold of the grave and crib' (p. 26). The spirit of the grotesque belonged to the world of popular festivities of the Middle Ages, and inform comic tradition.
[2] Interview with Wendy Jones, 8 April 1964, Today in the South and West, BBC; BBC Written Archives, Caversham.
[3] Alexander Walker reviewing Rutherford's performance in Murder, She Said, cited in Dreadnought with Good Manners (Merriman, 2009, p. 225).

summer skirt made from furnishing material as I do?' (Rutherford, 1972, pp. 216–217). Rutherford admired the fashions of the swinging sixties, believing that 'Fashions have become ageless' and proudly quoting Roy Boulting's description of her as 'the original flower child' (Rutherford, 1972, p. 216). In this respect her appearance worked to confirm the conventional and the archaic, whilst cultivating a sense of eccentricity in transgressing age-related norms.

Normative perceptions of female ageing were also challenged by Rutherford's frenetic and highly physical acting style, with her distinctive facial mannerisms and commanding vocal presence. An implacable energy is central to many of Rutherford's film roles, most notably the frenetic Madame Arcati in *Blithe Spirit* (1945), who waxes lyrical about cycling uphill, declaring, 'Just knack again. Down with your head, up with your heart, and you're over the top like a flash and skimming down the other side like a dragonfly.' Rutherford was a particularly dynamic elderly detective as Miss Marple, doing the twist and riding in a hunt in *Murder at the Gallop* (1963), and engaging in a swordfight in *Murder Ahoy*. In her role as Nurse Carey in *Mad about Men* (1954), Rutherford dived into a lagoon to pursue a kleptomaniac mermaid who had stolen her nurse's cap, refusing the offer of a stunt double.

This anachronistic energy and determination informed a persona which evoked fabled figures of authority and leadership. One review of her performance as the irascible head teacher Miss Whitchurch in *The Happiest Days of Your Life* (1950) describes her as 'looking like Queen Boudica at a difficult dress fitting' (Rutherford, 1972, p. 91), whilst Geoffrey Macnab likens her to Hannibal 'about to lead her troops over the Alps' (Macnab, 2000). Rutherford was uncertain about the role, comparing the headmistress to 'a trumpeting steam-roller' who 'flattened' her adversary, head teacher Godfrey Pond (Alastair Sim) (Rutherford, 1972, p. 88). She added that 'I had never before lent myself to a more disgraceful exhibition of ruthless feminism', wanting to distance herself from the character and her 'ruthless' feminist tendencies on the one hand but clearly being proud of the performance, citing a review which praises her performance 'as a headmistress before whom an atomic bomb might quail' (Rutherford, 1972, p. 89). Rutherford acknowledges this aspect of her persona in her autobiography, in stating her desire to be Jane Russell, for 'She has that elemental, savage quality which I simply adore. I think I have a little of that too' (Rutherford, 1972, p. 220).

The British Eccentric

Rutherford was held to be emblematic of a British type which harnessed the mismatch between age, gender, and traits. *Time* magazine described her as 'the ultimate symbol of resourceful, tweedily eccentric British womanhood, of the old gals who go stamping across the heath in the wild rain, looking for stuffed shirts to poke with their umbrellas' (Time, 1963). Her eccentricity was central to her persona, as promoted in wider publicity and press. One obituary listed her 'endearing eccentricities' citing how 'she claimed that she wore cloaks because they suited her billowing personality; when she wore hot water bottles under her cloak for winter travels, and [...] asked engine drivers to fill them up for her?' (*Evening News*, 1972).

The 'extraordinary' plays a key role in distinguishing a star from other performers. Rutherford's persona resided primarily in the confluence of eccentricity and otherness in contrast to the normative perception of stardom, which is configured around glamour and desire. Rutherford's persona resonates with the sense of being 'other', drawing on ancient archetypes which have defined female ageing, such as the witch, one critic describing her as having 'the air of enjoyment of an accredited witch whose magic has worked'.[4] The witch is typically delineated by characteristics associated with female ageing: she is a grotesque, whose appearance is as distorted as her behaviour. The witch is aligned with the natural world, at one with natural elements, being an outcast from the civilised world, roaming the countryside at night, preferring the company of her familiars to the human world. Rutherford wrote about how she could relate to Madame Arcati, as '[s]he was a wholesome woman who got down to business and worshipped fresh air' (Rutherford, 1972, p. 48). In a similar vein, Rutherford's autobiography reiterates her love for fresh air, 'wild' swimming, and walking in the countryside, sometimes at night-time and with her 'cloak flying behind' her (Rutherford, 1972, p. 66). Rutherford's persona, both publicly and privately, is informed by an eccentricity which deliberately cultivates a sense of 'otherness'.

The success of *Blithe Spirit* early on in her film career was to imprint Rutherford's persona with the eccentricity and supernatural powers of Madame Arcati. She playfully described herself as being inhabited by the spirit of the medium, as she assumed the character's habit of nibbling on

---

[4] Cited in *Dreadnought with Good Manners* (Merriman, 2009, p. 219).

cucumber sandwiches during her filming breaks, stating that by this time she 'completely identified' herself with the character (Rutherford, 1972, p. 51). Rutherford prepared for the role by visiting several seances, having initially turned down the role for fear of offending mediums, writing that 'though I do not entirely understand spiritualism, I feel that as many people take it seriously, I had no right to make fun of sincere professional mediums' (Rutherford, 1972, p. 47). Many of Rutherford's roles are characterised by having powers beyond the normal, or an affiliation with the supernatural or animal world, much like a witch with her familiars. In *English without Tears* (1944) Lady Christabel Beauclerk is an impassioned ornithologist, elaborately impersonating a nightingale in her opening scene; in *An Alligator Named Daisy* (1955) she plays a pet shop owner who attempts to communicate with animals using a trumpet and stethoscope; and in *Just My Luck* (1957) she plays the menagerie enthusiast Mrs. Dooley, who keeps an elephant outside the front door. In all these roles Rutherford appears to possess the ability to commune with the animal world, whereas in some of her other roles she has an innate ability to commune with the world of the supernatural and mythological, whether it be ghosts in *Castle in the Air* (1952) or a mermaid in *Miranda* (1948) and *Mad about Men* (1954).

The persona of the 'cracked old lady' was central to her performances, as eccentricity shaded into suggestions of a benign madness. With some of her characters this was manifested in a monomania: being obsessed with a particular cause or subject which drives the character on into excessive behaviour. Madame Arcati has dedicated herself to being a medium, her 'otherness' being figured in her total absorption in her calling, being heightened by the contrast with the urbane sophistication of her hosts, Charles (Rex Harrison) and Ruth Condomine (Constance Cummings). Indeed, Arcati is outraged by the suggestion that she is an 'amateur', seeing herself as a professional medium, whose whole life has been dedicated to her profession, having had her first trance when she was 4 years old.

The Older British 'Lady'?

Durgnat observed that the eccentrics 'glorified' are 'usually' 'upper-class in origins and either of independent means or firmly ensconced in authority [...] variations on old-fashioned father and aunt figures'. Rutherford's breakthrough stage role was as Aunt Bijou, a dotty old lady partial to betting on the horses to relieve the tedium of her existence in a crumbling Irish mansion, in the 1938 production of *Spring Meeting*.

The essence of this role was to be the bedrock of Rutherford's career on stage and screen: the eccentric ageing spinster, often an aunt figure, lovable and unpredictable, from the upper echelons of society. The spinster persona allowed the breadth to indulge the eccentricity that this status implies, in being outside the norm, although Rutherford herself was not a spinster, having married actor Stringer Davis in 1945. Biographer Eric Keown described Rutherford's persona as 'The universal aunt [...] emerging shining from her chrysalis, a rare and most lovable specimen' (Keown, 1956, p. 24). The character of the aunt suggests an unmarried older member of the family, a benign character whose single status has allowed her to develop an individuality—to the point of eccentricity. She is essentially a queer member of the family, who has departed from the normative life path for a woman, in not being married, or having children. Zoe Brennan argues that the portrayal of 'the old woman as grandmother/spinster is an extension of the virgin/whore dichotomy that recurs throughout Western culture', the grandmother tending to be a positive figuration, whilst the spinster is a 'demented and isolated woman, a "Miss Havisham" figure who lives in the past and cannot cope with the present' (Brennan, 2005, p. 2). The aunt allows for a confluence of these two figurations, which is particularly apt for its purpose as a comic character: lovable yet eccentric.

Rutherford's casting as the village spinster was a persistent aspect of her persona, embodying George Orwell's apocryphal image of Englishness: 'the old maids biking to Holy Communion through the mists of the autumn morning' (Orwell, 2000, p. 139). The figure of the cycling old maid symbolises continuity, timelessness, a sense of 'doing the right thing' as she wends her way to church. Roles such as Miss Marple and Madame Arcati located Rutherford within the context of the English village, as a spinster of the parish who dedicates herself to good works, an archetypal figuration of the middle-class, ageing, single woman. Her off-screen persona fed into this role, with press reports of her good works such as her 'mothering' of Borstal boys, presenting radio appeals for charities, and even presenting a religious reading on the radio for the BBC.[5] Russell Berman argues that the ideal of the village community contains 'a yearning not essentially for pastness but for a genuine community of pleasure, loyalty, and freedom, a charismatic community' (Berman, 1989, p. 122). In her guise as the 'village spinster' Rutherford embodies such a community, and

---

[5] Writing in 1956, Eric Keown decried the extent to which she was typecast by 'film moguls' as 'an eccentric parish-worker' (Keown, 1956, p. 31).

offers a figuration of 'pleasure, loyalty, and freedom'. Her eccentricity is animated by her status and behaviour, moreover the licence to be intensely distinctive and accepted.

The wartime propaganda comedy *The Demi-Paradise* (1943) cast Rutherford as village do-gooder Rowena Ventnor, a central role in the film's mission to evoke 'the traditional idiosyncrasies and foibles of the English' (*Kinematograph Weekly*, 1943). Her work is to dedicate herself to the community in the figure of the 'universal aunt', loved and respected by all. She is a commanding figure as she marshals the cast of the pageant, in her cloak and robes, brandishing a staff, barking out commands. Her role in defining Englishness is foregrounded, as she is represented as resilient and inspirational in her energetic commitment to organising the pageant. The mismatch of genteel female ageing and combative leadership is exploited for comic effect, the oddness of these characters being commensurate with their spinster status.

Rutherford's figuration of female ageing is circumscribed by a distinctive sense of national identity, specifically an upper middle class Englishness, which is redolent of Empire and Victorian values, a nostalgia for a supposed golden era of British supremacy and power. Being born in 1892, she was a relic of Victorian times, a child of the era of Empire, who could recall an early childhood in India. In her autobiography, Rutherford refers to herself as 'essentially English' and certainly cultivated this image in her public persona (Rutherford, 1972, p. 36). She portrayed herself as a creature of habit, who had distinctive rituals, having to transport her teapot, 'tea caddy and egg cozies' on overseas trips (Rutherford, 1972, p. 157). For the American audience, Rutherford's persona was structured around a figuration of quintessential Britishness, being described as 'Mrs John Bull' in a 1963 profile in *Time* magazine (Time, 1963). She is 'so British that by comparison with her, even John Bull himself seems the son of a miscegenetic marriage', her defining traits being a 'fresh-air fiend in sensible shoes who parries with her nose and charges with her chin. She likes to scrunch into wicker chairs and sniff sea air. She has average tastes, nonexotic pleasures'. In contrast to the lithesome ethereality of the likes of Julie Christie and Vanessa Redgrave, the emerging starlets of Swinging London, Rutherford off-screen is a figuration of British tradition and reliability being predictable, 'sensible', and unstoppable. This is the persona which animated her performance as Miss Marple: 'A formidably blocky torso stands draped in a regular tarpaulin of a sweater descending over a tweedy skirt of indefinite length [...] The effect is of a warmly bundled English bull-dog'.[6]

Bruce Babington observed that Hollywood tended to deploy British stars 'in ways that accentuated their Britishness (usually Englishness)', for whatever stars may 'mean in the larger cinema', with reference to Hollywood, 'they signify more complexly in relation to their original environment' (Babington, 2001, p. 22). In her later roles Rutherford tended to be cast as a relic of the British upper class by Hollywood— for example, as Lady Vivian in *On the Double* (1961) and the Duchess of Brighton in *The VIPs*. These characters were a distillation of a key aspect of British identity for an American audience: an affectionate caricature of ageing aristocracy, benign yet largely redundant, keying into a broader perception of Britain's declining potency as a world power. John Huston's perception of post-war Britain blames its decline on the ageing woman, ranting that 'The young Englishmen are all women-haters, because they live under a regime of terrifying old ladies, ruled over by a scarcely seductive girl guide. London's no city for men—it's a spinster's capital' (Durgnat, 1970, p. 185).

As Aunt Dolly in *I'm All Right Jack* (1959), Rutherford took this aspect of her persona to an extreme, in line with the film's satirical intentions. The character is true to the spirit of Orwell, who reflected that wartime Britain was a country which resembled 'a rather stuffy Victorian family [...] It is a family in which the young are generally thwarted and most of the power is in the hands of the irresponsible uncles and bedridden aunts' (Orwell, 2000, p. 150). One review described Aunt Dolly as 'impregnably smug and reactionary', horrified by her nephew's decision to betray his upper-class roots, and work in industry (*Monthly Film Bulletin*, 1959). She takes direct action in the face of Windrush's strike action, transported in her furs and chauffeured car to demand that her nephew cross the picket line and return to work. Youthful idealism and rebellion are suppressed by this Orwellian aunt, as he is caught in the crossfire between employers, unions, and even politicians, losing his girlfriend as well as his job.

---

[6] Melvin Maddocks in *The Christian Science Monitor*, cited in Rutherford's autobiography (Rutherford, 1972, p. 178).

Rutherford and Marple: A Perfect Fit?

Rutherford's performance of the role of Miss Marple made her a very different character from that envisaged by Agatha Christie. The figure of the 'universal aunt' casts her shadow over this role, as Rutherford recounts in her autobiography how Marple had been based 'to some extent on a little aunt of [Christie's] who in no way resembled me physically [...] a fragile, pink and white lady' (Rutherford, 1972, p. 176). Christie was unhappy about the casting, although the film's producer, George Brown, opines that 'Miss Marple in the book was nothing like so interesting a character as the character we could provide for the screen' (Merriman, 2009, pp. 231–232). The first film of the series *Murder She Said* (1961) was an adaptation of the 1957 novel *4.50 from Paddington*, in which Jane Marple plays a background role, judging herself too frail and elderly to physically carry out the investigation. Instead she sends for a younger friend, Lucy, who takes a job as a maid at the home of the troubled Ackenthorpe family, gathering information and finding clues, supervised by Marple from a safe distance. Christie describes Marple as 'an elderly, frail old lady [...] Although, for her age, her health was good, yet she *was* old', perceived by others as 'fluffy, dithery in appearance but inwardly as sharp and as shrewd as they make them'. Rutherford's energetic forceful performance of the role actually combines three characters from the book: Miss Marple, Lucy, and Miss Marple's friend Mrs. McGillycuddy, who witnesses the murder on the train. Rutherford's Marple displays the acuity and indomitable spirit of her namesake, combined with the practical skills and energy of the much younger Lucy. Her performance of old age dispenses with the physical shackles which hold Miss Marple back, making the character central to almost every scene of the film as compared to the withdrawn elderly figure in the book (Fig. 15.1). She demonstrates an indomitable physical ability which matches her mental energy, as she effortlessly takes control of the Ackenthorpe household, cooking, tidying, nursing, playing golf, even masquerading as a railway worker in order to scout the line for clues (and clambering over a high wall). The climax of the film involves her putting herself in danger as she lures the murderer to a confession, on the brink of being killed herself. Christie's Miss Marple physically withdraws and applies her wisdom from a distance, defined by her exemplary codes of 'dignified behaviour'. In contrast, Rutherford's Marple is wise but *refuses* to disengage from the wider world, making it a point to be everywhere and do everything she can to engage in her quest for the truth.

Fig. 15.1 Rutherford in *Murder She Said* (1961)

Rutherford's persona evokes the familiar and the ordinary, reprising figurations of the middle class, middle aged, or elderly woman which are instantly recognisable to the British audience. This is the persona which is also established in publicity materials, seeking to construct her as homely and contented, depicted in an armchair or her garden, yet her exceptional nature is established in details of her poetry reading tour of Europe and her energetic exploits, including scaling a mountain in Canada and 'having a quick "splasher" in Highgate Ponds' (Strutton, 1957). Ellis states that 'the star is present in the same social universe as the potential film viewer. At the same time the star is extraordinary, removed from the life of mere mortals, has rarefied and magnified emotions', creating a 'contradictory star image' (Ellis, 1982, p. 97). To this end, posthumous biographies, profiles and reviews have sought to emphasise Rutherford's tragic family background, her battles with depression, and her tendency to befriend various waifs and strays, including her biographer and 'adopted' transsexual daughter, Dawn Simmons. The interest in Rutherford has gone beyond her roles and fixated more on her personal tragic narrative, helping to perpetuate her fame beyond the grave, becoming the subject matter of plays, performances and autobiography.[7]

---

[7] For example, Timothy Spall's performance as Rutherford in the television play *For One Night Only* (Bilbow, 1993), Andy Merriman's *Dreadnought with Good Manners* (Merriman, 2009), being the basis for the BBC radio play *A Monstrous Vitality* (Merriman, 2011), and

Rutherford commented that 'in my film life I invariably get landed with edgy parts', in contrast to her private life where she was 'invariably described as "gentle", "ladylike" or "nice"—rather dull-sounding adjectives, I feel' (Rutherford, 1972, p. 87). She relished the 'nice meaty part[s]' she had been given.[8] Rutherford's flourishing film career was endemic of a wider phenomenon in post-war British film, identified by Raymond Durgnat, who wrote of 'British cinema's extraordinary difficulty, not in finding, but in developing, starlets, female, assorted, innumerable' whilst '[r]oles abound for such excellent character actresses as Flora Robson, Brenda de Banzie, Margaret Rutherford, Kathleen Harrison, and Thora Hird', before noting as an aside that this was 'in complete contrast to the equal and opposite Hollywood imbalance, all optimism, glamour and little character' (Durgnat, 1970, p. 185). Such character actresses enjoyed a longevity of career which eluded conventional stars, as ageing augmented their quiddity. British youth and glamour could rarely compete with the 'real thing', the Hollywood starlet, whereas the character actress articulated an authenticity and sense of nationhood cultivated by British film in an attempt to compete with Hollywood. Rutherford's performances offered pleasures of transgression, challenging the rigidity of social boundaries regarding behaviours related to age and gender. The socio-cultural climate of wartime and post-war Britain, combined with the generic framework of comedy, created the environment for her successful career in film, not in spite of her age, but *because* of her performance of age, gender, and social class.

References

An Alligator Named Daisy. (1955). Film. Directed by J. Lee Thompson. [DVD]. UK: Rank.
Babington, B. 2001. *British stars and stardom.* Manchester: Manchester University Press.
Bakhtin, M. 1984. *Rabelais and his world.* Bloomington: Indiana University Press.

---

more recently, Philip Meeks's play *Murder Margaret and Me* (2013), which dramatizes the friendship between Rutherford and Agatha Christie.

[8] Rutherford would reject roles if she didn't feel there was enough to them. She initially turned down the role of the duchess in *The VIPs* as she felt that 'the character [...] had no beginning, middle or end. There was simply nothing there for me to get my teeth into' (Rutherford, 1972, p. 192).

Berman, R.A. 1989. *Modern culture and critical theory: Art, politics and the legacy of the Frankfurt school.* Wiscousin: Madison.
Bilbow, T. 1993. *Without walls, for one night only: Margaret Rutherford.* London: Channel 4.
Blithe Spirit. (1945). Film. Directed by David Lean. [DVD]. UK: General Film Distributors.
Brennan, Z. 2005. *The older woman in recent fiction.* Jefferson, NC: McFarland & Company.
Castle In The Air. (1952). Film. Directed by Henry Cass. UK: Associated British.
Durgnat, R. 1970. *A mirror for England.* London: Faber & Faber.
Dusty Ermine. (1936). Film. Directed by Bernard Vorhaus. [DVD]. UK: Wardour.
Ellis, J. 1982. *Visible fictions.* London: Routledge & Keegan Paul.
English Without Tears. (1944). Film. Directed by Harold French. UK: General.
Evening News. (1972, May 22). The five famous chins of lovable Dame Margaret. *Evening News.*
I'm All Right Jack. (1959). Film. Directed by John Boulting. [DVD]. UK: British Lion
Just My Luck. (1957). Film. Directed by John Paddy Carstairs. [DVD]. UK: Rank.
Keown, E. 1956. *Margaret Rutherford.* Aberdeen: Rockliff.
Kinematograph Weekly. (1943, November 18). Kinematograph Weekly.
Macnab, G. (2000, July 29). A quivering lip and a blithe British spirit. *Independent: Review,* p. 11.
Mad About Men. (1954). Film. Directed by Ralph Thomas. [DVD]. UK: General.
Merriman, A. 2009. *Margaret Rutherford: Dreadnought with good manners.* London: Aurum Press.
―――― 2011. *A monstrous vitality.* London: BBC.
Miranda. (1948). Film. Directed by Ken Annakin. [DVD]. UK: General.
Monthly Film Bulletin. (1959, October). I'm all right Jack. *Monthly Film Bulletin.* 26 (309). p. 133.
Morey, A. 2011. Grotesquerie as marker of success in aging female stars. In *In the limelight and under the microscope: Forms and functions of female celebrity,* eds. S. Holmes, and D. Negra. Continuum: New York.
Murder Ahoy. (1964). Film. Directed by George Pollock. UK: MGM British.
Murder At The Gallop. (1963). Film. Directed by George Pollock. [DVD]. UK: MGM British.
Murder She Said. (1961). Film. Directed by George Pollock. [DVD]. UK: MGM British.
On The Double. (1961). Film. Directed by Melville Shavelson. USA: Paramount.
Orwell, G. (2000). The Lion and the Unicorn. In *Essays,* ed. S. Orwell and I. Angus. London: Penguin.
Rutherford, M. 1972. *Margaret Rutherford, an autobiography as told to Gwen Robyns.* London: W. H. Allen.

Strutton, B. (1957, October 9). Queen of comedy on a "stamper" to Australia. *The Australian Women's Weekly*, p. 3.
The Demi-Paradise. (1943). Film. Directed by Anthony Asquith. [DVD]. UK: General.
The Happiest Days Of Your Life. (1950). Film. Directed by Frank Launder. [DVD]. UK: British Lion.
The VIPs. (1963). Film. Directed by Anthony Asquith. UK: MGM British.
Time. (1963, May 24). Mrs John Bull, Ltd. *Time*.
Variety. (1964, September 30). Murder Ahoy. *Variety*.
Whelehan, I. 2010. Not to be looked at: Older women in recent British cinema. In *British Women's Cinema*, eds. M. Bell and M. Williams. Abingdon: Routledge.
Zec, D. (1972, May 23). Blithe spirit. *Daily Mirror*.

CHAPTER 16

This Never Happened to the Other Fellow: The Fluctuating Stardom of James Bond and George Lazenby

Jaap Verheul

Following the decision of Sean Connery to retire from the role after *You Only Live Twice* in 1967, producers Harry Saltzman and Albert Broccoli decided to cast George Lazenby, an unknown Australian actor and model, to play the part of secret agent 007 in *On Her Majesty's Secret Service* (*OHMSS*) (Fig. 16.1), the series' 1969 follow-up. During the film's production, Lazenby decided to withdraw from the franchise, expressing closer affinity with the emerging counterculture of the late 1960s, which he perceived as antithetical to the then allegedly outmoded British spy. When Lazenby thus attended the world premiere of *OHMSS* with long hair and a beard, he was criticized by the British press for his 'very un-Bond-like' appearance, which would come to define his only take on the Bond persona. Lazenby's performance was met with a mixed response, with some critics praising his physical presence while others disapproved of his poor acting skills and lack of charisma. If the character of James Bond became a lasting cultural icon over the past fifty years, Lazenby was consistently defined as the 'non-Bond', the one who did not fit the part, and the one to fill the gap left by Sean Connery and the then-unavailable Roger Moore.

J. Verheul
Department of Cinema Studies, New York University,
New York, United States of America

Fig. 16.1 Poster for *On Her Majesty's Secret Service* (1969) (courtesy of the Kobal Collection at Art Resource, New York)

Since the release of *OHMSS*, however, revisionists have increasingly celebrated the idiosyncratic qualities of Lazenby's performance. Compared to Connery's wit and self-assurance and Moore's cartoonesque campiness, Lazenby's dry and physical interpretation is now seen as a crucial contribution to *OHMSS*'s attempt to bring the Bond series back to the presumed realism of Ian Fleming's novels, as a precursor to the more grounded approaches to the Bond persona by Timothy Dalton and Daniel Craig, and as a signifier of the constantly shifting connotations of the Bond phenomenon. As a result, Lazenby's star image has been revitalized over the past four decades. Chronicling Lazenby's transformation from the archetypal non-Bond into the quintessentially modern James, this chapter argues, firstly, that star studies must acknowledge the failed production of stardom, and secondly, that Lazenby's reappraisal warrants further examination of the fluctuations in the star images of both actors and their on-screen personas.

BIG FRY HAS COME TO TOWN

Born in New South Wales, Australia, in 1939, George Lazenby moved to London in 1964 to become a car salesman. During one of his shifts, he was spotted by fashion photographer Chard Jenkins, who convinced him that he could make a profitable career as a mannequin. Lazenby soon became one of Britain's most successful models, and his appearance in television commercials for Fry's chocolate cream bars contributed substantially to his celebrity in the United Kingdom. If the popular advertisements for Cadbury, Fry's rival, had featured a Bond-inspired Milk Tray Man, Fry hired Lazenby as the crate-carrying Big Fry Man to offer the British audience, according to Roy Pierce-Jones, a more convincing surrogate for the Bond persona, for Lazenby's outback virility closely resembled Sean Connery's suave machismo. Consequently, Dyson Lovell, a casting director, believed Lazenby could be groomed for the role of 007 and suggested him to Bond producer Harry Saltzman. To prepare for his first audition, Lazenby ordered Connery's uncollected Savile Row suit and visited his barber at the Dorchester Hotel. Peter Hunt, the first-time director of *OHMSS*, was impressed by Lazenby's semblance to Connery and seized the opportunity to transform the untrained actor into a global icon of British masculinity (Pierce-Jones, 2010, pp. 365–366; Barnes & Hearn, 2000, pp. 82–84; Giammarco, 2002, pp. 94–96; Coleman, 1968, p. 5).

Hunt ordered Lazenby to collaborate with a vocal trainer to mitigate his Australian accent and to improve his proper British speech, while he tested his aspired idol for four months against four other candidates who were equally unknown to the wide audience and equally inexperienced when it came to acting. During the screen tests, Lazenby again impressed the director and producers with his rugged physique and fighting skills. Broccoli subsequently awarded him the role of 007 and offered him a seven-year contract that, in spite of Lazenby's reluctance to accept it, remained open to him until the release of *OHMSS* in 1969. When the new James Bond was formally introduced to the international press at the Dorchester Hotel on 7 October 1968, director Peter Hunt stressed that Lazenby's lack of acting experience constituted a minor detail only: 'He has many other attributes which I require. I am not saying he is an actor. There is a great deal of difference between an actor and a star' (Australian Non-Actor, 1968, p. D14). Lazenby's authority as the new 007 would be further undermined when a second press conference revealed that Lazenby's co-star and Bond girl, Diana Rigg, who was already an established celebrity in the 1960s due to her performance as secret agent Emma Peel in the popular spy series *The Avengers*, had signed a contract for £50,000 and would thus earn almost twice as much as the film's intended star (Pierce-Jones, 2010, p. 366; Barnes & Hearn, 2000, p. 84; Giammarco, 2002, p. 97).

Rebel With(out) a Cause

The rather derogative presentation of Lazenby mirrored the troubled production of *OHMSS*. After Sean Connery had announced his retirement, Saltzman planned to adapt *The Man with the Golden Gun* (1974) with Roger Moore. The political instability in Cambodia and the unavailability of the already well known Moore, who had just signed up for another season of the popular television series *The Saint* (1962–1969), nonetheless obstructed the film's further development. The producers consequently shifted their attention toward *OHMSS* and the casting of a new lead. From the outset, Broccoli and Saltzman had thus instituted Lazenby as a surrogate James who was neither Sean nor Roger. This, in turn, generated tensions on-set. An extensively covered feud emerged between the inexperienced and unknown Lazenby and the accomplished and celebrated Rigg, who, as Tracy Draco, would introduce a more independent and intelligent female protagonist to the mythology of Bond. In addition, Peter Hunt was more concerned with the film's elaborately designed action sequences while he also sought to distance himself from his lead to recreate the solitude that defines the Bond character in *OHMSS*. This lack of direction created animosity between Hunt and Lazenby, which lingered into the post-production process, when Hunt casted voice actor George Baker to dub Lazenby's performance as Bond's undercover persona, the London College of Arms's genealogist Sir Hilary Bray, for he regarded Lazenby's thick Australian accent irreconcilable with Bond's and Bray's Britishness (Barnes & Hearn, 2000, pp. 85–86; Giammarco, 2002, pp. 99–101).

Same Old James?

If *OHMSS*'s producers and director went to great lengths to question their new star, Lazenby did little to convince them of his suitability for the role. On-set, George acted as a prima donna, assured of his stardom because he was a successful model and had secured the part of the then globally popular Bond. 'I have made a happy discovery: I AM James Bond', Lazenby declared in 1969 (Watts, 1969, p. 1F). Yet, *OHMSS* concerned Lazenby's debut in the world of cinema, and his lack of acting experience and proven star power did not legitimize his celebrity lifestyle. The playboy displayed a similar level of arrogance during his contract negotiations. United Artists had offered their intended star a contract for seven years, which included a slate of productions to be realized between each Bond feature, but three months into the production, Lazenby had only signed a letter of intent, which augmented the producers' mistrust of their new 007. Saltzman's and Broccoli's apprehension was justified, for when United Artists urged them to reach a decision on Lazenby, the latter announced that *OHMSS* would end his tenure as James Bond.

Unlike Sean Connery, Lazenby did not seek greater financial compensation but, instead, terminated his affiliation with the series for personal considerations. In an interview with the *Los Angeles Times*, he expressed his frustration about the way he had been treated by Saltzman, Broccoli, and Hunt: 'They made me feel like I was mindless. [...] They disregarded everything I suggested simply because I hadn't been in the film business like them for about a thousand years' (Latest 007, 1969, p. 2). Furthermore, after his agent had advised him to leave the franchise, Lazenby also articulated his affinity with the emerging counterculture of the late 1960s. He publically rejected the Bond persona, identifying the secret agent as archaic in a liberated decade of anti-establishment, anti-imperialism, and non-violence. 'Bond is a brute', he announced. 'I will never play him again. Peace man—that's the message now' (James Bond Brute, 1969, p. 6-A). To further solidify his newfound rebellious stance, Lazenby appeared at the world premiere of *OHMSS* at the Leicester Square Odeon on 18 December 1969 with long hair and a beard, which, antithetical to the conservative conceptualization of the impeccably dressed and clean-cut James, not only added to his feud with Broccoli and Saltzman but also enshrined him in the public's imagination as the quintessential non-Bond (Barnes and Hearn, 2000, pp. 86–91; Giammarco, 2002, p. 102).

If *OHMSS*'s producers and director had positioned Lazenby as the non-Bond, Lazenby himself further contributed to this incommensurability by emphasizing his personal discrepancies with the Bond character. This dual incongruity informed, in turn, the semiotic level of Lazenby's take on Bond as well as the film's discourses of marketing, promotion, publicity, and reception. On the level of the film text, James Chapman (2007) argues, the introduction of the unknown Lazenby as the new James Bond constituted the greatest challenge for the filmmakers. According to Chapman, *OHMSS* deploys various textual references to emphasize its continuity with the Connery years. The most explicit allusion occurs at the end of the pre-title sequence in which Lazenby whimsically acknowledges that 'This never happened to the other fellow'. Chapman posits that this innuendo invites the audience to accept Lazenby as Connery's ineludible heir. 'While the film itself acknowledges that Lazenby is *not* Connery', he asserts, 'it is at great pains to show that Lazenby *is* James Bond' (Chapman, 2007, p. 114). Consequently, Miss Moneypenny describes the Australian macho as the 'same old James, only more so'. The filmmakers imply further continuity through the opening titles, which display the heroines and villains from the five preceding Connery entries, through the lingering theme music from those films, and through a scene in which Bond, while clearing out his office, stumbles upon some of the most notable gadgets from Connery's reign. These allusions, Chapman posits, suggest that 'while the actor may change, James Bond himself remains constant' (p. 115).

Yet this emphasis on continuity also casts Sean Connery's shadow over Lazenby's performance. What is more, *OHMSS*'s extra-textual discourses explicitly connected Connery to Bond at the levels of casting, production, marketing, promotion, merchandising, publicity, and reception. First, during the casting process, Saltzman, Broccoli, and Hunt made no secret of the fact that they were essentially scouting for a new Connery. 'We were looking for someone with the same sort of qualities', Broccoli explained. 'Lazenby is everything we hoped for and more' (Watts, 1969, p. 1F). Rather than deciding on an experienced performer capable of re-interpreting the Bond persona according to his own dramatic skills, they selected Lazenby because they thought he looked the part, for he physically resembled Connery and was not an established actor or star, which meant that he could be moulded to fit Connery's take on the character. 'I haven't a clue why they chose me', Lazenby declared during his presentation to the press in October 1968. 'It's probably because basically they wanted a person who will work with them, who hasn't got his own ideas' (Ross, 1968, p. G17). This desire to turn Lazenby into a surrogate Connery lingered into the production process, during which director Hunt required Lazenby to change his performance to resemble Connery's style more closely. Disillusioned, Lazenby would later identify Connery's enduring presence as a reason to abandon the franchise. Feeling 'a little embarrassed at being Sean's stand-in', he proclaimed that the producers and director 'were teaching [me] to walk like Connery, master the Connery mannerisms and the Connery style' (Arnold, 2006, p. A18; Wisehart, 1978, p. E23).

In like manner, the promotion and marketing of *OHMSS* minimized Lazenby's contribution. After Lazenby had announced he would leave the series after just one outing, he was removed from the posters for *OHMSS* for the American market and replaced with a silhouette, while his name was relocated to the bottom and subordinated to the real star of the picture: 'James Bond 007'. Hence, if the poster for *You Only Live Twice* staunchly declared that 'Sean Connery *is* James Bond', Lazenby's presence was reduced to the point of anonymity, made explicit in the posters that presented to the audience a new Bond without a face. The uncertainty over Bond's future appearance also cumulated in a relatively minor merchandising campaign. As one of the first global franchises, the Bond brand had relied on merchandising to generate additional revenues. Yet, when Lazenby retired from the role, Saltzman and Broccoli decided to limit *OHMSS*'s tie-ins to the soundtrack and the film edition of Ian Fleming's source novel, a decision that turned the few items produced for the film into valuable collectables on the fan circuit. Finally, Lazenby's decision to resign and to grow long hair and a beard only added to his friction with the production team. Consequently, Saltzman and Broccoli removed their new star from *OHMSS*'s promotion in the United States and replaced him with Diana Rigg, who had already become a household name overseas (Pfeiffer & Worall, 2000, pp. 74–75).

Announcing the arrival of a new, Australian James, the press also expressed its scepticism and incessantly referred to Lazenby as a 'non-actor', chosen only because Connery had left the franchise and positioning him as inferior to his Scottish predecessor. *The Guardian* introduced Lazenby as 'the man who is succeeding Sean Connery' while gently reminding the reader that 'the waiting showbiz reporters had difficulty in restraining their natural urge to chant "Big Fry has Come to Town"' (Coleman, 1968, p. 5). This derogatory attitude continued during *OHMSS*'s production and promotion, as journalists considered Lazenby's bohemian lifestyle as unprofessional and suggested that his behaviour had created conflicts on-set. When *Los Angeles Times* reporter Wayne Warga gathered with Lazenby two months after the release of *OHMSS*, he identified Lazenby as 'bearded, long of hair and about as un-Bond as one can get', confessing it was difficult to tell if the new James Bond deserved 'either a congratulatory pat on the back or a good swift kick on the back side' (Warga, 1970, p. D18).

Notwithstanding this antagonism, Chapman (2007) reminds us that the critical reception of *OHMSS* and Lazenby's performance was, contrary to popular belief, generally mixed rather than hostile, although the initial aversion by no means mitigated. 'I can't help missing Sean Connery with his saturnine mask and his flat delivery of the throwaway line', the *Sunday Times*'s Dilys Powell declared. 'His successor, George Lazenby, I find too amiable; one doesn't get the rasping indifference to danger which used to combine so happily with the sybarite's tastes in drink' (Powell, 1969, p. 36). The film's more mixed reviews commonly celebrated Peter Hunt's technical skills but persisted in their scepticism about Lazenby's take on Bond. Pauline Kael famously hailed *OHMSS* and its action thrills as 'marvellous fun' while referring to the new 007 as 'quite a dull fellow' (Kael, 1969). The *Boston Globe*'s George McKinnon similarly called the film 'handsomely produced' but still proclaimed that Lazenby 'has a bland manner which doesn't project from the screen with the rugged force of his predecessor' (McKinnon, 1969, p. 29). In spite of this vicious retaliation, some were also eager to defend the new 007. *The Hollywood Reporter* praised Lazenby for bringing 'new youth and humour to a role which had begun to look and act tired' under Connery's tenure (Chapman, 2007, p. 120). In like manner, the *Evening Standard*'s Alexander Walker also hinted at Connery's laissez-faire attitude and acknowledged that 'George

Lazenby is almost as good as James Bond as the man referred to in his film as "the other fellow"' (Walker, 1969).

THE NAME IS BOND

The mixed critical response signifies, on the one hand, the enduring influence of Sean Connery's performance on Bond's star image and, on the other hand, the fluctuating connotations of the Bond persona and its impersonators. In its 1969 review of *OHMSS*, *Variety* already envisaged this impasse as it asserted that Lazenby 'doesn't have [Connery's] physique, voice and saturnine, virile looks whose impact on the screen completely fused with the image of Bond with Connery. That image still persists after seeing Lazenby in the role' (Rick, 1969). Audiences worldwide reacted in accordance and expressed their disappointment with both the film and its already forsaken star. Yet Chapman (2007) reminds us that, while the film's box-office revenues paled in comparison to the five preceding Connery entries, it still emerged as one of the year's most profitable releases. The public and critical perception, which, since its release in 1969, had maintained that *OHMSS* had been an artistic and economic failure, consistently ignored this relative commercial success. Consequently, *OHMSS* and its Aussie were soon pushed to the margins of Bondology (Chapman, 2007, pp. 121–122).

Since the release of *OHMSS* in 1969, however, revisionists have begun to acknowledge Peter Hunt's refined film making and in particular the film's memorable action sequences, handsome cinematography, and razor-sharp editing, a trademark of Hunt, which also determined the distinctive pace of the previous Bond films he had worked on as an editor. In addition, Lazenby's performance, centred on his imposing physique, is now seen, firstly, as a grounded and visceral effort to bring the franchise back to its basics after the lush excess of *You Only Live Twice*, and as a vital reconceptualization of the Bond persona after Sean Connery had grown visibly detached from the rather one-dimensional character. 'Good as he was', Clancy Sigal wrote ten years after the release of *OHMSS*, 'I suspect Connery would have been incapable of credibility in the scene where 007 refuses to sleep in the snowbound farmhouse with his fiancée Diana Rigg' (Sigal, 1979, p. 8). In a 1994 editorial for *The Independent*, Martin Sterling also defended the Australian and argued that his performance, 'derided by critics as wooden, was, in retrospect, an object lesson in fluidity compared with the humourless stiffness of prevailing 1990s action-adventure stars like [Jean-Claude] Van Damme and [Steven] Seagal' (Sterling, 1994).

Secondly, Lazenby's take on 007 rejected, in retrospect, the cartoonesque campiness of Roger Moore's reign as the British superspy while it anticipated the more restrained interpretation by Timothy Dalton in the 1980s and the more physical rendition by Daniel Craig in the 2000s. According to the *Toronto Star*'s Mark Dillon, 'Lazenby got the role for his looks and credibility in fight scenes—the latter point giving him the edge on subsequent Bonds until Daniel Craig. And the fact that he wasn't a star allowed for a more vulnerable character that could fall in love and actually look scared when in danger' (Dillon, 2012, p. E6).

Thirdly, Lazenby's remarkable vulnerability, and the public's newfound appreciation for Bond's romantic sensitivity, also signifies the fluctuating connotations of the Bond persona. 'As notions of masculinity, of sex, and the relations between men and women have changed', Hal Hinson posited in the *Washington Post* in 1987, 'Bond has changed too. In some respects, his transmutations as a mythic figure over the years [...] are as reliable a barometer of those changes as any in the culture' (Hinson, 1987, p. F4). Indeed, due to these changing socio-cultural conventions, Lazenby's interpretation acquired new gravitas over the years. 'Lazenby's Bond is more cerebral than Connery's', Peter Howell argued in the *Toronto Star*, 'almost pretentiously so, and also more sensitive. He's a physical and sensual animal [...] but he's close to tears at one point and Rigg's very capable Tracy comes to his aid' (Howell, 2012, p. E1). In the *National Post*, Katrina Onstad similarly lauded the Australian's modern characterization of Bond's masculinity. If 'Connery's alpha Bond hit the screen in 1962, before the full swing of the sexual revolution', *OHMSS* 'reflected the shifting cultural moods', while Lazenby, 'perhaps without trying, captured the Bond blankness, all manly smirk and open, pansexual breeziness' (Onstad, 2002, p. AL1).

As a result of this threefold revisionism, Lazenby's star image has been revitalised. Bond fan Steven Popper stated that 'not only did Lazenby portray Bond convincingly, he also convincingly portrayed him in love' while managing 'to make the fight and action scenes believable' (Popper, 1994). Articulating a widely shared sentiment, Bond aficionado Ian Alterman declared in the *New York Times* that 'many Bondophiles consider Mr. Lazenby's single performance better than any of those of Roger Moore or Timothy Dalton. [...] All he had to bring to the role was his real self, his minimal acting skills and a zest for the Bond character' (Alterman, 1998,

p. ST5). Partly due to this newfound recognition of Lazenby, *OHMSS* is now the favourite entry of many Bond devotees, and the former Australian model has become a fashionable guest at fan conferences all over the world. Last but not least, the failed production of Lazenby's stardom has been constructed into an attraction in and of itself, and he is now frequently invited to give his professional opinion on the franchise, the choice of its lead, and his own failure to live up to the role. Moreover, his name has become synonymous with neglected and forgettable acting efforts in popular entertainment franchises, and it is thus no surprise that the *Daily Show*'s John Oliver referred to Pope Benedict the Sixteenth as 'the George Lazenby of the papacy' (Flanagan, 1996, p. D10; Odell, 2003, p. G37).

Fluctuating Stardom

Lazenby's initial failure and subsequent success has profound implications for the study of stardom. If Richard Dyer's *Stars* (1979) introduced semiotics and sociology to star studies as it focused on the social, institutional, and economic conditions of stardom, scholarship has since been dominated by a more in-depth investigation of the audience's engagement with stars and by a detailed examination of stardom as an industrial process. Extending these dominant strands, I want to argue that, firstly, Lazenby's case study demonstrates the further need to examine the failed production of stardom. If, as Paul McDonald has argued, 'star and brands serve the same commercial function—to distinguish between products while also preserving assurance by continuity', Lazenby's star image initially appeared incommensurable with the already well-established brand of Bond (McDonald, 2013, p. 46). This, in turn, warrants the second question of how to analyze an actor's star image when the on-screen persona—James Bond—constitutes the text's star and thus overshadows him. In the case of *OHMSS*, the destructive influence of Bond's star image on Lazenby's indicates the semiotic significance of the character-as-star, which is further complicated by the fact that the film's character-as-star— James Bond—had been constructed through the enduring star image of another actor: Sean Connery. In addition, the shift in public perception from Lazenby-as-the-non-Bond to Lazenby-as-the-Daniel-Craig-*avant-la-lettre* signifies the fluctuations in the star images of both actors and their on-screen personas. Indeed, on a semiotic level, the reappraisal of George can only be assessed in relation to Roger's jubilantly camp rendition of 007 in the 1970s and 1980s.

An in-depth examination of extra-textual factors remains important nonetheless. Lazenby's secondary position to Diana Rigg begs the question of how to analyze stardom when the text's intended star is subordinated to another actor or actress. In addition, Lazenby's rebellious stance is itself crucial to an understanding of his initially failed star image, and it merits, as Melanie Bell (2016) reminds us, a closer investigation of the agency of screen stars. Indeed, the bankruptcy of Lazenby's star image cannot be assessed without recognizing his own role in shaping and rejecting the Bond persona. Finally, Lazenby's newfound celebrity also reveals the audience's agency in constructing, rejecting, and reconstructing star images. As Paul McDonald has argued, 'Whatever range of representations and identities are available and circulate in the film market through stardom [...] emerge from the dialectical exchange between what the industry offers and what the audience chooses to pay for' (McDonald, 2013, pp. 39–40). The overwhelming commercial success of Daniel Craig's *Casino Royale* (2006) and *Skyfall* (2012) indicates that millennial Bond aficionados desire a 007 defined by emotional depth and raw physicality. Lazenby already embodied these qualities in *On Her Majesty's Secret Service*, and it is thus not surprising that both the film and its star resonate more strongly with millennial audiences than they did in the late 1960s.

While star studies have traditionally emphasized the influence of context on the meaning of the film star as text, George Lazenby's fluctuating stardom demonstrates that the dynamic semantics of the film text, and of the enduring Bond character in particular, also affect the social and cultural significance of the actor or actress as star. In the case of Lazenby, the semiotic, industrial, social, and cultural modifications to James Bond's star image explain the initial criticism and subsequent reappraisal of his impersonation of Britain's most illustrious secret agent. Indeed, as Martin Shingler has argued, 'Changing persona[s] demonstrat[e] the extent to which film stars occupy different relations with social groups and historical contexts as they age [...]. It also suggests that the process of identifying a star's cultural significance necessarily involves mapping the shifts that take place over the course of their career' (Shingler, 2012, p. 174). If Lazenby was, at first, dismissed for not being Connery or Moore, his transformation from the non-Bond to the quintessentially modern Bond reflects the fluctuations in both Bond's and Lazenby's star images. Now this never happened to the other fellows. Right, Timothy?

References

Alterman, I. (1998, January 4). George Lazenby as 007. *New York Times*, p. ST5.
Arnold, W. (2006, November 19). A common bond. *The Gazette*, p. A18.
Australian Non-Actor Chosen to Play James Bond. (1968). *The Washington Post*, p. 9.
Barnes, A., and M. Hearn. 2000. *Kiss Kiss Bang! Bang! The unofficial James Bond film companion*, Revised and Updated Second edn. London: B T Batsford.
Bell, M. 2016. *Julie Christie (Film Stars)*. London: British Film Institute.
Casino Royale. 2006. Film. Directed by Martin Campbell. [DVD]. USA: MGM Home Entertainment.
Chapman, J. 2007. *Licence to thrill: A cultural history of the James Bond films*, Second edn. London: I.B. Tauris.
Coleman, T. (1968, October 8). 007 Mk2. *The Guardian*, p. 5.
Dillon, M. (2012, October 19). The best Bond film? We have a contender: 007 Magazine recently affirmed On Her Majesty's Secret Service as the best James Bond film. It's not an outlandish claim. *Toronto Star*, p. E6.
Dyer, R. 1979. *Stars*. London: British Film Institute.
Flanagan, K.F. (1996, November 17). Double-O Heaven. *The Observer*, p. D10.
Giammarco, D. 2002. *For your eyes only: Behind the scenes of the James Bond films*. Toronto: ECW Press.
Hinson, H. (1987, July 26). James Bond, Agent of Our Fantasies. *The Washington Post*, p. F1.
Howell, P. (2012, October 20). Greatest Weapon is His Changing Face. *Toronto Star*, p. E1.
James Bond 'Brute', Star Gives Up Role. (1969, December 13). *The Miami News*, p. 6-A.
Kael, P. (1969, December 27). On her majesty's secret service. *The New Yorker*.
Latest 007 Seeking to End His Bondage. (1969, November 24). *Los Angeles Times*, p. 2.
McDonald, P. 2013. *Hollywood stardom*. Chichester: Wiley-Blackwell.
McKinnon, G. (1969, December 22). New '007' pretty good, so is 'Secret Service'. *Boston Globe*, p. 29.
Odell, M. (2003, January 19). It's Fame... But not as they knew it. *The Observer*, p. G37.
On Her Majesty's Secret Service. 1969. Film. Directed by Peter Hunt. [DVD]. USA: MGM Home Entertainment.
Onstad, K. (2002, November 19). In Lazenby's hands, he was the spy who loved series: James Bond. *National Post*, p. AL1.
Pfeiffer, L., and D. Worrall. 2000. *The essential Bond: The authorized guide to the world of 007*. London: Boxtree.

Pierce-Jones, R. 2010. The men who played James Bond. In *James Bond in world and popular culture: The films are not enough*, eds. Weiner R.G., Whitfield. B.L., and Becker J. Newcastle Upon Tyne, UK: Cambridge Scholars Publishing.
Popper, S. (1994, December 20). Letter: Believable Bond. *The Independent*.
Powell, D. (1969, December 21). A Bond honoured. *Sunday Times*, p. 36.
Rick. (1969, December 17). On her majesty's secret service. *Variety*.
Ross, M. (1968, October 25). He traded in auto selling for 007 job. *Los Angeles Times*, p. G17.
Shingler, M. 2012. *Star studies: A critical guide*. London: Palgrave Macmillan.
Sigal, C. (1979, June 25). Spy with a saving grace. *The Guardian*, p. 8.
Skyfall. (2012). Film. Directed by Sam Mendes. [DVD]. USA: MGM Home Entertainment.
Sterling, M. (1994, December 14). Licence revoked. *The Independent*.
The Man with the Golden Gun. (1974). Film. Directed by Guy Hamilton. [DVD]. USA: MGM Home Entertainment.
The Saint. 1962–1969. Television series. Created by Leslie Charteris. [DVD]. United Kingdom: Network.
Walker, A. (1969, December 16). Review. *London Evening Standard*, p. 36.
Warga, W. (1970, February 1). Movies: Why the new 007 gave up role after only 001 film. *Los Angeles Times*, p. D18.
Watts, G. (1969, April 6). New agent 007 says 'I AM James Bond'. *The Hartford Courant*, p. 1F.
Wisehart, B. (1978, September 10). 007 rises, falls, then rises again. *Chicago Tribune*, p. E23.
You Only Live Twice. (1967). Film. Directed by Lewis Gilbert. [DVD]. USA: MGM Home Entertainment.

CHAPTER 17

Don't You Forget about Me: Molly Ringwald, Nostalgia and Teen Girl Stardom

Frances Smith

The Simple Minds' '(Don't You) Forget about Me' plays poignantly over the concluding scenes of John Hughes's classic *The Breakfast Club* (1985) as the five teenagers, 'the brain, the athlete, the basket case, the princess and the criminal', finally part ways after their revealing detention. Viewers have certainly not forgotten John Bender's (Judd Nelson) fist defiantly raised against authority as he strides through the playing fields at the end of this transformative Saturday. To the—doubtless—bafflement of many present-day teenagers, the scene continues to be referenced in contemporary Hollywood teen movies, attesting both to the lasting resonance of the scene and to the unarguably pervasive trend for nostalgia.[1] The film's stars, too, have not been forgotten. Immortalised as the Brat Pack, these young actors, principally comprised of the casts of *The Breakfast Club* and *St. Elmo's Fire* (1985) were seen to embody the

---

[1] Despite being almost 30 years old, the scene features prominently in *Pitch Perfect* (2012).

F. Smith
School of European Languages, Cultures and Society,
University College London, London, UK

© The Editor(s) (if applicable) and The Author(s) 2016
L. Bolton, J.L. Wright (eds.), *Lasting Screen Stars*,
DOI 10.1057/978-1-137-40733-7_17

era's youth (Blum, 1985).[2] Nonetheless, it is Molly Ringwald, the star of three films either directed, written, or produced by John Hughes in the mid 1980s, who remains 'cauterised' by the decade (Lee, 2007, p. 66). Despite an eclectic and successful career encompassing jazz, literature, and journalism, in addition to prominent roles in film and television, Ringwald remains perpetually 'time cast', her image set permanently as an icon of the 1980s (Lee, 2010, p. 53).

Ringwald's status as an embodiment of the mid 1980s contrasts with the fortunes of Jon Cryer, Andrew McCarthy, and James Spader, all of whom played prominent roles in Ringwald's 1986 star vehicle, *Pretty in Pink* (1986). Indeed, all three of her male co-stars have since enjoyed successful careers in American film and television, in which their teen movie beginnings are but a footnote on a long and varied CV.[3] Conversely, Ringwald's female co-star, Ally Sheedy, the 'basket case' of *The Breakfast Club* and star of *St. Elmo's Fire,* remains primarily known for her teen roles. Certainly, Sheedy never possessed Ringwald's star power. However, their similar fates attest to a peculiarity of teen girl stardom, and potentially, the construction of idealised teen femininity that prevents successful transition into successful adult stardom. Although Sheedy and Ringwald have largely been permitted to age on screen, their cultural status remains firmly tied to a particular moment in the 1980s.

Owing to her popularity and enduring cultural status, this chapter will focus solely on the changing stardom and cultural status of Molly Ringwald. As such, I explore the nostalgic pull of girlhood and its ability to prevent a lasting stardom in womanhood. Two recent studies are significant in this regard: Gaylyn Studlar's work on girlhood in classical Hollywood cinema and Sarah Projansky's study of 'spectacular girlhood'. The former argues that female stars are 'juvenated', with their youth becoming the 'primary means through which consumers and subjects alike are addressed (Studlar, 2013, p. 6). In turn, Projansky demonstrates the unique symbolic potency of girlhood and argues that girlhood 'clings' to female celebrities who achieved fame during their childhood years (Projansky, 2014, p. 20).

---

[2] Blum's term has come to be associated with a wider group of actors than the journalist originally intended. The notion of a Brat Pack was coined as a result of a night out spent in the company of Judd Nelson and Rob Lowe, during which Blum watched the stars drink boisterously and pick up women. Brat Pack was never intended to encompass Ringwald. See Blum, D. (1985).

[3] Jon Cryer is a lead in successful sitcom *Two and a Half Men* (CBS, 2003–2015), while Andrew McCarthy and James Spader both maintain diverse careers in film and television.

This study of lasting stardom aims to elucidate the complex mechanisms through which Ringwald is perpetually constructed in a particular vision of 1980s girlhood. In order to do so, this essay will first examine Ringwald's stardom as established in her mid-1980s hits, before assessing the role of nostalgia and the symbolic power of girlhood in continuing to signify that same construction of youth in the present.

In order to gauge the potency of Ringwald's construction of girlhood, it is necessary first to examine her roles in *Sixteen Candles* (1984), *The Breakfast Club*, and *Pretty in Pink*, the three films either written, produced, or directed by John Hughes that first brought her to public attention in the mid 1980s. John Hughes, of course, is widely credited with the creation of the modern teen movie. Indeed, Timothy Shary argues that 'no other director has so thoroughly affected the way that young people are shown in films' (Shary, 2005, p. 72). For Adrian Martin, Hughes's works are distinct for their undramatic, even banal content (Martin, 1994, p. 67). Many teen movies of the early 1980s portrayed teenagers undergoing unusual adolescent experiences, such as a quest for greatness in the performing arts as in *Fame* (1980), or being the subjects of a gruesome murder in *Friday the 13th* (1980). In contrast, Hughes tapped into 'teendom's silent majority of average, middle-class, suburban kids' (Martin, 1994, p. 67). As will become apparent, Martin's characterisation of Hughes's work as portraying the life of the average middle-class teenager provides an important context in which to view Ringwald's construction of girlhood.

Ringwald starred firstly in *Sixteen Candles* as Sam Baker, a middle-class teenager whose parents have forgotten her birthday, and who is in love with Jake Ryan (Michael Schoeffling), who initially seems out of her league. A year later, in *The Breakfast Club,* she played homecoming queen, Claire Standish, whose detention revealed the paradoxical loneliness and vulnerability of that exclusive position. The Ringwald-Hughes cycle concluded with *Pretty in Pink,* with Ringwald as Andie Walsh, a working-class scholarship student positioned literally at the wrong side of the tracks. These films, and the constructions of femininity with them, were enormously popular at the time of their release, and undeniably possess a lasting cultural resonance.[4] One reason for Ringwald's fandom was the way in which she was able to embody a wide variety of teenage girls—from

---

[4]February 2015 marked 30 years since the release of *The Breakfast Club*, an anniversary that was celebrated with a restored theatrical release and a gala event at the SXSW festival.

working class to upper-class—and find pathos in each of their situations. That she did so in films released in consecutive years, always situated in the Midwest, America's heartland, allowed Ringwald to become a universal composite of American girlhood.

Ann De Vaney has been among the most vehement critics of Hughes's treatment of femininity as embodied by Ringwald, arguing that these films 'reinscribe domesticity and deference to male authority' as the rightful domain of femininity (De Vaney, 2002, p. 204). For De Vaney, then, these films can be regarded as part of a retrograde, backlash discourse. Other critics find a greater complexity in Hughes's depictions of femininity. Jonathan Bernstein's study of the 1980s teen movie singles out Hughes's films as the exception to girls' typical roles simply to 'display good-natured tolerance in the face of stalking, voyeurism or fumbled attempts at seduction (Bernstein, 1997, pp. 173–174). Instead, according to Bernstein, Hughes depicts girls 'railing against cliques and caste systems' (Bernstein, 1997, p. 5), and calling attention to the acute social divisions that were becoming increasingly apparent during the 1980s. Elsewhere, Anthony C Bleach highlights the contribution of Ringwald herself to Hughes's idiosyncratic treatment of gender and class (Bleach, 2010, p. 25). Notably, he observes that in all three films in which she features, it is Ringwald's characters who, regardless of their own class background, 'struggle within or against the class constraints erected within their narratives (Bleach, 2010, p. 25). As such, Ringwald's characters can be seen to contest, rather than uphold, dominant values.

Pauline Kael's description of Ringwald as an embodiment of 'charismatic normality' has provided an important touchstone for 1980s and contemporary commentators alike (Kael, 1992, p. 133). Charismatic normality can be distilled into three distinct features: vulnerability, moral uprightness, and authenticity. These attributes find echoes in what Gaylyn Studlar identifies as the persistent themes of juvenated stardom—that is, stardom that regardless of the star's true age, continues to communicate via the medium of youthfulness:

> the girl's anticipation of the virtues of womanliness [...] the need for the girl to grapple loss, victimisation [...] innocence as a counterforce to precocious sexuality and the demand that the girl be recognised for her emotional and cultural value. (Studlar, 2013, p. 236)

These qualities are found in Ringwald's characters in the films she made with John Hughes. However, her charismatic normality—and indeed, her status as a juvenated star—is expressed to its fullest potential in *Pretty in Pink*. Here, Ringwald plays Andie, a working-class scholarship student at a private high school whose vulnerability is demonstrated through her victimisation by the school's 'richies', who regard her as little more than a 'mutant'. Andie is morally upright in her care of her indolent father (Harry Dean Stanton) and when she angrily confronts Blane for having retracted his earlier invitation to the prom in such a cowardly and deceptive manner. Finally, her authenticity is expressed in the film's closing scenes, wherein Andie attends the prom, wearing a dress resourcefully crafted out of gifts from her father and her employer and friend, Iona (Annie Potts), neither sacrificing the character's subcultural affiliations nor her family ties. Hughes's films not only construct Ringwald as a figure of idealised, virtuous girlhood but one that corresponds with Studlar's conceptualisation of a construction of femininity frozen in time.

Both on- and off-screen, authenticity emerges as a key feature of Ringwald's stardom. On-screen, critics remarked on the actor's skills in realistically conveying her characters.[5] For his part, Hughes's direction and screenplays likewise contributed to the apparent authenticity of Ringwald's performance. To ensure that his scripts had the feel of real teen experience, Hughes spent time with his young actors, and talked to them about their hobbies, fears, and their tastes in music.[6] Ringwald, in particular, was key to Hughes's writing process, as he reportedly taped her photo to his typewriter as he wrote the screenplay for *Sixteen Candles*. As a consequence, Ringwald was widely perceived to be performing as herself in the characters she portrayed.

The correspondence between Ringwald and her characters, and thus, her authenticity, was played up in an interview given with Richard Corliss at the height of her stardom in 1986. Spending the day with Ringwald, Corliss comments on her family's 'modest, cluttered, comfortable', home and joins her for a trip to her local mall (Corliss, 1986, p. 68). His interview calls attention to the central contradiction of her stardom: Corliss attempts to paint Ringwald as an all-American 'everygirl', yet she had been acting since the age of six, and younger still, when she guest-starred in her father's jazz band.[7] Already a huge box-office draw and gracing the front

---

[5] See, for instance, Kael (1992), Corliss (1986), and Ebert (1986).

[6] One product of these discussions was the inclusion of the Psychedelic Furs' song 'Pretty in Pink' in the eponymous film.

[7] In 1974 Ringwald recorded 'I Wanna Be Loved by You', an album of Dixieland jazz for her father's band, the Fulton Street Jazz Band.

of a mainstream news magazine, Ringwald had yet to graduate from high school (Corliss, 1986, p. 171).

Ringwald's constructed authenticity resembles Richard Dyer's influential observation that 'stars are both ordinary and extraordinary', as representations of widespread social values, whilst at the same time exceptional to the majority (Dyer, 1979, p. 24). In an interview several years later, Ringwald herself attests to the disparity between her urban, travelled, acting lifestyle and the portrayal of ordinary, suburban adolescence portrayed in her films (Blackwell, 2012, n.p.). Tellingly, Corliss argues that the vulnerable, morally upright, authentic Ringwald embodies the 'exemplary California teen' (Corliss, 1986, p. 72). In addition to presenting her as an embodiment of idealised girlhood, Corliss's comments demonstrate the very constructedness of Ringwald's ordinariness. Aligning the star with California, Corliss positions Ringwald alongside a tradition of ambitious youth, whose aspirations can only be satiated by incorporation into the Hollywood machinery. In contrast, Ringwald's characters largely reside in the suburbs of Chicago, recalling Hughes's own Midwestern youth.

The cover of *Time* magazine, in which the interview appeared, attests not only to the significance of Ringwald's style, which she has since described as a poor imitation of Diane Keaton's androgynous clothing (Ringwald, 2014c, n.p.). Ringwald's style was widely imitated by hordes of 'Ringlets'. Indeed, Corliss is amused by a pair of teens who, seeing Ringwald at their local mall, assume it is merely 'one of those people who dress like her', rather than the real McCoy (Corliss, 1986, p. 70). On the cover, the strong orange/red hues are echoed in the shade of lipstick and the red frame of the cover. In turn, the delicacy of her white, lace blouse, recalling Victorian ideals of girlhood, are offset by her dark eye make-up and striking blue jewellery. Caught between feminine ideals of the past and the postmodern referentiality of the 1980s, this is the epitome of Ringwald's style, and it is echoed in her characters' costumes.

Costumes were one of the key elements that Hughes granted Ringwald control over and, as a consequence, her style is present in all three of her signature characters. Nonetheless, it is in *Pretty in Pink* where Ringwald's style is examined to its fullest extent. As Rachel Moseley notes, from the film's opening scenes, lingering close-ups call attention to the details of Andie's clothing (Moseley, 2002, p. 398). Ringwald's style is comprised of thrift-shop finds intermingled with her own creations and accessorised by copious jewellery. Her pearls, smart jackets, and dress evoke norms of conventional feminine dress of the past, while the clashing colours, patterns, and layers of her outfit create what Duckie (Jon Cryer) memorably describes as her 'volcanic ensemble', marking her clothing as excessive (Smith, 2013, p. 120). As a result, the character can be seen to play on the norms of conventional feminine dress. In turn, the film ends with Andie attending the prom alone, wearing a striking handmade dress of her own design. The pink, distinctly 1980s dress constitutes the guarantor of Andie's—and by extension, Ringwald's—vulnerability, authenticity, and moral uprightness.

Ringwald's idiosyncratic, bricolage style can be seen to correspond with what Kaja Silverman deems a characteristically 1980s tendency for 'anachronistic self-fashioning', or more simply, 'retro' (Silverman, 1986, p. 151). For Silverman, the wearers of retro fashion complicate the division between old and new, inserting themselves into a series of cultural and historical references that are invoked ironically, in quotation marks (Silverman, 1986, p. 151). The subversive potential of retro fashion was apparent in *Pretty in Pink* in which Andie and Duckie wore the fashions of the past to excess so as to effect an implicit mockery of the conservative values typically associated with the wearers of such clothing. Because there is such a clear correspondence between Ringwald's style and that of her characters, it is possible that a look back to ideas of femininity of the past is built into Ringwald's star image itself.

Both Ringwald's style and her authenticity have been central to her status as an object of popular nostalgia. Particularly significant in this regard is the star's lack of glamour, which is regarded as part of a tendency to 'do things differently then' (Freeman, 2014, n.p.). Indeed, Hughes's writing process described above, using no less an icon of analogue, hipster authenticity than the typewriter, speaks to perceptions of a past filmmaking age more attuned to the sensibilities of an individual than the focus group driven works that dominate today's Hollywood landscape.[8] In contrast to the teen stars of today,[9] journalist Hadley Freeman describes Ringwald as 'not skinny, not-blow-dried, not flaunting flesh' (Freeman, 2014, n.p.). However, just as Ringwald's styles themselves refer back to the past within her 1980s films, so to was the star's lack of glamour part of

---

[8] As fans of *Pretty in Pink* will know, however, Hughes was not immune from such influences. He reportedly changed the ending of the film in response to test audiences who wanted Andie to end up with Blane rather than Duckie.

[9] Freeman declines to name specific stars. Nonetheless, we might think of how Ringwald differs from Selina Gomez, Elle Fanning, or Chloe Grace Moretz.

her original star persona. In *Sixteen Candles,* Sam compares herself negatively to two tall blonde women, more typical icons of the silver screen: prom queen, Caroline and her sister, Ginny. In contrast, it's telling that Ringwald's suitors, Jake in *Sixteen Candles* and Blane in *Pretty in Pink* (Andrew McCarthy) both remark, 'Don't you think she's got something?' to which their less discriminating friends inevitably respond in the negative. Desiring Ringwald in these films speaks to the discernment of these male characters. In turn, she remains today an icon of Generation X hipster nostalgia.

The Ringwald-Hughes cycle was extraordinarily successful and cemented the image of both parties in the popular imagination. Nonetheless, feeling that she was now 'ready to graduate high school', Ringwald refused Hughes's offer to cast her in his latest film, *Some Kind of Wonderful* (1987) to pursue other, more adult projects (Meroney, 2010, n.p.).[10] Instead, she signed an unusually lucrative deal with United Artists, allowing her full control of the productions for which she was cast (Lee, 2007, p. 101). After cementing her credentials as a serious actor with an uncredited role in Jean-Luc Godard's production of *King Lear* (1987), the later 1980s saw Ringwald star in *The Pick-Up Artist* (1986), *For Keeps* (1988), and *Fresh Horses* (1988). These films, respectively, featured Ringwald's characters engaging in one-night stands, getting pregnant, and committing adultery in order to flee an abusive husband—a far cry from the plucky heroines she had played in Hughes's contained worlds.

These later productions were all released to a muted critical and popular reception. Nonetheless, writing in the *Chicago Sun-Times,* Roger Ebert praises Ringwald's 'natural' performances in all three films (Ebert, 1987 n.p.; 1988a, n.p.; 1988b, n.p.). Tellingly however, he comments that *The Pick-Up Artist* prevents the star's 'natural charm' from shining through (Ebert, 1987, n.p.). As Studlar points out, charm is a quality particularly associated with the juvenated female star (Studlar, 2013, p. 11). Indeed, Shirley Temple is frequently cited as charming the adults whom she encounters in her films.[11] To be charming, Studlar argues, is to

---

[10] According to an interview in *The Atlantic* (2010), Hughes was upset at Ringwald's decision to refuse the role of Watts, eventually played by Mary Stuart Masterson, in *Some Kind of Wonderful*. Ringwald felt the role was too generic, reminiscent of films in which she had acted in the past. Shary echoes Ringwald's criticism of *Some Kind of Wonderful*, describing it as a 'similar story [to *Pretty in Pink*] with the genders switched' (Shary, 2005, p. 74).

[11] See, for instance, Studlar's example, taken from *Stand up and Cheer* (1934). Temple 'charms the US Secretary of Amusement' (Studlar, 2013, p. 61).

be 'suggestive of qualities that create pleasure or satisfaction that is not serious, intellectual or important but pleasing, delightful and attractive' (Studlar, 2013, p. 11). Charm's valorisation of simple pleasure over qualities that accrue from experience and intellect indicate its specific connection to youthful femininity.

Ebert's comments on Ringwald's charm are symptomatic of the complexity of both the female star's transition between childhood and adulthood, and the particular space occupied by Ringwald in the cultural imaginary. Further, in continuing to describe the actor in terms that denote girlhood, Ebert's remarks can be seen to demonstrate the audience's reluctance to relinquish their perception of the star as a girl. Indeed, as stated previously, Projansky observes that girlhood 'clings' to women who achieve fame in childhood (Projansky, 2014, p. 20). Elsewhere, Susan Sontag argues that in contrast to men, for whom a wide spectrum of looks is culturally acceptable, 'Only one standard of female beauty is sanctioned: the girl' (Sontag, 1972, p. 107). As such, even while Ringwald ostensibly performs adult roles, she continues to be seen as citing the norms of girlhood. Indeed, we might go as far as saying that this is the only form of femininity that her audience will accept. Studlar cites Mary Pickford as an example of a woman who, having begun her career as a child actor in 1909, continued to masquerade as a girl throughout the 1910s and 1920s (Studlar, 2013, p. 13). Unlike Ringwald, Pickford's masquerades are clearly intentional, a way of continuing to mine a lucrative seam. Conversely, in the 1990s, Ringwald sought expressly to transcend her roots as a teen girl star.

The reluctance to accept the normal fact of Ringwald's transition to womanhood can be elucidated by the role of discerning nostalgia in her lasting stardom. In recent cameo roles, the significance of her appearance is only apparent to those who recognise Ringwald for her earlier work. In the TV movie *Since You've Been Gone* (1998) Ringwald briefly appeared as a guest at a high-school reunion.[12] Named Claire, the role is clearly intended to imagine a possible future for her character in *The Breakfast Club*. Three years later, a cameo in *Not Another Teen Movie* (2001) saw Ringwald play a sardonic air steward. Granted a moment of direct address to her contemporary audience, she remarks, "We all know where this is going. Fucking teenagers." As Lee notes, this scene allows Ringwald temporarily to break through from the past, as an adult, to supply a wry look at her image frozen in the 1980s (Lee, 2007, p. 94).

[12] I am grateful to Timothy Shary for this observation.

These cameo appearances notably coincide with Ringwald's return to the USA from France in 2002, and her resulting need to rebuild her acting career. She has since taken on stage roles on Broadway and the West End, established a fledging career as a writer, and released a further jazz album. Despite attempts to distance herself from her teen movie beginnings—by appearing in the press as visibly pregnant, for instance—all new projects are foreshadowed by her mid-1980s girlhood. Of course, Ringwald is at least partly complicit in this process. *Getting the Pretty Back* (2010), the title of Ringwald's first book, alludes to the actor's heyday, while her jazz album, *Except Sometimes*, features a cover of '(Don't You) Forget about Me'. In turn, her most prominent role of late has been in *The Secret Life of an American Teenager* (ABC Family, 2008–2013), in which she plays Annie Juergens, the mother of the lead, Amy (Shailene Woodley). Like her earlier cameos, this role too is a knowing nod to her teen stardom, since it acknowledges both Ringwald's former status as a teen star, as well as the fact of her ageing. Had the series been made thirty years earlier, it seems likely that Ringwald would have taken the lead role.

Since September 2014, Ringwald has served as an agony aunt in the *Guardian's Weekend* magazine, a position that grants her the opportunity to reflect on her 1980s persona and her status in the present. In response to a reader concerned that a friend is copying her image, Ringwald recalls the fans who imitated her own 'weird style' and advises the reader not to be too concerned (Ringwald, 2014c, n.p.). In another case, her advice to a mother convinced of the inadequacy of her son's foreign girlfriend prompts Ringwald, as an experienced elder, to recall her initially faltering relationship with her former French in-laws (Ringwald, 2014a, n.p.). This recent role, which allows her to assume aspects of both her past and present identities, can be seen to demonstrate Ringwald's increasingly complex relationship with her own past.

There is, undoubtedly, an element of misty-eyed nostalgia in Ringwald's recruitment as a wise confidante who can be trusted to provide sound advice. This, perhaps, is the role her virtuous protagonists provided for some teenagers. However, as previously stated, even at the very height of Ringwald's stardom, commentators noted an anachronistic element to her star image. Corliss likens her character in *Pretty in Pink*, Andie Walsh, to Andy Hardy, a clean teen played by Mickey Rooney between 1935 and 1946. As such, Corliss regards the virtuousness of Ringwald's persona as characteristic of the retro tendencies of the 1980s, wherein trends from earlier decades were repackaged for popular consumption. Lee agrees, arguing that Ringwald's characters contrast with the era's 'nihilistic consumption, corruption and hedonism' (Lee, 2010, p. 52).

Ringwald's ability to repackage gendered ideals from the past is likewise apparent in her idiosyncratic, bricolage teenage styling. As a result, Ringwald can be seen to be caught in a complex nexus of symbolic notions of girlhood, womanhood, and femininity. In contrast to Studlar's contention that the figure of the girl stands in for ideological continuity (Studlar, 2013, p. 19), Ringwald's contradictory image of youthfulness, virtuousness, nostalgia, and rebellion can be seen to demonstrate how, despite superficial changes to images of femininity, contemporary representations nevertheless retain powerful allegiances to earlier incarnations.

Molly Ringwald's stardom demonstrates the lasting symbolic potency of girlhood and the difficulty of the transition to a construction of womanhood. Ringwald's 'charismatic normality' presented her as an authentic 'everygirl' with whom millions of 1980s teenagers could readily identify. Nonetheless, her vulnerability, moral uprightness, and authenticity (best demonstrated in *Pretty in Pink*) recalled the Victorian ideals of femininity and that era's cult of the girl, to which many embodiments of girlhood in classical Hollywood are so clearly indebted. While Ringwald has aged, she has not been able to transcend her girlhood. As the star ruefully noted in response to a reader feeling alienated from her daughter, 'No-one is a teenager forever. Except me' (Ringwald, 2014b, n.p.).

References

Bernstein, J. 1997. *Pretty in pink: The golden age of teen movies.* New York: St. Martin's Griffin.
Blackwell, M. (2012, August 11). Molly Ringwald: Your former teenage crush. *The Observer.* Available from: http://www.theguardian.com/film/2012/aug/11/molly-ringwald-interview [Accessed: 25 July 2014].
Bleach, A.C. 2010. Postfeminist cliques? Class, postfeminism and the Molly Ringwald-John Hughes films. *Cinema Journal.* 49(3): 24–44.
Blum, D. (1985). Hollywood's Brat Pack. *New York Magazine.* 10 June. Available from: http://nymag.com/movies/features/49902/ [Accessed: 11 August 2014].
Corliss, R. (1986, May 26). Well, hello Molly Ringwald! Meet Hollywood's new teen princess. *Time.* 127 (21). pp. 66–74.
De Vaney, A. 2002. Pretty in pink? John Hughes Reinscribes Daddy's girl in homes and schools. In *Sugar, spice and everything nice: Cinemas of girlhood*, eds. F. Gateward, and M. Pomerance. Detroit: Wayne State University Press.

Dyer, R. 1979. *Stars*. London: BFI Publishing.
Ebert, R. (1987, September 18). Review: *The Pick-Up Artist. The Chicago Sun-Times*. Available from: http://www.rogerebert.com/reviews/the-pick-up-artist-1987 [Accessed: 30 July 2014].
——— (1988a, January 18). Review: *For Keeps.The Chicago Sun-Times*. Available from: http://www.rogerebert.com/reviews/for-keeps-1988 [Accessed: 13 December 2015].
——— (1988b, March 4). Review: *Fresh Horses.The Chicago Sun-Times*. Available from: http://www.rogerebert.com/reviews/fresh-horses-1988 [Accessed: 13 December 2015].
Fame. (1980). Film. Directed by Alan Parker. [DVD]. USA: MGM.
For Keeps. (1988). Film. Directed by John G Avilden. [DVD]. USA: TriStar Pictures.
Friday the 13th. (1980). Film. Directed by Sean S. Cunningham. [DVD]. USA: Paramount Pictures.
Freeman, H. (2014, July 21). Why I'd like to be ... Molly Ringwald in *Pretty in Pink. The Guardian*. Available from: http://www.theguardian.com/film/filmblog/2014/jul/21/molly-ringwald-pretty-in-pink-role-model [Accessed: 25 July 2014].
Fresh Horses. (1988). Film. Directed by David Anspaugh. [DVD]. USA: Weintraub Entertainment Group.
Kael, P. 1992. *Hooked: Film Writings 1985–1988*. New York: Marion Boyers Publishers.
King Lear. (1987). Film. Directed by Jean-Luc Godard. [DVD]. USA: Cannon Group.
Lee, C. 2007. Going nowhere? The politics of remembering and forgetting Molly Ringwald. *Cultural Studies Review*. 13(1): 89–104.
——— 2010. *Screening generation X: The politics and popular memory of youth in contemporary cinema*. Aldershot: Ashgate.
Martin, A. 1994. *Phantasms: The dreams and desires at the heart of our popular culture*. Melbourne: McPhee Gribble.
Meroney, J. (2010, August 19) Molly Ringwald's revealing interview on John Hughes, not being Lindsay Lohan and more. *The Atlantic*. Available from: http://www.theatlantic.com/entertainment/archive/2010/08/molly-ringwalds-revealing-interview-on-john-hughes-not-being-lindsay-lohan-and-more/61085 [Accessed: 2 August 2014].
Moseley, R. 2002. Glamorous Witchcraft: gender and magic in teen film and television. *Screen*. 43(4): 403–422.
Not Another Teen Movie. (2001). Film. Directed by Joel Gallen. [DVD]. USA: Columbia Pictures.
Pitch Perfect. (2012). Film. Directed by Jason Moore. [DVD]. USA: Brownstone Productions.
Pretty in Pink. (1986). Film. Directed by Howard Deutch. [DVD]. USA: Paramount Pictures.

Projansky, S. 2014. *Spectacular girls: Media fascination and celebrity culture.* New York: New York University Press.

Ringwald, M. 2010. *Getting the pretty back: Friendship, family and finding the perfect lipstick.* New York: It Books.

—— (2014a, October 3). Ask Molly Ringwald: My son's dating the wrong woman. *The Guardian.* Available from: http://www.theguardian.com/lifeandstyle/2014/oct/03/worried-about-sons-relationship-ask-molly-ringwald [Accessed: 8 January 2015].

—— (2014b, October 17). Ask Molly Ringwald: My daughter loves celebrities and shopping. I don't. *The Guardian.* Available from: http://www.theguardian.com/lifeandstyle/2014/oct/17/my-daughter-likes-celebrities-shopping-ask-molly-ringwald [Accessed: 8 January 2015].

—— (2014c, November 28). Ask Molly Ringwald: My friend keeps copying me. Do I let her steal my identity? *The Guardian.* Available from: http://www.theguardian.com/lifeandstyle/2014/nov/28/ask-molly-ringwald-friend-copying-steal-identity [Accessed: 8 January 2015].

Shary, T. 2005. *Teen movies: American youth on screen.* London: Wallflower Press.

Silverman, K. 1986. Fragments of a fashionable discourse. In *Studies in entertainment: Critical approaches to mass culture*, ed. T. Modleski. Bloomington: Indiana University Press.

Since You've Been Gone. (1998). Film. Directed by David Schwimmer. [DVD]. USA: Miramax Pictures.

Sixteen Candles. (1984). Film. Directed by John Hughes. [DVD]. USA: Channel Productions.

Smith, F. 2013. 'Rethinking the Norm: Judith Butler and the Hollywood Teen Movie.' Unpublished PhD Thesis. University of Warwick, UK.

Some Kind of Wonderful. (1987). Film. Directed by Howard Deutch. [DVD]. USA: Paramount Pictures.

Sontag, S. (1972, September 23). The double standard of aging. *The Saturday Review.* pp. 29–38.

Stand Up and Cheer. (1934). Film. Directed by Hamilton MacFadden. [DVD]. USA: Fox Film.

St Elmo's Fire. (1985). Film. Directed by Joel Schumacher. [DVD]. USA: Sony Pictures Home Entertainment.

Studlar, G. 2013. *Precocious charms: Stars performing girlhood in classical Hollywood cinema.* Berkeley: University of California Press.

The Breakfast Club. (1985). Film. Directed by John Hughes. [DVD]. USA: Distributor.

The Pick-Up Artist. (1986). Film. Directed by James Toback. [DVD]. USA: Amercent Films.

The Secret Life of an American Teenager. (2008–2013). ABC Family.

Two and a Half Men. (2003–2015). CBS.

CHAPTER 18

Redundancy and Ageing: Sylvester Stallone's Enduring Action Star Image

Glen Donnar

Sylvester Stallone's star image extends across five decades, since his authorial breakthrough in *Rocky* (1976), with its emblematic features including his iconicity as an action star and association with hypermasculinity, hyperbolic (bodily) spectacle, and monosyllabic mumbling. Broadly speaking, Stallone's stardom grew from the mid 1970s until 1990 as a star, screenwriter, and director of five *Rocky* films and star of the *Rambo* series. In the first half of the 1990s he relinquished writing and direction, appearing merely as an action star in a series of progressively less successful action blockbusters, including *Judge Dredd* (1995) and *Assassins* (1995). After Stallone attempted to shift his star image by playing against type in the late 1990s in films such as *Cop Land* (1997), his 'lean period' stretched through the early 2000s as he struggled to interest audiences in characters that acknowledged their advancing age. However, Stallone's vaunted (and perhaps desperate) return to his early franchises from the mid 2000s and the surprising subsequent success of *The Expendables* series since 2010 have unexpectedly extended his stardom.

Thank you to Chris Holmlund for early conversations and encouragement in the formation of the essay.

G. Donnar
School of Media and Communication, RMIT University, Melbourne, UK

Stallone's career also includes an explicit, self-reflexive engagement with his star image and filmography, and the genres and tropes with which he is most associated. This self-reflexivity is integral to his endurance as a screen and cultural icon. His recent revival in *The Expendables* series (2010, 2012, 2014) and the mid-2000s franchise returns to his most defining characters, Rocky Balboa and John Rambo, reiterate and cultivate this engagement, numerously restaging and reworking iconic moments, catchphrases and music. This is not a new phenomenon, however, as Stallone makes playful self-referential jokes about Rambo all the way back to *Tango and Cash* (1989), in which he plays a fashion-conscious narcotics detective, Ray Tango and states, 'Rambo is a pussy'. Despite this, and *The Expendables*' knowing levity and recycled catchphrases, Stallone's engagement has often been serious and earnest, exemplified in not only Rocky's repeated return to the steps of Philadelphia's Museum of Art, such as in *Rocky II* (1979) but also in documentary footage that accompanies the end credits of *Rocky Balboa* (2006) of the innumerable fans who spontaneously re-enact the iconic filmic moment. A key part of Stallone's longevity is linked to production and exhibition trends that continue to favour sequels and franchises—a feature of his stardom that he conspicuously (and unsuccessfully) avoided during his 'lean period'—and amplify the nostalgia associated with his franchise revivals and the intensified self-reflexivity of the all-star collective *Expendables* films. Audience nostalgia certainly appears a core reason for *The Expendables*' success, as Chris Holmlund (2014) identifies, especially in light of the commercial and critical failures of subsequent solo, non-franchise outings. All testify to Stallone's lasting cultural significance but equally expose persistent anxieties about redundancy and ageing that have always shaped his star image.

Stallone's multifaceted involvement in his films and star image remains under-appreciated, as Holmlund (2014) observes in *The Ultimate Stallone Reader*, specifically employing an auteurist perspective to analyse Stallone's importance and interrogate his star image. This shaping and control of his star image through his screenwriting and direction is long-standing, from writing and directing throughout the *Rocky* and *Rambo* series to directing *Rocky Balboa* and the first *The Expendables*. Paul Ramaeker (2014) also asserts Stallone's endurance is equally tied to his capacity to adopt and adapt to changed contemporary action styles. In short, Stallone's cultural-cinematic iconicity, his generic and star self-reflexivity, and his authorial status and control all contribute to the longevity of his stardom. However, associated with discourses of redundancy in relation to 1980s action stars and the newly minted 'geri-action' subgenre, Stallone's late commercial resuscitation demands that we review, rethink and perhaps recast his overall star persona and reasons for its laudable longevity. I contend that Stallone's late revival in 'geri-action' and his famed film franchises rather than superficially appending notions of redundancy and ageing onto his action star identity, actually reveals the integral and long-standing importance of each to his star image since the mid 1970s and early 1980s, generically as an action star performer and narratively via culturally and professionally redundant and aged characters.

Despite acting, writing, and directing across a diverse range of genres, including romantic comedy and musicals, Stallone's star image is indelibly defined by, if not equated with, action stardom, and most particularly, in action, sports, and war films. Indeed, considerations of Stallone's enduring action star image routinely focus on what Tasker (1993) terms 'muscular cinema', a body of 1980s action films that showcase and celebrate the hyperbolic muscularity of their stars, most notably starring Stallone and Arnold Schwarzenegger. Stallone's 'hard-bodied' persona (Jeffords, 1994) is also consistently linked to Reagan-era American culture, politics, and foreign policy, associated with the desire to 'remasculinise' Cold War America, post-Vietnam. Stallone's films also represent the vanguard of the cultural counter to perceived threats to white male hegemony following post-1960s cultural shifts and 1970s economic instability. Elmwood (2005), for example, asserts that *Rocky* (1976) complexly counters various emasculating economic and cultural impacts, in the awkward 'mutual remasculinisation' of elevated white masculinity and preservation of African American advances (while reaffirming traditional gender values). Gallagher (2006, p. 52) also argues that the *Rambo* series recurrently 'cast male predicaments in melodramatic terms', complicating claims that 1990s action films predominantly co-opted 'feminine' qualities to preserve (white) male hegemony. This complication is arguably more than temporal, as a reconsideration of an element of Rambo's enduring iconicity demonstrates. Rambo's ritualised pre-battle 'suiting up'—the obligatory montage invoking the symbolic unity of man and/as weapon, as he collects weaponry and drapes ammunition over his body, effectively weaponising the 'hard body'—seemingly signals an ideal masculinity, emphasising his musculature through putting on his headband. Yet in *Rambo: First Blood Part II* (1985), Rambo fashions his headband from a strip of the traditional dress that his killed Vietnamese would-be lover had earlier used to dress his wound, incorporating the feminine to facilitate retributive violence (Fig. 18.1). In line with Susan Jeffords et al. (1994), Rambo's

Fig. 18.1 Rambo Ao Dai Headband

assumption ambiguously displays not only the persistent wounding of the muscled action star body but also its 'feminisation'—fetishised, objectified, and vulnerable—in the service of 'remasculinisation'.

Numerous scholars, including O'Brien (2012), writing recently about *Die Hard* (1988), have noted the obsolescence often associated with Stallone's characters, and white male protagonists more generally, in 1980s action, with protagonists whose gender and professional relevance are explicitly questioned in a world that seemingly no longer values or needs the characteristics associated with either. Yet, even though the desire to 'remasculinise' and reassert cultural and professional worth highlights persisting and unalleviated anxieties, as Gallagher (2006) recognises, scholarly discourse typically submits to reading Stallone's films as violently redemptive or recuperative texts—of wounded white male and imperilled nation alike.[1] Supposed career side moves, even in Stallone's non-action films, similarly engage with this predominant 'hard-bodied' action star image, whether by inverting it in *Cop Land* or caricaturing it in *Antz* (1998). While his films are now being reread as less straightforwardly conservative or Reaganite, with Mattes's (2013) recent re-reading

---

[1] Holmlund notes the complexity of Stallone's demarcation as 'white', with Tasker (2014, p. 250) arguing that Rocky's status as an Everyman outsider whose struggles, 'suggesting tropes of self-invention in the context of American mythology', establish the Italian American as representing the nation, well before the Cold War conceit of *Rocky IV* (1985). The equation of Stallone's iconic characters *with* the nation and their struggles *with* traditional white masculinity marks another fundamental aspect of his star image. It is likewise evident in the characterisations of the oft-abandoned lone warrior, John Rambo, who is otherwise attributed mixed 'Indian' German heritage.

of *Cobra* (1986) representing just one intervention, the scholarly focus on 'muscularity' continues to dominate and frame discourse on Stallone's star image. However, this not only underestimates the under-appreciated authorial status that Holmlund's collection seeks to celebrate but also the integral relation of Stallone's star image and its longevity to persistent evocations of redundancy and ageing, expiration, and aged-ness.

'I'M EXPENDABLE': STALLONE'S GENERIC AND NARRATIVE REDUNDANCY

The intimate relation of Stallone's image to redundancy functions in multiple ways: generically, narratively, as an action star, and as an ageing action performer. Redundancy is a recognised—and oft-maligned—feature of genre films, and particularly of Stallone's 1980s action genre successes. Redundancy as repetition is what marks out generic terrain. The repetition or overlapping of tropes, themes, images, and/or expressions creates predictability, and is even apparent in promotional materials such as film posters. In the *Rocky* and *Rambo* series, numerous tropes and themes recur: being 'used (up)' by anonymous and distant powerful others; the underdog struggling against overwhelming odds; the isolated warrior battling and besting seemingly overwhelming numbers; montages of the building and 'suiting up' of the body; and the wounding and self-repair sequences. This redundancy is also stylistic: beyond employing flashbacks to recall the protagonist's travails, the *Rocky* films consistently open with a recap of the conclusion of the previous franchise instalment. Such predictability is key to generic formation and articulation and yet leads inexorably towards symbolic exhaustion, with the nostalgic returns to iconic scenes and images in his recent franchise revivals at once celebratory and mournful. Ultimately, generic redundancies become excessive, and a genre must adapt and transform or become mired in self-reflexive parody, each ambiguously evident in the knowing levity of *The Expendables*.[2]

Redundancy also implies being *in excess*, no longer being needed or useful. To be, or be made, redundant is to be marked unnecessary and superfluous, and deprived of one's job and associated worth, a point not

---

[2] For example, the third instalment of *The Expendables* more directly engages with elegy and loss, with the shooting of one Expendable compelling Barney to dismiss the rest, fearful (and hoping to avert the inevitability) that they will meet the same fatal end as preceding members.

only central to Stallone's defining characters, Rocky and Rambo, but the star life of 1980s action performers defined by hyperbolic physicality.[3] Stallone's action star persona is iconically defined by his characters' various perceived cultural, economic, and professional redundancies, including their subsequent resistance. In *First Blood Part II*, for example, Rambo declares it is because 'I'm expendable' that he is sent back into Vietnam to search for possible POWs. Stallone's longevity largely lies in his repeated identification with and portrayal of marginalised 'blue collar' white masculinities. Globally distributed by Hollywood, Stallone's star image nonetheless paradoxically turns on (and arguably exploits) the perceived impacts of economic and cultural change on working-class white males—derided, unfashionable, and undesirable—post-1960s, post-Vietnam and, more recently, post-recession. Stallone's characters are routinely downtrodden and written-off, beaten and abandoned, and bear an insistently reiterated 'outsider' or 'underdog' status. Yet more than this, Stallone's films have long been read as social commentaries on 'the victimisation of the working class' (Kellner, 1995, p. 65, cited by Boyle & Brayton, 2012, p. 482). Rocky, for example, is often twinned with the decline and dilapidation of American cities and particular neighbourhoods, all struggling against threatened economic and cultural redundancy. This most pointedly recurs in *Rocky Balboa* (2006), in which an aged Rocky's acknowledged crestfallen status—a retired widower who nightly recounts his glory days for his restaurant customers—is reflected in and produced by the blighted urban environment that repeatedly serves as his background. Indeed, Stallone's mid-1990s decline is in part linked with a series of specialist-expert blockbusters, including *Judge Dredd* and *Assassins*, in which his characters' prowess is immediately foregrounded and celebrated rather than a necessary response to threat. This shift from culturally and professionally redundant characters, along with his unquestioned star power and action genre successes, compromised audience sympathies for his typically beleaguered 'outsider' characters. In this sense, *Cop Land* actually marks a symbolic return to redundancy rather than the conscious attempt to diversify his star persona it is routinely considered to be (see Gates, 2010, for example). In the film, Stallone's characters' customary professional redundancy is exemplified by his beleaguered sheriff in a town primarily inhabited—and controlled—by New York Police Department (NYPD) officers. Stallone's

[3]Boyle and Brayton (2012; see also Tasker, 2014) likewise explore the first *Expendables* in relation to notions of 'expendability' in post-recession America.

comeback since the mid 2000s is arguably, much like his ascendance, culturally aligned with American economic uncertainty and destabilised white masculinities, particularly in view of the 2008 financial crisis, as well as perceived American military failure in Iraq and Afghanistan.

The centrality of the redundant American working-class male is reiterated by repeated societal-military redundancy, from traumatised Vietnam veteran Rambo in *First Blood* (1982) to 'used-up' (and equally used) ex-Special Forces and former military contractor Barney Ross, in *The Expendables* series. Stallone's characters rail against these perceptions and experiences of redundancy, but much more ambivalently and with much less success than popular opinion recognises. They seemingly offer fantasies of ascendance and of return (for victory), and restored white masculine vitality and (narrative) centrality, encapsulated in Rambo's desired Vietnam do-over in *First Blood Part II*: 'Do we get to win this time?' However, Rambo's question is meekly delivered, and defers to the authority of his 'maker', Colonel Trautman (Richard Crenna), who 'masculinises' the plaintive question in his assertive reply, 'This time it's up to you'. These uncertain fantasies of reinvigoration and victory are, and can only be, partially fulfilled. Although Rocky's body is spectacularly defiant and resilient, triumphant in its declared capacity to endure, he is defeated at the end of both *Rocky* and *Rocky Balboa*. And at the close of *First Blood*, Rambo breaks down and seeks the consoling fatherly embrace of the colonel before submitting to imprisonment. His defining franchise characters, now including Ross in *The Expendables*, remain at the behest of larger, distant forces—trained, shaped, and abandoned by powerful, anonymous others when their usefulness has been exhausted. Thus, rather than the symbolic, 'muscular' arm and embodiment of reinvigorated American military-political strength he is often argued to represent, Stallone's defining characters are also more generally victims of the consequences of American military, cultural, and economic globalisation and imperialism. Their physical traumas reflect and manifest those conditions that already marginalise them and their struggles, most notably in the physical torture they masochistically endure rather than transcend. Even in *Cop Land*, where his sheriff character ultimately resists his (acquiescent) redundancy by confronting the corrupt NYPD officers that dominate life in his jurisdiction, his redundancy as a would-be 'husband'—of a woman he once saved from drowning, but who married one of the NYPD officers—is cemented when she again/still rejects him.

Being Past It: Redundancy as (Geri-)Action Star

This notion of redundancy as being in excess, no longer needed and deprived of one's job, is also particularly pertinent to the figure of the transnational action star, and especially the 1980s action star defined by hyperbolic muscularity, as Boyle and Brayton (2012) similarly observe. Scholarship on ageing action star bodies, largely initiated by Holmlund's (2002) work on Eastwood, is growing, particularly in relation to Stallone et al. (see Gates, 2010; Boyle & Brayton, 2012). Tasker (2014), most notably, argues that the ambivalent admiration now accorded to Stallone's body is as shaped by changes in celebrity culture and notions of authenticity in action cinema as by ageing. However, I believe ageing is under-recognised as an integral rather than emergent feature of Stallone's 1980s action star image. That is, rather than primarily a recent development associated with franchise resuscitations and films like *The Expendables*, themes of ageing have long been central to Stallone's star image, ever since and including his breakout role as a 'past it' fighter in *Rocky*.[4] My focus, therefore, is not on ageing per se, but ageing as a form of redundancy, centred on perceptions of being aged, 'past it', or 'used up'.[5] While the (action) star's career maturity often concludes in this trajectory, Stallone's most iconic characters have always needed to counter the perception they have passed their supposed 'use-by' date. In *Rocky*, Balboa is already labelled a 'too old', 'never-has-been' local boxer who had foregone any shot at 'the title'—at least until those qualities and skills previously derided are, much like Rambo's, cynically and ambiguously sought. Moreover, the series thematises ageing, with Rocky uneasily vacillating across bodily, work- and age-related redundancies throughout, variously linked to injury and rebuilding, retirement, and comeback, financial security and ruin, and fame and obscurity.

This persistent relation of Stallone's star image to age and expiration is thus reinvigorated (though masked) in the recent emergence of the so-called 'geri-action' subgenre, and particularly *The Expendables*.[6] This late

---

[4] This reading of Stallone's revival has admittedly been encouraged by Stallone's repeated comparison of Rocky's life with his own age and desire to remain relevant, observed in Gates (2010) and Ramaeker (2014).

[5] Holmlund notes that *Rocky* also thematises maturing emotionally, or 'growing up', especially in relation to his courtship of his later wife.

[6] It is also evident in his franchise revivals of Rocky and Rambo. However, outside the franchise revivals, which profit on the accumulated weight of their history, only Stallone's

resurgence extends not only his star image but also includes the characteristics identified as crucial to his enduring star image: his iconicity, generic self-consciousness, star persona self-reflexivity, and authorial hand. However, it more intriguingly disavows and yet displays Stallone's redundancy as 'hard bodied' action star through numerous significant shifts in his 'muscular' star image. *The Expendables* films mark the shift from a highly individualistic star image to a collective one, a point Holmlund (2014; see also Gates, 2010) identifies as key to their box-office success.[7] The 1980s action star's waning powers—both audience drawing and physical—now mandate a multi-generational ensemble star cast, covering multiple markets and action subgenres. Stylistically, and akin to wider contemporary Hollywood trends, the films hybridise (and cannibalise) other action subgenres, such as martial arts and wrestling, and markets and periods, like 1990s Hong Kong action and 2000s actions aesthetics. This savvy market positioning maximises the films' audience and demographic appeal, but arguably also evidences motivating anxieties about capacity and worth that exceed those typically attributed to action cinema's much discussed hypermasculine self-presentation. Commercial survival necessitates teaming with fellow—and likewise aged—luminaries of 1980s white cinematic masculinity, such as Schwarzenegger, Bruce Willis, and Chuck Norris (Fig. 18.2); stars popular in key international markets, most notably Jet Li with Chinese-speaking audiences and martial arts fans; and younger would-be action stars, like Liam Hemsworth and Ronda Rousey, in a mutually beneficial association, where the older stars lend their action star gravitas and the younger their muscular vitality and access to youth audiences. In order to endure, Stallone's star persona now even seeks to disavow the professional redundancy (in this instance as action performer) on which his stardom paradoxically revolves and depends, generically and narratively.

A number of recent shifts likewise threaten Stallone's laudatory longevity as an action star. The 1980s action hero's masculinity is largely defined and narrated via the spectacle and/or transformation of the body, either in its building up, its (return to an) ideal status or its spectacular wounding or beating, all key to Stallone's star image. Yet the aged 'geri-action' body

multi-generational, all-star collective, *The Expendables*, have succeeded, with *Bullet to the Head* (2012), *Grudge Match* (2013) with Robert De Niro, and *Escape Plan* (2013), with Arnold Schwarzenegger, failing commercially and critically.

[7] Ramaeker (2014, p. 49) even identifies this shift in the use of more dispersed cross-cutting in the climactic battle in *Rambo* (2008), positioning the aged Rambo as one amongst a team of mercenaries rather than a lone warrior.

Fig. 18.2 Stallone (centre) in *The Expendables* (2010)

is decidedly concealed and the site of spectacle wholly displaced in *The Expendables* and *Rambo*. Gilligan (2012, p. 177) notes a shift in recent science fiction and action cinema whereby the construction and performance of masculine identities has been displaced from the body onto clothing and gadgets. While part of a broader cinematic trend, the concealment of the star body in 'geri-action' nonetheless represents a telling shift in the presentation, or absence thereof, of formerly idealised 1980s action bodies.

In Stallone's 'geri-action' films, the aged action body, although remaining impressively muscled, is now largely hidden, with Stallone's ageing body now clothed—concealed rather than showcased. Even the archive of promotional materials, while seeking to invoke the stability and persistence of genre tropes and Stallone's star image by referencing earlier iconic images, subtly admits deterioration and growing anxiety rather than return and reinvigoration. The promotional poster for *Rambo* (2008) clearly recalls the iconic image from *Rambo III* (1988) of Rambo's muscled torso, shot from behind, glistening and unmarked, as he 'suits up' for battle. However, Rambo's body is now not only covered by a T-shirt but he is wounded and his head downcast, weighed down both by a life lived violently and in the wasted aftermath of battle. Similarly, lingering shots or conventional montages of the muscled male body 'suiting up' for war are now routinely excised from the subgenre, with *Rambo* (2008) instead fetishising the production of a weapon. Even the de-emphasising of masochistic and tortuous bodily suffering that Holmlund (2014) cannily observes in *The Expendables* signals the redundancy of the 'hard-bodied' 1980s action star. This torture of the muscled body, contorted in beautiful agony and pain, was integral to Stallone's embodied screen identity, exemplified in *First Blood Part II* when Rambo is repeatedly electrocuted by a sadistic Russian officer. Although his body is badly beaten in each *Expendables*, and the physical travails of action stardom and age alike writ large on face and body in *Rocky Balboa* and *Rambo*, the reticence to showcase the 1980s action body-in-suffering concedes the trope has reached its expiration. Stallone no longer wants to show—and perhaps audiences no longer desire to see, much less linger over and gaze upon— the 1980s action body enduring suffering because it reveals its ageing and consequent redundancy too readily, and more profoundly than a self-deprecating quip or insult from a fellow 1980s action luminary. The very reticence that seeks to extend Stallone's longevity ultimately confirms the generic redundancy so anxiously disavowed.

Even more suggestively, the site of spectacle is displaced from the body not only onto preposterously large guns (oversized even by 1980s action standards), but a preponderance of ostentatiously oversized, outfitted, and decorated vehicles. Vehicles are fetishised throughout each of the *Expendables*. They are the first object seen on-screen in each, and fragmented, objectified, and lingered on in place of the now-aged and veiled, muscled 1980s action body. His oversized guns are also no longer indicative of 'muscularity', such as in *First Blood Part II*, but compensatory, dwarfing the now-hidden 'hard body' in *Rambo* and *The Expendables*— and in spite of the increased physical size of Stallone's steroid-enhanced body since the early 2000s (Tasker, 2014). The hyperbolic spectacle of the destructive 'hard body' is equally displaced onto more agile and mobile bodies, such as Jason Statham in *The Expendables* and multiple younger would-be stars in *The Expendables 3*. The intimate association with guns and explosions is a long-standing part of the 1980s action star's toolkit, but their significance and size in *The Expendables* is figured vastly differently for the aged action star, as Tasker (2014) likewise recognises. No longer appendages, a reflection and extension of the star's muscled body and power, they—like the younger star bodies—now seek to distract our attention from the concealment of the ageing star bodies, while still delivering the requisite 'muscular' apparatus of action cinema that Jennifer Baker (2009, cited by Holmlund, 2014) describes. Ramaeker (2014) further identifies Stallone's astute use of contemporary style in *Rocky Balboa* and *Rambo*, via hyperbolised stylisation and intensified continuity, as both contemporising each franchise and evidence of Stallone's conscious positioning as what Holmund (2014) labels a 'commercial *auteur*'. However, the deployment of intensified continuity not only seeks to extend Stallone's longevity *as* action star-*auteur* but also conceals the star's aged body and diminished action capacities, masking his attenuated agility and speeding him up.

Conclusion

Sylvester Stallone's defining characters and action star image insistently resist—and now seek to disavow—redundancy, age, and expiration. Yet his star image is nonetheless integrally founded and dependent upon each. It remains tempting to read Stallone's late career revival as redemptive, and symptomatic of the stubborn persistence oft associated with his star persona. However, albeit impressive, it more registers the physical and cyclical exhaustion of a particular type of star and genre. Although Stallone's authorial labours continue to generically and commercially extend his star life and resist redundancy, he acknowledges the latter through ever greater and anxious hypermasculine efforts, buttressing the ageing body with ever more affected (and distracting) guns, vehicles, and explosions. Stallone's star image laudably endures, and will do so as long as we watch his films, but now does so only tenuously as an action star performer of attenuated agility and power. Stallone and the 1980s action subgenre he represents move inexorably towards exhaustion and a conjoined 'use-by' date, his now-concealed action body admitting the inevitable redundancy of an undeniably ageing star body intimately aligned with generic 'muscularity'. Sylvester Stallone will not submit without a fight, as Rocky (and Stallone) reiterates in paternal advice to his young son in *Rocky IV* (1985) that life demands 'going one more round, when you don't think you can'—or perhaps *should*, as the prospects of *The Expendables 4*, *Rambo: Last Blood*, and a *Rocky* spin-off ambivalently and spectacularly attest.

References

Antz. (1998). Film. Directed by Eric Darnell and Tim Johnson. [DVD]. USA: DreamWorks Home Entertainment.

Assassins. (1995). Film. Directed by Richard Donner. [DVD]. USA: Warner Home Video.

Boyle, E. and Brayton, S. (2012). Ageing Masculinities and 'Muscle Work' in Hollywood Action Film: an Analysis of *The Expendables*. *Men and Masculinities*. 15 (5), pp. 468–485.

Bullet to the Head. (2012). Film. Directed by Walter Hill. USA: Icon Film Distribution.

Cobra. (1986). Film. Directed by George P. Cosmatos. [DVD]. USA: Warner Home Video.

Cop Land. (1997). Film. Directed by James Mangold. [DVD]. USA: Miramax Home Entertainment.

Die Hard. (1988). Film. Directed by John McTiernan. [DVD]. USA: 20th Century Fox Home Entertainment.

Elmwood, V.A.. 2005. 'Just some bum from the neighbourhood': the resolution of post-civil rights tension and heavyweight public sphere discourse in *Rocky*. *Film & History*. 35(2): 49–59.

Escape Plan. (2013). Film. Directed by Mikael Håfström. [DVD]. USA: Entertainment One.

First Blood. (1982). Film. Directed by Ted Kotcheff. [DVD]. USA: Artisan Entertainment.

Gates, P. 2010. Acting His Age? The Resurrection of the 80s Action Heroes and their Ageing Stars. *Quarterly Review of Film and Video*. 27: 276–289.

Gallagher, M. (2006). 'I married Rambo': Action, Spectacle, and Melodrama. In: *Action Figures*. New York: Palgrave Macmillan.

Gilligan, S. 2012. Fragmenting the Black Male Body: Will Smith, Masculinity, Clothing, and Desire. *Fashion Theory*. 16(2): 171–192.

Grudge Match. (2013). Film. Directed by Peter Segal. [DVD]. USA: Warner Home Video.

Holmlund, C. (2002). The aging Clint. In: *Impossible bodies: Femininity and masculinity at the movies*. London: Routledge, pp. 141–56.

———, ed. 2014. *The Ultimate Stallone Reader: Sylvester Stallone as Star, Icon, Auteur*. New York: Columbia University Press.

Jeffords, S. 1994. *Hard Bodies: Hollywood Masculinity in the Reagan Era*. New Brunswick, NJ: Rutgers University Press.

Judge Dredd. (1995). Film. Directed by Danny Cannon. [DVD]. USA: Hollywood Pictures Home Entertainment.

Mattes, A.M.. 2013. Turning the gun on America: *Cobra* and the action film as cultural critique. *The Australasian Journal of Popular Culture*. 2(3): 457–470.

O'Brien, H. 2012. *Action Movies The Cinema of Striking Back*. Wallflower: Short cuts. London.
Ramaeker, P. 2014. Staying Alive: Stallone, Authorship and Contemporary Hollywood Aesthetics. In *The Ultimate Stallone Reader: Sylvester Stallone as Star, Icon, Auteur*, ed. C. Holmlund. New York: Columbia University Press.
Rambo. (2008). Film. Directed by Sylvester Stallone. USA: Sony Pictures Releasing.
Rambo: First Blood Part II. (1985). Film. Directed by George P. Cosmatos. [DVD]. USA: Artisan Entertainment.
Rambo: Last Blood. (n.d.). Film. USA: Lionsgate.
Rocky. (1976). Film. Directed by John Avildsen [DVD]. USA: 20th Century Fox Home Entertainment.
Rocky II. (1979). Film. Directed by Sylvester Stallone. [DVD]. USA: MGM Home Entertainment.
Rambo III. (1988). Film. Directed by Peter MacDonald. [DVD]. USA: Lionsgate Home Entertainment.
Rocky IV. (1985). Film. Directed by Sylvester Stallone. [DVD]. USA: MGM Home Entertainment.
Rocky Balboa. (2006). Film. Directed by Sylvester Stallone. [DVD]. USA: Twentieth Century Fox Film Corporation.
Tango and Cash. (1989). Film. Directed by Andrey Konchalovskiy. [DVD]. USA: Warner Home Video.
Tasker, Y. 1993. *Spectacular Bodies: Gender, Genre and the Action Cinema*, 2nd edn. London and New York: Routledge.
——— 2014. Stallone, Ageing and Action Authenticity. In *The Ultimate Stallone Reader: Sylvester Stallone as Star, Icon, Auteur*, ed. C. Holmlund. New York: Columbia University Press.
The Expendables. (2010). Film. Directed by Sylvester Stallone. USA: Roadshow Film Distributors.
The Expendables 2. (2012). Film. Directed by Simon West. USA: Roadshow Films.
The Expendables 3. (2014). Film. Directed by Patrick Hughes. USA: Roadshow Films.
The Expendables 4. (n.d.). Film. USA: Lionsgate.

SECTION 6

Reflections Beyond the Screen

CHAPTER 19

Still Famous: Fixing the Star Image of Diana Dors in the Photography of Cornel Lucas

Linda Marchant

This chapter will analyse the role played by still photographs in maintaining the legacy of the star persona, focussing on images made in the 1950s by photographer Cornel Lucas (1920–2012) of British actress Diana Dors (1931–1984). Lucas was head of still photography at Pinewood Studios for the Rank Organisation in Rank's heyday of film making in the 1950s. Although he left Pinewood in 1959, his career continued across six decades and his images have been published, collected, and exhibited throughout his working life and posthumously. He remains the only stills photographer to win a British Academy of Film and Television Arts (BAFTA) award for his Outstanding Contribution to British Cinema (1998) and his work has been celebrated with a lifetime retrospective at the National Portrait Gallery in London (2005) among many other exhibitions. Lucas made many thousands of images, working daily within the film industry, and his photographs chart the careers of many different actors including Kenneth More, David Niven, and Joan Collins, but his pictures of Diana Dors from the 1950s, which continue to be circulated today, provide rich examples to illustrate the relationship between the photograph and the lasting nature of stardom.

Diana Dors was a talented, vivacious star of the period, whose sense of fun, cheeky humour, and eccentric publicity stunts sealed her place in the hearts of British fans, but whose bombshell looks also provided a

L. Marchant
School of Art and Design, Nottingham Trent University, Nottingham, UK

© The Editor(s) (if applicable) and The Author(s) 2016
L. Bolton, J.L. Wright (eds.), *Lasting Screen Stars*,
DOI 10.1057/978-1-137-40733-7_19

sense of glamour with a wider, more international appeal. She has been described as one of the stars whose 'publicity narrative almost eclipse their screen career' (Babington, 2001, p. 21), as well as a star whose 'image moved beyond the level of representation to become symbolic, a public monument' (Cook, 2001, p. 167). I will argue that the continuing publicity narrative of stills photography is central to extending the longevity of the film persona. Although often simply categorised together as 'stills' to emphasise their difference from the moving image, there is a range of still types, each of which contributes in a different way to extend the legacy of the star. Covering publicity stills, film star portrait, and action stills, this chapter will analyse how each particular type of image contributes to 'fixing' the star image for both their contemporaneous audiences and extending it through future circulation.

In the Glare of Publicity

The term 'publicity stills' broadly covers images made by stills photographers to keep the stars' faces in news and magazine coverage. Publicity stills captured stars at events, openings, at home, in seasonal outfits (termed 'calendar art' by Finler, 1995, p. 104), on fashion shoots and behind the scenes on-set, as well as the stories when filming was happening. For stars under a studio contract, it was important to be kept in the public consciousness (see Finler, 1995; Vieira, 1997; Basinger, 2009; McDonald, 2013), so stills photographers played a significant role in the 'industrialised cultural production of stardom' (McDonald, 2013, p. 14). When films were in production and during release, the film was the story to report. Outside these times it was equally important to maintain star currency and value for future income, as well as providing work for photographers.

The photographs released were controlled to present an 'image' of a star that the studio wished to promote, the texts of promotion to which Dyer refers to as 'part of the deliberate creation/manufacture' and the 'most deliberate, direct, intentioned and self-conscious' construction (1998, p. 60). If we examine Lucas's publicity stills of Dors, we can begin to see three distinct ways in which they function to fix aspects of the star image. They firstly establish a recognisable visual 'image' for the star. Secondly, they construct a 'personality' in the way she is depicted for an audience who has never met the star in person (see for example Lusted, 1991; Dyer, 1998). This construction can of course be shifted through the ways in which they

Fig. 19.1 Diana Dors (c) Cornel Lucas. Reproduced by kind permission of Cornel Lucas Collection. Image supplied by BFI National Archive

are presented and represented photographically. Lucas explains this process in relation to one of his images of Howard Keel:

> At the time of the photograph, he was seeking to break away from the musical mould and switch to straight parts. For this sitting we therefore departed from his usual clean-cut look, for something a little unexpected. (Lucas, 1988, p. 14)[1]

---

[1] See also Vieira (1997) on MGM photographer George Hurrell, where he explains the change in perception brought about by Hurrell's images of Norma Shearer.

Fig. 19.2 Diana Dors, Venice, May 1955. (c) Cornel Lucas. Reproduced by kind permission of Cornel Lucas Collection

Finally, the publicity still also functions to attract and maintain the star's fan base, providing a sense of connection and community, which in Diana's case often reflect a humorous, working class connection. As interviewer and writer Tony Bilbow commented, 'Her friends in the one-and-nines gave her a friendly wink that said, "Good for you, Di—tell 'em to get stuffed!"' (Bilbow, 1990, p. 1).

Fixing the 'Image'

Lucas's images trace the journey to reach the established look of Diana Dors as the curvaceous British blonde bombshell. As photographer for the Rank Organisation's Company of Youth (known as the Rank Charm School), Lucas first photographed Diana along with other emerging stars such as Joan Collins, Honor Blackman, and Donald Sinden. Described by Sarah Street as 'the only institutional attempt within the British film industry to present a conscious strategy of stardom' (Street, 2009, p. 173), Charm School subjects were photographed by Lucas in a Hollywood style but on rationed British budgets. Behind the scenes for photographers, the equipment, sets and costumes were less lavish and expensive than in America, with materials often still being subject to post-war rationing. However, lighting styles, poses, and make-up followed the codes and glow of Hollywood film portraiture. Early images of Diana Dors depict a young brunette wearing a dark fur hat with the shadows of her lashes falling across her face,[2] or a smiling brunette Diana in 1949, standing in fake snow, wearing a skating skirt, fur wrap, and heels.[3]

It took a while, and a few changes in image from this coyer brunette Diana for the confident, polished Diana Dors to appear in the photographs, and this journey is charted on the reverse of the photographs found in the British Film Institute archives as well as the front. The captions on the back of images provide copy for publication or information for the magazines to which they were sent. These descriptors, often published alongside the visual image, become lodged in the minds of the viewer, describing the star as 'lovely',[4] 'promising',[5] and a 'picture of grace, charm and beauty'[6] in her fledgling career. The photographs show her as smiling, engaging, and fresh-faced and the costumes depicted are simple, if skimpy. The epithets gained in grandeur and glamour: 'DIANA DORS—the sizzling glamour-queen of the screen. At 23, she's the most glittering, talked-about star in Britain. She has the shine, the sparkle, the poise of star quality'.[7] Visually, the images show Diana as more in control, often taken from a slightly lower angle to emphasise her shape. Her clothes in the images become more sculpted, tighter fitting, and lower cut on the bust, a more elaborate and lavish depiction of sparkle and glamour.

This shine and sparkle is evident in this photograph by Lucas, which was originally used as a publicity shot for the film *An Alligator Named Daisy* (1955). It has been widely circulated in a number of forms, demonstrating how the publicity image endures. Depicting Diana in a costume from

---

[2] Image PP1699-9, BFI Stills Collection.
[3] Image MP3097, BFI Stills Collection.
[4] Image MP3097, BFI Stills Collection.
[5] Image MP 2884, BFI Stills Collection.
[6] Image MP3098, BFI Stills Collection.
[7] Image 282.P.17, BFI Stills Collection.

the film, it appeared in *Picture Show* magazine on 8 September that year.[8] The photograph focusses on the glamour of the star rather than the acting role or performance. Lucas's image uses a key light falling from high from the left, throwing highlights onto the shine and blondeness of her hair, naked shoulder, bust and left hip, accentuating her femininity, softness, and curves. The background uses curtaining and upholstered satin, reminiscent of a headboard, hinting at a bedroom setting. Her almost-smile, her pose, and an expanse of skin hint at sexuality and accessibility, although this is counterbalanced with her prominent ring on her wedding finger and a bridal veil—all references to the film's storyline. The photograph was used by Rank as one of the 10-inch by 8-inch promotional images for Dors, and also as one of a number of postcards produced by the studio to send to fans writing in for photographs of their favourite stars. Other appearances of this particular image are as a free giveaway postcard within the *Empire News and Sunday Chronicle* (July 1956) to promote Dors's 'Hollywood Diary',[9] and also with the background removed in a Channel 4 publication about Dors released six years after her death (Bilbow, 1990). It represents a young, blonde, beautiful, and glamorous image of Diana Dors, which circulates freely in the contemporary world of the Internet.

How is this image (and many similar ones, including from the same shoot, identifiable by the jewelled dress strap) used to fuel her enduring legacy? One significant and interesting example is the Facebook page 'Re-Introducing Diana Dors—Official Fan Page', run by Seán Flynn (2014). Through the page, and the forthcoming website/database and book, Flynn is able to share photographs, information, stories, and news (such as DVD releases) about Diana and the many stars with whom she was connected. At the time of writing, there are over 4,500 followers of the page.

When asked why he had chosen the title of 're-introducing' Diana Dors, Flynn points to how the images help to sustain her legacy:

> The original title was 'Out of the Shadows—Re-Introducing Diana Dors.' I chose this title as I believe that up to that point, Diana's career, especially had been left in the shadows, and that much of the mythology, exagger-

---

[8] This article was held in an archive as a cutting from the newspaper, without page numbers and author details.

[9] 'Diana Dors's Hollywood Diary' was a short-lived column in the *Empire News and Sunday Chronicle* starting 15 July 1956. Dors promised "to serve up something hot from Hollywood" for the newspaper which was eventually merged into the *News of the World* in 1960. The insert postcard was an archive find, without the accompanying newspaper for specific dates.

tions, and untruths about her life were pushed to the fore, casting a large shadow over what had been an impressive career in film, television, stage and music. So over time, be it through photographs or information, I have made it the project's mission to remind the public about Diana's life work. And very slowly, examples of her work have been released on DVD or Blu-Ray, not only to the delight of old fans but introducing her to a whole new generation of fans. (Flynn 2014 Personal Interview).

Two photographs from this shoot have been posted to the page. Comments show admiration for the glamour and 'look' of Diana, while other images garner comments about her talent, her personality and personal fan stories relating to her. In a digital world it is possible to quantify the contemporary reach of these photographs in this particular context. Each image enjoyed 124/125 'likes', and maybe more significantly, was shared to the pages of other users 37 and 53 times respectively. If each user has 100 followers who will see the photograph, and possibly share with their own followers, it is easy to see the potential reach of this 1950s image to this contemporary audience.

Flynn also points out how modern-day celebrity adoption also extends the legacy of the star through the visual photograph. Singer Perrie Edwards, from the 2013 X-Factor winning band Little Mix, posed in front of a 1950s publicity shot of Diana blown up into giant print form. The photograph was posted on the Little Mix Tumblr site on 4 September 2013, with the caption, 'At a photoshoot with the beautiful Diana Dors [...] @samcoxy seems to think we look alike! Perrie <3' (Little Mix, 2013). Flynn observes, 'What has increased the lasting appeal of Diana Dors image, is how it has been embraced by today's stars [...] When the [Edwards] photograph went viral, the interest in Diana Dors grew considerably.' (Flynn 2014 Personal Interview). Further research shows that this single image received 118,000 'likes' on the Little Mix Tumblr, and was reblogged to many fan sites. Little Mix followers are a young, mainly female demographic who may not have seen Diana's image previously so the image is not representing Dors to them per se. However, some of the comments available show that the photograph is understood to be of a beautiful, glamorous, film star, and one whose image is sufficiently significant and 'current' to be visually echoed by Perrie, with her blonde hair, deep-coloured lips, darkened eyes, and confident pose. Photographs perform 'an instantaneous abduction of the object out of the world into another world, into another kind of time—unlike cinema, which replaces the object, after the act of appropriation, in an unfolding time similar to that of life.' (Metz, 1985, p. 84). The image of

Diana within the Perrie photograph is therefore abducted from the world of the 1950s and brought into the contemporary yet simultaneously historical world of stardom. The two can now co-exist in time and place through the object of the photograph itself. The image of Diana within the Perrie photograph functions as the fetish object, and for Metz, this other kind of time memorialises 'loved beings who are no longer alive' and the photograph is 'always active later' (Metz, 1985, p. 84) as the photograph is shared.

SHOWING AND SHARING: REVEALING PERSONALITY AND BUILDING COMMUNITIES

Aside from her glamorous looks, publicity stills of Diana often either implied or displayed her sense of fun and humour for the viewers. This sense of fun is depicted in many of Lucas's photographs of her, such as a series of Christmas publicity shots of her wearing a Santa hat and pretending to capture her own self-portraits. He worked closely with Diana and her husband/manager Denis Hamilton, building a rapport and understanding of their working practices and Diana's personality that he shared through his photographs.

> The mischievous alchemy between the two [Diana and Denis Hamilton] enabled her to establish a reputation that at times upstaged Hollywood. I found Diana a most amusing and talented actress, who brought tears, joy and wonderment into many people's lives, and who possessed a very good sense of humour. (Lucas, 1988, p. 92)

Lucas took many publicity images of Diana, but none were more famous, or infamous, than the shots of her wearing her 'mink' bikini whilst on a gondola at the Venice Film Festival in May 1955,[10] 'an incident which has become as legendary as Marilyn Monroe's famous billowing skirt in *The Seven Year Itch*' (Wilder, cited in Cook, 2001, p. 173).

Diana had asked Lucas to be in attendance on the Lido to shoot a 'special picture'. Once in position, she removed her long coat to reveal the fur bikini to waiting photographers, Lucas in the best position. The image appeared 'on the front page of newspapers all over the world' (Lucas, 2005, p. 158.) and remains part of her 'myth', which is most frequently cited in articles and writing about her life. The image serves to encapsulate the star persona of Diana

---

[10] It was rabbit rather than mink, but the latter has the glamour factor and was the story which circulated.

Dors within one frame. We see her glamorous lifestyle as an international film star depicted in her outfit and the location. Her friendly down-to-earth persona is represented by her cheery wave to her fans and finally, the humour and cheekiness of her persona are evidenced in her actual undertaking of such exploits. A 'contrived but still ingenious Rank publicity stunt' (Macnab, 2000, p. 139) possibly, although other accounts recall it as Diana's idea, it has also become part of her lasting legacy. The photograph proves the event took place; it gives viewers from any time period or context of viewing proof both of the myth's existence and of the veracity of the event. And this proof, in the form of photographic evidence, can continue to circulate or be preserved in a photograph more than through any type of evanescent news footage.

The image helps to establish and maintain an impression of her personality. 'She is already assured of a small place in the social history of our time. She has made the unlikely commodity of sex-appeal a British export' (*Daily Mail*, 2 May 1956).[11] It was a daring, risqué but humorous stunt and cemented her as a firm favourite with her British fan base. Visually, the images exuded the glamour and sex appeal which writers such as Geraghty and Street point out as atypical of British film portrayals of women presented to British audiences during the 1950s. But this was always tempered with a tongue-in-cheek twist. Her glamour and looks gave her international appeal, but her humour marks her as British. Unlike Hollywood sex symbols of the time, Diana's projected persona takes the more British approach of not taking herself, or her image, too seriously. She is self-aware in a similar way to that of Marilyn Monroe and Jane Russell but self-deprecating, using the type of harmless fun and humour in line with Britishness as represented in the Rank Organisation's *Doctor* series of films, and as in the quote cited below.[12] Geraghty points this out as Diana's 'sex symbol paradigm', noting that 'for film audiences in the 1950s, she could be seen as one of "us" not one of "them"; and her performance, in and out of the films, could be enjoyed more because of it' (Geraghty, 1986, p. 345). This includes her photographic performances. Newspaper interviews of the time frequently supported these views:

> That is why she turned down a long term Hollywood offer; 'I have been a Dumb Blonde long enough in England without competing in the American

---

[11] This article was held in an archive as a cutting from the newspaper, without page numbers and author details.

[12] In the 1950s, these were *Doctor in the House* (1954), *Doctor at Sea* (1955), and *Doctor at Large* (1957).

market, which is overstocked with my type already' (*Evening Standard*, 25 July 1953).[13]

These publicity stills are central to a presentation of a star image which displays a form of national identity, becoming a point of connection for various communities through the photograph's circulation.

COMMUNITIES OF ART: ON THE GALLERY WALL

Cornel Lucas's career as a film photographer encompassed all aspects of stills photography, but his speciality, and his own lasting legacy, has been for his film star portrait photographs. In terms of still photography within the film industry, these are 'gallery portraits' or 'gallery stills', which in modern times have been returned to the gallery: the art gallery or museum collection. Film star portraits as representations of familiar, loved, icons, certainly attract audiences: *Glamour of the Gods*, a 2011 exhibition of movie star photographs from the John Kobal Collection, attracted 87,000 admission-fee-paying visitors to the National Portrait Gallery, an audience some 60% higher than anticipated (National Portrait Gallery, 2012). The contribution of these images to the star legacy relates to a combination of factors: from the very nature of film portraiture itself, the skill of the maker, and the prestige afforded to the context of art in the gallery or museum space. As early Hollywood film photographer Ruth Harriet Louise advertised in 1922: 'Won't you visit my studio, and let me perpetuate your personality' (Abrams, 2011).[14]

FILM STAR PORTRAITS

This image of Diana (Fig. 19.3), taken by Lucas in 1954 depicts her in costume from the film *As Long As They're Happy* (1955). Unusually, as Lucas is renowned for his sepia-toned images, this is photographed in colour, shot using a cool blue background to highlight the hot red dress. It is designed, however, to reproduce equally well in black and white. The glint of the diamond bracelet on her arm towards the back of the shot, for

---

[13] This article was held in an archive as a cutting from the newspaper, without page numbers and author details.

[14] An advertisement appearing in a 1922 business directory, requesting actors to have their portraits taken by soon-to-become Metro-Goldwyn-Mayer (MGM) Portrait Photographer Ruth Harriet Louise.

Fig. 19.3 Diana Dors. (c) Cornel Lucas. Reproduced by kind permission of Cornel Lucas Collection

example, gives clear definition and differentiation from the background if shown in colour or monochrome. The photograph has been widely exhibited, often alongside the Mink Bikini shot, both as part of exhibitions of Lucas's work and in other curated exhibitions such as *British Blondes* (2003 National Portrait Gallery), thereby illustrating both the humour and the sex in Dors's persona.[15] It has been published in artist monographs and is held in the National Portrait Gallery Collection.

Portraiture is a complex genre within photography, often raising questions about its ability to either capture the inner essence of the sitter or to merely reflect a surface reality of the subject photographed. Film star portraits, however, often intentionally aim to create a fantasy rather than to seek any inner essence or surface truths. The aim for the movie star photographer is to sell an image which helps to create a connection between viewer and

---

[15] 2014 *Cornel Lucas: Photo Noir*, National Theatre. 2011 *Cornel Lucas*, Chris Beetles Fine Photographs. 2005 *Shooting Stars*, National Portrait Gallery, London. 2003 *British Blondes*, National Portrait Gallery

subject. The art of these photographers involves the careful and creative construction of the codes of meaning outlined in Dyer's notion of the ordinary/extraordinary paradox. The stills photographers communicate star quality and a connection to the audience, which is often mixed with emotion, aspiration, and familiarity: in Dyer's terms, 'Stars are constructed as being "ordinary" (like "us"), yet simultaneously distinctive and "special"' (Holmes, 2005, p. 10). In this image of Diana we see the extraordinary: a glittering, glamorous dress and glinting diamonds reminiscent of the costumes of Marilyn Monroe and Jane Russell in *Gentlemen Prefer Blondes* (1953), yet familiar to the film-going public of the time.

'Being a photographer means not only to look, but to sustain the gaze of others' (Bellon cited in Darke, 2007, p. 45). The portrait in the gallery setting encourages the viewer to look, and the creative and aesthetic traditions of the film portrait are on display as much as the photographic subject. If the film still has a similar function to a painting, an 'attempt to combine standstill with a narrative dimension and dramatic intensity' (Jacobs, 2010, p. 381), the studio film portrait has the same legitimacy and intent as the painted monarch's portrait. These photographic portraits have status, and thus have a recognised, and *enduring*, place on the gallery wall. The gallery is a space for contemplation, and it is both the skill of the photographer and the connection to subject which are promoted by positioning the work in this prestigious milieu. The constructed photographic film star portrait is created in order to connect the desires of an audience and the appearance of a recognisable face layered with performance, characters played and emotions evoked. The significance of performance in the image links closely with representations in the action or scene still.

Performance and Stillness: The Action Still

The action still is perhaps the most familiar example of the still photographer's work. Originally shot on-set and circulated to magazines and cinemas, they were designed to distil the action of the film, present it to a potential audience, and encourage that audience into cinemas. Lucas's earlier work in the industry included working on-set for many action stills, but as his career advanced, he was able to specialise in the more prestigious gallery work, his speciality by the time Diana Dors worked with Rank. As the action still is essential to the construction of the legacy of

Fig. 19.4 Production still of Dors in *Yield to the Night* (1956) © 1956 STUDIOCANAL Films Ltd

stars such as Dors, however, I will include a final image here which was not made by Lucas.[16]

The action still does not only depict the scene but also captures the acting performance. One of Dors's most critically acclaimed acting roles was that of Mary Price Hilton in *Yield to the Night* (1956).

This still (Fig. 19.4) is one of the most circulated images from the film. It depicts the condemned Mary Hilton on her prison bed, awaiting her fate. The 1956 *Yield to the Night* campaign sheet for cinema managers featured such performance stills, depicting the strength and intensity of Diana's performance as well as more glamourous portraits of the star, made by Lucas. The 'selling approach' was boldly stated: 'SELL—the new Diana Dors in 'Yield to the Night', the most glamorous star of British films proves she is also an outstanding dramatic actress.'[17] The still emphasises the understated, subtle depth of her performance. Her face clear of make-up is recognisable yet focuses on performance not the 'image' of Diana more commonly depicted. Unlike depictions of Diana in publicity stills and portraits, in this image she is separated from her audience. The

---

[16] The photographer is unconfirmed (as was often the case), but there are a number of possibilities. The stills photographer for the film is listed on IMDb as George Higgins. *Cine Technician* magazine from April 1956 also lists W. Penn as publicity stills photographer alongside Higgins, and Peter Hammond as unit press representative. Frank Buckingham was the resident photographer at Elstree studios at the time.

[17] *Yield to the Night* 1956 Campaign Sheet.

bars of the prison headboard stand as signifiers for her prison bars and throw her out of the direct glare of the photographer's lens. Her hand, curled into a fist, is centre focus and acts as a barrier to the viewer. She is hidden from plain view, imprisoned by the frame and foreground of the image. In fixing the otherwise moving performance, the viewer can shift between the 'narrative dynamics' of the film action and the 'iconic stillness' of the photograph (Jacobs, 2010, p. 380). The performance is 'embalmed' to use Barthes's term, preserved to be viewed, circulated, studied, reviewed, and recirculated any time the photograph is seen. This particular image was introduced to new audiences through use on the cover of The Smiths compilation album, *Singles*, released by WEA in 1995 some forty years after the making of the photograph and eleven years after Diana's death.

Lucas and Dors: Still Famous

In this particular study, Lucas's virtuosity as a photographer, coupled with Diana Dors's looks and talent, the dedication of those who remember her work and career, and those who continue to display or reappropriate her image demonstrate how 'looker and looked at [are] locked together in the eternity of a still' (Darke, 2007, p. 45). When drawing the strands of film still photography together, we can conclude that there is a synergy in how they function to preserve the legacy of stardom. In a digital world, sharing images of people and subjects we are interested in forms communities of viewers who continue to look. Publicity images functioned at the outset to make the star known to the public, to become familiar, and thus remembered. Action stills preserve the legacy of the actor's performance, allowing time and motion to be suspended within the frame, ready to be enacted by the gaze of the viewer. And finally, the quality of the portraits made by film photographers such as Lucas merits a place for display in the art gallery. Prestige, importance, and lasting significance for both the subject and the image result from display in exhibition spaces and provide the public with a contemporary space for contemplation and admiration of the star image.

REFERENCES

Abrams, M. (2011, July 24). Star Maker: The photographer Ruth Harriet Louise. Telegraph [Online]. Available from http://www.telegraph.co.uk/culture/8562691/Star-maker-the-photographer-Ruth-Harriet-Louise.html [Accessed 17 December 2014]

An Alligator Named Daisy. (1955). Film. Directed by J. Lee Thompson. UK: J. Arthur Rank Film Distributors.

As Long as They're Happy. (1955). Film. Directed by J. Lee Thompson. UK: General Film Distributors.

Babington, B. 2001. *British stars and stardom: from Alma Taylor to Sean Connery.* Manchester: Manchester University Press.

Basinger, J. 2009. *The star machine.* New York: Vintage Books.

Bilbow, T. 1990. *Diana Dors.* London: Channel 4 Television.

Cook, P. 2001. The trouble with sex: Diana Dors and the blonde bombshell phenomenon. In *British stars and stardom: From Alma Taylor to Sean Connery*, ed. B. Babington. Manchester: Manchester University Press.

Darke, C. (2007). Once more into the zone. *Vertigo* 3(6): 45.

Doctor at Large. (1957). Film. Directed by Ralph Thomas. UK: J. Arthur Rank Film Distributors.

Doctor at Sea. (1955). Film. Directed by Ralph Thomas. UK: J. Arthur Rank Film Distributors.

Doctor in the House. (1954). Film. Directed by Ralph Thomas. UK: General Film Distributors.

Dyer, R. 1998. *Stars.* London: BFI.

Empire News and Sunday Chronicle. (1956, July).

Finler, J. 1995. *Hollywood movie stills. The golden age.* London: B.T. Batsford Ltd.

Flynn, S. (2014). Re-introducing Diana Dors–official fan page. [Facebook]. Available from: https://www.facebook.com/REINTRODUCINGDIANADORS?fref=ts [Accessed 16 July 2015].

Gentlemen Prefer Blondes. (1953). Film. Directed by Howard Hawks. [DVD]. USA: 20th Century Fox.

Geraghty, C. 1986. Diana Dors. In *All our yesterdays: 90 years of British cinema*, ed. C. Barr. London: British Film Institute.

Holmes, S. (2005). 'Starring…Dyer?' Re-visiting star studies and contemporary celebrity culture. *Westminster Papers in Communication and Culture.* [Online] 2 (2). pp. 6–21.

Jacobs, S. (2010, October 4). The history and aesthetics of the classical film still. *History of Photography.* 34. pp. 373–386.

Little Mix. (2013). [Tumblr]. Available from: http://instagram.com/p/d2BdnxuGbd/?modal=true [Accessed 31 August 2014].

Lucas, C. 1988. *Heads and tales: The film portraits of Cornel Lucas*. Luton: Lennard Publishing.
—— 2005. *Shooting stars: Camera portraits*. Bath: English Group.
Lusted, D. 1991. The glut of the personality. In *Stardom industry of desire*, ed. C. Gledhill. London: Routledge.
Macnab, G. 2000. *Searching for stars: Stardom and screen acting in British cinema*. London: Cassell.
McDonald, P. 2013. *Hollywood Stardom*. Malden, MA: Wiley-Blackwell.
Metz, C. (1985). Photography and Fetish. *October*. 34, pp. 81–90.
National Portrait Gallery. (2012). *Annual Report and Accounts 2011–2012* [Report]. Available from: https://www.gov.uk/government/uploads/system/uploads/attachment_data/file/229184/0365.pdf [Accessed 23 September 2014].
Street, S. 2009. *British national cinema*. London: Taylor and Francis.
Vieira, M. 1997. *Hurrell's Hollywood portraits: The Chapman collection*. New York: Harry N. Abrams.
Yield to the Night. (1956). Film. Directed by J. Lee Thompson. UK: Associated British-Pathé.

CHAPTER 20

From Action Babe to Mature Actress: The Place of Humanitarianism in Angelina Jolie's Lasting Screen Career

Joshua Gulam

Since assuming the role of goodwill ambassador for the United Nations High Commissioner for Refugees (UNHCR) in August 2001, Angelina Jolie has met with refugees and internally displaced persons in over twenty countries, lobbied high-ranking politicians, including US President Barack Obama, and documented her hands-on experiences of humanitarian crises in numerous public appearances and interviews, as well as a series of journal entries that was published in 2003. This on-the-ground campaigning, along with her extensive donations to causes around the globe, has earned the actress high praise from aid workers and journalists, in addition to various accolades: Jolie currently holds the title of Special Envoy to UNHCR—a position she has occupied since April 2012—and is regularly ranked among the most influential stars by the press (Forbes, 2012).

In this same period, Jolie's screen image also underwent a number of transformations: moving from the wild child persona of early films *Gia* (1998) and *Girl, Interrupted* (1999), to her emergence as a major action star in the early 2000s, with notable leading roles in *Lara Croft: Tomb*

J. Gulam
School of Arts, Languages and Cultures,
The University of Manchester, Manchester, UK

Raider (2001) and *Mr. & Mrs. Smith* (2005); while, most recently, the actress has combined her action star turns with voice work in family-friendly animation (*Kung Fu Panda* (2008)), as well as low-key performances in dramas such as *Changeling* (2008).

Jolie's humanitarianism has been instrumental to each of these transformations, working to reinforce established aspects of her screen image, while also adding new associations that have contributed to her enduring appeal: since scoring her first major commercial hit in 2001 (*Lara Croft: Tomb Raider*), Jolie has featured regularly on *Forbes*'s annual list of the top-earning Hollywood actresses, achieving the number-one spot in 2009, 2011, and 2013 (Pomerantz, 2013).

The charitable and political activities of movie stars are often dismissed as an exercise in public relations—something Jolie herself was accused of in 2006, when she appeared to use her UNHCR duties to offset the scandal surrounding her romance with *Mr. & Mrs. Smith* co-star, Brad Pitt. However, despite the routine nature of such readings among both scholars and journalists (Dieter & Kumar, 2006; Hyde, 2009), few have provided in-depth accounts of how campaigning might assist or extend a star's career.

This chapter looks at the relationship between Jolie's work for various causes and the development of her film career. I concentrate on the period 2007–2014, starting with her starring role in *A Mighty Heart* (2007) and ending with her biggest box office hit to date—*Maleficent* (2014). This period is significant because it spans Jolie's mid to late thirties, an age when the opportunities for female film stars tend to decline. I argue that Jolie's humanitarianism was pivotal to her screen stardom in these years, feeding into her films in ways that brought both critical approval and commercial rewards.

1998–2006: Breaking into the A-List

Jolie rose to prominence in the late-1990s, with her Oscar-winning portrayal of a teenage psychiatric patient in *Girl, Interrupted*. The role of Lisa Rowe—a 'sociopath' who torments the other patients on her ward—established Jolie as a promising talent, with Roger Ebert (2000) commenting upon the film's release: '[She's] emerging as one of the great wild spirits of current movies'. This reputation as a raw and uncompromising actress corresponded with contemporary media coverage of her private life. Indeed, at the same time that she received critical acclaim for *Girl, Interrupted*, Jolie cultivated an off-screen image as 'Hollywood's wild child', achieving notoriety for her love of knives, as well as her sexual experimentation and substance abuse (Richardson, 2000).

After winning a Best Supporting Actress Oscar for *Girl, Interrupted*, Jolie abandoned the edgy and intimate roles that had first brought her to popular attention, opting to work almost exclusively in action films. From 2001 to 2006, she played ass-kicking heroines in a succession of blockbusters: *Lara Croft: Tomb Raider*; its 2003 sequel, *Cradle of Life*; and the husband-and-wife assassin movie *Mr. & Mrs. Smith*. These three films grossed over $900 million in cinemas, establishing Jolie as one of the biggest action stars of the decade (Box Office Mojo, 2014).

Although Jolie's work in action movies has been fundamental to her success, propelling her into the elite band of stars who can command $15 million per picture, it posed certain obstacles to her acting career as she moved into her mid thirties. The first of these concerns the relatively short-lived nature of female stardom within the action genre. While actors like Sylvester Stallone and Bruce Willis have continued to work in blockbuster action films into their fifties and sixties, few female action stars can lay claim to such longevity. Jolie is one of the few actresses who have consistently starred in big-budget action films in her mid thirties, achieving success in the genre as recently as 2010 when *The Tourist* (2010) and *Salt* (2010) grossed a combined total of $570 million. Actresses working in the action genre therefore exhibit a more acute version of the short shelf-life that afflicts most female stars. Paul McDonald (2012, pp. 30–31) notes how the commercial fortunes of female stars tend to decline at an earlier age than their male counterparts. Likewise, Peter Kramer (2003, pp. 201–203) observes a general downturn in the box office performance of female stars when they reach 35.

With their physically active but hyper-sexualised heroines, *Mr. & Mrs. Smith* and the *Tomb Raider* films are examples of a subgenre that Marc O'Day (2004, pp. 204–206) has dubbed the 'action babe cinema'. O'Day differentiates characters like Lara Croft from the earlier action heroines of the 1970s and 1980s—characters such as Ripley in *Alien* (1979)—due to the way in which they combine sexual spectacle with empowerment, through an emphasis on both their feminine figure, and their martial arts expertise. This doubled emphasis on the heroine's physique results in a particularly narrow window of opportunity for female stars in the action babe cinema because, as O'Day explains, 'the [genre] demands an actress who is "young"—(usually in her twenties or early thirties)'.

The second obstacle relates to the critical reception of these action films. While critics often marvelled at Jolie's ability to match the muscular presence of her male counterparts, her action films received poor reviews overall. Indeed, the actress was herself subjected to criticism in these years, earning Golden Raspberry nominations for both *Tomb Raider* films. As she turned 32 in June 2007, Jolie therefore had to contend with both diminishing opportunities in the action genre, and the fact that her critical standing had declined: she was no longer seen as the same daring young actress of the late1990s.

From the *Heart*: Jolie's Mature Acting Phase

A Mighty Heart, directed by Michael Winterbottom and co-produced by Brad Pitt, marked the beginning of a new phase in Jolie's film career, where she diversified beyond the action babe cinema. *Heart* depicts the events surrounding the death of Daniel Pearl, an American journalist who was kidnapped and beheaded by al Qaeda operatives while on a writing assignment in Karachi in 2002. Jolie stars as Daniel's wife, Mariane Pearl, who wrote the 2003 memoir from which *Heart* is adapted. Shot in a naturalist style, the film details Mariane's efforts to locate her husband, as she works with the local authorities and the CIA to uncover details of Daniel's disappearance.

Reviewing *Heart* for *USA Today*, Claudia Puig (2007) hailed the film's 'intelligence', setting aside praise for the way it handled a difficult subject without 'sensationalism'. For Puig, Jolie was vital to this success, giving the film 'its lifeblood'. Although *Heart* underperformed at the box office, realising only a minor profit on its $16 million budget, other critics tended to agree with Puig's assessment. For example, Peter Howell (2007) awarded *Heart* four stars, adding that 'Jolie is central' to the film's 'honesty and courage'. These reviewers praised Jolie's performance for its 'understatement', 'nuance', and 'maturity', qualities rarely associated with the actress prior to 2007.

Curiously, a recurring theme across these reviews was Jolie's philanthropy. P. David Marshall (1997, p. 110) explains that a connection to political and charitable causes 'deepens the character profile of the celebrity', adding 'possible connotations of depth, intelligence, and commitment' to her/his public persona. This was certainly evident in the press reception of *Heart*, where Jolie's on-the-ground campaigning helped to authenticate her portrayal of Mariane. A July 2007 segment on CBS, for example, explicitly made the connection between acting and humanitarianism when it prefaced a review of *Heart* with details of Jolie's work for refugees, concluding: 'It's that ability to empathize with others that's key not only to this role but to her life in general' (Smith, 2007). Likewise, a pre-release article in the *Independent* framed Jolie's 'serious' performance against the background of her previous field missions to Pakistan: Jolie first visited Pakistan in May 2005 to tour Afghan refugee camps on the outskirts of Peshawar and Islamabad, returning five months later to visit the site of the October earthquake in Kashmir (Palmer, 2007). From the perspective of these reviews, Jolie's performance in *Heart* was the culmination of her extensive campaigning since 2001: the work of a socially conscious actress, whose first-hand experience of humanitarian crises gave her a strong grasp of the complex geopolitics depicted in the film, as well as its setting.

As a semi-independent drama based on real-life events, *Heart* was a far cry from the blockbusters for which Jolie was best known prior to 2007. Unsurprisingly, then, many reviewers expressed skepticism about her casting in such a 'serious', character-driven film. For example, the *Washington Post*'s Ann Hornaday (2007) wrote, 'Jolie is a star of such stratospheric proportions that the chances of her disappearing into a character seem slim'. Yet, Hornaday, like many reviewers, went on to qualify her initial assessment: '[I]t turns out she is the perfect choice to play Mariane because her persona as a UN representative [...] so seamlessly meshes with the global consciousness that the Pearls represent'. Jolie's humanitarianism helped to mitigate concerns about her casting, therefore, with her campaigns counteracting not only the poor reviews that she had received in previous years but also the negative associations wrought by her celebrity.

In several respects, Jolie's campaigns for UNHCR were consistent with her performances in the action babe cinema. For example, the star's field missions to Pakistan and other exotic locales evoked elements of her role as a globe-trotting archaeologist/adventurer in the *Tomb Raider* films (like Jolie, the humanitarian, Lara travels to hazardous regions around the world). At the same time, this UNHCR work shifted the terms of her representation. Photographs from Jolie's UNHCR field missions around this time show the actress engaged in intimate conversations with refugees [Fig. 20.1]. In these images, Jolie models a range of facial expressions,

Fig. 20.1 Jolie near Islamabad (courtesy of UNHCR/J. Redden)

from deep regret at the sight of human suffering to captivation and delight as she is given the opportunity to interact with diverse groups of people. The focus here is on the star's compassion, her ability to understand and share the feelings 'of distant Others' (Bell, 2013, p. 4). The effect of this footage in terms of Jolie's star discourse, then, was to move her away from the Lara Croft role, by reinterpreting her strong female image in terms of an emotional rather than a physical strength. These texts also offered a departure from her hyper-sexualised representation in the action babe cinema, with photographs from Jolie's field missions showing her dressed in baggy T-shirts, jeans, and/or some form of regional dress, clothing that contrasted sharply, in other words, with the tight vest and shorts worn by Lara Croft.

Heart offered a cinematic articulation of these broader shifts within Jolie's image. At the simplest level, Jolie's character aligned neatly with the transnational dimensions of her humanitarianism: a mixed-race French journalist living in Pakistan (she is of Afro-Cuban and Dutch heritage), Mariane evoked aspects of the global citizen image that Jolie projects through her UNHCR work. Furthermore, the role appeared to speak reflexively to the UN's goal of promoting international co-operation. In the film's climactic scene, Pearl preaches a sense of understanding and forgiveness that crosses national borders, calling on the international community to conceive of the costs of terrorism not just on the narrowly defined West but also on countries like Pakistan.

In *Heart*, Mariane is heavily pregnant throughout the search for her husband, while she is also shown together with her child in a flash-forward sequence. *Heart* therefore allowed Jolie to play out elements of her own family life at this time, drawing on her status as the mother of two adopted children—Maddox and Zahara, who were adopted from Cambodia and Ethiopia, respectively. Reviews often made the link between Jolie's motherhood and that of Mariane, citing this as further evidence of her 'perfect' fit for the role (Hornaday, 2007). Significantly, these critics tended to conflate Jolie's motherhood with her humanitarianism. One reason for this was the fact Jolie's adopted children were from countries she had previously visited as part of her campaigning.[1]

Another reason for this conflation of motherhood and humanitarianism is the tendency for female celebrity campaigners to be valued as 'motherly nurturers' (Wilkins, 2014, p. 4). Indeed, Jolie is the latest in a long list of female stars—Audrey Hepburn, Mia Farrow, and Madonna—whose humanitarian activities have been framed in maternal terms (Trope, 2012). Continuing this tradition, promotional images from her 2005 field missions show Jolie flanked by children. Moreover, the actress encourages this blurring of the familial and philanthropic when she uses the same vocabulary of global citizenship to describe her high-profile adoptions as she does for her UNHCR campaigns, declaring, 'I want to create a rainbow family. That's children [...] from different countries' (Daily Mail, 2006). Such comments and photographs play a role in driving the media obsession with Jolie's status as a revered celebrity 'mom'. Whether depicting her public or her private life, the focus of these texts is the star's depth of feeling.

Recent scholarship about celebrity humanitarianism has explored the gendered dynamics of this phenomenon (Wilkins, 2014). Katherine Bell (2013), for example, observes how the tendency to present (white) female campaigners as mothers not only reinforces traditional gender stereotypes, but also invokes colonial discourses which construct the imperial project as a mission to 'raise' the Third World, where the majority of celebrity campaigning is directed toward Africa. Jolie has herself been the subject of such criticism. Most notably, the star courted controversy in May 2006 over her decision to give birth to daughter Shiloh in Namibia. Jolie and her partner, Pitt, were accused of using their star power to obtain privileged access to the Namibian government, access that allowed the couple's security team to conduct door-to-door searches to locate unauthorized members of the media (Barron, 2009).[2] Journalist Marina Hyde (2009, p. 178) dubbed the event 'Apocalypse Brangelina', for instance, compar-

---

[1] Jolie's foundation, the Maddox Jolie-Pitt Foundation, has funded development projects in Cambodia and Ethiopia.

[2] Jolie and Pitt sold the US rights to the first photographs of Shiloh to *People* magazine for $4.1 million, which they donated to charity (Hyde, 2009).

ing Jolie and Pitt's actions to those of Walter E. Kurtz, the megalomaniacal army colonel in *Apocalypse Now* (1979). However, these blunders, and the problematic gender and racial discourses they activate, have largely gone unremarked upon in the press reception of Jolie's humanitarianism. For the most part, she has been celebrated for using her empowered mother image to 'do good' (Forbes, 2012; Smith, 2007).

Deborah Jermyn (2012, p. 44) explains how the mother is 'one of the few character types that has remained relatively available' to Hollywood actresses over 50. Although Jolie is still in her early forties, her career—with its succession of mother roles in *Heart*, *Changeling*, and *Maleficent*—has shown traces of the kind of typecasting of 'mature' female stars that Jermyn identifies. These film roles, intricately tied to her family life and humanitarianism, are one of the ways in which Jolie has altered her on-screen image to accommodate her maturing stardom, allowing her to age in a fashion that both Hollywood and the wider culture deems 'appropriate'.

Jolie's UNHCR campaigns have been crucial in laying the foundations for a long film career, therefore, one which extends beyond the period when she can no longer realistically play characters like Lara Croft. Perhaps most importantly, these activities facilitated her return to serious dramatic films, where there are more opportunities for actresses in their late thirties and forties. In 2008 Jolie cemented her status as a serious actress with her Oscar-nominated performance as a single mother in the period drama *Changeling*. More recently, Jolie took a break from acting to pursue a career behind the camera, making her directorial feature debut with *In the Land of Blood and Honey* (2011), a film about Bosnian Muslim women imprisoned in Serbian rape camps during the Bosnian War (1992–1995). However, Jolie's campaigning has contributed not just to the critical acclaim that she earned for these serious dramas but also to her enduring popularity in action-adventure blockbusters.

MALEFICENT'S BLOCKBUSTING ACTIVISM

After a three-and-a-half-year absence, Jolie made a successful return to the big screen when the children's fantasy *Maleficent*, in which she stars as the eponymous protagonist, grossed $70 million during its opening weekend. The film is a live-action reinterpretation of the Disney classic *Sleeping Beauty* (1959), with Jolie playing the queen fairy who casts a sleeping curse on the new-born princess, Aurora, a curse that can only be broken by 'true love's kiss'. While the 1959 Maleficent was a one-dimensional villain, Jolie's character is drawn in more complex and sympathetic terms, casting the curse only after her wings are brutally removed by Aurora's father, King Stefan. In a further twist on the traditional fairy-tale narrative, the 2014 film centres on the relationship between Aurora and Maleficent: guilt-ridden by her decision to curse an innocent baby, Maleficent vows to protect Aurora from harm, and ultimately comes to act as a surrogate mother for the princess throughout her childhood. Indeed, it is Maleficent's kiss which breaks the curse in the final act, confirming both her love for the princess, and her status as the film's heroine.

On 1 September 2014, worldwide ticket sales for *Maleficent* surpassed $750 million, making it Jolie's biggest commercial hit at the age of 39. Although *Maleficent* was marketed as a Disney picture, Jolie featured prominently in the promotional campaign as the studio sought to build anticipation through her return to acting. Early posters for *Maleficent* showed Jolie in close-up, for instance, wearing the black cape and horns of her character. In contrast to her costume, Jolie's skin is porcelain white in these posters, while the red of her lips is digitally enhanced to provide a shot of vivid colour. This monochrome aesthetic foregrounds Jolie's facial features, suggesting that her 'famous hornet-stung lips' are as iconic as her character's horns (Richardson, 2000, p. 93). These posters are also significant in terms of the broader development of Jolie's star image. The emphasis here is on the face, rather than the body, reinforcing the extent to which Jolie has moved from the hyper-sexualised image of her action babe years. At the same time, however, the blood-red color of the lips invokes themes of carnality and temptation. Elements of Jolie's earlier personae remain present, then, existing alongside her new roles as mother and humanitarian.

In his review of *Maleficent* for the *Washington Post*, Michael Cavna (2014) noted how the film is 'deepened by the meta-narrative of [Jolie's] own life', referring to the way in which the plot draws on both her bad-girl-gone-good image, and her motherhood, an allusion that is made explicit by the casting of Jolie's own daughter, Vivienne Jolie-Pitt, as the four-year-old Aurora. Yet, the plot also folds in elements of the star's humanitarianism. In the film, Maleficent acts as guardian of the Moors, a magical realm populated by various creatures and wildlife. As guardian of the Moors, Jolie's character must defend her home against the constant threat of human invasion. In an early action sequence, Maleficent fends off an army of marauding soldiers, using her wings to propel her enemies backward [Fig. 20.2]. The camera frames Jolie in medium long shot, cap-

Fig. 20.2 Maleficent's wings

turing the full expanse of her wings. Although this shot recalls the physical prowess of Jolie's action roles, it also invokes the saintly image that she has cultivated in her UNHCR campaigns: Maleficent comes to the rescue of the other magical creatures, using her spectacular abilities to help those who cannot protect themselves. Jolie's costume in this sequence is also significant: barefoot and wearing a long, flowing dress, Maleficent is simultaneously winged adventurer and earth mother, action star and humanitarian.

In a June 2014 interview for *Woman's Hour*, Jolie established a series of parallels between *Maleficent* and her recent campaigns to raise awareness of sexual violence in conflict.Indeed, the interview was part of the star's work to promote the Global Summit to End Sexual Violence in Conflict (ESVC). Held in London in June 2014, ESVC was a four-day summit where Jolie gave the opening address. Speaking about the scene in which Maleficent's wings are torn from her body, Jolie confirmed that this was intended as 'a metaphor for rape', commenting, 'The core of [*Maleficent*] is abuse' (Wallace, 2014). With these comments, Jolie sought to take advantage of a correlation that emerged between her ESVC appearance and her latest film to merge these two star projects together in a fashion best described as 'synergistic'.

Alison Trope (2012, p. 188) argues that it is common for stars to 'directly align their artistic […] output with the causes they support'.

Media coverage of this type of campaigning—so often skewed towards the star's output and not the cause—prompts the question, 'Who stands to gain more?' Jo Littler (2008, p. 241) notes how humanitarian campaigning offers an 'extremely cost-effective' way for a star to gain wide exposure for her/his brand, for example. The experiences of Jolie, by and large, serve to uphold such a reading: her work with UNHCR added new associations to her star image as she moved into her mid thirties; and these associations have, in turn, been pivotal to the way in which Jolie has expanded her on-screen brand in this period, moving beyond the action babe cinema into other genres. Indeed, the branding opportunities generated by celebrity campaigning were certainly evident in the case of *Maleficent*, where Jolie's ESVC interview corresponded with Disney's efforts to market the film as an edgy, revisionist fairy tale with cross-generational appeal.

Rather than simply transferring political energy onto the pop-culture sphere, the star's comments also used the film and its broad appeal to mediate and amplify the campaign against sexual violence in conflict. Jolie's on-screen performances are crucial to the affective power that she wields as a campaigner. *Maleficent* and several earlier films, including *Heart* and the *Tomb Raider* franchise, engage a number of discourses that overlap with her ESVC campaigns. Indeed, it is the strong female image that she projects in these films that animates much of what Jolie now does as a humanitarian, rendering her campaigns visible for audiences who might otherwise be unaware of such issues. More than just self-promotion, Jolie's ESVC interview illustrates how stars are able to exploit connections between their films and their campaigning to advance not only their own brands but also those of the causes they support. While Jolie's efforts to align her humanitarianism with her films have not always been successful (both *Heart* and *In the Land of Blood and Honey* underperformed commercially), this strategy has played a significant part in several career milestones. Foremost among these milestones was *Maleficent*, a film which bucked the trend of diminishing box-office returns for female stars over 35.

Conclusion

At a time when almost every Hollywood star appears to support one or more causes, it is important to study how the films and campaigns of these individuals intersect (Gulam, 2014). This chapter has examined the place of humanitarianism in Jolie's lasting screen career, endeavouring to show how the star's work with UNHCR featured in her transition from action babe to mature actress. Although Jolie's willingness to speak out on various issues has brought its fair share of criticism (Hyde, 2009), it has also contributed to her enduring appeal. This was apparent in the case of her recent decision to publicly disclose the details of her preventative double mastectomy. In a *New York Times* op-ed published in May 2013, Jolie revealed how she chose to undergo surgery because of her high risk of developing breast cancer: she is a carrier of the 'faulty' BRCA1 gene (Jolie, 2013). The response to Jolie's announcement was generally positive, with various commentators praising her 'thoughtfulness' and 'bravery' (Hollywood Reporter, 2013). What this incident clarifies is how a star's interventions into important issues—health debates, humanitarian crises, and so on—have the potential to reinforce pre-existing aspects of her/his star persona, while also adding new qualities that can aid career longevity. In her real-life campaigning, as on the big screen, Jolie has projected an image of 'strong', 'compassionate' female stardom, which has both adapted to her maturing years, and demonstrated sustained popularity.

References

A Mighty Heart. (2007). Film. Directed by Michael Winterbottom. [DVD]. USA: Paramount Vantage.

Alien. (1979). Film. Directed by Ridley Scott. [DVD]. USA: Twentieth Century Fox.

Apocalypse Now. (1979). Film. Directed by Francis Ford Coppola. [DVD]. USA: United Artists.

Barron, L. 2009. An actress compelled to act: Angelina Jolie's Notes from My Travels as celebrity activist/travel narrative. *Postcolonial Studies*. 12(2): 211–228.

Bell, K. 2013. Raising Africa?: Celebrity and the rhetoric of the White Saviour. *PORTAL Journal of Multidisciplinary International Studies*. 10(1): 1–24.

Box Office Mojo. (2014). *Angelina Jolie*. [Online] Available from: http://www.boxofficemojo.com/people/chart/?id=angelinajolie.htm [Accessed: 17 September 2014].

Cavna, M. (2014, June 1). 'MALEFICENT': Angelina Jolie soars with $70 M debut at box office. *Washington Post*. [Online]. Available from: http://www.washingtonpost.com/news/comic-riffs/wp/2014/06/01/maleficent-angelina-jolies-villainous-screen-return-soars-with-70m-debut-at-box-office/ [Accessed: 17 September 2014].

Changeling. (2008). Film. Directed by Clint Eastwood. [DVD]. USA: Universal Stduios.

Daily Mail. (2006, October 26). Angelina set to adopt another baby. *Daily Mail.* [Online]. Available from: http://www.dailymail.co.uk/tvshowbiz/article-412751/Angelina-set-adopt-baby.html [Accessed: 29 September 2014].
Dieter, H., and R. Kumar. 2006. The downside of celebrity diplomacy: The neglected complexity of development. *Global Governance.* 14(3): 259–264.
Ebert, R. (2000, January 14). Girl, interrupted. *Chicago Sun-Times.* [Online]. Available from: http://www.rogerebert.com/[Accessed: 17 September 2014].
Forbes (2012, August 22). The World's most powerful couples. *Forbes.* [Online]. Available from: http://www.forbes.com/[Accessed: 24 September 2014].
Gia. 1998. Television Movie. Directed by Michael Cristofer. [DVD]. USA: HBO.
Girl, Interrupted. (1999). Film. Directed by James Mangold. [DVD]. USA: Columbia Pictures.
Gulam, J. 2014. Film stardom, gender and philanthropy: Sharon Stone at the world summit of nobel peace laureates. *Celebrity Studies.* 5(3): 360–363.
Hollywood Reporter. (2013, May 14). Angelina Jolie's 'Brave' double mastectomy decision. *Hollywood Reporter.* [Online]. Available from: http://www.hollywoodreporter.com/news/angelina-jolies-double-mastectomy-hollywood-522173 [Accessed: 9 September 2014].
Hornaday, A. (2007, June 22). A blow to the heart. *Washington Post.* [Online]. Available from: http://www.washingtonpost.com/wp-dyn/content/article/2007/06/21/AR2007062102504.html. [Accessed: 9 September 2014].
Howell, P. (2007, June 22). Heart and soul. *Toronto Star.* [Online]. Available from: Factiva.com. [Accessed: 24 September 2014].
Hyde, M. 2009. *Celebrity: How entertainers took over the world and why we need an exit strategy.* London: Harvill Secker.
In the Land of Blood and Honey. (2011). Film. Directed by Angelina Jolie. [DVD]. USA: Sony Pictures.
Jermyn, D. 2012. 'Glorious, glamorous and that old standby, amorous': The late blossoming of Diane Keaton's romantic comedy career. *Celebrity Studies.* 3(1): 37–51.
Jolie, A. 2003. *Notes from my travels.* New York: Pocket Books.
——— (2013, May 14). My medical choice. *New York Times.* [Online]. Available from: http://www.nytimes.com/2013/05/14/opinion/my-medical-choice.html?_r=0 [Accessed: 9 September 2014].
Kung Fu Panda. (2008). Animated film. Directed by John Stevenson and Mark Osborne. [DVD]. USA: Paramount Pictures.
Kramer, P. 2003. 'A woman in a male-dominated world': Jodie Foster, stardom, and 90s Hollywood. In *Contemporary Hollywood stardom*, eds. T. Austin, and M. Barker. London: Arnold.
Lara Croft: Tomb Raider. (2001). Film. Directed by Simon West. [DVD]. USA: Paramount Pictures.

Lara Croft Tomb Raider: Cradle of Life. (2003). Film. Directed by Jan de Bont. [DVD] USA: Paramount Pictures.

Littler, J. 2008. 'I feel your pain': Cosmopolitan charity and the public fashioning of the celebrity soul. *Social Semiotics.* 18(2): 237–251.

Maleficent. (2014). Film. Directed by Robert Stromberg. [DVD]. USA: Walt Disney Studios.

Marshall, P.D. 1997. *Celebrity and power: Fame in contemporary culture.* Minneapolis: University of Minnesota Press.

McDonald, P. 2012. *Hollywood stardom.* Oxford: Wiley & Sons.

Mr. & Mrs. Smith. (2005). Film. Directed by Doug Liman. [DVD]. USA: Twentieth Century Fox.

O'Day, M. 2004. Beauty in motion: Gender, spectacle and action babe cinema. In *Action and adventure cinema,* ed. Y. Tasker. London: Routledge.

Palmer, M. (2007, September 8). Angelina almighty. *Independent.* [Online]. Available from: Factiva.com [Accessed: 25 September 2014].

Pomerantz, D. (2013). *Angelina Jolie Tops Our List of Hollywood's Highest-Paid Actresses.* [Online]. Available from: http://www.forbes.com/sites/dorothypomerantz/2013/07/29/angelina-jolie-tops-our-list-of-hollywoods-highest-paid-actresses/ [Accessed: 15 September 2014].

Puig, C. (2007, June 24). Jolie gives 'Mighty Heart' its lifeblood. *USA Today.* [Online]. Available from: http://usatoday30.usatoday.com/life/movies/reviews/2007-06-21-mighty-heart_N.htm [Accessed: 5 May 2014].

Richardson, J. (2000, February). Angelina Jolie and the torture of fame, *Esquire,* pp. 91–157.

Salt. (2010). Film. Directed by Philip Noyce. [DVD]. USA: Columbia Pictures.

Sleeping Beauty. (1959). Animated film. Directed by Clyde Geronomi. [DVD]. USA: Walt Disney Studios.

Smith, T. (2007, June 22). Angelina Jolie discusses 'A Mighty Heart'. *The Early Show* [Television] CBS. Available from: Factiva.com [Accessed: 24 September 2014].

The Tourist. (2010). Film. Directed by Florian Henckel von Donnersmarck. [DVD]. USA: Columbia Pictures.

Trope, A. 2012. Mother Angelina: Hollywood philanthropy personified. In *Commodity activism: Cultural resistance in Neoliberal Times,* eds. R. Mukherjee, and S. Banet-Weiser. New York: NYU Press.

Wallace, E. (2014, June 10). Angelina Jolie, William Hague, and sexual violence in conflict. *Woman's Hour.* [Radio] BBC Radio 4. Available from: http://www.bbc.co.uk/programmes/b0460hz8 [Accessed: 22 September 2014].

Wilkins, K. (2014). Celebrity as celebration of privatization in global development: A critical feminist analysis of Oprah, Madonna, and Angelina. [Online]. *Communication, Culture & Critique.* Available from: http://onlinelibrary.wiley.com/ [Accessed: 11 March 2015].

CHAPTER 21

Rearticulating Bruce Lee and His 'Hip Hop Fury' in Fan-Made Videos

Dorothy Wai-sim Lau

INTRODUCTION

No Chinese movie star's name has perpetuated for so long a time and with such great intensity as Bruce Lee, 'the world's most idolised star' (Hu, 2010, p. 166). Lee reached his greatest success after starring as the lead in only four martial arts movies including *The Big Boss* (1971), *Fist of Fury* (1972), *Way of the Dragon* (1972), and *Enter the Dragon* (1973). His tragic and unexpected death[1] at 32 shocked fans of Chinese cinema and martial arts communities all over the globe. Despite the short filmography, Lee's cinematic fame sustains decades beyond his premature death. To this day, the international public uses various accessible means to recall and recode Lee's star image, engaging with a range of fan activity beyond the cinema. Audiences continue to fervently discuss, distribute, and recycle Lee's texts and pieces of his legacy, as if they, in Brian Hu's words, 'refus[e] to let go of the memory of Bruce Lee' (2010, p. 166).

Bruce Lee's bond with hip hop is a prominent aspect of his stardom, frequently noted by scholars, critics, and fans. A number of critical works

[1] While producing *The Game of Death* in 1973, Lee suddenly died from what his doctors officially announced as a 'death by misadventure', and autopsies showed his brain had swollen considerably due to cerebral edema.

D.W.-s. Lau
Academy of Film, Hong Kong Baptist University, Hong Kong, China

have explored the relationship between Bruce Lee and hip hop, including M. T. Kato's *From Kung Fu to Hip Hop: Globalization, Revolution, and Popular Culture* (2007), which asserts Bruce Lee's prominent place and cultural legacy in hip hop (pp. 176–178). In view of global capitalism, Kato argues how Lee's movies and the self-sufficiency of the 'hip-hop nation' offer a 'new social relationship', an 'alternative to those imposed by dominant institutions' (p. 6). Kato also demonstrates how the art of Lee serves as 'a progressive foundational concept of the hip-hop aesthetics' to many hip hop artists (p. 176). As 'the first global Chinese film star' (Berry, 2006, p. 218), Lee attained fame not only in Chinese communities but also with African American audiences, making him the martial arts actor who, possibly, enjoys the most popularity among African Americans.

The impetus of this chapter is the question how Bruce Lee and his hip hop-propelled persona are recalled and recoded as they are transposed from cinematic space to cyberspace. The phenomenon of cyber obituaries began to appear shortly after the emergence of computer-mediated communications (Wahlberg, 2009, p. 224). The prevalence of fast broadband infrastructures and free image-editing software, that became popular in the late 1990s, allow ordinary users to easily search, poach, copy, and share texts (Russo, 2009). Fans can post clips obtained from other websites or favourite movie clips from DVDs, or even mix the variously sourced footage into a single video. They can also set the images to musical tracks that are taken from a different source. All these technologies have given rise to fan vids, which appear and stand out as an extension and renewal of earlier forms of fan-based memorial culture. Vids refer to the montages of visual material culled from mass media source texts and set to music. By fusing music with images, 'vidders' (creators of vids) separate songs from their original contexts to create new meanings (Russo, 2009). Fans post memorial vids on cyber platforms and invite other users to comment, sharing knowledge and exchanging ideas about the star, while collaboratively reinventing the star discourse. Lee's persona, as a result, escapes the threat of being 'frozen in immortality' (Hu, 2010, p. 166) by reappearing vigorously and relentlessly in the Web-based fan circuits all over the world, reviving and strengthening Lee's currency as a global star.

This chapter will examine how fan vids preserve and reimagine Bruce Lee's star persona by rearticulating Lee's connection with hip hop in original yet familiar ways. I adopt YouTube, the most popular video hosting site among vidders, as the primary site of investigation. To limit the corpus of analysis, I performed a keyword search on YouTube, on 9 July 2014, of the phrase 'Bruce Lee tribute video'. I focus on the first two videos generated from the result list (sorted by most viewed), *Bruce Lee Tribute Video* (which I refer to as 'fan vid #1'[2]) and *Bruce Lee 'Be Like Water'—A Tribute (40 Year Anniversary)* (which I refer to as 'fan vid #2'[3]). The analysis will show how Lee's rebellious screen image (verified by fan vid #1) and the freestyling and multiple sampling of martial arts (verified by fan vid #2) reveal an affinity to hip hop culture. I will attempt to argue that fan vids work to sustain Lee's hip hop connection, allowing the star to reappear in the global fan circuit as contemporary, compelling, and vibrant even though he has been dead for four decades. In addition, fan vid #1 is a fan-generated text that lies outside the corporatised milieu, whereas fan vid #2 is an 'official' one, created by BruceLee.Com (the online address of the official Bruce Lee site).[4] This analysis will then provide clues as to how fans and Lee's family contextualise Lee's star image differently, as official monuments of celebration and as cultural expressions effected by the 'vernacular memory' (Wahlberg, 2009, p. 218).

Bruce Lee and Hip Hop

Lee's connection to hip hop arguably stems from America's fascination with Hong Kong martial arts in the 1970s. Benefiting from the unprecedented domination of foreign films on American cinematic screens that, according to David Desser (2000), happened in May 1973[5] (pp. 20–21), publicity for films like *Deadly Duo* (1971) and *The Water Margin* (1972), both directed by Chang Cheh, appeared in the *Amsterdam News*,[6] the most widely circulated black newspaper in New York City. Not only were martial arts films distributed theatrically throughout Chinatowns, they were also commonly shown in black communities in cities such as New York

---

[2] Accessed at: https://www.youtube.com/watch?v=kqrivEdB8K4 [1 July 2014].
[3] Accessed at: https://www.youtube.com/watch?v=a8o0Xk5LSAg [1 July 2014].
[4] BruceLee.Com is a website engineered by personal management of Lee since 2010. It is part of the system of production and circulation of 'official' star images and narratives.
[5] During the week of 16 May 1973, a handful of films, such as *Fist of Fury* (1972), *Deep Thrust: The Hand of Death* (1972), and *Five Fingers of Death* (1973) were ranked the top three on *Variety*'s box-office list. According to Desser (2000), this was a rare instance where a number of foreign films, starring non-white actors, were extremely well received at the US box office.
[6] This newspaper, the oldest African American newspaper in the United States, was founded in 1909 and continues to be published to this day, under the name, *New York Amsterdam News*.

and Washington DC. Furthermore, the popularity of a handful of 'kung fu' films notably influenced Blaxploitation, an American subgenre targeted to the urban black audience, and although short lived, attained box-office success and an enduring influence on American cinema through such low-budget cult films as *Scream Blacula Scream* (1973) and *The Mack* (1973) (Ongiri, 2005, p. 252).

As a representative figure of the rebel culture (Kato, 2007, p. 107), Lee was a source of inspiration to the emerging hip hop scene in that period. Hip hop culture has different expressions including graffiti, rapping, beat-boxes, and breakdancing, constituting an intervention into mainstream culture. Originating in the 1970s as a ghetto youth subculture in the New York city boroughs, especially in the Bronx, it grew properly among the African American, Caribbean American, and Latin American young people (Gateward, 2009, p. 53), whose opportunities were truncated and histories and identities were gravely oppressed. Asian martial arts offered an alternative lifestyle and state of mind to insurgent youth (Kato, 2007, p. 94).

A number of pioneering practitioners such as Daniel Lee, Jhoo Rhee, Ed Parker, and Bruce Lee were able to afford the authentic teachings of different Asian martial arts, developing an awareness of the self and serving against any systematic formation of a collective identity. In this regard, Lee's movies share a similar ideological foundation and social reality to those movies circulated in the African American community, especially Blaxploitation. Lee's films reveal stories about Chinese people attempting to negotiate their identities, mainly through physical prowess and aggression, with respect to Japanese (as in the case of *Fist of Fury*), European (as in the case of *Way of the Dragon*), and white American powers (as in the case of *Enter the Dragon*), validating what Kato phrases, 'the paradigm of kung fu as a rebel culture' (Kato, 2007, p. 96). Key to this, as will be demonstrated later, is the freestyle nature of martial arts, especially the type of martial arts performed by Bruce Lee and hip hop's improvised origins.

Bruce Lee Tribute Video (Fan Vid #1)

On YouTube many fan vids present a modern fusion of Lee's hip hop identity by intercutting Lee's screen performance with hip hop music. On 28 September 2008, a Web user named D/Vision uploaded the video entitled *Bruce Lee Tribute Video* (fan vid #1), for the purpose of—as the title directly indicates—paying tribute to the superstar. Online for nearly six years, the video entry proved quite popular, attracting 4,174,650 views (at the time of my original search). Approximately seven minutes long, fan vid #1 is an assemblage of footage from *Enter the Dragon* (1973), Lee's fourth feature film, a co-production between Warner Brothers in America and Golden Harvest in Asia, becoming, as Kato stated, 'one of the first projects under the strategic paradigm of global capitalism' (Kato, 2007, p. 98). Directed by Robert Clouse, the movie was released in the United States on the sixth day after Lee's death, and marked Lee's final cinematic appearance.

The vidder extends Lee's character from the diegetic cinematic world to the African American youth subculture by cutting movie footage to hip hop music. The sonic space of the vid is filled by three musical pieces: 'Till We Meet Again' and two soundtracks from the albums titled *Epicon* and *Avenger*, produced by Immediate Music, a USA-based trailer music company. The song 'Till We Meet Again' lasts less than one-third of the video length, yet its limited length does not imply its insignificance. It serves as the opening audio cue, setting the stage, subtly, for the elucidation of Lee's martial arts persona in relation to hip hop culture. The song is performed by Grammy Award-winning rapper Mr. Cheeks, featuring Stephen Marley, son of the renowned reggae artist Bob Marley. Like the vid itself, 'Till We Meet Again' was intended as a memorial, a ballad written in remembrance of Freaky Tah, who, with Mr. Cheeks, was a member of a hip hop group called the Lost Boyz. The lyrics reveal the deep relationship between the colleagues, resonating beyond Freaky Tah's death. The lyrics articulate Mr. Cheeks's sorrowful emotion, combined with his salute, over the loss of a companion. However, the song cut to fan vid #1 includes no lyrics but merely musical cues. The void of lyrical space signifies that music alone plays a crucial role in identifying the paralleled memories of Freaky Tah and of Bruce Lee. Putting aside the literal signification of the lyrics, the vidder makes music the dominant aesthetic form that rearticulates Lee's kinetic self-expression with respect to the loss of Freaky Tah. As Francesca Coppa argues, fan vids use music to further analyse the pre-existing images and even to tell new stories.[7] The vidder renews, if not pluralises, Lee's star appeal by reinterpreting his screen personality—the source material of star

---

[7] Coppa (2008) further corroborates her thesis by pointing out, journalist, Jake Coyle's false assumption in an *Associated Press* article ('The Best Fan-Made Music Videos on YouTube', 15 January 2008) that fans who make fan music videos intend to use video to illustrate the music, rather than using the music to convey the story of the video.

discourse—in the non-diegetic realm. Despite its brief duration, the use of 'Till We Meet Again' is noted by users, including 'Drumadldol', who wrote in March 2013: 'The intro song is Mr. Cheeks till we meet again. I hope it helps everyone who wanted to know hola back if it helped', showcasing his knowledge of hip hop music through the reference to the song and the user's use of hip hop vernacular. This comment, alongside the video post, frames and constitutes Lee's stardom with respect to hip hop culture.

Fan vid #1 also reveals an emphasis on Lee's body, central to his unique charisma (Berry, 2006, p. 218). The body is a focal point in kung fu films (Gateward, 2009, p. 65), allowing training scenes to underscore a rise to power and control. A majority of fan vid #1's content belongs to the fight scenes in *Enter the Dragon*, such as the martial arts competition, the underground base combat, and the mirror room duel between Lee and Han, demonstrating Lee's unmatched fight choreography. Many shots register the body's expressive possibilities by exhibiting Lee's iconic image and demeanour—bare-chested body, bending muscles, shouting with fury. Battling either bare-hand or with weapons like the *nunchaku*, 'the weapon of popular defense' (Kato, 2007, p. 41), Lee uses his body, stringently trained and tightly manipulated, as an instrument to attack and defeat the evildoers and oppressors. The intense sense of discipline and stress on physical prowess carry significance in the cultural imperatives of African Americans (David, 2012). As Gateward suggests, for many African Americans, the body is the tool to negotiate the experiences of marginalisation and advance the power of ethnic monitories, 'a site of resistance' as well as the primary resource and the means for self-articulation (2009, pp. 64–65). The physical training, as a process of becoming, permits powerless, colonised people to gain power (Gateward, 2009, p. 65). Thus, fan vid #1 displays the possibilities and alternatives to the oppressive regimes that Lee's body signifies, advocating the identification of the star in African American culture. While some fans prefer Lee, in *Fist of Fury*, as a confrontational screen personae, the vidder presents Lee's character in *Enter the Dragon* as a better fit, ideologically and pertinently, to hip hop culture, expressing his/her alternative outlook about the star personality. Although *Enter the Dragon* is utilised in the video I am examining, the centrality of *Fist of Fury* to Lee's star image, and crucially for this chapter, his outsider position deserves to be discussed further.

As Chris Berry posits, *Fist of Fury*, among Lee's films, is his 'most evidently nationalistic work' (2006, p. 220). In the setting of semi-colonised Shanghai, Lee plays the role of Chen Zhen, a student of Huo Yuanjia, founder of the jinqu martial arts school, seeking to avenge his master's death from rival Japanese people. The Japanese sneer at Zhen with a sign bearing the 'Sick Men of Asia' (*dongya bingfu*) slogan. This is reminiscent of an earlier scene in *Fist of Fury* when Lee tries to enter a park off limits to the inhabitants but is stopped at the gate by the guard, who points to the sign which reads 'No Dogs or Chinese'. Lee leaps several feet in the air and breaks the sign with a single kick. This scene serves as both a narrative and visual climax with Chen Zhen presented as a patriotic hero that all Chinese threatened by imperialism would be keen to associate themselves with. Departing from the general understanding, the vidder devotes his/her reading of Lee's on-screen persona, choosing *Enter the Dragon* to copy and rework Lee's culturally subversive image. In *Enter the Dragon*, Lee plays the role of a member of the international police working in the service of a British intelligence agent to combat a well-off criminal named Han. As Vijay Prashad illuminates with regard to *Enter the Dragon*'s release in India, contrasting the film with the Bond series, '[W]ith his bare fits and his *nunchakus*, Lee provided young people with the sense that we could be victorious, like the Vietnamese guerrillas, against the virulence of international capitalism' (2003, p. 54), although Prashad ignores the fact that Lee works with an MI-5 agent in the film. Fan vid #1 displays how Lee's screen performances promoted a culturally subversive image against oppressive regimes, but one that rose, through Lee's bodily strength, to become a heroic image. The video also illustrates that vidders are empowered to create their own meaning through the use of stars' materials and the manipulation of popular texts. D/Vision employs hip hop music to memorialise Lee as a figure of resistance through his taut and resilient body, fully demonstrated in his films.

'Be Like Water': Fan Vid #2

Lee's hip hop connection is demonstrated through not only his on-screen image but also his off-screen persona. Fans and critics celebrate Lee's genuine martial arts prowess, sustained by a reflective philosophical foundation, illustrated in fan vid #2, (*Bruce Lee 'Be Like Water'—A Tribute (40 Year Anniversary)*), which is a commemorative text of the star from his official website. This approximately 5-minute-long fan vid has attracted more than 400,000 views since its launch on YouTube on 19 July 2013 and the time of writing. The vidder uses digital production techniques such as lap dissolves, superimposed images, and multiple frames to create a montage following the timeline of Lee's life from his youth to his death. Different types of images—movie stills, press interviews, family photographs, gym-room practice, and his performance in the Long Beach competition[8]—are all repurposed, with cinematic effects, to pay compliment to Lee. The majority of the content appears in black and white, a visual aesthetic akin to documentary, a genre defined by the conveying of real life rather than fiction. Distinct from the previous video which emphasises Lee's cinematic appearances, this vid represents Lee in a way that his off-screen persona overshadows his on-screen presence.

The visual materials in this vid pinpoints Lee's appeal as a martial arts actor-philosopher, a quality that distinguishes Lee from his counterparts. One may argue that Lee's martial arts would not have been as popular and complete without the profound philosophical basis that he attached to them. As a martial artist, Lee is famous for an amalgam of physical prowess and philosophical wisdom. Attending philosophy courses, in addition to his drama major, at the University of Washington, Lee was able to synthesise the thoughts of East and West from Lao Tzu, Plato, and Descartes into a unique personal philosophy of self-knowledge. Throughout media appearances, Lee offered insight on life, human understanding, and state of mind, solidifying his public personality as a genuine martial artist, while also moving beyond his screen image.

In fan vid #2, this aspect of Lee's persona persists, mainly evidenced through Lee's philosophical narration from an interview on *The Pierre Berton Show* in 1971. The edited sequences of his 'water' analogy to martial arts serve as the structural skeleton of the vid, together with sundry still images filling up the other content space. The vid opens with Lee's speech in the interview, in which he states, 'Empty your mind, be formless, shapeless, like water. Water can flow, or it can crash. Be water, my friend.' This speech, originating from the four-episode TV series *Longstreet* in 1971, included as the opening voiceover of fan vid #1, is delivered through Lee's monologue.[9] The vidder of fan vid #1 presents the monologue alongside Lee's movie footage exhibiting his screen persona as a martial arts fighter, whereas the creator of fan vid #2 edited the speech from the interview footage, underscoring Lee's philosophical statement and his status

---

[8] The Long Beach competition is an international karate and martial arts tournament held in Long Beach, California since August 1964.

[9] 'Empty your mind, be formless, shapeless, like water. If you put water into a cup, it becomes the cup. You put water into a bottle and it becomes the bottle. You put it in a teapot, it becomes the teapot. Now water can flow or it can crash. Be water, my friend' (*Longstreet*, 1971).

as a philosopher. The 'water' analogy exemplifies the essence of jeet kune do, a martial arts system invented by Lee and meaning, literally, 'the way of the intercepting fist', which suggests liberation from form or 'style'. Combining various martial arts techniques to create a unique system, jeet kune do could be described as freestyle martial arts (Smith, 2011). Lee dissolves the classical, rigid disciplines of kung fu and rebuilds them with practicality, fluidity, and flexibility, encouraging martial arts practitioners to transcend the boundary of a single technique and attempt a more fluid sort of kinetic approach to martial arts.[10]

This suggests jeet kune do can be seen as conceptually interlocked with hip hop (Yang, 1998, p. 94). In a *Vibe* article about Lee, Jeff Yang attempts to 'reset' hip hop to its conceptual foundation through an analogy with jeet kune do:

> Because the art of Jeet Kune Do was motivated by practicality, it evolved like hip-hop: it began in the old school—spares, freestyle, with nothing separating the master from the rhythm. And then, only after locking down the basics, did Lee start sampling the best of what other disciplines had to offer, biting on world flavours like Muay Thai, Jiu Jitsu, and Tae Kwon Do. Even toward the end of his days, Lee was still remixing. (p. 94)

The 'formless' and 'shapeless' paradigm of martial arts coincides with hip hop: from the beginning, hip hop, as a musical form, breaks from existing genres like rock, funk, and soul by sampling pre-existing sounds, layering and looping until a new groove is formed (Strauss, 1999, p. 240). What jeet kune do and hip hop have in common is the creativity and autonomy of self-expression, in addition to discipline and expertise. As Imani Perry has noted, the martial artist's

> combination of discipline, dexterity, excellence, mysterious tradition, and improvisational fighting ability seduces the MCs and listeners because of hip hop culture's love of improvisation, difficulty, and the kind of expertise that makes the difficult appear smooth and easy. (2004, p. 132)

---

[10] This point is made clear by Lee's speech in Berton's interview, heard in fan vid #2 after about one minute and twenty seconds. As Lee professes: 'Styles tend to ... err ... separate men because they have their own doctrines, and then the doctrines became the gospel truth, you know? Then you cannot change, you know? And ... but if you do not have style, we just say, here I am, you know, as ... as a human being, how can I express myself, totally and completely. Now that way ... you won't create a style because style is a crystallisation, you know what I mean, that way is a process of continuing growth' (*The Pierre Berton Show*, 1971).

Among the existing images of Bruce Lee directly suggestive of this jeet kune do/hip hop 'remix' connection is the confrontation between Lee and Kareem Abdul-Jabbar in *Game of Death* (1973) (Kato, 2007, p. 178). This scene evokes a sense that the masters of kung fu and basketball both participate in 'freestyle' combat, not confined to a single framework.

Lee's martial arts philosophy underscoring 'freestyle' and sampling of multiple martial arts is not only articulated in the monologue of fan vid #2 but also embodied in the music (and similar to fan vid #1). The song 'Be Like Water', which plays throughout the entire video, was inspired by Lee's 'water' theory and draws immediate association with Lee's martial arts doctrines. The song was written exclusively to commemorate the fortieth anniversary of Lee's death, and the single was released in July 2013 as part of the soundtrack of *No Way As Way*, a documentary film about Lee, produced and distributed in the United States. 'Be Like Water' is performed by London-based singer and songwriter Mozez, whose music is trip hop,[11] a fusion of hip hop and electronica that emerged in the early 1990s as a genre of electronic music that combines several musical styles (Cinquemani, 2002). Therefore, fan vid #2 appropriates, foregrounds, and rejuvenates Lee's martial arts persona, marked by jeet kune do, with hip hop consciousness by blending Lee's images with Mozez's music. Suffice to say, the amalgam of hip hop, martial arts, and Lee's persona renews the star discourse of Lee readily available.

Conclusion

The above analysis examines how hip hop serves as a prominent component in fans' tributes of Bruce Lee in cyberspace. Fan vids entail a dynamic discursive space where Lee is reincarnated in the fan-generated, multifaceted texts. The two vids analysed demonstrate how fans and official sources reshape Lee's star personality in the contemporary cultural milieu. The first vid focuses on Lee's status as martial arts actor whereas the second vid stresses Lee's persona as a martial arts philosopher. Yet, both vids promote Lee's connection with hip hop, an entirely different cultural system from Chinese martial arts. By editing hip hop music to the *Enter the Dragon* footage, the vidder of fan vid #1 restages the dynamics

---

[11] Mozez is a member of the successful British trip hop band called Zero7. Trip hop's drum-based breakdown is similar to hip hop music.

between Lee's rebel persona and African American experiences, while the vidder of fan vid #2 utilises images from Lee's personal life with the song 'Be Like Water', stressing Lee's martial arts philosopher persona. Both vids rejuvenate the star's hip hop tie in creative and eclectic fashions, unveiling key continuities between modes of star discourse on the Web and earlier media.

Lee's persona is under endless reworking from fans, leading to a new hybrid star phenomenon. Lee does not appear to 'freeze' in a coherent, already-known star image. Instead, his image has been remade, demonstrating the ability of fans, through the World Wide Web, to revise, diversify, and complicate a star image, and create new ways of ensuring that star personas endure in the contemporary era.

References

Berry, C. 2006. Stellar transit: Bruce Lee's body or Chinese masculinity in a transnational frame. In *Embodied modernities: Corporeality, representation, and Chinese cultures*, eds. F. Martin, and L. Heinrich. Honolulu: University of Hawai'i Press.

Bruce Lee. (1971, December 9). The Pierre Berton show, *Canadian Television Network*.

Cinquemani, S. (2002). Album review: DJ shadow: Endtroducing [Online]. Available from: http://www.slantmagazine.com/music/review/dj-shadow-endtroducing [Accessed: 26 May 2015].

Coppa, F. (2008). Women, *Star Trek*, and the early development of fannish vidding. *Transformative works and cultures*. 1. Available from: http://journal.transformativeworks.org/index.php/twc/article/view/44/64 [Accessed: 3 August 2014].

David, J. (2012). How Bruce Lee has influenced black culture. *The Grio*. [Online]. Available from: http://thegrio.com/2012/07/20/how-bruce-lee-has-influenced-black-culture/2/[Accessed: 3 January 2015].

Deadly Duo. (1971). Film. Directed by Chang Cheh. Hong Kong: Shaw Brothers.

Deep Thrust: The Hand of Death. (1972). Film. Directed by Feng Huang. USA: American International Pictures.

Desser, D. 2000. The kung fu craze: Hong Kong cinema's first American reception. In *The cinema of Hong Kong: History, arts, identity*, eds. P. Fu, and D. Desser. Cambridge: Cambridge University Press.

Enter the Dragon. (1973). Film. Directed by Robert Clouse. USA: Warner Bros. Pictures & Golden Harvest/Fortune Star.

Fist of Fury. (1972). Film. Directed by Lo Wei. Hong Kong: Golden Harvest.

Five Fingers of Death. (1973). Film. Director by Chang-hwa Jeong. Hong Kong: Shaw Brothers.

Gateward, F. 2009. Wong Fei-Hung in Da House: Hong Kong martial-arts films and hip-hop culture. In *Chinese connections: Critical perspectives on film, identity, and diaspora*, eds. S. Tan, P. Feng, and G. Marchetti. Philadelphia: Temple University Press.

Hu, B. 2010. Bruce Lee after Bruce Lee: A life in conjectures. In *Chinese film stars*, eds. M. Farquhar and Y. Zhang. London: Routledge.

Kato, M.T. 2007. *From kung fu to hip hop: Globalization, revolution and popular culture.* Albany, NY: State University of New York Press.

Longstreet: The way of the intercepting fist. (1971, September 16). American Broadcasting Company.

No Way As Way. (2013). Film. Directed by Shannon Lee. USA: Warner Brothers.

Official Bruce Lee. (n.d.). Available from: http://www.brucelee.com/ [Accessed: 27 July 2014].

Ongiri, A. 2005. Bruce Lee in the ghetto connection: Kung fu theatre and African Americans reinventing culture at the margins. In *East main street: Asian American popular culture*, eds. S. Dave, L.N. Shilpa, and O. Tasha. New York: New York University Press.

Perry, I. 2004. *Prophets of the Hood: Politics and poetics in hip hop.* Durham, NC: Duke.

Prashad, V. 2003. Bruce Lee and the anti-imperialism of kung fu: A polycultural adventure. *Positions: East Asia cultures critique* 11(1): 51–90.

Russo, J.L. 2009. User-penetrated content: Fan video in the age of convergence. *Cinema Journal.* 48(4): 125–130.

Scream Blacula Scream. (1973). Film. Directed by Bob Kelljan. USA: American International Pictures.

Smith, J.P. (2011). MMA Godfather Bruce Lee's 15 Best Videos on the Net. [Online] *BleacherReport.com.* Available from: http://bleacherreport.com/articles/707581-mma-godfather-bruce-lees-15-best-videos-on-the-net [Accessed: 2 July 2014].

Strauss, N. 1999. Rap and rock. In *The vibe history of hip hop*, ed. A. Light. New York: Three Rivers.

The Big Boss. (1971). Film. Directed by Lo Wei. Hong Kong: Golden Harvest.

The Game of Death. (1973). Film. Directed by Bruce Lee. Hong Kong: Golden Harvest.

The Mack. (1973). Film. Directed by Michael Campus. USA: Cinerama Releasing Corporation.

The Water Margin. (1972). Film. Directed by Chang Cheh, Wu Ma and Pao Hsueh-li. Hong Kong/USA: Shaw Brothers, New World Pictures.

Wahlberg, M. 2009. YouTube commemoration: Private grief and communal consolation. In *The YouTube reader*, eds. P. Snickars, and P. Vonderau. National Library of Sweden: Stockholm.

Way of the Dragon. (1972). Film. Directed by Bruce Lee. Hong Kong: Golden Harvest.

Yang, J. (1998, August). Immortal combat. *Vibe*, p. 90–94.

INDEX

A

The Adventures of Quentin Durward (1955), 93
ageing, 4–5, 61, 86, 99, 101, 102, 106–109, 178, 181, 185, 203, 204–207, 209–211, 214, 240
  in European art-house cinema; Dyer's views, 115; female star body, Mulvey's comments on, 116, 123–4; fetish, Marxist and Freudian theorisations of, 123; Haneke's films (*see* Haneke, Michael); photographic and film technology, Sontag's discussion of, 124; photographic images, 118; stardom, mythological and Olympian aspects of, 115
  Mason, James (see Mason, James)
  Stallone, Sylvester (see Stallone, Sylvester, redundancy and ageing)
Age Of Consent (1969), 143
Agneepath (1990), 18
Ajtay, Andor, 48
Alien (1979), 279
Along for the Ride (2000), 102
AmeriKKKa's Most Wanted (1990), 56
Amour (2012)
  authorial agency, declaration of, 116
  depiction of death, 118–20
  female star body, ageing process of, 116, 117, 125–6
  intimate mode, 117
  Parisian haute-bourgeoisie couple, focus on, 117
  realist aesthetic codes, 116
  Trintignant and Riva, casting of, 120–2
An Alligator Named Daisy (1955), 208, 266
Anand (1971), 13, 16
anti-Jewish acts of 1938–1941, 43
Antz (1998), 248
Apger, Virgil, 190
Apocalypse Now (1979), 283
Are We Done Yet? (2007), 64
Are We There Yet? (2005), 64
The Artist (2011), 128
Asian martial arts, 294
As Long As They're Happy (1955), 271
Assassins (1995), 245, 250
The Avengers, 220

B

Babington, Bruce, 211, 262
Bachchan, Amitabh, 3
 advertising campaigns, 19, 21
 angry young man persona;
    alignment with Karna, 15–16;
    all-round entertainer, 13;
    anti-hero, 15; macho super-
    hero, 17–18; middle-class
    values, 23–4; Mishra's
    comments on Bachchan's
    appeal, 16; performance style,
    16; physique, 20; proletarian
    figure, 15–17; socio-political
    crisis, 14–15; urban vista,
    19–20; working-class
    consciousness, 15
 Bofors gun scandal, 12
 contemporary persona, 18–19
 event management, 19
 in experimental roles, 18
 extra-cinematic media undertakings, 11
 fan culture, 11
 film and entertainment productions, investments in, 19
 as guest/supporting actor, 18
 Hindi cinema, domination of, 11
 in *India Poised: Our Time Is Now* campaign, 21-2
 Kaun Banega Crorepati (KBC), 19–21
 in national politics, 12
 press, relationship with, 12
 product endorsements, 19
 public interest campaign, 21
 in romantic and familial films, 18
 social media presence, 11, 23
 transcendence, 24
 voted as 'Greatest Super-Star of the Millennium' (1999), 11
Banderas, Antonio, 104, 105

Barbershop (2002), 59–60
Barbershop 2: Back in Business (2004), 59, 60
The Barretts of Wimpole Street (1934), 78
Barthes, Roland, 118, 174
Bataan (1943), 92
Batman (1966–1968), 94
Beckett, Samuel, 128, 132-134, 136, 137
Before I Forget (1981), 149
Bell, Melanie, 227
Bender, John, 231
Bernstein, Jonathan, 234
Bhuvan Shome (1969), 13
The Big Boss (1971), 291
Bigger Than Life (1956), 143
Big Night (1996), 32
Blackman, Honor, 264
Blaxploitation, 294
Bleach, Anthony C, 234
Blithe Spirit (1945), 204, 206
The Blue Idol (1931), 43
Bode, Lisa, 174
Body Double (1984), 100, 102, 103
Bofors gun scandal, 12
The Bonfire of the Vanities (1990), 100, 103
Boogie Nights (1997), 101
Born Yesterday (1993), 104
Botany Bay (1953), 144
Boy on a Dolphin (1957), 31
Boys Town (1938), 175
Boyz N the Hood (1991), 56–8
Brando, Marlon, 5
 acting style and public persona, 193
 'after-market,' 190
 complicated sensuality, 192
 masculinity, 192
 MasterCard 'Priceless' campaign, commercial for, 194–7
 Merkin's reflection on, 192

on-screen and off-screen images, 190, 193
personification and impersonation, 196
professional legacy, 191
The Breakfast Club (1985), 231–3, 239
A Breath of Scandal (1960), 31
British Academy of Film and Television Arts (BAFTA), 261
Broccoli, Albert, 217, 220
A Bronx Tale (1993), 32
Bruce Lee 'Be Like Water'—A Tribute (40 Year Anniversary), 297–300
Bullock, Sandra, 100
Burton, Tim, 7
The Buster Keaton Story (1957), 4
  conclusion, 131
  critics, 130
  entertainer biopic, 129, 132
  focus on Keaton's rough childhood, 130
  faded stardom, 128
  Keaton's acceptance of his screen mortality, 131
  pre-credit text, 129
  star retirement picture, 131

C

calendar art, 262
Camille (1936), 85
Captains Courageous (1937), 175
Casino Royale (2006), 227
Castle in the Air (1952), 208
Caught (1949), 143–4
Celebrity, 57, 85, 102, 103, 116, 190–192, 197, 198, 219–221, 227, 252, 268, 280–281, 283, 287
Changeling (2008), 278
Chapman, James, 222–225
Charles, Ray, 189

Cheeni Kum (2007), 18
Cherry 2000 (1987), 103
Chicago (musical), 106
Christopher Columbus (1992), 191
Citizen Kane (1941), 107
Clift, Montgomery, 95
Clouse, Robert, 295
Cobra (1986), 249
Cocoon (1985), 35
Code Unknown (2002), 117, 124
Collins, Joan, 264
companionate marriage, 77
Complicated Women (2000), 72
Connery, Sean, 217, 220, 221
Conspirator (1949), 92
Coolie (1983), 15, 20
Cooper, Gary, 92, 95
Cop Land (1997), 245
Coppa, Francesca, 295
Cops (1922), 130
Corliss, Richard, 107, 235, 236, 240
Costume, 11, 93, 107, 193, 236, 266, 271, 272, 285, 286
Cradle of Life (2003), 279
Craig, Daniel, 219, 225
Crazy in Alabama (1999), 103, 108
Crosby, Bing, 2
The Crowd Roars (1938), 91
Cryer, Jon, 232
Cube, Ice, 3
  AmeriKKKa's Most Wanted (1990), 56
  Are We Done Yet? (2007), 64
  Are We There Yet? (2005), 64
  Barbershop (2002), 59–60
  Barbershop 2: Back in Business (2004), 59, 60
  community, 59–61
  Cube Vision productions, co-founder of, 56
  cultural identity, 64

Cube (*cont.*)
 as Doughboy in *Boyz N the Hood*
  (1991), 56–8
 First Sunday (2008), 59, 60
 Friday (1995), 58, 59
 Friday after Next (2002), 59
 gangster (gangsta) rap, 56–7
 The Glass Shield (1995), 58
 Higher Learning (1995), 58
 industry *vs.* ideology, 61–3
 21 Jump Street (2012), 64
 22 Jump Street (2014), 64
 The Longshots (2008), 59, 60
 Lottery Ticket (2010), 59
 Next Friday (2000), 59
 Ride Along, 64
 vs. Smith, 55
 Straight outta Compton (2014), 64
 Trespass (1992), 58
Cube Vision, 3, 56, 58, 62, 64

D
Dalton, Timothy, 219, 225
Dankó Pista (1940), 50
Deadly Duo (1971), 293
Deadly Spring (1939), 44
Dean, James, 86, 87, 193
Death Valley Days (1952–1970), 94
de Banzie, Brenda, 214
Deewar (1975), 13
Deleuze, Gilles, 135, 137
The Demi-Paradise (1943), 210
Deneuve, Catherine, 7
Depp, Johnny, 7
The Desert Fox (1951), 144
Desk Set (1957), 179
The Detectives (1959–1962), 94
De Vaney, Ann, 234
Diaz, Cameron, 100
Die Hard (1988), 248
Dillon, Mark, 225

The Divorcee (1930), 76, 77
Doody, Alison, 101
Dors, Diana, still photography,
  273–274
 exhibitions, 261
 film star portraits, 271–2
 fixing images; image captions, 266;
  legacy, 267; modern-day
  celebrity adoption, 268; Perrie
  photograph, 268; post-war
  rationing, 266; Rank Charm
  School, 264; Street's comment,
  264
 gallery portraits/still, 271
 publicity stills; Bilbow's comment,
  264; connection and
  community, 264; Keel's image,
  263; news and magazine
  coverage, 262; personality, 262;
  recognisable visual image, 262;
  studio contract, 262
 quality, portraits, 274
 glamourous lifestyle, 269;
  Hamilton, Denis, 269; national
  identity, 271; photographic
  performances, 270; self-
  portraits, 269; sex symbol
  paradigm, 270
Do the Right Thing (1989), 57
Dr. Fischer of Geneva, 142, 143,
  149–52
Durgnat, Raymond, 214
Dyer, Richard, 3, 6, 12, 16, 17, 24,
  29, 41, 44, 46, 47, 48, 58, 73,
  74, 88, 104, 115, 177, 178, 226,
  236, 262, 272

E
Eat with Me (1980), 34
Ebert, Roger, 100, 235, 238–239, 278
Emmy (1934), 49, 50

End Sexual Violence in Conflict (ESVC), 286
English without Tears (1944), 208
Enter the Dragon (1973), 291, 295–7
ethnicity, 29, 31–2
The Expendables (2010), 245, 246, 249, 251–6
Ex-Wife (1929), 77

F
The Fall of the Roman Empire (1964), 148
Fan Magazines, 29, 47, 71, 73–75, 76, 81, 91, 160, 162–164, 166–168
Farrow, Mia, 283
Father of the Bride (1950), 180
Fear City (1984), 100, 102
female employment, 76
fetish, 123–4
Fifty Shades of Grey (2015), 105
Film (1965), 128, 132–7
    as allegories of stardom, 135–6
    Beckett's notes on, 132–3
    failure, 134
    Keaton's interpretation of, 136–7
    philosophical concern, 133
    sections, 133–4
Film Chamber, Hungary, 43
Film Fund (1925), 42
First Blood (1982), 251
First Sunday (2008), 59, 60
Fist of Fury (1972), 291, 296–7
Ford, Harrison, 106
Forever (1921), 161
For Keeps (1988), 238
Foster, Jodie, 101
The Four Horsemen of the Apocalypse (1921), 166
A Free Soul (1931), 76
Fresh Horses (1988), 238
Friday (1995), 58, 59
Friday after Next (2002), 59
Friday the 13th (1980), 233
From among the Waves (1943), 45

G
Gable, Clark, 41, 86, 89, 95
Game of Death (1973), 300
gangster (gangsta) rap, 55–57, 61
Gardner, Ava, 7
Garland, Judy, 86, 95
Gassman, Vittorio, 30
Gaynor, Janet, 90
Georgy Girl (1966), 143, 147–8
Gia (1998), 277
Girl, Interrupted (1999), 277–9
The Glass Shield (1995), 58
global capitalism, 292, 295
Godard, Jean-Luc, 238
Goddard, Mark, 94
Golden Raspberry Awards, 101
Gone with the Wind (1939), 86
Graham, Heather, 101
Grant, Cary, 92
Griffith, Melanie, 4
    Citizen Kane (1941), 107
    in *Body Double* (1984), 100
    in *The Bonfire of the Vanities* (1990), 100
    in Lolita (1997), 106–107
    in *Chicago* (musical), 106
    contradictions, 107
    in *Crazy in Alabama*, 108
    in *Fear City* (1984), 100
    in *Hawaii Five-0*, 106
    Hedren, daughter of, 99
    Kramer's analysis of star making, 100–1, 108
    motherhood and resilience, 109
    in *Night Moves* (1975), 99–100

Griffith (*cont.*)
  nominations for Worst Actress 'Razzies,' 101
  off-screen life, 104–5
  Raising Hope (2010–2014), 106
  RKO281 (1999), 107
  in *Roar* (1981), 100
  star image, elements of, 99, 101;
    female genealogy, 105–6;
    physical appearance, 102–3;
    vulgarity, 103–5
  in *Stormy Monday* (1988), 100
  in *Working Girl* (1988), 100, 101
Grumpier Old Men (1995), 3, 28
Grumpy Old Men (1993), 28, 35
  ethnic food, preparation and consumption of, 33–4
  ethnic revival, 29, 31–2
  sexualisation, 34–7
Guddi (1971), 16
Guerrero, Ed, 62, 63, 64
Guess Who's Coming to Dinner (1967)
  career culmination, 174
  film's paternalistic approach, 174

H
Haneke, Michael, 4
  Amour (2012); authorial agency, declaration of, 116; depiction of death, 118–20; female star body, ageing process of, 116, 117, 125–6; intimate mode, 117; Parisian haute-bourgeoisie couple, focus on, 117; realist aesthetic codes, 116; Trintignant and Riva, casting of, 120–2
  Code Unknown (2001), 117, 124
  Hidden (2005), 117, 124
  image-making technology, 117, 124–5

Saxton's views on, 116–17
Harlow, Jean, 87
Harris, Mark, 173, 184
Harrison, Kathleen, 214
Hawaii Five-0, 106
Hayward, Susan, 41, 122, 123
Heavenly Bodies, 6
Hedren, Tippi, 99, 100, 105
Hepburn, Audrey, 147, 283
Hepburn, Katharine, 71, 174, 175, 177, 178–180, 182, 183
Hidden (2005), 117, 124
Higher Learning (1995), 58
High Society (1956), 1, 2
hip hop
  Cube, Ice (see Cube, Ice)
  Ice-T, 55
  and Lee; Asian martial arts, 294; black communities, 293–4; *Bruce Lee 'Be Like Water'—A Tribute (40 Year Anniversary)*, 297–300; *Deadly Duo* (1971), 293; *Enter the Dragon* (1973), 291, 295–7; *Fist of Fury* (1972), 291, 296–7; global capitalism, 292; Hong Kong martial arts, 293; Kato's *From Kung Fu to Hip Hop: Globalization, Revolution, and Popular Culture* (2007), 292, 294, 295, 296, 300; rebel culture, 294; *The Water Margin* (1972), 293
  Shakur, Tupac, 55
Hird, Thora, 214
Hiroshima mon amour (1959), 120, 121
Hollywood Cavalcade (1939), 128–9
Holm, Celeste, 2
Holmlund, Chris, 245–246, 248, 248–249, 252–253, 255, 256
Howell, Peter, 226

Hughes, John, 231–4
Hum (1991), 15
humanitarianism
  Jolie, Angelina; 1998–2006 films, 278–80; *Maleficent* (2014), 284–7; mature acting phase, 280–4
  public relations, 278
  UNHCR, 277
Human Wreckage (1923), 162, 164
Hungarian film industry
  anti-Jewish acts of 1938–1941, 43
  domestic films, 42
  Film Fund (1925), 42
  growth of, 42
  vs. Hollywood, 42
  Hungarian star system, hybrid model, 43
  Hungarian talkies, 42
  Hunnia, state ownership of, 42–3
  Jávor, Pál (see Jávor, Pál)
  Magyar Filmiroda, establishment of, 42
  state investment, 42
Hunnia, 42–3
Hunt, Peter, 219, 224, 225
Hurrell, George, 263
Hyde, Marina, 283
Hyppolit, the Butler (1931), 43

I
I Cannot Live without Music (1935), 45–6
Ice-T, 55
Indiana Jones and the Last Crusade (1989), 101
Inherit the Wind (1960), 176–9
In the Kitchen with Love (1972), 34
In the Land of Blood and Honey (2011), 284
It Happened One Night (1934), 89

It's a Mad, Mad, Mad, Mad World (1963), 176
It's a Wonderful Life (1946), 86
Ivanhoe (1952), 93

J
'James Bond 007,' 217, 219–21, 223–5, 227
Janky Promoters (2009), 63
Jávor, Pál, 3
  arrest and deportation, 51
  audience vote for, 44
  The Blue Idol (1931), 43
  criticism, 50
  as crosser of class boundaries, 48
  in *Emmy* (1934), 49, 50
  end of career, 51
  fan response, 47
  Film Chamber, suspension from, 44
  in *Hyppolit, the Butler* (1931), 43
  national identity, 49
  off-screen life, 47
  vs. Páger, 49, 50
  physical presence, 41
  pride, 44
  report on his police interview, 46–7
  as romantic lead, 41, 44
  social mobility, 47–8
  as stage apprenticeship, 43, 44
  star body and persona, 45–6
  in state-controlled film sector, 41
  Székely's remarks on, 44–5
  temperamental characters, 49
The Jazz Singer (1927), 129, 131
Jermyn, Deborah, 5, 284
Johnny Eager (1941), 92
Johnson, Dakota, 105, 106
Jolie, Angelina, 6
  1998–2006 films, 278–80

Jolie (*cont.*)
  Maleficent (2014); action roles, 285; ESVC, 286; facial features, 285; media coverage, 286; on-screen performances, 287; promotional campaign, 285
  mature acting phase; action-adventure blockbusters, 284; action babe cinema, 281; colonial discourses, 283; critical acclaim, 284; global consciousness, 281; international co-operation, 282; media obsession, 283; motherhood, 283; on-the-ground campaign, 280
The Jolson Story (1946), 129
Joyride (1977), 102
Judge Dredd (1995), 245, 250
Judgment at Nuremberg (1961), 176–181
Julius Caesar (1953), 144, 152
21 Jump Street (2012), 64
22 Jump Street (2014), 64
Just My Luck (1957), 208

K
Kabhi Alvida Naa Kehna (2006), 20
Kabhie Khushi Kabhie Gham (2001), 19
Kael, Pauline, 145, 148, 176, 178, 182, 224, 234, 235
Kato, M.T., 292, 294, 295, 296, 300
Kaun Banega Crorepati (*KBC*), 19–21
Keaton, Buster, 4
  The Buster Keaton Story (1957) (*see The Buster Keaton Story* (1957))
  Cops (1922), 130
  Film (1965), 128, 132–7; as allegories of stardom, 135–6; Beckett's notes on, 132–3; failure, 134; Keaton's interpretation of, 136–7; philosophical concern, 133; ruining of time in, 137; sections, 133–4
  in *Hollywood Cavalcade* (1939), 128–9
  in publicity still as paragon of the Greek physical ideal, 127
  in *Sunset Boulevard* (1950), 127
  tragic-comic cameo, 127
Keaton, Diane, 236
Keel, Howard, 263
Kelly, Grace, 1, 2, 5, 95, 147
Kerkorian, Kirk, 95
King Lear (1987), 238
Knights of the Round Table (1953), 93
Kotlowitz, Robert, 183
Kramer, Stanley; 'mature pictures of substance,' 176–7; 'message movies,' 174; as mouthpiece, Tracy, 177–9; romantic comedies, 179; self-promotion, 184
'kung fu' films, 294
Kung Fu Panda (2008), 278

L
Lady of the Night (1925), 73–5
Lady Possessed (1952), 144
Lara Croft: Tomb Raider (2001), 277–9
Late (1943), 49
Lazenby, George, 6
  Chapman comments on, 222
  Connery, Sean; laissez-faire attitude, 225; suave machismo, 219
  counterculture, 217
  derogatory attitude, 223
  early life, 219
  idiosyncratic qualities, 219
  imposing physique, 225

as James Bond in *OHMSS*; Bond persona, 221, 224, 227; Bray's comments on, 220; fluctuating connotations, 224, 225; Ian Fleming's novel, 219; on-screen personas, 227; post-production process, 220
Jenkins, Chard, 219
rugged physique and fighting skill, 220
Saltzman's and Broccoli's apprehension, 221
socio-cultural conventions, 226
20,000 Leagues under the Sea (1954), 144
Lee, Bruce, 6, 301–2
   African American audiences, 292
   The Big Boss (1971), 291
   cyber obituaries, 292
   death, 291
   and hip hop; Asian martial arts, 294; black communities, 293–4; *Bruce Lee 'Be Like Water'—A Tribute (40 Year Anniversary,* 297–300; *Deadly Duo* (1971), 293; *Enter the Dragon* (1973), 291, 295–7; *Fist of Fury* (1972), 291, 296–7; global capitalism, 292; Hong Kong martial arts, 293; Macnab, Geoffrey, 149, 204, 206, 270 Kato's *From Kung Fu to Hip Hop: Globalization, Revolution, and Popular Culture* (2007), 292, 294, 295, 296, 300; rebel culture, 294; *The Water Margin* (1972), 293
   Way of the Dragon (1972), 291
   web-based fan circuits, 292
Let Us Be Gay (1930), 76
Little Mary (1937), 49

Little Mix Tumblr site, 268
Lolita (1997), 106–107
Lolita (1962), 143, 145–147
The Longshots (2008), 59, 60
Longstreet (1971), 298
Loren, Sophia, 3
   as age-defying sex symbol, 28
   American star persona, 30–1, 38
   awarded Golden Lion for career achievement, 30
   in *Boy on a Dolphin* (1957), 31
   in *A Breath of Scandal* (1960), 31
   as embodiment of smouldering sensuality, 28
   in *Grumpier Old Men* (1995), 28; ethnic food, preparation and consumption of, 33–4; ethnic revival, 29, 31–2; sexualisation, 34–7
   international popularity, 30
   national identity, 29–30
   in *Prêt-à-Porter* (1994), 28
   private life, media coverage of, 27
   public persona, media coverage of, 27
   signifying function, 29
Lost in Space (1965–1968), 94
Lottery Ticket (2010), 59, 63
Louise, Ruth Harriet, 271
Lovell, Dyson, 219
Lucas, Cornel, 6, 261–274

M
The Mack (1973), 294
Macnab, Geoffrey, 149, 204, 206, 270
Mad about Men (1954), 208
Madonna, 283
Magnificent Obsession (1935), 90–1
Mahabharata, 15–16
Main Azaad Hoon (1989), 15
Maleficent (2014), 278

Mandingo (1975), 143
The Man in Grey (1943), 143
Ma nuit chez Maud (1969), 120
The Man with the Golden Gun (1974), 220
Marie Antoinette (1938), 79–80
Marley, Bob, 295
Marley, Stephen, 295
Married to the Mob (1988), 35
Marti, Adrian, 233
martial arts
   African Americans, 292
   black communities, 293
   formless and shapeless paradigm, 299
   hip hop culture, 295
   Hong Kong, 293
   philosophy, 300
   water analogy, 298, 299
Mason, James, 4–5
   in *Caught* (1949), 143–4
   as critic of British cinema, 148–9
   death, 141
   The Desert Fox (1951), *Daily Mirror* report on, 144
   Dr. Fischer of Geneva, 142, 143, 149–52
   as exceptional and versatile character actor, 142
   failure, 144
   in *Georgy Girl* (1966), 143, 147–8
   Before I Forget (1981), 149
   international career, 143
   interviews and profiles, 149
   in *Lolita* (1962), 143, 146, 147
   in *North by Northwest* (1959), 143, 145
   Odd Man Out (1947), 142
   off-screen persona, 142
   as romantic villain, 141
   screen persona, 142, 143
   The Sea Gull (1968), 148
   The Seventh Veil (1945), 142, 143, 147
   in *The Shooting Party* (1985), 142, 149–52
   A Star is Born (1954), 142, 146
   tributes and appraisals, 141, 142, 153
   in unsympathetic roles, 144
MasterCard's rebranding strategy, 194–7
Mastroianni, Marcello, 29
McCarthy, Andrew, 232
McDonald, Paul, 189, 190, 227, 262, 279
A Mighty Heart (2007), 278, 280
Milk Money (1994), 102
Miranda (1948), 208
Mohabattein (2000), 19
Monroe, Marilyn, 86, 87, 189, 194, 269, 270, 272
   fetish, 123
   sexuality, embodiment of, 104
Moonstruck (1987), 32
Moore, Demi, 100
Moore, Roger, 217, 220
Morin, Edgar, 115, 135
Morituri (1965), 191
Moseley, Rachel, 236
motherly nurturers, 283
Motion Picture Production Code, 72, 80, 88, 162, 167, 169
Mr. Cheeks, 295
Mr. & Mrs. Smith (2005), 278, 279
Muqqaddar ka Sikandar (1978), 20
Murder Ahoy (1964), 204, 206
Murder at the Gallop (1963), 206
Murder She Said (1961), 212–14
My Big Fat Greek Wedding (2002), 32
My Cousin Vinny (1992), 35

N

Namak Halal (1982), 15
Naremore, James, 193
National Portrait Gallery, 271

Negra, Diane, 29, 31, 32, 33, 37
Negri, Pola, 163
New York Police Department (NYPD), 250
Next Friday (2000), 59
Niggaz Wit Attitude (NWA), 56, 58
Night Moves (1975), 99–100, 102
Nishabd (2007), 18
Nobody's Fool (1994), 102
Norris, Chuck, 253
North by Northwest (1959), 143, 145
Nostalgia, 32, 137, 165, 167–169, 181, 183, 185, 210, 231, 233, 237–241, 246
Not Another Teen Movie (2001), 239
Notorious (1946), 145

O
O'Connor, Donald, 128
Off-screen image/persona, 28, 29, 30, 45, 46, 47, 86, 87, 88, 89, 92, 103, 104, 108, 119, 128, 142, 148, 149, 153, 162, 175, 180, 182, 190, 193, 209, 211, 235, 279, 297, 298
Odd Man Out (1947), 142, 143
Once Upon A Time in the West (1968), 146
On Her Majesty's Secret Service (OHMSS) (1969), 217, 218, 220, 224, 225, 227–8
On the Waterfront (1954), 191, 192

P
Pandora and the Flying Dutchman (1951), 143
The Paradine Case (1947), 145
parallel cinema, 13
Perkins, Anthony, 7
Perry, Tyler, 62

Pickford, Mary, 168, 239
The Pick-Up Artist (1987), 238
The Pierre Berton Show (1971), 298
Pitt, Brad, 280
Poitier, Sidney, 174, 178, 179, 184
Ponti, Carlo, 29
pop rap, 56
Presley, Elvis, 189
Prêt-à-Porter (1994), 28
Pretty in Pink (1986), 232, 233, 235
Prince Valiant (1954), 144
The Prisoner of Zenda (1952), 144
Projansky, Sarah, 232, 239

Q
Quo Vadis (1951), 85, 93

R
Rambova, Natacha, 163
Rank Charm School, 264
rap music, 56
Rebel without a Cause (1955), 193
Sofia Loren's Recipes and Memories (1998), 34
The Reckless Moment (1949), 143, 144
Regan, Ronald, 12
Reid, Wallace
  Anderson's work on, 159
  Anglo-American, 159
  cross-genre stardom, 161
  death reportage, 159, 161–2
  domestic recuperation and film revival, 164–6
  fan magazines, memorialisation in, 168–9
  in *Forever* (1921), 161
  Hollywood scandal, 161
  morphine addiction, 160, 161
  on-screen and off persona, 160–1

Reid (*cont.*)
  questions of individual character, 162
Remember Valentino: Remembrances of the World's Greatest Lover, 168
Ride Along (2014), 2, 64
Rigg, Diana, 220, 225, 227
Ringwald, Molly, 5
  'anachronistic self-fashioning,' 237
  authenticity, 235
  charismatic normality, 234, 241
  costumes, 236
  cultural imaginary, 239
  cultural status, 232
  girlhood, 233
  ideological continuity, 241
  natural performances, 238
  nostalgia, 233, 239, 240
  retro tendencies, 240
  teen femininity, 232
  womanhood, 232
  writing process, 237
Riva, Emmanuelle
  in *Amour* (2012), 116, 120, 121
  in *Hiroshima mon amour* (1959), 120, 121
  in *Three Colours: Blue* (1993), 120–2
RKO281 (1999), 107
Roar (1981), 100
Roberts, Julia, 100
Robson, Flora, 214
Rocky (1976), 245
Rocky Balboa (2006), 246, 250
Romance of Ida (1934), 44
Romeo and Juliet (1936), 78
Rope (1948), 145
Rose Hobart (1936), 137
Rose, William, 179–82, 184
Rourke, Mickey, 2–3
Russell, Jane, 270, 272
Rutherford, Margaret, 5–6
  as Aunt Dolly in *I'm All Right Jack* (1959), 211
  Berman, Russell, 209
  in *Blithe Spirit* (1945), 204
  in British comedies (late1940s and 1950s), 204
  conventional femininity, 204
  as the Duchess of Brighton in *The VIPs* (1963), 211
  in *Dusty Ermine* (1936), 203
  eccentricity, 207–8
  Eric Keown comments on, 205–6
  as Lady Vivian in *On the Double* (1961), 211
  as Miss Marple in *Murder She Said* (1961), 212–14
  as Miss Whitchurch in *The Happiest Days of Your Life* (1950), 206
  as Mrs. John Bull, 203
  narrative function, 204
  as Nurse Carey in *Mad about Men* (1954), 206
  Orwell, George, 209
  physicality, 205–6
  post-war Britain, 211
  public persona, 210
  ruthless feminism character, 206
Ryan, Jake, 233
Ryan, Meg, 7, 100

S
Saat Hindustani (1969), 13
Salary: 200 per Month (1936), 44, 45
Salt (2010), 279
Saltzman, Harry, 217
Santana, Carlos, 194
Sárdy, János, 48
Sarkar (2005), 19
Sarkar Raj (2008), 19
Sarkar series (2005, 2008), 19

Satte Pe Satta (1982), 18
Schwarzenegger, Arnold, 247, 253
Scream Blacula Scream (1973), 294
The Sea Gull (1968), 148
self-articulation, 296
The Seventh Veil (1945), 142, 143, 147
The Seven Year Itch (1955), 86, 269
sexual equality, 77
Shakti (1982), 18
Shakur, Tupac, 55
Sharaabi (1984), 18
Shary, Timothy, 233
Shearer, Norma, 4
   Academy Award, 71
   analysis of, 72–3
   Basinger's work on, 72, 81
   family background, 74
   fan magazines, mention in, 73, 81
   Lady of the Night (1925), 73–5
   marriage to Thalberg, 71, 73, 75–8
   in pre-Code films, 72, 79
   Schickel's work on, 72
   star image, 73, 74
   widowhood (1936–1942), 71, 78–81
Sheedy, Ally, 232
Shehanshah (1988), 18
The Sheik (1921), 166
Shingler, Martin, 3, 23, 228
Shining Through (1992), 107
Sholay (1975), 13–15
The Shootist (1976), 29
The Shooting Party (1985), 142, 149–52
Silverman, Kaja, 237
Sinatra, Frank, 1, 2
Since You've Been Gone (1998), 239
Sinden, Donald, 264
Singin' in the Rain (1952), 128, 131
Singleton, John, 57
Sin in Soft Focus (1999), 72

Sixteen Candles (1984), 233, 235, 238
Skyfall (2012), 227
Sleeping Beauty (1959), 284
Slumdog Millionaire (2009), 24
Small Time Girl (1936), 90
Small, Pauline, 27, 29, 36
Smith, Will, 55
Some Kind of Wonderful (1987), 238
Something Wild (1986), 102, 103, 107
Son of the Sheik (1926), 159, 160
Sontag, Susan, 124, 239
Spader, James, 232
Stallone, Sylvester, redundancy and ageing, 6
   action blockbusters, 245
   (geri-)action star; aged action star, 255; hyperbolic muscularity, 252; intensified continuity, 256; professional redundancy, 253; work- and age-related redundancies, 252
   auteurist perspective, 246
   'feminisation,' 248
   generic and narrative; economic and cultural redundancy, 250; *The Expendables*, 245, 246, 249, 251–6; hyperbolic physicality, 250; hypermasculine self-presentation, 253; societal-military redundancy, 251; symbolic exhaustion, 249
   'muscular cinema,' 247
   'mutual remasculinisation,' 247
   remasculinisation, 248
   self-reflexivity, 246
Standish, Claire, 233
Stanwyck, Barbara, 86, 87, 146
A Star is Born (1954), 142, 143, 146
The Star Machine (2007), 72, 81, 262
Stars (1979), 74, 115, 226, 236
Stars (1998), 41, 47, 48, 177, 178, 262

Stars (2004), 58
St. Elmo's Fire (1985), 231, 232
Stewart, James, 7, 86, 92
Stormy Monday (1988), 100, 102
Strabler, Johnny, 194
Straight outta Compton (2014), 64
A Stranger among Us (1992), 107
Strangers May Kiss (1931), 76, 78
A Streetcar Named Desire (1951), 191, 192
studio contract, 262
Studlar, Gaylyn, 159, 160, 161, 162, 232, 234, 235, 238, 241
Sunset Boulevard (1950), 116, 127

T
Tah, Freaky, 295
The Talking Robe (1941), 44
Tango and Cash (1989), 246
Tasker, Yvonne, 247, 248, 252, 255
Taylor, Robert, 4
  in *The Adventures of Quentin Durward* (1955), 93
  Alexander's quotes on, 94
  in *Bataan* (1943), 92
  in *Camille* (1936), 85
  career, 86, 88
  in *Conspirator* (1949), 92
  contract with Metro-Goldwyn-Meyer (MGM), 86
  in *The Crowd Roars* (1938), 91
  death, 87, 95
  in *Death Valley Days* (1952–1970), 94
  in *The Detectives* (1959–1962), 94
  in diverse range of genres, 86
  early life, 89
  extra-filmic merchandise, dedication of, 86
  film fan magazines, appearance in, 88–9, 95
  Hinxman's article on, 93–4
  in *Ivanhoe* (1952), 93
  in *Johnny Eager* (1941), 92
  Knights of the Round Table (1953), 93
  as lost/forgotten star, 85
  Magnificent Obsession (1935), 90–1
  marriage to Stanwyck, 86, 87
  Picturegoer magazine article on, 93–4
  private life, 87
  publicity material on, 89
  in *Quo Vadis* (1951), 85, 93
  in *Small Time Girl* (1936), 90
  star persona, 87–8
  television listings magazines, appearance in, 95
  in *Undercurrent* (1946), 92
  The Wild Bunch (1969), 95
  in *A Yank at Oxford* (1938), 91
Thalberg, Irving, 71, 73, 75–8
The Tourist (2010), 279
They Were Sisters (1945), 143, 147
Three Colours: Blue (1993), 120–2
To His Coy Mistress, 121
Tracy, Spencer, 5, 95
  auteurist criticism, 177
  Crowther's critical reviews of, 173, 179, 182, 184
  as Drummond in *Inherit the Wind* (1960), 180
  in *Guess Who's Coming to Dinner* (1967) (*see Guess Who's Coming to Dinner* (1967))
  as Haywood in *Judgment at Nuremberg* (1961), 180
  Irving Thalberg Award, 179
  nostalgia, 183
  obituaries, 182
  personal idealism, 183
  studio system, 173
Trespass (1992), 58

Trintignant, Jean-Louis
  in *Amour* (2012), 116, 120–1
  in *Ma nuit chez Maud* (1969), 120
Trishul (1978), 20
True Grit (1969), 146
True Love (1989), 32
The Tutoress (1945), 52
Two Much, 104

U
Undercurrent (1946), 92
United Nations High Commissioner for Refugees (UNHCR), 277
Uray, Tivadar, 48

V
Vincendeau, Ginette, 29, 30, 41, 43
Valentino, Rudolph, 5
  death reportage, 159, 162–3
  ethnic masculinity, 159
  fan magazines, memorialisation in, 160, 167–8
  feminine desire, 163
  The Four Horsemen of the Apocalypse (1921), 166
  'Latin lover,' 159
  The Sheik (1921), 166
  Son of the Sheik (1926), 159, 160, 166–7
  spiritual presence, 163
The Verdict (1982), 148

Victoria Regina, 79
The VIPs (1963), 204

W
water analogy, 298–300
The Water Margin (1972), 293
Wayne, John, 29, 194, 196
Way of the Dragon (1972), 291
West, Adam, 94
Whatever Happened to Baby Jane? (1962), 116
The Wicked Lady (1945), 143, 149
The Wild Bunch (1969), 95
The Wild One (1953), 192–4
Willis, Bruce, 253, 279
Winterbottom, Michael, 280
The Wizard of Oz (1939), 86
A Woman's View (1993), 72
The Women (1939), 80–1
Working Girl (1988), 100, 101, 103

Y
A Yank at Oxford (1938), 91
Yield to the Night (1956), 265, 273
You Only Live Twice (1967), 217
YouTube, 292, 294, 295, 297

Z
Zanjeer (1973), 13

MIX
Papier aus verantwortungsvollen Quellen
Paper from responsible sources
FSC® C105338

If you have any concerns about our products,
you can contact us on
ProductSafety@springernature.com

In case Publisher is established outside the EU,
the EU authorized representative is:
**Springer Nature Customer Service Center GmbH
Europaplatz 3, 69115 Heidelberg, Germany**

Printed by Libri Plureos GmbH
in Hamburg, Germany